MW00794852

Language of the Snakes

SOUTH ASIA ACROSS THE DISCIPLINES

Edited by Muzaffar Alam, Robert Goldman, and Gauri Viswanathan

Dipesh Chakrabarty, Sheldon Pollock, and Sanjay Subrahmanyam, Founding Editors

Funded by a grant from the Andrew W. Mellon Foundation and jointly published by the University of California Press, the University of Chicago Press, and Columbia University Press

For a list of books in the series, see page 309.

Language of the Snakes

Prakrit, Sanskrit, and the Language Order of Premodern India

Andrew Ollett

UNIVERSITY OF CALIFORNIA PRESS

University of California Press, one of the most distinguished university presses in the United States, enriches lives around the world by advancing scholarship in the humanities, social sciences, and natural sciences. Its activities are supported by the UC Press Foundation and by philanthropic contributions from individuals and institutions. For more information, visit www.ucpress.edu.

University of California Press
Oakland, California

Suggested citation: Ollett, Andrew. *Language of the Snakes: Prakrit, Sanskrit, and the Language Order of Premodern India*. Oakland: University of California Press, 2017. doi: https://doi.org/10.1525/luminos.37

Library of Congress Cataloging-in-Publication Data

Names: Ollett, Andrew, 1986- author.
Title: Language of the snakes : Prakrit, Sanskrit, and the language order of premodern India / Andrew Ollett.
Description: Oakland, California : University of California Press, [2017] | Includes bibliographical references and index. |
Identifiers: LCCN 2017018705 (print) | LCCN 2017019745 (ebook) | ISBN 9780520968813 (ebook) | ISBN 9780520296220 (pbk. : alk. paper)
Subjects: LCSH: Prakrit literature—History and criticism. | Prakrit languages. | Sanskrit literature—History and criticism. | Language and culture—India.
Classification: LCC PK4994 (ebook) | LCC PK4994 .O45 2017 (print) | DDC 891/.3-dc23
LC record available at https://lccn.loc.gov/2017018705

26 25 24 23 22 21 20 19 18 17
10 9 8 7 6 5 4 3 2 1

यस्या मे शान्तिराद्यायामाख्यायां यवनायते |
तस्यै सर्वस्वभूताया इदं सर्वं च सर्वदा ॥

CONTENTS

LIST OF ILLUSTRATIONS

LIST OF TABLES

ACKNOWLEDGMENTS

I'm thankful to a great number of people at Columbia University, Harvard University, and the University of California Press for support, comments and suggestions. These include participants in the MESAAS post-MPhil seminar (Nasser Abdurrahman, Omar Farahat, Yitzhak Lewis, Wendell Marsh, Timothy Mitchell, Casey Primel, Kenan Tekin, Sahar Ullah), the INCITE program at Columbia (coordinated by Bill McAllister), in whose basement office the majority of this book was written, the South Asia Graduate Student Forum (Fran Pritchett, Jay Ramesh, Joel Bordeaux, and Joel Lee), and my colleagues at the Society of Fellows (Alexander Bevilacqua, Stephanie Dick, Alisha Holland, Abhishek Kaicker, Ya-Wen Lei, and Adam Mestyan). My research would not have been possible without the support of the staff at MESAAS and GSAS at Columbia, including Jessica Rechtschaffer, Michael Fishman, Irys Schenker, Sandra Peters, and Kerry Gluckmann. I also thank the staff at Harvard's Society of Fellows: Yesim Erdmann, Kelly Katz, Diana Morse, and Ana Novak. Bill Nelson produced the map in chapter 2. I thank Whitney Cox, Owen Cornwall, Irene SanPietro, Dalpat Rajpurohit, David Shulman, and Anand Venkatkrishnan for feedback at various points over the life of this project. Yigal Bronner, Allison Busch, Jack Hawley, and Sudipta Kaviraj were generous with comments and suggestions when this book was a dissertation. The late Barney Bate introduced me to much of the literature that is cited in these pages. Sheldon Pollock provided constant support and guidance; it was he who encouraged me to begin this project in the first place. The Lalbhai Dalpatbhai Institute of Indology, the Bhandarkar Oriental Research Institute, the Asiatic Society in Kolkata, and the Nepalese–German Manuscript Cataloguing Project all provided important manuscript materials.

1

Prakrit in the Language Order of India

What historical a priori *provided the starting-point from which it was possible to define the great checkerboard of distinct identities established against the confused, undefined, faceless, and, as it were, indifferent background of differences?*

—MICHEL FOUCAULT, *THE ORDER OF THINGS*[1]

"It should be understood that the people of India have a number of languages," Mīrzā Khān observes in his *Gift from India* in 1676, "but those in which books and poetical works may be composed—such as would be agreeable to those who possess a refined disposition and straight understanding—are of three kinds."[2]

With these words, addressed to the son of the Mughal emperor Aurangzeb, Mīrzā Khān articulated the age-old schema of the *bhāṣātraya,* the "three languages." This was one of the most enduring ways of representing language in India. Of course, then as now, India was one of the most linguistically diverse places on earth. But the sense that Mīrzā Khān assigns to the schema of three languages is that these three alone answer to the purposes of textuality, and especially the higher purposes of textuality to which he alludes.[3] Mīrzā Khān's three languages are Sanskrit, Prakrit, and the vernacular (*bhākhā*). He is simply reframing what was common knowledge in India. The three slots in the schema were not arbitrary: for nearly fifteen hundred years, they had been filled in more or less the way that Mīrzā Khān describes.[4] But let's now turn to his description of Prakrit:

> Second, Parākirt. This language is mostly employed in the praise of kings, ministers, and chiefs, and belongs to the world, that is to say, the world that is below the ground; they call it Pātāl-bānī, and also Nāg-bānī, that is, the language of the lowest of the low, and of reptiles of mean origin, who live underground. This language is a mixture of Sahāskirt, mentioned above, and Bhākhā, to be mentioned next.[5]

On originally reading this passage, I had two reactions. The first was that of my inner historian, who recognized that Mīrzā Khān's description was remote from what I knew about Prakrit—and, more important, what was known about Prakrit even in Mīrzā Khān's time. Nobody ever represented it as a language of the snakes, except, as I later found out, a handful of other authors from the seventeenth and eighteenth centuries.[6] Given that this linguistic tradition began, as I'll argue here, around the first century, Prakrit was only known as the "language of the snakes" at the tail end of its long history. Hence I wondered what Mīrzā Khān's sources might have been. But my second reaction was to the description itself. Mīrzā Khān begins in a register of descriptive ethnography ("the people of India have a number of languages") and then transports us to a snake-infested subterranean realm. Prakrit, he tells us without a hint of contradiction, is the language of the lowest of the low and yet used to praise the highest of the high. At this point, the question of Mīrzā Khān's sources gave way to another question: what would it mean for Prakrit to be the language of the snakes anyway? It is obviously not a language in the sense of the *Linguistic Survey of India:* we can't send a field linguist into the underworld and have him ask the resident serpents how they say a couple dozen words. Is Mīrzā Khān simply reporting folk beliefs or myths? Does this mean that we have left the surface of the earth for good, and retreated into a fantastic realm of imaginary language? Or can we—should we—try to recover some shards of historical truth from Mīrzā Khān's account?

This passage, as Foucault famously said of Borges's Chinese encyclopedia, shatters the familiar landmarks of our thought. Not because it presents a completely new picture of language, but because it presents the utterly familiar picture of the three languages in an uncanny way.[7] Instead of asking how we can accommodate Mīrzā Khān's remarks within "this world," the world of truths to be discovered by social science, we are led to ask what worlds the language practices he describes belong to. Where can we accommodate them, if not within the familiar landmarks of our thought? Among experts, the question of the "reality" of Prakrit, or Sanskrit for that matter, has been debated for more than a century: where, when, and among whom did these languages exist, and what was their mode of existence? Were they spoken or written, natural or artificial? What kinds of histories do they have, and how can they possibly be related to other kinds of histories—of spoken language, for example, or of society and politics, or of literature and the imagination?

This book addresses these questions by telling the story of the mysterious snake-language. Prakrit is not just a curio in the cabinet of India's languages. It is the key to understanding how literary languages worked in premodern India as a whole, and it provides an alternative way of thinking about language—about its modes of existence, its unity and diversity, its sociality, and its imaginative possibilities. For the way we think about language today is almost completely bound up with the nation and its histories and aspirations: this is as true in linguistics departments, where national languages provide convenient labels for collections of differences, as it is among those who espouse some form of linguistic purism or chauvinism. Prakrit, by contrast, is a language without a people and without a place, between and beyond Sanskrit, the "language of the gods," and the vernacular, the "language of men."

LANGUAGE ORDERS

One important starting point for my investigation is Mikhail Bakhtin's observation that "[a] unitary language is not something which is given (*dan*) but is always in essence posited (*zadan*)."[8] We might think that we have answered the question "What is Prakrit?" with a series of descriptions: what are its grammatical features, what texts are written in it, who wrote those texts, and so on. For a language as little studied as Prakrit, much of this descriptive work remains to be done.[9] But Bakhtin's comment suggests that this is only the beginning. To ask "What is Prakrit?" is not just to ask what it is like, but to ask how, by whom, and for what purposes Prakrit was "posited" as a language over the course of its history.

Throughout this book I address these questions through the concept of a *language order.* This concept foregrounds the fact that languages interact with each other in such a way that it is impossible to characterize a language without reference to the other languages that fall within its cultural-historical horizons. It is, of course, possible to characterize a language in that way as a formal system, through the contrasts it articulates and its procedures of derivation. This was Ferdinand de Saussure's goal in delimiting "internal linguistics" from the study of all language-external phenomena.[10] Saussure's success in defining the object of linguistics as a formal system, however, has meant that comparatively little attention has been paid to the ways in which languages are posited in relation to each other. The term "language order" refers to the way that languages are ordered within a culture, to the recurrent patterns and schemas and tropes by which they are defined and represented, the names under which they are known, and the values with which they are associated. A language order provides the linguistic parameters for all manners of cultural practices, from scratching one's name on the wall of a cave to composing a text on poetics.

India was home to one of the premodern world's most productive and dynamic textual cultures, and one of its distinctive characteristics is its use of a small number of languages that stand, almost literally, outside of space and time. The practices of stability and continuity are well known in the case of Sanskrit: some families have been memorizing and reciting the exact same Sanskrit texts, down to the smallest details of accent, for more than twenty-five hundred years. But they apply mutatis mutandis to Prakrit as well. The Prakrit that Rāma Pāṇivāda wrote in eighteenth-century Kerala was self-consciously identical to the Prakrit that Rājaśekhara wrote in tenth-century Kannauj, which was in turn self-consciously identical to the Prakrit that Hāla wrote in first- or second-century Maharashtra.

These are, of course, limit cases, but premodern India was exceptional in the stability of its textual languages, and thus it is an important site for thinking about how languages are posited as unitary over the course of their history.

Another characteristic of the textual culture of premodern India, which is less well known today but was certainly taken for granted and occasionally remarked upon by premodern Indians themselves, is the deep and systematic interrelation between textual languages, not just on the level of their linguistic form but on the level of the practices, discourses, and imaginative worlds that they co-constitute. Even languages that modern linguistics has taught us to think of as genetically distinct, such as Sanskrit and Kannada, were situated by the people who wrote in them within a continuous, if capacious, frame of conceptualization and analysis. This frame anticipates in certain respects the twentieth-century concept of the "linguistic area."[11]

Language, in short, was *ordered* in premodern India in a way that seems to have few parallels, premodern or modern. That is why, necessary though it is to describe and account for this order, it seems preferable at this stage of research to simply state it as a fact, and to allow its features to emerge over the course of this book. At the foundation of this language order was a dichotomy between Sanskrit and Prakrit. Built upon this "schema of co-figuration," as I have learned to call it from Naoki Sakai, are a range of other schemas: the three languages, such as we encountered above in Mīrzā Khān; the three and a half languages; the four languages; the six languages. Amid this apparent arithmetic confusion—which I discuss in detail in chapter 5—it is important not to lose sight of the fact that all of these schemas situate languages in complex relations with each other, and differentially assign them over the entire field of textual production.

Such a structure is certainly not hidden. It is explicitly announced in some of the most influential and well-read works of Indian literature, such as Daṇḍin's *Mirror of Literature* (ca. 700 CE)—"the text can be Sanskrit, Prakrit, Apabhramsha, or mixed"—and it reaches down into every letter of every text.[12] Nevertheless, only a few scholars have thought critically about the language order of premodern India as a whole, especially as a condition for the emergence and articulation of particular language practices. Sudipta Kaviraj discussed the history of the "internal economy of language" in India in an attempt to account for some of the differences between the imagination of language in the domain of the political in modern India and in modern Europe. And Sheldon Pollock's theorization of Indian literary culture depended on identifying its internal structure and principles, among which is the principle of "literary language as a closed set."[13]

I am not claiming that this language order is absolutely unique or exceptional. What I am claiming, however, is that it is important not to assume that any particular framework that was developed in and for the modern West will completely account for the ordering of language practices in premodern India. The idea of a language order allows us to remain theory-neutral and prevents us from being theoretically naïve. A survey of the wide range of phenomena that linguistic anthropologists have placed under the rubric of "language ideology" shows, first of all, that hardly any of this work addresses the non-modern non-West, and secondly, that much of this work attempts to reduce the organization of language to putatively more basic categories such as prestige, distinction, legitimacy, and identity.[14] Whether or not this reductive maneuver is justified by the facts in a given case, the ways in which language is embedded in social and political life does need to be carefully—I would say: philologically—recovered from the facts, rather than assumed as a given. There is no default language order.[15]

In the exploration of what language is, and what it means, in the non-modern non-West, we must not assume, for concepts that have become thoroughly naturalized in the modern West, "a victory, or the right to a victory." This phrase betrays that my own thinking about language orders has been guided by a broadly Foucauldian perspective, especially as applied to language by Naoki Sakai. I think of language orders as "discursive spaces" in which the production of texts is "controlled and dominated by presupposed conditions" which are, however, immanent in the discursive spaces themselves and not tyrannically imposed upon them from without; the spaces accommodate "regimes of narrating, reciting, listening, writing, reading, and translating and writing," each of these a "set of protocols and rules" that determine how these actions are to be performed.[16]

PRAKRIT AS A CLASSICAL LANGUAGE

This book presents Prakrit as a critical component of a complex of cultural practices that have to do with language. These language practices, as I call them, are centered on the domain of literature, since it is largely in and through and for literature that languages like Prakrit are cultivated, but they extend far beyond it. It is convenient and appropriate to call this complex of language practices "classical," since they form part of what people generally recognize as classical Indian culture.

It is difficult to define the classical with precision in any cultural context, but one signal characteristic of classical Indian culture is the use of Sanskrit as the preeminent language of political and literary expression. Even on this criterion, the temporal, geographic, and social boundaries of classical culture are still very fuzzy. But this fuzziness allows us to imagine a "core domain" of classical culture found in educated and often elite circles of South Asia throughout the first millennium CE, which largely coincides with what Sheldon Pollock has theorized as the "Sanskrit cosmopolis," alongside a number of other domains.[17] Hence "classical" easily applies to practices of the court of Harṣa of Kannauj in the seventh century: this king, the subject of a famous historical poem in Sanskrit by Bāṇa, was the author of several Sanskrit plays based on older story-cycles. But it also applies to the practices of Buddhist monasteries of the Tarim basin of the middle of the first millennium, where monks translated Buddhist literature in Sanskrit into Khotanese and Tocharian, or of the courts of eastern Java in the early second millennium, where poets reimagined the great works of Sanskrit literature. Hans-Georg Gadamer's definition of the classical, as a "notable mode of being historical, the historical process of preservation that, through constantly proving itself, allows something true to come into being," evokes several features that apply to the cultural complex under discussion here: its historicality, its monumentality and exemplarity, its interpenetration with political, ethical, and aesthetic ideals.[18]

When I call Prakrit "critical," I mean, first, that it was one of the main languages of classical Indian culture, and second, that understanding Prakrit is crucial for understanding the language order of classical India. I will explain the first point in this section, and the second in what follows.

To get a first impression of what Prakrit was in this context, we can ask one of classical India's most remarkable intellectuals, who also happened to be one of its most famous kings: the Pāramāra overlord Bhoja, who ruled from Dhārā, in what is now Madhya Pradesh, in the first half of the eleventh century. Bhoja produced, or at least had a hand in producing, important works in Sanskrit on the topics of Yoga, architecture, Tantric Shaivism, grammar, and literary theory. In one of his works of literary theory, *Necklace of Sarasvatī*, he listed Prakrit as one of a handful of languages in which literature can be composed. As an example, he cited the following verse:

> tujjha ṇa jāṇe hiaaṃ maha uṇa maaṇo divā va rattiṃ va
> nigghiṇa tavaï balīṇaṃ tui juttamanorahāi aṃgāiṃ

> I do not know your heart.
> But as for me, cruel one,
> love torments my body,
> wracked with longing for you,
> ever more severely
> day and night.[19]

This verse comes from Kālidāsa's *Recognition of Śakuntalā*, composed around the beginning of the fifth century CE, a classic of Indian literature if ever there was one. At this point in the play, King Duśyanta has married the heroine, Śakuntalā, and returned home—soon to forget about his new bride altogether as a result of a curse—while Śakuntalā remains at the hermitage where she was raised. Grieved by separation, she is advised by her friends to send a message to the king. And the message is the verse quoted above.

Bhoja was writing about a thousand years into the history of Prakrit as a literary language. By this time there were dozens, if not hundreds, of texts he could have chosen. But he picked this verse because it supports his point that the principle of suitability (*aucitya*) informs the choice to employ one type of language (*jāti*) over another. What kind of suitability might Bhoja have had in view? For one thing, *Recognition of Śakuntalā* is a stage play, and one convention of the genre is that different characters speak different languages based on their gender and social status. Male characters of a high status typically speak Sanskrit, while male characters of a lower status, and most female characters, speak Prakrit. If you know only one thing about Prakrit, this is likely to be it: that Prakrit serves to represent the speech of characters who do not speak Sanskrit, that it is the language conventionally assigned to women, children, low-lives, and the uneducated. Thus Prakrit's association with "the lowest of the low" according to Mīrzā Khān. The verse Bhoja quotes is suitable in the very superficial sense that it adheres to the generic conventions of the play.

Despite the fact that Prakrit is now generally associated with these snippets of dialogue in Sanskrit stage plays, Prakrit was also used as the primary language of other types of texts—single-verse lyrics, longer narrative poems, historical poems, and romances. Prakrit was, in other words, the language of Prakrit literature. And that literary tradition, by most accounts, began with an influential anthology of single-verse poems, compiled by Hāla around the first or second century, called *Seven Centuries*. Thanks in part to this text, the Prakrit language had a long-lasting association with the inward-looking themes of erotic lyric.[20] Bhoja quoted the verse from the *Recognition* because in it Śakuntalā expresses her love for Duśyanta in a type of language that is eminently "suitable" for this purpose. Everything about this verse—its language, its meter, its theme of love-in-separation, its meta-literary character (it is composed as a message), and its studied earnestness—evokes the rich world of Prakrit poetry beyond the world of Kālidāsa's play.

Prakrit was not just a part of the classical Indian world. Prakrit texts were themselves classics. They continued to be read and studied, in some cases more than a thousand years after they were composed. Among theorists of literature in India, they represented more clearly than almost any other texts literature's affective and suggestive powers. As most students of Sanskrit literature know, the ninth-century theorist Ānandavardhana elaborated his revolutionary concept of "suggestion" by citing Prakrit verses. Many of these verses are taken from the *Seven Centuries* of Hāla, but some are taken from the now-lost *God of Five Arrows at Play*, a Prakrit poem that Ānandavardhana himself composed in order to illustrate aspects of his poetic theory. Ānanda develops his argument in his *Light on Suggestion* by first producing a reading of the following verse from *Seven Centuries*:

bhama dhammia vīsattho so suṇao ajja mārio teṇa
golāaḍa-viaḍa-kuḍuṃga-vāsiṇā daria-sīheṇa

Go your rounds freely, gentle monk,
the little dog is gone.
Just today from the thickets by the Godā
came a fearsome lion and killed him.[21]

Ānanda cited this verse for the simple reason that what is "suggested," namely, that the monk should fear for his life, is the opposite of what is actually stated, namely, that the monk should go about his business without a care. Readers knew, in accordance with long-standing conventions for reading Prakrit poetry, that the speaker was a woman trying to get a flower-picking monk away from the place where she had arranged to meet her lover. This verse would continue to be discussed for centuries after Ānandavardhana by those seeking to refute or reinforce his theories, especially among the intellectuals of Kashmir. Bhaṭṭa Nāyaka, for example, added that the words "gentle monk" and "fearsome lion" are what allow the suggested meaning to get off the ground, and Mahimabhaṭṭa attempted to reduce the suggestion in this verse to a case of garden-variety inferential reasoning. Abhinavagupta and Mammaṭa defended Ānandavardhana's interpretation.[22]

The lyrics of the *Seven Centuries* helped to establish Prakrit as a literary language in the early centuries of the common era. In fact, they helped to establish the category of "literary language" itself. Over the next several centuries, Prakrit texts such as *Hari's Victory* and *Rāvaṇa's Demise*, by the Vākāṭaka kings Sarvasena (late fourth century) and Pravarasena II (early fifth century) respectively, would become models for the courtly epic, rich in description and poetic tours de force. Meanwhile, Prakrit was the preferred language, for much of the first millennium, for the fictional romance. One of the earliest examples of this genre is Pālitta's *Taraṅgavatī*, probably composed in the first or second century. Subsequent romances include the Haribhadra's *Story of Samarāditya*, Uddyotana's *Kuvalayamālā*, and Kautūhala's *Līlāvatī*, all from around the eighth century. Throughout this period, Prakrit continued to be used in plays, in the dual functions noted above: to represent the speech of certain kinds of characters, and to introduce elements of lyric and song.

As a language of systematic knowledge, Prakrit's scope was more limited. But in light of Sanskrit's near-total dominance of this domain, it is remarkable that Prakrit was used at all. We notice, first of all, that Prakrit was employed as the language of systematic knowledge about Prakrit literature: in grammar and lexicography, in metrics, and in the analysis of figures of speech. Although Sanskrit eventually supplanted Prakrit in most of these discourses, they slightly complicate the story of Sanskrit as the exclusive language through which literary culture theorized itself. There are, besides, Prakrit texts on a range of "practical" subjects, ranging from alchemy and medicine to divination and gemology. One example is *Hara's Belt* by the tenth-century author Mādhuka, a wide-ranging compendium of procedures (*yogamālā*), such as casting love spells or treating snakebites. These texts slightly complicate the story of Prakrit as an exclusively literary language.[23]

Besides being used for literary and scientific texts, Prakrit was used for religious purposes, above all by the Jains. Jainism is a religion based on the teachings of Mahāvīra, an earlier contemporary of the Buddha, that teaches asceticism and restraint as the means of obtaining liberation from the cycle of transmigration.[24] It is largely as a Jain language that Prakrit is studied today. The boundaries between these three categories—literary, scientific, and religious—are fuzzy, but we can point to a number of key genres in this last category. One is the profusion of commentary on Jain canonical literature, unfolding through several layers (*niryuktis*, *bhāṣyas*, *cūrṇis*, and *ṭīkās*). It was probably in this domain that Prakrit was first employed as a textual language. Other genres include stories meant to inculcate Jain virtues, stories about important Jain figures, legendary and historical, hymns to the founders of the religion, and systematic expositions of Jain doctrine. Prakrit may be indispensable for studying Jainism, but Prakrit is hardly the only language that Jains used, nor did only the Jains use Prakrit for religious purposes. There are, for example, Shaiva *tantras* and Vaishnava devotional poems in Prakrit as well.[25]

Beyond being cultivated by members of disparate religious traditions, Prakrit was the language of a literature in which religious differences disappeared. It was, as Rājaśekhara and Bhoja said of literature more generally, common to all religious traditions.[26] No genre represented this better than the anthology or "treasury" (*kośa*). Prakrit anthologies were produced by Hindus, Buddhists, and Jains, and it is only a slight exaggeration to say that we would not be able to identify the religious identity of their authors but for the invocations and colophons. It is no exaggeration at all in the case of the author of a thirteenth-century *Message Poem* (*Sandeśarāsaka*), who calls himself "the lotus of his family in Prakrit poetry": only his hint that his family comes from "the land of the Muslims" allows us to decode the Prakrit name he gives us, Addahamāṇa, as ʿAbd ur-Raḥmān.[27]

Participants in the literary culture of India viewed Prakrit literature as an "inexhaustible treasury" that they held in common: after an initial investment by classical authors of the early first millennium, its resources—themes, figures, turns of phrase, even whole verses—were continually drawn down and replenished by poets, anthologists, and literary theorists. For example, the Jain monk Jineśvara included in his *Treasury of Gāthā-Jewels* (1194 CE) verses that had been circulating, in and outside of such anthologies, for nearly a thousand years. Jineśvara had no hesitation whatsoever about including verses in praise of Viṣṇu and Śiva in his collection.[28]

To summarize, Prakrit was a classical language in a number of overlapping senses. Prakrit texts were considered "classics" and studied for upwards of a thousand years, beginning in the first couple of centuries of the common era. Knowledge of the language and the literature was a key component of cultural fluency. Prakrit was cultivated across a vast swath of southern Asia, from Kashmir to Tamil Nadu, and from Sindh to Bengal, and it was at least known, if not studied, in Cambodia and Java as well.[29] Like Sanskrit, it was a language of literary intellectual culture, and cut across regions and religious traditions. If it was not cultivated as intensively or as broadly as Sanskrit was, it was nevertheless cultivated by those at the very apex of cosmopolitan culture, such as Bhoja and Ānandavardhana.

Yet Prakrit has unquestionably fallen from its earlier glory. To describe the state of Prakrit today, we might paraphrase what a medieval Jain monk said about one of the classics of Prakrit literature, *Taraṅgavatī* by Pālitta: nobody recites it, nobody asks for it to be recited, nobody talks about it; it has become the exclusive preserve of scholars; nobody else can do anything with it.[30] If people think of Prakrit at all, they generally think of it as a mild deformation of Sanskrit used exclusively in plays. And even the Prakrit portions of plays are always read in the Sanskrit translations, called "shadows" (*chāyās*), that are always printed alongside them, or sometimes even instead of them. In circumstances like these, the complex intertextuality of the verse from the *Recognition of Śakuntalā* mentioned above will inevitably fall flat. But Kālidāsa is lucky to have his texts read at all in the twenty-first century. The same cannot be said of Pālitta, whose *Taraṅgavatī* is lost, or Vairocana, whose *Brilliance of the Connoisseurs* remains unpublished. Even *Rāvaṇa's Demise* by Pravarasena struggles to find readers today, despite the fact that the Mughal emperor Akbar personally requested that this classic text be explained at his court.[31] Only a few Prakrit texts survive; of those that survive, not all have been published; and of those that have been published, few have attracted any kind of critical scholarship. What accounts for this neglect?

Prakrit is even more vulnerable than other classical languages to the various processes by which modernity dismisses, discounts, marginalizes, and fetishizes the non-modern. Take, for example, the official designation of "classical language" that the Government of India has, since 2003, bestowed upon Tamil, Sanskrit, Kannada, Telugu, Malayalam, and Odia. Prakrit is missing from this list and likely will remain missing for some time, despite the fact that it has a longer history of attestation than all of them, except for Sanskrit and possibly Tamil.

One reason for its absence is that it does not stand for a regional, national, ethnic, or even a religious identity that might serve as a bulwark against being forgotten. Prakrit texts are "homeless texts"; no one claims to own them and they figure in no one's cultural politics.[32] A handful of attempts to make Prakrit a more important component of Jain religious education are exceptions that prove the rule.[33] Another reason is that Prakrit is so deeply embedded in Sanskrit culture. It is widely seen as a dialect of Sanskrit, with the implication that it fails to be a language in the full sense of the word. Sanskrit has always cast its shadow—its *chāyā*—over Prakrit. Of all of the literary languages of South Asia, Prakrit alone was close enough to Sanskrit—both linguistically, in terms of their forms, and discursively, in terms of their co-occurrence in texts—to be read *as* Sanskrit. When we read a Sanskrit "shadow" of a Prakrit verse in modern editions, we are following a practice that was already in place in the tenth century, when Abhinavagupta translated every Prakrit verse he encountered in Ānandavardhana's *Light on Suggestion* into Sanskrit. Hence Prakrit was very rarely conceived of as a language unto itself, with its own distinctive practices and its own history.

DEFINING "PRAKRIT"

Before discussing the stakes of Prakrit's history, I must be very clear about what I mean, and don't mean, by the word "Prakrit." Over its history, this word has had a wider range of application than any other language name I can think of, and a productive discussion of Prakrit's history requires that we limit this range somewhat. In this section I discuss the scope of the term "Prakrit," its singularity or plurality, and the term "Mahārāṣṭrī," which has often been used as a synonym or near-synonym of Prakrit. This section will also double as a *précis* of the history of scholarship on Prakrit, since that narrative shows how the signification of "Prakrit" has shifted according to the priorities of scholarship.

William Jones's 1789 translation of the *Recognition of Śakuntalā* is often credited with introducing classical Sanskrit literature to the Western world. In doing so, it also introduced Prakrit, as the title page proclaims: "translated from the original Sanskrit *and Prakrit*."[34] Very soon afterwards, based exclusively on the evidence of the plays, "Prakrit" was understood as a vernacular language in contrast to Sanskrit, although there was considerable debate over whether it was a "real" or "fabricated" vernacular. In 1837, Christian Lassen, in his *Institutiones Linguae Pracriticae*, provided a systematic survey of Prakrit and its varieties following their description in Indian sources. He introduced Western audiences to premodern grammars of Prakrit, including the *Light on Prakrit* by Vararuci. Lassen drew attention to the ambiguity of the term "Prakrit": on the one hand, it referred to a group of closely related literary languages; on the other hand, it referred to one of these languages in particular—Prakrit *par excellence* (*Pracritica* κατ' ἐξοχὴν)—which alone was used as the primary language of entire poems.[35] It was not until the later nineteenth century that scholarly editions of these poems were brought out. Siegfried Goldschmidt edited *Rāvaṇa's Demise* in 1880, and Albrecht Weber edited *Seven Centuries* in 1881.[36] These works, which remain unsurpassed to this day, gave a clear picture for the first time of the second, more specific, sense of Prakrit. Around the same time, Richard Pischel undertook the study of premodern Prakrit grammars, in the course of which he edited two important works of the twelfth-century polymath Hemacandra, the *Garland of Regional Words* and the Prakrit section of his grammar (*Siddhahemacandra*). Georg Bühler aided the effort by editing another Prakrit lexicon, the *Prakrit Lakṣmī* of Dhanapāla. By 1900, Pischel had finished his magisterial grammar of Prakrit in all of its varieties, *A Grammar of the Prākrit Languages*.[37] Meanwhile, Weber's student Hermann Jacobi brought to light the vast literature of the Jains, much of which was written in Prakrit and closely related languages, and accompanied his editions, translations, and primers of this material with shorter linguistic and philological studies.[38] In this effort he was joined by Jain scholars in India, including Puṇyavijaya Muni and Jinavijaya Muni, who led an effort to publish the Prakrit texts found throughout the manuscript libraries of India. This effort continued throughout the twentieth century, and included A. N. Upadhye and H. C. Bhayani, to whom we are indebted for many fine editions.[39]

Jacobi represented a transition between two ways of conceiving and naming Prakrit. We can see this most clearly in his *Ausgewählte Erzählungen in Mâhârâshṭrî*, which was instrumental in introducing the language to the wider scholarly public. There he divided the "Indic languages," a family related by descent from a common ancestor, into three stages of development: Old Indic or Sanskrit, Middle Indic or Prakrit, and New Indic or Bhāṣā. The three-stage model is still generally accepted by linguists and philologists.[40]

Each stage has two names, which reflects Jacobi's commitment to the perspectives of what I call below a "natural" and "cultural" history of language. "Old Indic," "Middle Indic," and "New Indic" are "etic" names that nobody who used these languages would have recognized; they represent the natural historian's attempt to classify these languages along a single developmental continuum. "Sanskrit," "Prakrit," and "Bhāṣā" are "emic" names. They represent the languages that were picked out, named, and used for literary purposes. And they coincide exactly with the three languages that Mīrzā Khān identified. Later in his career, Jacobi would use "Prakrit" when writing in a literary-historical mode and "Middle Indic" when writing in a linguistic mode.

Jacobi's well-intentioned parallelism has given rise to a number of misunderstandings. One is that the etic and emic terms are synonymous. They aren't. "Middle Indic" and "Prakrit" are not just the modern and premodern ways of picking out the same languages, or even the same kinds of languages. What underwrites this false equivalence is the idea that any language that deviates from Sanskrit in any way is and always was Prakrit. I will call this a "broad" definition of Prakrit. There is some warrant for this idea within the Indian tradition, but one major problem with it is that it empties the categories of "Sanskrit" and "Prakrit" themselves of any concrete referentiality and employs them as transhistorical categories of language—refined versus unrefined, artificial versus natural—despite the fact that the processes that give meaning to these categories are, of course, historical.[41] Another misunderstanding is that Sanskrit, Prakrit, and Bhāṣā somehow follow each other in history. Jacobi was careful to avoid this suggestion by referring to stages of development (*Entwicklungsstufen*) rather than stages of attestation. Indeed, against the general expectation that linguistically "later" forms of a language are historically attested "later" as well, the entire linguistic history of India provides many striking counterexamples, including one that Louis Renou identified as the "great linguistic paradox of India": Middle Indic languages are attested in the inscriptional record centuries before Old Indic languages are.[42] Yet when we think of India's language practices as comprising a "simultaneous order," situations like this become less paradoxical, and we can more readily countenance a work like the eighth-century *Kuvalayamālā*: written largely in Prakrit ("Middle Indic"), with a sprinkling of Sanskrit verses ("Old Indic") and a few snippets of vernacular conversation ("New Indic").[43]

The broad definition is typically adopted by scholars concerned with the natural history of language: given the project of tracing the genealogical relationship between the ancient, medieval, and modern languages of India, a sufficiently broad term is needed to encompass all of the forms of speech that might figure in this genealogy.[44] Hence "Prakrit" becomes a cover term for languages that were never called Prakrit in ancient India: the languages of Ashoka's inscriptions; the languages of later inscriptions in India ("Monumental Prakrit," "*Leṇa* Prakrit," or "Stūpa Dialect") as well as in Sri Lanka ("Sinhalese Prakrit"); the language of the Theravāda Buddhist canon, now commonly known as Pali; the popular Sanskrit of Buddhist literature in the early centuries CE ("Buddhist Hybrid Sanskrit"); the language of birch-bark scrolls from northwestern India to Western China ("Gandhari Prakrit" and "Niya Prakrit," both generally called "Gandhari" these days); essentially, any piece of the linguistic puzzle between the Vedas and the appearance of the modern vernaculars, which is to say, the entire linguistic puzzle.[45] There are some good reasons for grouping these enormously diverse languages under the heading of "Middle Indic"; I am less sure that they should be grouped under the heading of "Prakrit."

For some scholars, including Richard Pischel and Oskar von Hinüber, "Prakrit" is a subset of "Middle Indic." It refers specifically to a set of literary languages, and Pischel took care to point out that this latter term did not simply mean "languages that happen to be used in literature," but rather "languages that are used *exclusively* in literature."[46] This narrow sense of "Prakrit" includes two distinct groups of languages. One is the "scenic Prakrits," which are used exclusively in plays. They are given names which suggest that they are related to particular regions—Śaurasenī, Māgadhī, Āvantī, and so on—although these regional associations are almost totally notional. These are secondary languages, to use Sheldon Pollock's term, in that they are never used as the primary language of a literary text.[47] They are also considered to be Prakrits only in a secondary sense, at least according to the earliest theorists.[48] The other group includes primary languages, and above all the language of literary classics like the *Seven Centuries*. As Daṇḍin said in his *Mirror of Literature*, "people know that Prakrit *par excellence* is the language based in Mahārāṣṭra, in which poems such as the *Building of the Bridge* (i.e., *Rāvaṇa's Demise*), an ocean filled with the jewels of good poetry, have been composed.[49]" As Daṇḍin's description suggests, this language too has an association with a particular region, namely, Mahārāṣṭra, and for this reason it is often called Mahārāṣṭrī. But we should not be misled into thinking that Mahārāṣṭrī bears the same relation to Mahārāṣṭra as the scenic Prakrits bear to the regions for which they are named. They are distinct language practices, with distinct histories and distinct connotations of the regional.

The narrow sense of Prakrit maps closely onto what premodern Indians meant by the word. And one of my contentions is that if we want to understand what Prakrit was, we need to start from what the people who actually used this word meant by it. The appearance of "Prakrit" as a language name and the literature it designates marks a major turning-point in the cultural history of language in India—a turning-point that is completely obscured if we continue to equate "Prakrit" with "Middle Indic." Moreover, "Prakrit" designated a language that had a stable identity, such that it was equally possible to compose Prakrit texts in the eighteenth century as in the first, and it therefore cuts clean across the linguistic periodization implied by "Middle Indic."[50] Prakrit, put simply, is what Prakrit texts tell us they are written in: when *Seven Centuries* proclaims that it is "Prakrit poetry" (*pāua-kavvaṃ*), when *Taraṅgalolā, Līlāvaī* or *Kuvalayamālā* proclaims that they are in the Prakrit language (*pāaa, pāaāe bhāsāe, pāiya-bhāsā-raiyā*), or when *Vajjālagga* includes a whole section on the beauty of Prakrit poetry, we know what they are referring to, and it's not a stage in the historical development of a family of languages.[51] "Prakrit poetry," says a verse in *Brilliance of the Connoisseurs*, "is like a beautiful courtesan: erotic, alluring, full of *rasa*, delicate, provoking excitement and desire, it captivates your heart."[52] The name of Prakrit was retroactively applied to the language of Jain scripture, and on occasion to the language of Buddhist scripture as well, but the historically and conceptually primary sense of the word remained the language of literary texts composed in the first half of the first millennium CE. Indeed, against those who argued that Buddhist scripture could be authoritative despite being composed and transmitted in Prakrit, the seventh-century philosopher Kumārila Bhaṭṭa claimed that the language was "not even Prakrit."[53]

UNLOCKING THE LANGUAGE ORDER

If Prakrit is indeed a "minor" language in a certain sense—whether that means being a subordinate part of a language order dominated by Sanskrit, or constituting a minority of textual production in premodern India—it is nevertheless a grave mistake to equate "minor" with "unimportant": "there is nothing that is major or revolutionary," Deleuze and Guattari assert, "except the minor."[54] Prakrit gives us an opportunity to reconceptualize and rehistoricize the language order of premodern India. It is the most important Indian language you've never heard of.

What we think of as the literature of classical India—its genres, its styles, its figuration, its tropes, and most of all the languages in which it was composed—exists within a framework that Prakrit texts played a crucial role in establishing. One of the organizing features of this framework was the contrast between Sanskrit and Prakrit, which gave each its name: *saṃskṛta* means "refined," and *prākṛta* "common."[55] This dichotomy came to inhere in the concept of language itself: to write a text in classical India meant to write it not just in language, but in a language. Any system of signs could be language, but only a well-defined cultural practice—defined, that is, by the exhaustive dichotomy of Sanskrit and Prakrit—could be *a* language. To simplify the picture slightly, prior to the first and second centuries CE, the limited evidence that coins and inscriptions make available to us presents a continuum of languages, but we have very little evidence for the names of these languages, or how people otherwise distinguished them. But after the second century, in order to count as a text at all, a text had to be written in one of a small set of languages that were named and defined in relation to each other, and by far the most important of these languages were Sanskrit and Prakrit.

Prakrit was a very different kind of language than Sanskrit, however. Prakrit was essentially "in-between": neither Sanskrit, the preferred language of learned discourse, nor a regional vernacular; this is why the threefold schema, such as we find it in Mīrzā Khān, is so often invoked. It was also ambiguous, being at once the language of a sophisticated and courtly literature and the language used to mimetically represent the speech of the unsophisticated and uncourtly, as Mīrzā Khān also suggests. For these very reasons it was, and remains, important for thinking about the tensions inherent in textual language practices: between the ideal of a transregional discourse and the ineluctable imprint of the regional; between the discursive figure of the author and the social figure of the speaker; between being circulated and being read, spoken, and understood.

The significance of Prakrit lies, further, in its role in the major historical articulations of language orders in India: specifically, the formation of the "Sanskrit cosmopolis" around the second century CE, and the process of vernacularization that began, or at least began in earnest, around the ninth century.[56] One of the foundations of the Sanskrit cosmopolis is the literature, called *kāvya*, through which its political, ethical, and aesthetic ideals were articulated and by which they spread. Prakrit's role in the development of this literature has been vastly underestimated. Scholars have largely looked for its origins in Sanskrit alone, either tracing its genealogy back to texts of Vedic Sanskrit, or positing a dramatic repurposing of Sanskrit from the liturgical to the expressive. Sometimes they have reached back into the Pali texts of the Buddhist canon.[57] I will take up an old but mostly forgotten suggestion that *kāvya* began as *kavva*, and that Sanskrit learned to be poetic from Prakrit.[58] My argument turns not so much on the chronological priority of Prakrit literature to Sanskrit literature, which remains doubtful in any case, but on the clear evidence that the constitutive features of *kāvya/kavva* in its earliest stages easily and frequently crossed the boundaries between these languages, and indeed other languages, such as Tamil.

Prakrit is similarly underappreciated as a catalyst of, and model for, vernacularization, the process by which vernacular languages come to be used for "books and poetical works" (to use a phrase of Mīrzā Khān's). I argue that Prakrit provided the regional vernaculars with the concepts with which to theorize themselves, including the concept of the regional itself (*deśya* or *deśī*). As profound as the differences are between Prakrit and the vernaculars in terms of the cultural work that each performed, it was often the case that the vernaculars were able to do this work at all only because of the example of Prakrit. Further, we can distinguish between two groups of languages that followed very different trajectories of vernacularization based on their relationship to Prakrit. Southern languages like Kannada and Telugu represented themselves in place of Prakrit in the framework that they took over from Prakrit grammar.[59] Northern languages, by contrast, represented themselves as largely continuous with Apabhramsha, a language that was in turn largely continuous with Prakrit (I consider it an "iteration" of Prakrit in chapter 5). So long as they could be accommodated into these older categories, newer categories more specific than simply "language" (*bhāṣā*) were rarely devised, and in stark contrast to the South, grammars—which depend upon and rearticulate such categorial distinctions—were never written.

NEW MODALITIES OF LANGUAGE

This book is not an attempt to translate the concepts and practices of language prevalent in premodern India into the terms in which we in the twenty-first century have grown accustomed to speaking of them. I offer a biography of Prakrit in part as a critique of some of the ways of thinking about language that are available to us, both within academic disciplines and beyond them into our own "vernaculars." We have many ready-made categories that are reflected in the adjectives that we frequently put before the word "language": literary, spoken, natural, artificial, vulgar, refined, technical, vernacular, cosmopolitan, national, prestige, elite, courtly, religious, and so on. But Prakrit stubbornly refuses to fit in most of them, or it fits into categories that we imagine to be mutually exclusive: the debate over its "artificiality," discussed below, is a case in point. This intractability suggests that the major traditions of modern thought about language don't provide sufficient resources to theorize what Prakrit was. And this doubt naturally leads us to wonder whether the same traditions come up short when it comes to other languages—even the ones with which they are most closely concerned.

Let me be clear about what those major traditions of modern thought about language are. The history and structure of language are the domain of linguistics.

The variation of language across social differentials is the province of sociolinguistics. Cultural attitudes about language are studied by linguistic anthropology. Literary history is probably most concerned with the use of language in literary texts, or what I will be calling textual language practices, and once upon a time, philology had similar concerns. All of these traditions share an ontology of language that is basically historicist (language is a thing that exists in, and inevitably changes over the course of, history) and that awards primacy to speech instead of writing (speech is a first-order, and writing a second-order, system of signs). There have been searching critiques of this ontology, but no serious alternatives have been offered.[60] Most problematically, although we have a descriptive *notion* of literary language—the kinds of language that are used in literary texts—this ontology leaves no space for a *theory* of literary language.[61] There is language itself and its use in a literary text. The theory of the former is linguistics; the theory of the latter is rhetoric or stylistics. But what if there was no "language itself" apart from its use in a literary text?

Prakrit in particular, and the language order of premodern India in general, represents a challenge to these widespread assumptions. Whatever spoken language it might have been "based on," and whatever this might mean, the practices of Prakrit for over a thousand years were *literary* practices. It cannot be reduced to a "vernacular" in the usual sense of the word, that is, a language of everyday communication.[62] Let's provisionally adopt the model of social-scientific approaches to language, in which features of language practices are a "dependent variables" that need to be reduced to and thereby explained by an "independent variable." In the case of Prakrit, what could these independent variables be? It was never a national language, and never possessed the kind of extension and boundaries that such languages are supposed to have. Nor was it the language of state administration, nor was it ever controlled by state institutions. It was never anyone's "mother tongue," and nobody ever thought of it as such; certainly nobody burned themselves in the street, or fasted to death, for Prakrit.[63] It was never the language of intersectarian dialogue, and only rarely that of learned discussion. It was a scriptural language only for a small minority—and even for them it was not the only such language.

How did it come to pass that in such a language, minor or not, literature would be written and studied by people of all religious persuasions throughout all of South Asia for a period of more than fifteen hundred years? Or, more important, how *could* this come to pass? How must a culture think of language, how must it organize it and determine it and articulate it in systematic knowledge, in order to do such things with it? Clearly, a theory of this kind of literary language would not merely treat it as a "modification" of spoken language for literary purposes, as it is usually conceived of, but as a language that does not stand in need of spoken language at all, either for its being or for its being known, and as a language that properly belongs to a literary culture, rather than to a community of speakers defined on social, religious, or political lines.

NATURAL AND CULTURAL HISTORIES OF LANGUAGE

I have often been asked whether I was studying Prakrit as a language or as a literature, and from my remarks above, it will be clear that I refuse the alternatives. In order to ask questions about the Prakrit language, one must first know what the Prakrit language is, where it is, how it is; one must know what it means for Prakrit to be a language. And in order to ask questions about Prakrit literature, one must know what this thing called "Prakrit" that qualifies and unifies it actually is. To see just how closely the linguistic and the literary are connected, we can consider two problems that have attended the study of Prakrit since its very beginning.

The first problem is whether the Prakrit text transmitted in the manuscripts available to us accurately represents the text that the author himself wrote. Should the transmitted text be emended on the basis of our knowledge of what Prakrit is "supposed" to look like? Or—given that this knowledge is necessarily derived from other texts transmitted in manuscript form—is the impulse to emend circular and hubristic?

Although the problem of circularity is familiar from other manuscript cultures, one thing that was never in dispute in regard to Prakrit is that the transmitted texts range from inaccurate to incomprehensible. Knowledge of Prakrit was evidently far more difficult for scribes to come by than knowledge of Sanskrit in the period in which most of our manuscripts were produced, that is, between 1300 and 1800, and in many cases scribes clearly had no idea what they were copying.[64] Furthermore, like Sanskrit, Prakrit was written in a variety of regional scripts, and each region, and sometimes each community, had its own orthographic conventions. The eighteenth-century scholar Ghanaśyāma complained loudly about a confluence of scribal error and scholarly cluelessness in one of his commentaries: instead of reading a circular mark as a sign of nasalization, "self-styled scholars" read it as a sign of consonantal doubling, and made censorious comments on the basis of their misreading.[65]

The question is thus not whether to emend the texts, but how, and in particular, whether we should revise the Prakrit of the manuscripts so that it matches the descriptions found in premodern grammars. In 1894, Theodor Bloch proposed to dispense with the Prakrit grammarians entirely: he argued that they could not be trusted to correctly describe the language of texts that were written centuries before them. Mārkaṇḍeya, for example, wrote in the late sixteenth century, describing a language that had been used as early as the first. Bloch was criticized by scholars such as Sten Konow, Richard Pischel, and Alfred Hillebrandt who argued—although not precisely in these terms—that the knowledge systematized in Prakrit grammars reflects the same knowledge that the authors of Prakrit texts actually possessed.[66]

The discovery of manuscripts of a number of previously unknown stage plays in Kerala at the beginning of the twentieth century put the problem into focus. Several scholars ascribed these plays to Bhāsa, an early playwright (fourth century CE or earlier) of whom no other works remain.[67] Does the Prakrit of these manuscripts, which diverges in several respects from the Prakrit taught by the grammarians and from the Prakrit of other plays, represent an older stage of the language? The early presumption was that these manuscripts do indeed transmit an "archaic" variety of Prakrit, which corroborates the ascription to Bhāsa. But recent work has shown that many of the alleged archaisms of "Bhāsa's Prakrit" appear in the manuscript traditions of other plays, and especially in South Indian manuscripts. These features have generally been edited out of the other plays, however, precisely because they conflict with the statements of the Prakrit grammarians.[68] The common wisdom now is to collect and report all of the possible manuscript evidence, and then to "chart a navigable course" between the manuscripts and the grammarians, although there are very few examples of what such a course would look like in practice.[69]

Let us suppose that we have an autograph copy of a Prakrit text, such as Rājaśekhara's *Karpūramañjarī* (early tenth century). Is the language in front of us Prakrit?

Not necessarily. Rājaśekhara might have made mistakes, which are only identifiable as mistakes if there is a standard external to the text against which the language of the text can be judged. In the context of our example, one such standard would be Prakrit grammar. In the late sixteenth century, the eminent Prakrit grammarian Mārkaṇḍeya faulted Rājaśekhara's Prakrit, and in 1901 Sten Konow again accused Rājaśekhara of "confusing" two dialects of Prakrit when in fact he should have had his characters speak Māhārāṣṭrī in verse and Śaurasenī in prose. But how do we know that this principle, which was first enunciated by Viśvanātha in the fourteenth century, would have been known to, or even intelligible to, Rājaśekhara in the tenth? Rājaśekhara himself never distinguishes between Māhārāṣṭrī and Śaurasenī, but instead imagines Prakrit as one language, or at least one kind of language, alongside Sanskrit, Apabhramsha, and Paishachi.[70]

This example simply illustrates the uncertainty we enter into once we begin to consider standards of language use external to the text. The grammarians are one such standard, but really they are only a proxy for the language practices that they codify and thus enshrine as normative. These are not conversational but textual practices; the language the grammarians sought to describe was that of the earliest classics of Prakrit literature, such as *Seven Centuries* and *Rāvaṇa's Demise*. Is this, finally, Prakrit?

Yes, I think, but this answer appears to have been fairly disappointing. On the one hand, texts such as *Seven Centuries*, with its sympathetic vignettes of village life, appear to offer a window onto the real language practices of real people.[71] On the other hand, they only appear to do so: they are, after all, still texts, and most of them are courtly and sophisticated texts. George Grierson, one of the most influential philologists of the early twentieth century, and the director of the *Linguistic Survey of India*, framed the question as follows:

> Unfortunately we cannot accept this literature as illustrating the actual vernaculars on which it was founded. To adapt them to literary purposes the writers altered them in important particulars, omitting what they considered vulgar, reducing wild luxuriance to classical uniformity, and thus creating altogether artificial products suited for that artificial literature which has ever been so popular in India. These literary Prakrits cannot, therefore, be considered as representing the actual speech of the people at any epoch, although they are based on it, and a veil is drawn by them between us and it which it is not always easy to lift.[72]

Grierson was not the first to distinguish between literary Prakrit and "real vernaculars." But his views can be taken as representative of a philological tradition that persists to this day. Essential to the Griersonian vision is that literary languages can be used as evidence for reconstructing the "real" languages that underlie them, so long as we are sensitive to the distortions that literary languages introduce. Grierson confusingly called these "real" languages Prakrits as well: "For centuries the Aryan vernacular language of India has been called Prakrit, *prākṛita*, i.e., the natural, unartificial language, as opposed to Sanskrit, *saṁskṛita*, the polished, artificial, language."[73] Prakrit, the language of our texts, thus becomes an imperfect sign for Prakrit, the language that is imagined to exist prior to it, both conceptually and historically. If this seems like a contradiction, then all we need to resolve it is time: "Originally Prākrits were the spoken languages of the people and their true vernaculars," A. M. Ghatage wrote in 1936. "In course of time they were refined and polished greatly with the help of the grammarians and they were made suitable for literary expression."[74]

There may seem to be a great deal of prevarication, not to speak of Orientalism, in Grierson's conception: Prakrit is what the timeless Indians have always called their unartificial language; it is also, by a constitutive contrast with this first sense, the artificial language in which they have composed the artificial poetry they all like so much. Yet Grierson was in good company when he considered Prakrit to be an "artificial" language. Félix Lacôte noted in 1908 that "the Prakrits, in the strict sense which the grammarians give to this term, have no linguistic reality, or more precisely, they only have an indirect one."[75] To be spoken is to be real. To be written, and especially to be written in accordance with a complex of literary and grammatical conventions, is to be artificial. "From the moment they started writing in Prakrit," Jules Bloch wrote in 1914, "the authors were prisoners of the literary and grammatical tradition."[76]

If a language is "linguistically real" to the extent that it represents the language that people really spoke, then Prakrit clearly poses a problem. Take the example of the *Kuvalayamālā*, a romance by the Jain monk Uddyotana, completed in 779 CE. In a well-known bazaar scene, the narrator quotes small bits of eighteen different languages, some of which sound remarkably similar to the spoken languages of today, and none of which remotely resemble the language of narration throughout the text that Uddyotana himself identifies as Prakrit.[77] It may well be the case that the gap between Prakrit and a "real" spoken language was smaller in the first century than it was in the eighth. But even then, we can only speak in a very vague and speculative way about the "real" language or languages on which Prakrit is based. And this, scholars widely concluded, is a shame. If Prakrit doesn't allow us to make substantive claims about the "real" languages of India, then what is it good for?

At the beginning of his *Grammar of the Prakrit Languages* (1900), which remains the standard reference work, Richard Pischel observed:

> The Prakrit languages are thus "artificial languages" (*Kunstsprachen*) insofar as they have been significantly modified by poets for literary purposes. But they are not "artificial languages" if it is thereby meant that they are whole-cloth fabrications of the poets. Entirely the same account applies to them as to Sanskrit, which was neither itself the general language of everyday life (*allgemeine Umgangssprache*) of educated Indians, nor is based on such a language, but certainly harkens back to a dialect spoken by people that was, for reasons of politics or religious history, elevated to the status of a general literary language (*Litteratursprache*).[78]

I would unpack Pischel's telegraphic comments as follows: people expect Prakrit to be a popular language because it isn't Sanskrit, but it never was such a language; rather, we should think about Prakrit in *the same terms* in which we think about Sanskrit, namely, as a language that lives in its abundant literature. His comparison makes it clear that artificiality, however we understand it, is not unique to Prakrit, but constitutes a general condition of literary languages in premodern India, and to some extent throughout the rest of the world. It has only become clearer since Pischel's time that whatever tradition we take up—the Vedas of the Brahmans, the Pali canon of the Buddhists, the Ardhamāgadhī canon of the Jains—we are always dealing with a language that has been heavily redacted, revised, and transformed, both intentionally and unintentionally. Pischel's little-appreciated maneuver was to admit the artificiality of Prakrit provisionally, not to discount it as a "philologically worthless" sign of some other language, but to reappraise artificiality itself as an essential feature of the regimes of reading and writing that constitute Indian textuality in general.[79]

We can now distinguish two competing conceptions of language history. August Schleicher, one of the founders of comparative philology, represents the first:

> Languages are organisms of nature; they have never been directed by the will of man; they rose, and developed themselves according to definite laws; they grew old, and

died out. They, too, are subject to that series of phenomena which we embrace under the name of "life." The science of language is consequently a science of nature; its method is generally altogether the same as that of any other natural science.[80]

Schleicher advocates for a *natural history* of language, which tells the story of how languages change over time according to general laws, and crucially *not* according to human will. This is the history that philology and linguistics have attempted, and still attempt, to produce. Sanskrit and Prakrit can only ever furnish indirect evidence, important though it may be, in this kind of history. For they do not represent the spontaneously evolving languages of common people, but fixed literary languages.[81]

The second conception is contained in Heinz Kloss's statement that "languages do not just grow and wither like plants."[82] Language is not just a natural object, but a cultural object. Language practices are cultural practices. And against those who claim that the *uses* of language are altogether distinct from the *structure* of a language itself, this perspective emphasizes that "languages themselves" are not immune to the categorizing, classifying, distinguishing, excluding, regularizing, and standardizing work of culture. Sanskrit and Prakrit can be the subjects of a cultural history of language, since they have been defined and deployed as cultural products all along. This approach does not ask how far the language of a given text can be used as evidence for a "real" language that exists outside of it, but what the real practices were that resulted in the text that we have in front of us. Cultural history complements natural history, but also corrects it. It prevents us from speculating about "the linguistic situation" on the basis of naïve assumptions about the relationship between spoken language and written texts, and it encourages us to account for the linguistic parameters of cultural production: what kinds of languages were Sanskrit and Prakrit, how were they known and represented to the people who actually used them, and why were these languages—and virtually no others—used in literary texts for almost the entirety of the first millennium CE?

INVENTING, FIGURING, KNOWING AND FORGETTING PRAKRIT

Language of the Snakes offers a biography of Prakrit from the perspective of cultural history. Although one might expect a "biography" of a language to be organized around the biological conceits of birth, life, and death, I have organized this book around the things that people did with Prakrit, the *practices* that gave it its historical being.

First of all, it had to be invented. The claim that Prakrit was invented, or even the more modest claim that it has a beginning, will seem counterintuitive so long as the prevailing notion of Prakrit is that it arose from the beginningless current of popular language. Accordingly, one important scholarly discussion of "Prakrit" begins by surveying attitudes toward language that can be recovered in Vedic texts and grammatical literature, including Patañjali's *Mahābhāṣya* (second century BCE).[83] By contrast, one of my contentions is that "Prakrit" only began when a set of cultural practices, possessed of a determinate form and commonly recognized by the name "Prakrit," came into existence. I argue that Prakrit emerged as such specifically in the context of the Sātavāhana empire of the Deccan, which lasted roughly from the early first century BCE to the early third century CE. Before this, we can identify all manners of "near-Prakrits"—plenty of Middle Indic dialects, and plenty of instances of the influence of Middle Indic speech on Sanskrit—but nothing that proclaims its linguistic identity as clearly and as consistently as the literature of the Sātavāhana period.

The argument for Prakrit's invention has two parts. Chapter 2 focuses on the inscriptions of the Sātavāhanas, their contemporaries, and successors. I argue that the use of a self-consciously literary style in these inscriptions belongs to a newly aestheticized vision of power that the Sātavāhanas articulated. By taking the latest epigraphic and numismatic evidence into account, I offer a detailed history of inscriptional language practices in the Deccan, which I use to critically revise some commonly accepted ideas about two related phenomena: the appearance of literary prose, and the appearance—and gradual domination—of Sanskrit in literary and political discourse. I argue, first, that a "language of power" formed part of the Sātavāhanas' cultural politics from the dynasty's beginnings, and second, that their conflicts with a competing dynasty, the Kṣatrapas, between 50 CE and 150 CE resulted in the contestation and redefinition of this language of power, and in particular, the use—at first experimental—of Sanskrit as such a language, in contrast to the Middle Indic favored by the Sātavāhanas.

Prakrit as we know it, however, belongs to a different domain of the Sātavāhanas' cultural politics. While they promoted one Middle Indic language as the medium of their inscribed "poetry of polity," they promoted another as the medium of courtly literature. This latter language was called "Prakrit." As I argue in chapter 3, the Sātavāhana court supported and directed a nascent literary culture that would, in turn, be defined by the aesthetics of the court. The works produced under the Sātavāhanas, such as *Seven Centuries* and *Taraṅgavatī*, would become the foundational texts of the Prakrit literary tradition, and of the Indian literary tradition more broadly. If this is not the whole story of the origins of classical Indian literature, it is nonetheless an important and neglected part of it. This chapter examines *Seven Centuries* in detail as a programmatic statement of the aesthetics of this new literary movement that was centered on the Sātavāhana court. I also argue in this chapter that courtly Prakrit and Jain Prakrit, which are almost always considered separate entities with separate histories, were in fact closely intertwined, as shown by the important contributions of the Jain monk Pālitta, the author of *Taraṅgavatī*, to *Seven Centuries*.

In chapter 4 I provide a conspectus of some of features of this literature in an attempt to define more clearly what it meant to write in Prakrit, whether it was Hindu kings or Jain monks doing the writing. I listen, first, to its prized aural qualities—its "sweet syllables"—and reflect on the poetic possibilities that its phonology opened up. Then I discuss the metrical forms that were employed in Prakrit literature: I argue that a new style of versification is a sign of the profound influence that Prakrit literature had on a number of textual traditions, since it redefined what it meant to compose in verse. Lastly, I examine some of the ways that Prakrit poems were collected and arranged in anthologies, and how this mode of presentation helped to constitute Prakrit literature as an intertextual field.

During and after its invention, Prakrit had to be figured: it had to be accommodated within a representational structure that would determine its limits and its relations to other languages. Prakrit was a constant and essential component of the threefold, fourfold, and sixfold schemas that mapped the language order of classical India. I examine a range of literary and literary-theoretical texts in chapter 5 to make this case, starting with Kālidāsa's image of the twofold speech of Sarasvatī. Being inscribed into the foundations of a broadly based linguistic imaginary gave Prakrit a classical status that it maintained for its entire subsequent history. It also assigned Prakrit a productively ambiguous status within the classical language order: it was identical to Sanskrit, yet opposite to it; both a language of high literature and, at least notionally, of "the lowest of the low"; unified as a category, yet divided into a seemingly arbitrary number of varieties and subvarieties.

Prakrit then had to be known. It needed to become an object of systematic knowledge, and in this case, of grammar, metrics, and lexicography. These discourses defined Prakrit, and they also provided the conditions for its transregional cultivation. They provided the conceptual tools for comparing Sanskrit and Prakrit, on the one hand integrating Prakrit more fully into a transregional episteme represented by Sanskrit, and on the other resulting in the recognition of "the regional" as a domain resistant to this kind of integration. As a result of these operations, Prakrit had one foot, so to speak, in the Sanskrit cosmopolis and the other in the nebulous domain of the regional. But as such, it provided an ideal model for vernacular literary cultures which sought to theorize themselves as both regional and cosmopolitan. My focus in chapter 6 is on the earlier Prakrit grammars, including fragments of the earliest grammars in Prakrit and Vararuci's *Light on Prakrit*, as well as some early grammars of Kannada and Telugu.

Finally, Prakrit had to be forgotten, to disappear from the face of the earth and take up residence, according to Mīrzā Khān at least, in the subterranean realm of the serpents. I relate its disappearance to the major reconfiguration of the language order that Prakrit itself had facilitated, the conceptualization and theorization of regional vernaculars: between the vernaculars and Sanskrit, which was given new roles to play, Prakrit was largely squeezed out of most of the genres in which it had been written. Although this reconfiguration took place over centuries, it is between the twelfth and thirteenth centuries that its impact on textual production in Prakrit becomes clear. Prakrit texts were abridged, summarized, translated and adapted into Sanskrit, Kannada, Telugu, and Braj Bhāṣā. It was kept alive in certain communities, including an ever-shrinking circle of learned Jain monks and the theatrical performers of Kerala, but interest in the language was increasingly antiquarian and scholastic. Authors no longer resorted to Prakrit in order to spin out a tale or recite a verse in literary gatherings. I end with the redetermination of Prakrit as the language of the snakes.

This book thus follows Prakrit over the course of its existence. The goal throughout is to show what that existence consisted in, rather than to document every single thing that it comprised. It is inevitable that there will be absences in such a project. I hope, however, to have established a foundation for a new kind of narrative about Prakrit, and about literary languages within and outside of India. This is not a study of any one text or genre, or a history of Prakrit literature, but an account of Prakrit's position within the language order of India. Some of the materials discussed here will be familiar to every student of Indian literature; some have been completely untouched by scholarship; some are presently available only in manuscript form. This book is intended as a critical reorganization of the way we think of Prakrit, one that shifts the focus away from our own made-to-order definitions and onto the structures that Prakrit was in actual fact embedded in: language schemas, language orders, textual traditions, and literary cultures. It is critical, not just toward particular classifications and historicizations of Prakrit, but toward the classifying and historicizing regimes that predetermine for us what kind of thing language is and thus what kind of thing Prakrit must be.

2

Inventing Prakrit

The Languages of Power

Opera naturale è ch'uom favella,
ma così o così, natura lascia
poi fare a voi, secondo che v'abbella.
—DANTE, *PARADISO* 26.130–132[1]

INTRODUCTION

Chapters 2 and 3 tell the story of how Prakrit began. I locate its beginning in the same set of transformations that made Sanskrit the preeminent language of culture and power in South Asia. In this story, Sanskrit and Prakrit are cognate cultural practices. Chapter 2 provides a historical and conceptual framework for those transformations, and chapter 3 places the emergence of Prakrit as a literary language within this framework.

Between 50 BCE and 250 CE, the language order of India changed dramatically. This period saw the emergence of a new kind of culture-power, as Sheldon Pollock has convincingly shown, as well as the emergence of a set of language practices that indexed and constituted it.[2] Certain languages were thus reinvented as "languages of power." Classical Sanskrit is the paradigmatic example: Sanskrit was already very old around 50 BCE, but its use as a language of literary and political self-expression, and the qualities of refinement and ornamentation that accompanied these uses, were very new. I argue that Prakrit was also an "old-new" language—a set of existing language practices that were reinvented by being deployed in new discursive contexts. The stable configuration of these two reinvented languages, Sanskrit and Prakrit, was the answer to a question that lies just beneath the surface of literary and political discourse around the turn of the millennium: if there is to be a "language of power," what should it be? Rather than focusing on a single moment of invention or reinvention, the story here focuses on the centuries-long process by which "languages of power" were continuously fashioned, defined, and contested.

A "language of power" can be a language used by political power as well as language that confers power on those that use it. This reflexivity is what Dante had in mind when he noted that what makes a language "illustrious" (*illustre*) is the fact that it both illuminates and is illuminated (*illuminans et illuminatum*).[3] This chapter is primarily based on the evidence of royal inscriptions, which exemplify this reflexivity. "Royal inscriptions" in this context are documents inscribed in stone—the only medium that survives from the period that concerns us here—issued on the authority of members of a royal family. In them, political power presents a particular kind of language in which it is itself presented.

Together with "private" inscriptions that refer to ruling kings, royal inscriptions are convenient for building up a historical framework. But we need to be cautious about what it is, precisely, they offer evidence for. Inscriptions have a distributed agency that makes it difficult to ask about the intentions of individuals: behind every instance of inscription stands a complex of actors (donors, officials, scribes, and so on), and, even more important, a cascade of previous instances, all of them linguistic acts that, in varying degrees, reaffirm and recalibrate the conventions of language. This makes them poor evidence for language practices at the level of individuals, but ideal evidence for language practices at the level of discourse. And it is this discursive level, and the longer-term transformation of language within it, that interests me here, rather than the question of what language particular persons or families "spoke." We must again be cautious about how language practices at this level should be characterized. In this crucial period of transition, the inscriptions themselves tell us precious little about the languages they are composed in—what they're called, how they're thought of in relation to others, and so on. By comparison, literary sources tell us quite a lot, but they are largely from a later period, and thus they represent a retrospective from a world in which the dichotomy of Sanskrit and Prakrit is taken for granted. But in the early centuries of the common era, I argue, this dichotomy was still very much being worked out, and we would do well to resist the temptation to characterize the inscriptional languages of this period in these terms.

My starting point is the fact, perhaps well known but very rarely remarked upon, that the Sātavāhana dynasty, which ruled most of central India between 50 BCE and 250 CE, is closely associated both with radical innovations in inscriptional discourse in this period and with the invention of Prakrit literature. This chapter will therefore largely stay within the geographic and temporal limits of the Sātavāhana empire, although some of the developments I discuss here have important parallels in the realm of the Kuṣāṇas to the north.[4] This story has three parts, which unfold roughly in sequence: first, the emergence of the very idea of a "language of power"; second, the competition among particular languages to achieve and monopolize this status; third, the consolidation of a stable language order in which each individual language is assigned a place.

One advantage of this account relates to what it is an account of: not the emergence of particular kinds of language use—for example, the use of Sanskrit in political inscriptions—but the emergence of a large-scale language order in which these uses find a place. Broadening the focus in this way allows us to see language practices that we would not otherwise see. Foremost among these previously invisible practices is Prakrit, which has almost always been treated as a fixed point of departure for the process of Sanskritization rather than as a practice in its own right, or as I argue here, a counterpractice to Sanskrit. The theory of Sanskritization itself will therefore have to be revised in light of these findings, and I offer some suggestions for revising it in the chapter's conclusion. Another advantage is that the genealogy offered here accounts for some of the unique features of the classical language order. Why, for example, is Prakrit used at all in the classical literature of India? The answer must refer, in part, to the background of language practices against which this literature took shape. Finally, where most accounts focus on a single moment of emergence, this account foregrounds the trajectories, some extending over centuries, in which language practices are defined, refined, and ordered, as well as the networks of discourse in which these individual moments are situated.

While much of the evidence marshaled here has long been known to scholarship, it has proven notoriously difficult to situate in a convincing historical narrative.[5] Recent research, however, has provided a relatively stable consensus regarding the chronology of the Sātavāhanas, at least starting from the reign of Gautamīputra Śrī Sātakarṇi in the last quarter of the first century CE.[6] Thanks to this chronology, we can for the first time construct a convincing picture of language and power in the generations before Rudradāman, whose Junāgaṛh inscription of 150 CE previously provided us with the first fixed date in the history of Sanskrit as a language of power. The chronology of the early Sātavāhana rulers remains very provisional, but it will do no damage to the argument if the developments that I provisionally assign to the early first century BCE in fact occurred several generations earlier or later. A tabular chronology can be found in appendix A and a bibliography of the inscriptions referred to in this chapter, as well as other historically significant inscriptions, can be found in appendix B.[7]

INVENTING A DISCOURSE

Nāṇeghāṭ, or "Coin Pass," is a narrow pass through the Western Ghats, a few hours north of Pune in today's Maharashtra, that connects the coastal lowlands with the Deccan plateau. Here, around the beginning of the first century BCE, the Sātavāhanas—a family that had recently established control over large parts of what is now Maharashtra, northern Karnataka, and western Telangana—created an unprecedented monument to their own power. A number of caves were

FIGURE 1. The Nāṇeghāṭ Cave in 2014 (photo by the author).

excavated from the face of the cliff. The largest of these contained portraits of the royal family, carved in deep relief into the back wall, and an inscription listing the sacrifices the family had performed, carved into the two side walls.[8] The monument provided a political reading of the physical geography of the region: whether entering or exiting the Deccan plateau, travelers would know who its overlords were.

The word "Deccan" derives from *dakṣiṇāpatha*, the "Southern Path," a network of overland trade routes dating back at least to the middle of the first millennium BCE. Starting around the first century BCE, the Sātavāhanas identified the Southern Path as the space of their political ambitions, and it underwent rapid economic integration and urbanization under their control.[9] Nāṇeghāṭ was a monumental argument for the Sātavāhanas being, as they claimed in the accompanying inscription and as they would define themselves for centuries afterwards, "Lords of the Southern Path" (*dakkhināpathapati*).[10]

The visual language of this argument was the rock-cut cave. This architectural form, introduced under the Mauryas two centuries earlier, became ever more closely associated with the Deccan under the patronage of the Sātavāhanas and other local dynasts.[11] The largest concentration of rock-cut caves in India, used by Buddhists during the first centuries BCE and CE, is in Junnar, quite close to Nāṇeghāṭ. Whereas every other rock-cut cave in the Deccan served a religious function, either as a living cell (*vihāra*) or meditation hall (*caitya*) for renunciant monks, the purpose of the cave at Nāṇeghāṭ seems to have been overtly and primarily political. The sculptural representation of contemporary rulers is without earlier known precedents in India,[12] and Nāṇeghāṭ's discursive representation of these rulers in a new kind of language—a poetry of politics, in stark and obvious contrast to the prosaic inscriptions of earlier kings—was likewise unprecedented. Soon, however, the Sātavāhanas, their allies, and their rivals were all advancing their respective claims to power in this new idiom.[13]

The portraits are now completely effaced, and the inscription is badly damaged. The visual focus of the back wall, and the subject of the inscription, appears to have been King Śrī Sātakarṇi and Queen Nāganikā. Although major questions remain about its interpretation, the inscription gives us an idea of what kind of power this couple aspired to exercise, and why this kind of power required a new kind of language to represent it.

The inscription can be divided into three parts. The first (lines 1–2 on the left wall) bore invocations and a date that is now lost; the second (lines 2–6 on the left wall), a eulogy (*praśasti*) of the Sātavāhana royal family, and the third (the remainder of the left wall and the entirety of the right wall), a list of Vedic sacrifices that the Sātavāhana royal family performed and their donations, on the occasion of those sacrifices, to the officiating priests and spectators.[14] The invocations are addressed both to Vedic deities such as Indra and post-Vedic deities such as Saṃkarṣaṇa and Vāsudeva (Balarāma and Kṛṣṇa), indicating a broad commitment to what would later be identified as *śrauta* and *smārta* varieties of Hinduism. In my reading, they also announce the major themes of the inscription, similar in function to the introductory verses of later texts.

With its introductory invocation to *dharma*, the inscription almost seems to refer to the controversy surrounding this important concept. For the renunciant monks with whom the rock-cut caves were primarily associated, it meant the teachings of people like the Buddha. Within the quickly ramifying Vedic tradition, *dharma* ranged in meaning from "the divine principle that gave legitimacy and meaning to a worldly ruler," to the god Varuṇa, the "lord of *dharma*," to the sacrifices enjoined by the Vedas themselves.[15] The other theme is *dakṣiṇā*, hinted at by the invocation to the four "world-protectors" (*lokapāla*s) beginning with Yama, the guardian of the southern direction. For *dakṣiṇā* refers both to the geographic south, and to the gifts made over to the Brahman priests who officiate at Vedic sacrifices. The word *dakṣiṇāpatha*, besides its conventional designation of the Deccan as a geopolitical space, was used in Vedic literature for the "southern path" in the place where the rituals were performed, along which the cows given to the sacrificing priests as *dakṣiṇā* were led during certain rites.[16] This phrase thus fuses the cosmic space of the ritual and the geographic space within which people and goods circulated.

Dharma and *dakṣiṇā* are the key terms in the vision of political power on display at Nāṇeghāt. The Sātavāhanas sought to be kings rather than de facto rulers, and their performance of the Vedic rituals of consecration and sovereignty—such as the *rājasūya* and *aśvamedha*—entailed a performance of their powers of redistribution. The coins issued by Śrī Sātakarṇi and Nāganikā on the occasion of one of their horse sacrifices (see figure 2), which are likely the same coins referred to in the inscription, similarly reflect the fusion of two kinds of authority, one enacted through ritual and another disseminated through the instruments of exchange.

One obvious but nevertheless crucial aspect of this kind of power is its construction through literary language. While previous rulers, most notably Aśoka, represented their power in inscriptional discourse, the Sātavāhanas were the first to do so in an unmistakably literary style.[17] The second section of the inscription consists of about three hundred syllables—most of them no longer legible—making up a single sentence. Its syntactic core, "sacrifices were offered" ([*ya*]*ñehi yiṭhaṃ*), is an abrupt conclusion to a breathless series of long compounds that describe the royal family. These words abound in figures of sound, and specifically the alliterative pairs that later authors would call *chekānuprāsa:* for example, *sagara-giri-vara-valāya pathaviya pathamavīrasa,* "the foremost hero upon the ocean- and mountain-girdled earth," or the title *dakhināpathapati* itself.[18] The final phrase, which probably refers to Śrī Sātakarṇi's queen, Nāganikā, consists of at least five carefully chosen compounds, each longer than the previous one: *māsopavāsiniya gahatāpasāya caritabrahmacariyāya dikhavratayaṃñasuṃḍāya yañāhutidhūpanasugaṃdhāya,* "fasting for months, practicing the austerities of the household, practicing chastity [appropriate to a widow], skilled in initiation, vows, and rituals, and fragrant with the incense she has offered in sacrifices." Note also the repetition of the word *yaṃña* in different senses within adjacent words, which would later be called *lāṭānuprāsa.*[19]

The style of this inscription is instantly recognizable to anyone familiar with the later tradition of literary prose. For the "essence of literary prose" was widely agreed to be a quality called "power" (*ojas*) that was defined by precisely the features we encounter in the Nāṇeghāṭ inscription: long compounds, a density of words, the repetition of words in various senses, and elaboration on a single subject, according to the earliest available discussion of the subject in the *Treatise on Theater* (early centuries CE).[20] In all of the literature prior to this inscription that we know of—whether in Sanskrit, Pali, or Ardhamāgadhī—there was nothing quite like it. Indeed, the extreme density of compound words that characterizes the powerful style is found in none of the Indo-European languages that they are related to, and possibly no other language in the world. Conversely, the stylistic continuities between this inscription and later literary prose in Sanskrit and Prakrit cannot

FIGURE 2. *Aśvamedha* coin of Śrī Sātakarṇi and Nāganika (courtesy of Shailendra Bhandare).

possibly be accidental. The origins of "power" as a quality of language can thus be traced to these early attempts to represent political power in language. It may have been imagined as a counterpart to the quality of "sweetness" (*mādhurya*), which had already been theorized in Aśoka's time, and which was the dominant quality of lyric poetry, above all the Prakrit lyric poetry that the Sātavāhanas themselves patronized.[21] We might say, speculatively, that the discourse of the Sātavāhanas was already being organized around the complementary principles of "power" and "sweetness" in the respective domains of political and literary expression.

Vocabulary formed another component of this new language of power. The basic concepts, such as unlimited sovereignty, were inherited from the Vedic models that the inscription itself invokes so vividly, as well as from the Buddhist models that operate behind the scenes. In this inscription, however, they are refashioned and made more universal, imaginative, and idealized. Thus, rather than depicting themselves as "wheel-turning" emperors (*cakravartin*) of ancient lore, the Sātavāhanas called themselves "those whose wheels are unstoppable" (*apratihata-caka*), an epithet that is condensed and allusive: the "wheels" in question are those of the royal chariot, but perhaps also the "spheres" of political influence theorized in works such as the *Treatise on Power*. This term quickly became part of the standard vocabulary of kingship within the Sātavāhana sphere of influence.[22] This vocabulary singles out qualities such as martial valor that are not tied to any particular tradition or imagination of kingship, and represents them through timeless epithets rather than the narration of specific events. Power is not something the ruler enacts on specific occasions; as the Nāsik inscription shows in greater detail (see below), it inheres in him always and essentially.

The final aspect of this inscription noteworthy here is the type of language it is written in. Although modern scholarship calls it Prakrit, it differs markedly from the literary Prakrit that would develop somewhat later in the Sātavāhana empire.[23] We have absolutely no evidence for the name that contemporaries would have used for the language of this inscription, the "actors' category." To use unambiguously "analysts' categories," it is a western variety of Middle Indic, clearly continuous with the language of Aśoka's inscriptions in western India, which had become an epigraphic lingua franca by the first century BCE, evidently without ever having been standardized in any systematic way. Just as important as its linguistic features are the places in and on which it appeared. The space in which this language circulated, its "linguistic volume," corresponded roughly to the space of the Sātavāhanas' political ambitions.[24] The surfaces on which it was inscribed were usually the walls of rock-cut caves (*leṇa*), or the architectural elements of a Buddhist *stūpa*. Inscription was a prerogative of donors. Thus, to be able to use this language in the first place, the Sātavāhanas had to be donors. This is one of the reasons why donation is foregrounded in representations of the Sātavāhanas, and it also accounts for why rulers so ostensibly devoted to *śrauta* rituals could also be represented, in subsequent generations, as donors to Buddhist communities. In fact, the Śrī Sātakarṇi eulogized at Nāṇeghāṭ may well be identical to the Sātavāhana king who is depicted, at a distance of more than three hundred miles and roughly a hundred and fifty years from Nāṇeghāṭ, in one of the reliefs at the Buddhist *mahācaitya* at Kanaganahalli in what is now northern Karnataka.

There, amid representations of other Sātavāhana rulers, we encounter a scene (figure 3) that a label inscription explains for us: in the same variety of Middle Indic employed at Nāṇeghāṭ, and substantially the same script, it reads: "King Sātakarṇi donates silver lotus flowers to the Great *Caitya*" *(rāyā sātakaṇ*[*i mahāce-*] (*t*)[*i*]*yasa r*(*u*)*pāmayāni payumāni oṇ*(*o*)*yeti*).[25]

The later traditions of royal eulogy (*praśasti*) and literary prose (*gadyakāvya*) that the Nāṇeghāṭ inscription anticipates are predominantly Sanskrit traditions. Indeed, after the third century CE, it was increasingly unthinkable to compose a royal eulogy in any language other than Sanskrit. It is therefore important to emphasize that at this point, in the first century BCE, composing such a text in Sanskrit was equally unthinkable. In fact, the earliest surviving Sanskrit inscriptions of any sort are not much earlier than this one.[26] Herman Tieken claimed that "there is something extremely absurd in the long enumeration in Prākrit of Vedic sacrifices and the fees paid to priests found in the Nānāghāṭ Cave Inscription . . . [w]ith it the Sātavāhanas seem to say: 'See how great and powerful we are despite the fact that we do not know Sanskrit.'"[27] Whether or not the Sātavāhanas themselves knew Sanskrit is unknowable and for our purposes irrelevant: what matters is that, in their world, political power never spoke Sanskrit. According to one explanation of this absence, Sanskrit was still regarded as a language of Vedic ritual and its associated discourses, and its separation from the world of politics and administration—and also writing—was enforced by religious sanctions.[28] Sanskrit, moreover, was never composed in the "powerful" style that characterizes

FIGURE 3. Sātakarṇi making a donation to Buddhist monks at Kanaganahalli (photo by the author, with the permission of the Archaeological Survey of India).

the Nāṇeghāṭ inscription. The dichotomy of Sanskrit and Prakrit as literary languages, I argue, was one of the final results of the process that the Sātavāhanas set in motion. At this stage in the process, the very concept of a "language of power" was new, and it was not grammatical features but stylistic and aesthetic qualities that constituted it.

The success of the Sātavāhanas' experiments can be gauged from the way they were imitated by their eastern rivals, the Mahāmeghavāhanas.[29] In a well-known inscription in the cave-complex at Udayagiri, near Bhubaneshwar in today's Odisha, King Khāravela provided a year-by-year summary of his rule in a "powerful" style similar to that of the Nāṇeghāṭ inscription, and in a nearly identical language.[30] Khāravela there claims to have invaded Sātavāhana territories—specifically Ṛṣika, in today's Khandesh—"without a care for Sātakarṇi," the ruler whom the Nāṇeghāṭ inscription memorializes.[31] Its "narrative compounds," which served to enrich the transregional language of power, are an outstanding feature of Khāravela's inscription, expressing an action in a compressed and rapid way appropriate to the powerful style.[32] Another feature is its carefully calibrated prose rhythm, which arises from joining together words of a similar prosodic shape.[33]

The concluding portion of the inscription, which is its most insistently literary, contains a number of echoes of the language used at Nāṇeghāṭ.[34] Whereas a Sātavāhana king was there described as *apratihata-cakasa,* "whose wheels are unstoppable," Khāravela is described as *apatihata-caka-vāhana-balo,* "whose wheels, mounts, and forces are unstoppable," a phrase that also echoes the family names of Mahāmeghavāhana Khāravela and his Sātavāhana rivals. And whereas someone at Nāṇeghāṭ was described as *aṃgiya-kula-vadhanasa,* "he who brings prosperity to the Aṅgika family," Khāravela is described as *ceta-rāja-vaṃsa-vadhanena,* "he who brings prosperity to the line of Ceta kings."

Khāravela's inscription also provides us with a better sense than we get at Nāṇeghāṭ, because it is better preserved, of the kind of power that this new language was increasingly associated with. Its byword is "all" (*sava-*): the king, though himself a Jain layman, "honors all religious traditions," "sponsors the reconstruction of all temples," and "gives food and drink to all residents, to all royal officers, to all householders, to all Brahmans, as well as to all of the Jain and Buddhist monks, at a cost of hundreds of thousands."[35] This is faint evidence, but evidence nonetheless, of an incipient cosmopolitan vision that would later need to be expressed in a cosmopolitan language.

THE QUESTION OF LANGUAGE

After a few generations of relative silence, the Sātavāhana rulers got back into the epigraphic habit around the middle of the first century CE. To this later period belongs the inscription of the Queen Mother, Gautamī Balaśrī, the longest and most literary of all the extant Sātavāhana inscriptions. I date it to around 103 CE, which would make it one of the earliest documents that is universally recognized to be a *praśasti,* a poem of praise.[36] In terms of its language, it clearly belongs to the discourse of power that took shape several generations earlier. But as the inscription itself tells us, something had happened in the

FIGURE 4. The "Queen's Cave" at Nāsik (photo by the author).

intervening years that fundamentally destabilized both the political order and the discursive practices of power. A completely different cultural politics underlies the inscriptions of the early first century BCE and the turn of the second century CE.

Gautamī Balaśrī financed the construction of what would be called "The Queen's Cave" in what was already a well-established complex of rock-cut cells for Buddhist monks on a hill outside of Nāsik. She used the prerogatives of patronage to inscribe onto its walls a long eulogy of her son, Gautamīputra Śrī Sātakarṇi, although he had died almost twenty years earlier. A fragmentary inscription from the base of a sculpture near the Buddhist *mahācaitya* at Kanaganahalli presents many parallels to the Nāsik inscription, and strongly suggests that there was an "official story" about Gautamīputra Śrī Sātakarṇi that was propagated throughout the Sātavāhana empire through inscriptions.[37]

And quite a story it was. The central portion of the queen's inscription reads as follows:

> . . . crusher of the pride and arrogance of the Kṣatriyas, destroyer of the Scythians, Greeks, and Parthians, levier of taxes in accordance with *dharma*, delighting not in harming living beings even when his enemies have committed misdeeds, bringer

FIGURE 5. Fragmentary stela from Sannati with inscription commemorating Gautamīputra Śrī Sātakarṇi (from Sarma and Varaprasada Rao 1993).

> of prosperity to the houses of Brahmans and the low-born, the exterminator of the Kṣaharāta line, the reestablisher of the glory of the Sātavāhana family, at whose feet the whole circle of kings bows, who put an end to the mixing of the four *varṇa*s, who was victorious in many battles over a confederation of enemies, whose flag of victory remained unconquered, whose capital city was impossible for enemies to assail, who inherited from his ancestors the loud sounds of royalty.[38]

The events here alluded to have been reconstructed with reasonable certainty from other inscriptions and from numismatic evidence. Starting in the second century BCE, groups of Scythians—hereafter Śakas, as they call themselves in their inscriptions—migrated into northern India from central Asia. The leaders of these Śaka groups typically styled themselves Kṣatrapas, which had previously referred to the military governors of the Achaemenid empire. One of these groups, calling themselves Kṣaharātas, established a small kingdom in what was now Gujarat. In the middle of the first century CE, a ruler named Nahapāna wrested a number of key sites from the Sātavāhanas, probably intending to control the trade between India and Rome, which was then at its peak volume. Eventually, however, Gautamīputra Śrī Sātakarṇi retook all of these sites from Nahapāna and the local kings who had thrown in their lots with him.[39]

The eulogy of Gautamīputra Śrī Sātakarṇi incorporates a diversity of styles, ranging from highly compact and composite to punchy and analytic.[40] It redeploys the figures of sound we encountered at Nāṇeghāṭ within new figures of sense: Gautamīputra Śrī Sātakarṇi's face, for example, is "as white as a lotus made to blossom by the rays of the sun" (*divasakara-kara-vibodhita-kamala-vimala-sadisa-vadanasa*). The version at Sannati includes a passage that plays on Gautamīputra's family name, as Khāravela did at Udayagiri: the king is "one whose forces and mounts are on the rise, one whose mounts are unstoppable, the Sātavāhana" (*samudita-bala-vāhanasa abhaga-vāhanasa sātavāhanasa*); at Nāsik he is described as "one whose mounts have drunk the water of the three oceans" (*ti-samuda-toya-pīta-vāhanasa*). The final scene of the queen's inscription at Nāsik features a final battle attended by all kinds of mythological beings, in which the hero ascends directly into heaven from the shoulders of his elephant. Almost every aspect of these inscriptions suggests deep and systematic connections with courtly poetry. Here it is sufficient to note, with A. B. Keith, that "the appearance of mannerisms of the later *Kāvya* . . . implies current familiarity with the themes."[41] It is, in other words, one of the earliest examples of *kāvya* available to us. And it appears that political discourse of the Sātavāhanas had a significant, if largely indirect, influence on the imagination of power in later *kāvya*.[42] This discourse is undoubtedly a "poetry of politics."[43]

What distinguishes Gautamīputra Śrī Sātakarṇi's eulogy, and what has so far kept it out of the history of courtly literature, is the fact that it is in neither Sanskrit or Prakrit. Nearly all of the Sātavāhana inscriptions fit the same description. Like the earlier inscriptions at Nāṇeghāṭ and Udayagiri, these inscriptions are very often said to be in Prakrit, but only in the sense that everything that is not exactly Sanskrit can be regarded as Prakrit. In fact, it was noted long ago that in their inscriptions, the Sātavāhanas "touch so closely upon Sanskrit that they seem rather to guard against it than to try to write it."[44] Their language is closer to standard Sanskrit than to the language that the Sātavāhanas themselves called Prakrit—if we credit the tradition that a Sātavāhana king compiled *Seven Centuries* (see chapter 3).

We must be careful to distinguish "our" questions regarding the language of Sātavāhana inscriptions from "their" questions. I am claiming that a "question of language" was posed abruptly in the middle of the first century CE: given that there is such a thing as a "language of power"—something established by the discursive practices of earlier generations of rulers—what might that language actually be? During this time, new practices were introduced, and old practices were invested with new meanings. And as a result, the stakes of language choice were entirely different at the time of Balaśrī's inscription at Nāsik than they were at the time of Nāganikā's inscription at Nāṇeghāṭ.

The most significant break with existing language practices in this period was the use of Sanskrit in political inscriptions. As we will see, this innovation must be attributed to the Kṣatrapas. And it is true that the Sātavāhanas overwhelmingly preferred to use Middle Indic in their inscriptions, while their Kṣatrapa opponents exhibited a greater willingness to use Sanskrit. We now know, however, that the Sātavāhanas did use Sanskrit in political inscriptions, if only rarely. The narratives of diametrically opposed cultural politics—of Kṣatrapas versus Sātavāhanas, foreigners versus native rulers, and Sanskrit versus Prakrit—need to be critically revised.

A pair of inscriptions sponsored by Nahapāna's son-in-law Uṣavadāta can serve as an example of the kind of experimentation that the Kṣatrapas engaged in, enabling us to better understand how and why Sanskrit came to figure in these experiments. One inscription, found on the wall of a Buddhist cave at Nāsik, exhibits the functional differentiation of language that would characterize many later inscriptions, where Sanskrit was used for "expressive" purposes and other languages for "documentary" purposes. The first part is a eulogy of Uṣavadāta in fairly correct Sanskrit, and the second part records in Middle Indic his donation of the cave and the accompanying cistern.[45] An inscription at Kārle, more than a hundred miles away, contains a parallel version of the eulogy of Uṣavadāta, but in Middle Indic rather than in Sanskrit.[46] The two texts are presented in table 1.

These inscriptions represent two sets of choices, and two sets of cultural-historical possibilities, regarding language use. The "Kārle path" involved the use of Middle Indic for any and all purposes that required permanent inscription; it was a direct continuation of the language practices of an earlier era. The "Nāsik path" involved a differentiation of language. Sanskrit was used to reinscribe portions of discourse that had already been inscribed in Middle Indic at Kārle, thus forming an association between Sanskrit and the permanence of iterability, and between Sanskrit and the kind of discourse that merited this permanence: the expressive self-representation of political power. The creation of distinct discursive functions for Sanskrit implied the relegation of Middle Indic to other functions: the specific, the documentary, the occasional. By calling these different sets of choices "paths," I mean to connect them to their longer-term effects. The "Nāsik path" leads somewhere: to the expansion of Sanskrit in political discourse at the expense of Middle Indic, to the devaluation and destabilization of Middle Indic, and to the redetermination of Sanskrit as not just *a* language of power but *the* language of power.

This reconfiguration occurred along aesthetic, and emphatically not religious, lines. Indeed Uṣavadāta's inscriptions represent an economy of religious donation that cuts across sectarian boundaries: according to the Nāsik inscription, Uṣavadāta purchased a field from a Brahman family, then donated it to the local Buddhist community along with a rock-cut cave, on the walls of which he recorded his prior donations to Brahmans. Some scholars have connected Uṣavadāta's self-professed religious motivations with his use of Sanskrit. "[T]he pressure to use Sanskrit," Johannes Bronkhorst writes, "went hand in hand with the pressure

TABLE 1 Comparison of the introductory portion of Uṣavadāta's inscriptions

Kārle [99]	Nāsik [100]	Translation
raño khaharātasa khata-pasa nahapānasa jā[ma] tarā [dīnī]kapūtena usabhadātena	*rājñaḥ kṣaharātasya kṣatrapasya nahapānasya jāmātrā dīnīkaputreṇa uṣavadātena*	By Uṣavadāta, the son-in-law of King Kṣaharāta Kṣatrapa Nahapāna, the son of Dīnīka,
tigosatasahasa[de]ṇa	*trigośatasahasradena*	the giver of three hundred thousand cows,
nadiyā baṇāsāyā s[u]-vaṇatathakarena	*nadyā bārṇāsāyāṃ suvarṇadānatīrthakareṇa*	who established a holy site on the river Bārṇāsā through a donation of gold,
... brahmaṇāna ca soḷa[sa] gāma[d]e[na]	*devatabhyaḥ brāhmaṇebhyaś ca ṣoḍaśagrāmadena*	who gave sixteen villages to the deities and Brāhmaṇas,
prabhāse pūtatithe brahmaṇāṇa aṭhabhāyāp[r]a-[dena]	*prabhāse puṇyatīrthe brāhmaṇebhyaḥ aṣṭabhāryāpradena*	who gave eight wives to the Brāhmaṇas at the holy site in Prabhāsa,
anuvāsaṃ pi tu satasahasaṃ bhojapayita	*anuvarṣaṃ brāhmaṇaśatasāhasrībhojāpayitrā*	who feeds hundreds of thousands of Brāhmaṇas every year,
	bharukacche daśapure govardhane śorpārage ca catuśālāvasadhaprati śrayapradena	who gave four-roomed rest houses in Bharukaccha, Dásapura, Govardhana, and Śūrpāraka,
	ārāmataḍāgaüdapānakareṇa	who has made gardens, tanks, and wells,
	ibāpārādādamaṇatāpīkarabeṇādā hanukānāvāpuṇyatarakareṇa	who has established free crossings at the Ibā, Pārādā, Damaṇa, Tāpī, Karabeṇā, Dāhanukā, and Nāvā rivers,
	etāsāṃ ca nadīnāṃ ubhato tīraṃ sabhāprapākareṇa	and who has established public watering stations on both banks of these rivers,
	piṃḍītakāvaḍe govardhane suvarṇamukhe śorpārage ca rāmatīrthe carakaparṣabhyaḥ grāme nānaṃgole dvātrīśatanāḷige ramūlasahasrapradena	who gave thirty-two thousand coconut-tree stems at the village Nānaṃgola to the assocations of *carakas* at Pīṃḍītakāvaḍa, Govardhana, Suvarṇamukha, and Śūrpāraka,
	govardhane trīraśmiṣu parvateṣu dharmātmanā ...	who was very pious in the Triraśmi hills at Govardhana ...

to accept the Brahmanical vision of society."[47] The problem with this argument is that a Brahmanical vision of society had never needed to be expressed in Sanskrit before; indeed, according to a strict "Brahmanical vision," the pressure should have gone the other way: Sanskrit, the language of solemn Vedic rituals, should never have been used for the political self-promotion of *arriviste* warlords like Uṣavadāta.[48] What did need to be expressed in Sanskrit, however, was verse. The use of Sanskrit for expressive purposes finds parallels in two other inscriptions, which together testify to the large geographic area in which these changes were taking place. An inscription from the reign of Śoḍāsa in Mathurā (early first century CE) has a date in Middle Indic and a verse in Sanskrit in the *bhujaṅgavijṛmbhita* meter. And a fragmentary inscription that was found close to the fragmentary eulogy of Gautamīputra Śrī Sātakarṇi mentioned above speaks of a deceased king—probably Gautamīputra himself—in Sanskrit verses in the *vasantatilaka* meter. This inscription probably dates to the period between 85 and 100 CE.[49]

The Sātavāhanas put an end to the Kṣaharātas, but did not thereby put an end to the language question of the first century CE. In their inscriptions—most explicitly in the eulogy of Gautamīputra Śrī Sātakarṇi—they represented their victory as a return of social and political order. But some of these inscriptions were done only a few steps from those of Uṣavadāta. According to the cultural logic that governed inscription, what was inscribed should not and could not be uninscribed: a verse in the contemporary *Seven Centuries* makes it clear that "letters carved on stone" were supposed to last forever.[50] The official documents of the "reconquista" reaffirm the traditional language practices of the Sātavāhanas; more precisely, they "traditionalized" practices that previously had no such cultural valence. The use of Middle Indic, which earlier generations had taken for granted, now contrasted with the incipient use of Sanskrit. Thus when the Sātavāhanas boasted of restoring social and political order, and did so in Middle Indic, they were proclaiming the restoration of a cultural order as well. They had been forced to take a stand on the language question.

The Sātavāhanas were well attuned to the possibilities of language as an instrument of culture-power, and for these purposes they gave their strongest support to languages other than Sanskrit: the inscriptional Middle Indic of their ancestors, employed for political literary prose, and the language of literature in the Deccan plains, used for courtly lyrics. This does not mean that they were in principle opposed to the use of Sanskrit for such purposes, or that they "attempted to preserve Sanskrit in its ancient and pristine sacral isolation."[51] In fact, there is some evidence that the Sātavāhanas experimented with political Sanskrit both during and immediately after their conflict with Nahapāna: while most of their inscriptions, as well as coin legends, are in Middle Indic, the aforementioned verse inscription found at Sannati, which probably refers to Gautamīputra Śrī Sātakarṇi, is in Sanskrit, and at least one coin of Gautamīputra Śrī Sātakaṛni with a Sanskrit legend has come to light.[52]

These experiments seem to have been short-lived, given that the Sātavāhanas would go on to rule for at least another century after Sātakarṇi's death, and they apparently used Middle Indic exclusively in their official documents throughout this period. But the experiments nevertheless allow us to see something important about the Sātavāhanas' cultural politics: they seem to have been less concerned about the strict confinement of Sanskrit to the ritual sphere than about the creation of a new sphere of culture-power in which Sanskrit did not already have a monopoly. It is ironic, albeit predictable in hindsight, that Sanskrit, once introduced into this sphere, would fill it to the exclusion of the languages that the Sātavāhanas themselves promoted.

Even after their victory over the Kṣaharātas, the Sātavāhanas had to adjust to a larger political reality in which their cultural practices, to whatever extent they were normative within their own empire, were not quite so normative outside of it. Most important, the Sātavāhanas found themselves in an uneasy alliance with the Kārdamaka rulers of Ujjayinī. Like the Kṣaharātas, these rulers were Śakas and called themselves Kṣatrapas, and like the Kṣaharātas they were receptive to the political power of Sanskrit. In 150 CE, the Kārdamaka ruler Rudradāman produced what has been seen as one of the founding documents of the Sanskrit cosmopolis: a long eulogistic inscription in Sanskrit literary prose carved onto the face of a rock at Junāgaṛh, in the Kathiawad peninsula of Gujarat.[53] The history surveyed so far, however, puts us in a position to see this inscription somewhat differently, not as the sudden emergence of a new kind of discourse, but as one step—albeit more of a leap—in the dialectical development of a language of power. To trace this development, we need to start from about a hundred years earlier.

Why were rulers like Uṣavadāta receptive to the political uses of Sanskrit in the first place?[54] The texts that survive do not give us access to their intentions. One suggestion has been that these foreigners faced a severe "legitimation crisis." Their rule, as the *Yugapurāṇa* conveys in no uncertain terms, was thought to signal the end of the world. Hence they turned to Sanskrit in order to publicly demonstrate their acceptance of the sociocultural authority of the Brahmans.[55] There are, however, good reasons to be skeptical of this theory, both the general model of legitimation through the instrumental use of cultural signifiers, and the specific claim that Sanskrit was such a signifier. As noted above, orthodox Brahmans, the putative audience of this political theater, might even have regarded political self-glorification as an illegitimate use of their sacred language. Another theory emphasizes the very illegitimacy, according to the traditional understanding, of these new practices: foreigners were able to use Sanskrit in new ways precisely because they did not feel themselves to be bound by the sociocultural norms that kept Sanskrit strictly within the sphere of Vedic ritual. "In wresting from the schools and liturgy of the Brahmans their mysterious language," Sylvain Lévi observes, these foreigners "raised up against the confused variety of local Prākrits an adversary which alone was capable of triumphing over it."[56]

My explanation relies on a distinction between discourse in Sanskrit, which necessarily involves a will to compose in Sanskrit, and discourse in "hybrid" languages—a term that has become standard despite problems with the metaphor of hybridity—which does not self-evidently involve such a will, however similar to Sanskrit such languages might appear to us. These practices are related to each other, but they are not two points on a sliding scale of "Sanskritization": the deliberate use of Sanskrit took place against a background of "hybrid" language practices. There are political aspects to both practices, but the motivations and strategies behind them might have been much more different than is usually thought. In particular, the use of "hybrid" languages does not necessarily betoken a desire for prestige, legitimacy, or even correctness.

Polities of the first century CE were transregional in two senses. The Sātavāhana empire, from its very beginnings, incorporated smaller areas into a political supraregion that the Sātavāhanas called "the Southern Path." The polities of the Kṣaharātas and Kārdamakas were organized as military governorships that migrated over enormous areas. In both types of polities, locally dominant language practices must have come in contact with each other at the highest levels of official discourse. And as these two types of polities confronted each other over the course of the first and second centuries CE, they borrowed, adapted, and contested each other's strategies for navigating the complexities of language use within their realms. The Kṣaharātas, for example, had used three scripts on their coins: Kharoṣṭhī, Greek, and Brāhmī, reflecting their movement from the northwest, where the erstwhile Indo-Greek kingdoms were located, to western and southern India. Upon contact with them, the Sātavāhanas adopted the practice of issuing portrait coins, something no previous Indian dynasty had done. These coins featured bilingual legends, with Middle Indic on one side and Tamil on the other.[57]

Sanskrit played an increasingly important role in the language practices of the Kṣatrapas, but probably more because of the fact that they were migratory and in need of a workable lingua franca than because of the fact that they were foreign and in need of legitimacy. All of the Kṣatrapas, including the family of Rājūvula at Mathurā as well as the Kṣaharātas and Kārdamakas, are associated with what has been called "Epigraphic Hybrid Sanskrit."[58] This name is modelled on what Franklin Edgerton called "Buddhist Hybrid Sanskrit," which encompasses any type of Sanskrit used by Buddhists that deviates in any degree from the standard Sanskrit defined by Pāṇini. Epigraphic Hybrid Sanskrit also encompasses any inscriptional language in which there is a mixture of standard Sanskrit forms with Middle Indic forms. The received wisdom is that this language represents an attempt to write in Sanskrit on the part of people who didn't actually know the language, and that what induced these people to make the attempt despite their ignorance was the cultural superiority of the Brahmans—and particularly the Brahmans of Mathurā, from where Epigraphical Hybrid Sanskrit is thought to have radiated.[59] The major flaw of this account is that it explains "hybrid" languages as a failure to write in standard Sanskrit, although in a few diagnostic cases we can be sure that people who wrote in "hybrid" languages were quite capable of writing in standard Sanskrit: this is the case, for example, in Uṣavadāta's Nāsik inscription, where Sanskrit and Epigraphical Hybrid Sanskrit appear side by side.

The "Sanskritization" of Middle Indic finds a better explanation in the fact that Sanskrit forms—which need not necessarily have been recognized as belonging to the Sanskrit language at all—were often the common denominator among the locally dominant languages that the Kṣatrapas encountered on their distant campaigns. Forms such as *kṣatrapasa*, which look "sanskritized" in comparison to forms such as *khatapasa*, may be reflect the influence of relatively conservative languages such as Gāndhārī. In this case, as in many others, the case ending may remain "unsanskritized" simply because all of the locally dominant languages agree.[60] On this account, Sanskritization did not begin as Sanskritization at all, but as a regression to the linguistic mean. A bottom-up explanation like this for a broadly based cultural phenomenon such as Sanskritization should be preferred on principle to top-down explanations that invoke the strategic use of cultural signifiers by a foreign elite. But they are not mutually incompatible: once the language of inscriptional discourse could be recognized as Sanskrit, which would perhaps involve its passing a certain threshold of "hybridity," one could choose to compose in Sanskrit.

Where we do actually encounter Sanskrit in the inscriptions of the first and second centuries—apart from verse, which is only ever inscribed in Sanskrit—it is a translation of an existing discourse. This can clearly be observed in Uṣavadāta's inscriptions, one of which is a translation into Sanskrit of the other. Both inscriptions, however, can be thought of more broadly as translations of a discourse of power that the Sātavāhanas had developed in previous generations. This is equally true of the mature political Sanskrit of Rudradāman, which is more indebted to Sātavāhana models of political discourse than it appears. All of the inscriptions prior to 150 CE that are dated to the reigns of Rudradāman, or his grandfather Caṣṭana, are simple memorials composed in Epigraphic Hybrid Sanskrit. At some point in the 140s, he gave his daughter in marriage to Vāsiṣṭhīputra Śrī Sātakarṇi, and she left a unique Sanskrit inscription in the Kānherī caves just north of today's Mumbai. It seems, however, that the marriage alliance did not prevent hostilities, and in his Junāgaṛh inscription Rudradāman claims to have "acquired fame by sparing Sātakarṇi, the lord of the Southern Path, because their relation was not remote, although he defeated him twice in a fair fight."[61] It is only after he entered into a marital alliance with the Sātavāhanas, and encountered their practice of a "poetry of polity," that he could have wanted, and been able, to produce the kind of inscription that he did at Junāgaṛh.[62] Rudradāman's reinvention of Sanskrit, which undoubtedly did "turn it into an instrument of cultural-political power of a new sort," took place in a context where discourses of power were being borrowed, adapted, transformed, and ultimately used against each other.[63]

One advantage to seeing this reinvention as a kind of translation is that it privileges the connections between political Sanskrit and political Middle Indic—and the literary style and ornamentation that had come to define the latter—over the connections between political Sanskrit and religious Sanskrit. We all know that Vedic and classical Sanskrit are quite different. To the question of what, specifically, makes classical Sanskrit different, our answers would have to include its courtly ethos, its aestheticized and idealized view of the world, its rich inventory of figures of sound and sense, and its use of well-defined literary styles. All of these features appear for the first time in Middle Indic inscriptions. From this perspective we can see classical Sanskrit as a translation of the expressive discourses in Middle Indic that the Sātavāhanas helped to define, promote, and patronize.[64]

THE LEGACY OF THE SĀTAVĀHANAS

The Sātavāhana empire disintegrated around the second quarter of the third century CE, and over the course of the following century, what Sircar has called the "Age of Prakrit" in inscriptions—I would prefer to call it the "Age of Middle Indic"—ended as well.[65] In some places, the transition to the "Age of Sanskrit" was fairly immediate, as if all resistance to using Sanskrit as a public and political language disappeared with the Sātavāhanas themselves. The Śakas of Ujjayinī and their Ābhīra allies might have seen the demise of the Sātavāhanas as a victory for their own cultural politics. As an example, just a few steps away from the Queen's Cave at Nāsik, a Śaka woman named Viṣṇudattā recorded a donation in Sanskrit during the reign of the Ābhīra king Māḍharīputra Īśvarasena.[66] In much of South India, however, the transition to the "Age of Sanskrit" took much longer, as the successors of the Sātavāhanas carefully negotiated their legacy. Yet even here, dynasties that began by issuing official documents in Middle Indic—the Vākāṭakas, the Kadambas, the Pallavas, the Śālaṅkāyanas—would all come to use Sanskrit for this purpose by the fifth century.

The choice to follow the cultural model of the Sātavāhanas or the Kṣatrapas of Ujjayinī, and thus to follow the "Kārle path" or the "Nāsik path," was an important part of this process, which we can see most clearly among the Ikṣvākus of Vijayapurī (modern Nāgārjunakoṇḍa). The Ikṣvākus were the direct successors of the Sātavāhanas in the Krishna valley of today's Andhra Pradesh, and there are continuities in the way they represented themselves. A large number of inscriptions related to the founding of a monastic complex in the city contain a dual eulogy to the Buddha and to the founder of the Ikṣvāku dynasty, Śrī Cāntamūla, that resembles and at some points echoes the Sātavāhana inscriptions in language and style.[67] At the same time, the Ikṣvākus pursued marital alliances with the Kṣatrapas of Ujjayinī, after which there appears to be a trend toward the use of Sanskrit in inscriptions.[68] A somewhat later inscription clearly demonstrates the continuing and parallel influence of these two families, Sātavāhanas and Kārdamakas, on the imagination of power at Vijayapurī: a local official named Śivaseba noted in Sanskrit his installation of an image of Viṣṇu Aṣṭabhujasvāmin, "which neither the king Śaka Rudradāman of Avanti nor Viṣṇurudraśivalānanda Sātakarṇi of Vanavāsa"—belonging to a family of Sātavāhana epigones—"were able to move from its original location at Sañjayapurī."[69] The legacy of the Sātavāhanas is explicitly invoked in other South Indian inscriptions. The Tāḷagunda inscription of the Kadambas, from the middle of the fifth century, refers to a temple that "pious kings such as Sātakarṇi, seeking to obtain the highest good, faithfully revered."[70]

Another aspect of the process of transition was the regionalization of Middle Indic. Middle Indic as a language, the Brāhmī script in which it was written, and the practices of inscription more generally were part of a cultural complex that the Sātavāhanas brought to the regions over which they ruled, although there were often preexisting traditions of inscription, and these elements remained quite stable over three centuries of Sātavāhana rule. By the middle of the third century CE, these regions were no longer subject to any centralized authority. Inscriptions in those regions continued to make use of Middle Indic and the Brāhmī script, but in ways that diverged from the transregional standards of the Sātavāhanas. What we see in a wide variety of post-Sātavāhana inscriptions, rather than the sudden emergence of regional languages, are forms of Middle Indic with amplified regional particularities, a language which was "neither wholly popular, nor entirely regulated."[71] Ikṣvāku inscriptions, for example, sometimes change initial *s* to *h*, and sometimes write etymological voiced stops as voiceless. Both are clearly features of a South Dravidian substrate.[72] Many inscriptions of this period exhibit features that are also found in literary Prakrit, but which are more likely to be taken from the spoken language of the Central Deccan than from literary texts: the change of initial *y* to *j*, the converb in *-ūṇa*, the loss of contrast between retroflex and dental nasals, or the locative in *-amhi*.[73] These tendencies are neither inexorable nor irreversible: regionalisms can be found in an early inscription of Viṇhukaḍḍa Cuṭukulānanda Sātakarṇi, a ruler of northern Karnataka, but not in a later inscription of the same ruler.[74]

One final trend in post-Sātavāhana inscriptions helps us to understand the transition to the "Age of Sanskrit." Increasingly these inscriptions feature formulas, prayers, and verses, and in increasing proportions. These are the fragments of discourse that stood outside of their own time and might have been, and in fact often were, iterated across inscriptions. And these fragments are mostly written in Sanskrit: this includes seals and auspicious phrases, invocations, royal genealogies, and imprecatory verses. The most stringent discursive regularity of all is that verse of any kind, in any inscription, is in Sanskrit.[75] As we have already seen, the distinction between Sanskrit and Middle Indic engenders new discursive functions: Middle Indic becomes the language of the occasional, that which is strictly delimited by time and place, while Sanskrit becomes the language of the permanent. This distinction clearly leads to a kind of inflation: if all inscription is meant to be permanent in some sense, then why should one ever use the language of the occasional and impermanent?[76]

The outcome of these processes was the total obsolescence of Middle Indic as an inscriptional language. If it was unthinkable to use Sanskrit to commemorate political power at the beginning of the Sātavāhana empire, it was unthinkable not to use Sanskrit within a few generations of its dissolution. The way that the Sātavāhanas represented political power, however, far outlasted the languages in which they represented it. They stand at the beginning of the genealogy of political eulogy (*praśasti*) in India, a discursive form in which culture and power were co-constitutive, and thus one of the most important forms of the Sanskrit cosmopolis.[77] The influence of the Sātavāhana rulers, "whose mounts have drunk from the water of the three oceans," can be heard even in the titles given to the Gupta emperor Candragupta II, "lord of the three oceans" and "one whose glory has tasted the water of the four oceans," who was after all related by marriage to the Vākāṭakas, once feudatories of the Sātavāhanas and at the time of Candragupta II their most powerful successors.[78]

CONCLUSIONS

The foregoing account has implications for the way we think of two interrelated phenomena, the Sanskritization and literarization of discourse, which are important to any story we might want to tell about culture and power in premodern India.

Sanskritization is a general term for the process by which a discourse that had previously been in some other language more or less completely comes to take on features of Sanskrit. It has almost always been studied in relation to sets of evidence that are limited by medium, region, and sect, for example the birch-bark scrolls belonging to Buddhist communities in Gandhāra, although it is acknowledged to have been an "overall linguistic trend which transcended sectarian divisions."[79] Sanskritization is still commonly described, if not quite conceptualized, as a process of "hybridization," although the limitations and liabilities of hybridity as a governing metaphor are increasingly well known. A hybrid is often so called simply because it does not fit into the categories that we have grown accustomed to using. And often widely divergent uses of language are grouped together as constituting a "hybrid" for precisely this reason, and hence philologically and historically important distinctions are lost.[80]

The tendency has been to look for Brahmans behind every process of Sanskritization, and to postulate them when they can't be found. There are some striking contradictions and equivocations in this approach: the same Brahmans who are said to have so vehemently resisted the "culture of writing" introduced by Buddhism, and to have declared that Sanskrit must never be written down, are also said to have somehow come to defend, not just a culture of writing, but a culture of writing Sanskrit in particular, which thereby "regained its status of a religiously legitimized literary language."[81] The developments discussed in this chapter allow us to be more specific and more circumspect about the relations between script, language, religion, and social identity.

From the perspective of the agents involved in them, it may even be inaccurate to call these processes "Sanskritization" to begin with. First, although the language practices that we identify with Sanskrit had been around for quite a long time, the recognition of those practices as constituting a distinct language with the name "Sanskrit" is in all likelihood a product of this very period.[82] The first evidence of a clear differentiation between Sanskrit and non-Sanskrit in inscriptions is found in Uṣavadāta's Nāsik record. Second, it was possible to produce Sanskrit-like forms simply by defaulting to the forms that would have been recognized or recognizable across the large regions that the political actors of the first and second CE traversed. And hence many of the practices we consider to be "Sanskritized" or "hybridized" do not necessarily reflect a will to write in a language called Sanskrit at all. Third, scholarship generally fails to distinguish between the preconditions and causes of Sanskritization. If Brahmans, prestige, and the need for legitimation were all these processes required, there is no reason why they should have occurred in the first and second centuries CE, or indeed why they should not be occurring right now. It is only when we look at cultural changes, and above all the creation and contestation of a poetry of politics between the Sātavāhanas and the Kṣatrapas, that we can understand the genuinely new roles that Sanskrit and its others occupied in the first century, and the complex ways in which these roles redetermined the languages that occupied them.[83] The evidence simply does not permit a reduction of language practices to religious determinants.

Literarization is a slightly more elusive phenomenon. In the usage of Sheldon Pollock, it is the process by which a language is rendered appropriate for literary expression, as distinguished from literization, the process by which a language is put into writing.[84] In the context of discourse as a whole, rather than of particular languages, I assign literarization a slightly different meaning: the process by which an existing discourse takes on "literary" features, whatever those features are and however they are defined, or by which a new discourse characterized by these features is created (see the conclusion to chapter 3). I have traced the literarization of the language of inscriptions, starting from the early first century BCE to the fourth and fifth centuries CE, when the authors of political inscriptions could explicitly and unproblematically call their compositions "literature" (*kāvya*). The key actors in this history are the Sātavāhanas, who were the first and among the most influential practitioners of the poetry of politics. The literarization of political discourse

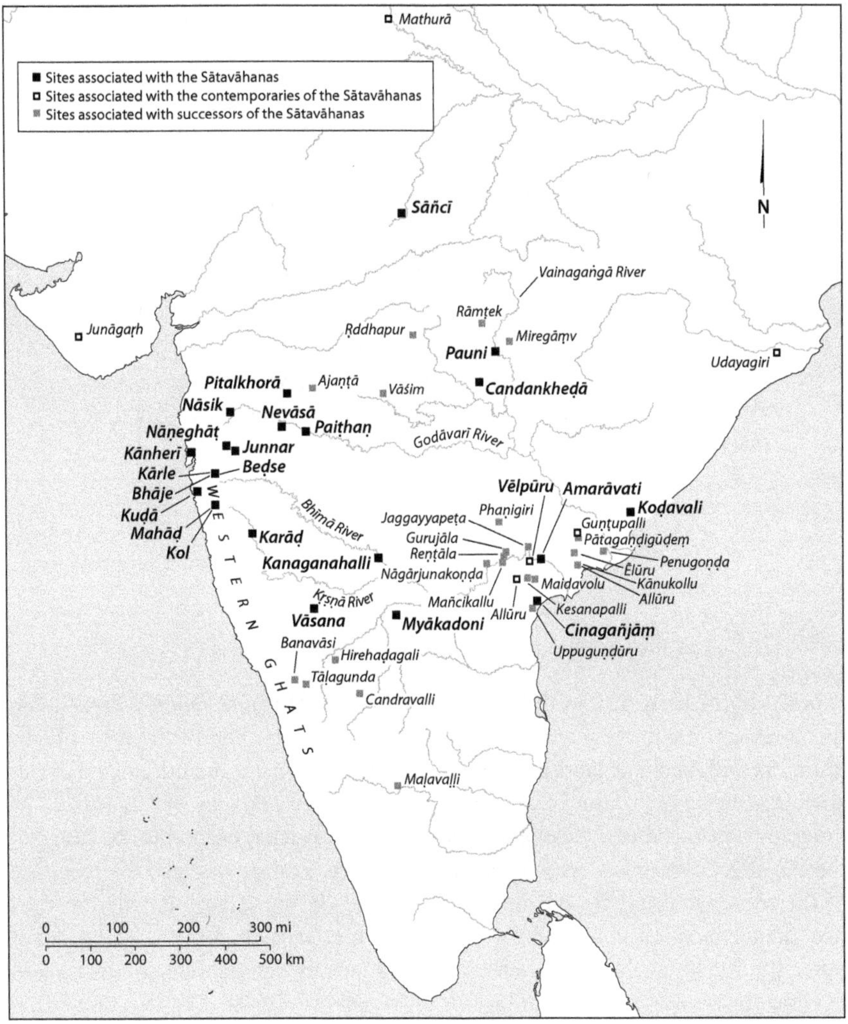

FIGURE 6. Important Sātavāhana sites.

over which they presided ran parallel to the literarization of literary discourse, or in other words, the emergence of a discourse that was conscious of itself as literature. This was *pāuakavva,* Prakrit poetry, and its emergence and relation to the wider field of textual production is the subject of the following chapter.

3

Inventing Prakrit

The Languages of Literature

Consciousness finds itself inevitably facing the necessity of having to choose a language. With each literary-verbal performance, consciousness must actively orient itself amidst heteroglossia, it must move in and occupy a position for itself within it, it chooses, in other words, a "language."

—M. M. BAKHTIN, *THE DIALOGIC IMAGINATION*[1]

THE TWO HISTORIES OF PRAKRIT LITERATURE

A précis of the early history of Prakrit literature might run as follows: Prakrit was the language of courtly poetry in the Deccan in the first half of the first millennium CE, and its major landmarks include *Seven Centuries*, an anthology of lyrics attributed to a king of the Sātavāhana dynasty named Hāla, as well as *Hari's Triumph* by Sarvasena and *Rāvaṇa's Demise* by Pravarasena, both epics by kings of the Vākāṭaka dynasty in present-day Maharashtra. Prakrit was also the language of the texts produced by Jain monks in around the same period, whether they take the form of commentaries on a canonical text, recastings of the narratives of other traditions (such as *Wanderings of Vasudeva* by Saṅghadāsa, a Jain version of Guṇāḍhya's *Great Story*, or the *Deeds of Padma* by Vimala, a Jain version of the *Rāmāyaṇa*), or entirely new stories (such as Pālitta's *Taraṅgavatī*).

This chapter focuses on the "also." What I offer here is not just a reading of Prakrit's earliest known works, but an attempt to read them together, as works that represent and define "Prakrit" in the singular. The way that the history of Prakrit literature has usually been told—to the limited extent that it has been told at all—splits it into two histories. One of these is "courtly" and "Brahmanical," and the other is "popular" and "Jain."[2] This bifurcation is not just a convenient way of organizing texts and authors which, like most such conveniences, can easily become facile and reductive. It has become foundational to the way Prakrit is understood today—as a generic term for two groups of languages and their associated literary practices that do not have much to do with each other. This separation of Prakrit's history into "Jain" and "non-Jain" strands, however valid it may be for understanding the literary production of a later period, is deeply misleading for the earliest period. It may well be the case that these strands are so closely intertwined that we might have to abandon the vocabulary of separation altogether. This is very plausibly the case for the Prakrit-producing literary culture of the western Deccan: the "non-Jain" *Seven Centuries* and the "Jain" *Taraṅgavatī* were in all likelihood produced by some of the same people in the same court.

The two histories of Prakrit converge upon a very obscure but very important period. The standard literary histories represent the first centuries of the common era as a "dark age": few literary productions survive from this period, and of those that do survive, almost nothing specific is known about their dates, authors, and places of composition. The idea of a "dark age" belongs to the same figure as that of a "golden age" under the Guptas in the fourth and fifth centuries proposed by Max Müller in the 1880s.[3] Although Müller's chronology is now completely discredited, the idea of a "golden age" had more staying power. We can briefly consider two discoveries that did more than anything else to discredit Müller's theory. Georg Bühler's work on Indian inscriptions convinced him that the literary practices that Müller associated with the Guptas had existed for centuries prior to them. And the discovery of Aśvaghoṣa's poems, which likewise antedated the Guptas by several centuries, meant that golden-age poets like Kālidāsa were not the first of their kind.[4] These discoveries had the effect of reframing Müller's "golden age," not as a period, but as a set of cultural practices that distinctively characterize that period; these practices might have existed, and according to Bühler did exist, long before that period. Even with this reframed idea, however, there is a danger that any history of Indian literature will have to refer to the practices of the golden age, and that everything will be classified as either an instance of such practices or a precursor to or epigone of them, with the evaluative dimensions that both of these terms imply.

For these reasons, although the history of Prakrit literature is very closely bound up with the history of Sanskrit literature, I do not want to take "Sanskrit literature" for granted as the lens through which we understand and historicize the former. I will therefore try to avoid narratives of the "pre-classical," a practice that both leads to and fails to itself become classical.[5] These narratives hold that Prakrit literature is a precursor to Sanskrit literature, embodying the same style, themes and outlook, but in a less developed and less sophisticated way, or rather represents what Sanskrit literature had to turn away from in order to become refined and courtly.

At the same time, however, I do want to focus my narrative upon a specific set of cultural practices: those of *kāvya,* commonly but not unproblematically rendered as "classical," "courtly," or "belletristic" literature. The form of the word *kāvya* implies that we are dealing in the first instance with Sanskrit. My contention is that the emergence of Sanskrit *kāvya* cannot be separated from the emergence of Prakrit *kavva,* that the two are linked in a strong sense. One is not straightforwardly derivative of the other. Rather, the multidirectional translation of themes, styles, and genres between languages was a crucial part of the practice of literature in this early period. This is not simply to gainsay the historical priority of Sanskrit as a language of *kāvya.* Hermann Jacobi had long ago refuted a version of the argument that classical Sanskrit literature was made up of translations from Prakrit originals.[6] Nor is it simply to interrupt the continuity of Sanskrit textuality from the oral hymns of the *Ṛgveda* to the courtly lyrics of Kālidāsa and beyond. It does mean, however, that non-Sanskrit texts, and above all Prakrit texts, need to be taken much more seriously when the origins and early development of *kāvya* are discussed. And it refocuses this discussion, too, from a question of historical or ethnohistorical priority (which texts, which authors, which languages were the first, or were believed to be the first, to realize this new discursive form?) to a question of historical possibility (what are the sociocultural contexts within which this new form of discourse could arise?).

One of my motivations for refocusing the discussion is, admittedly, my doubt that a convincing answer to the first question can ever be found. We have heard that Vālmīki's *Rāmāyaṇa* is the first *kāvya,* but that Aśvaghoṣa's poems are the first *kāvya*s that can be placed in history; that Patañjali knew about *kāvya* already in the second century BCE; that the *caṅkam* poems represent a Tamil tradition of *kāvya* that antedates and influences the Sanskrit and Prakrit tradition; that there may be further precedents in Vedic literature, and so on. On top of this, I have argued in chapter 2 that the inscriptions of the first and second centuries CE represent a transformation in inscriptional discourse from mundane and pedestrian to elevated and literary, and that we must describe some of these inscriptions, both Sanskrit and Middle Indic, as *kāvya.* The multiplicity of possible beginnings, far from sinking the whole enterprise of theorizing the beginnings of a practice, suggests that we should ask about the role that each of these putative beginnings plays in a broader "*kāvya* movement" that spanned the subcontinent and embraced Sanskrit, Prakrit and quite possibly Tamil in its early stages—the first and second centuries CE—and eventually came to include languages as disparate as Tocharian, Sinhala, and Javanese.

What I call the "*kāvya* movement" is one component of what Sheldon Pollock has called the "Sanskrit cosmopolis." This was a cultural-political formation, lasting roughly from the second to the twelfth century and spreading over much of southern Asia, that was imagined through the universalizing discourses of Sanskrit.[7] The history of Prakrit literature, together with the history of inscriptions, suggest that cosmopolitan culture was not originally or essentially indexed to Sanskrit language practices. My argument in this chapter is that the Sātavāhanas and their successors in the Deccan channeled cultural energies into Prakrit literature, and that this literature represented an ideal of courtliness and sophistication that increasingly came to define cosmopolitan culture in South Asia per se. The forms of literary discourse, like those of inscriptional discourse, "Sanskritized" as they spread throughout South Asia. Significantly, however, the process of Sanskritization did not push Prakrit literature into obsolescence: in contrast to the Middle Indic of inscriptions, Prakrit remained a possible means of literary expression for more than a thousand years. Further, by foregrounding the separation of courtly poetry from religious storytelling, the two histories of Prakrit provide a way of talking about one set of tensions inherent in the "Sanskrit cosmopolis": literature and its forms of knowledge were imagined to be the common property of groups that had mutually exclusive religious commitments, and were thus a site of intense appropriation, contestation, and exclusion.

A constellation of criteria distinguish the "Jain" and "non-Jain" histories of Prakrit from each other, and it will be useful briefly to review these schematically. The themes of love and heroism are prominent in both kinds of literature, but in Jain Prakrit these are explicitly subordinated to the theme of liberation. The principal genres of courtly Prakrit are the single lyric verse (*muktaka*) and a kind of epic that later authors would call the "great poem" (*mahākāvya*); the former is typically in the *gāthā* meter, and the latter in the *skandhaka*. The principal genre of Jain Prakrit is the story (*kathā*), whether told in verse or prose or a mixture of the two. Courtly Prakrit, especially the epic, is highly stylized and makes use of a range of figures of sound and sense, whereas the literary pretensions of Jain Prakrit are less conspicuous. The language of Jain Prakrit has always seemed distinctive to modern scholars, not only for its archaism and the influence of Ardhamāgadhī, the language of the Jain scriptures, but because it was written in a special orthography that employed the letter *y* as a hiatus filler. These linguistic and orthographic differences are related to different histories of transmission: different groups of people were reading, studying, commenting upon, and referring to these texts. The history of transmission is in turn related to their different social sites: courtly Prakrit, of course, being associated with royal courts and the networks of literary culture they sustained, and Jain Prakrit with temples, religious schools, and pilgrimage sites. Finally, these different locations point toward the different actors involved in each tradition: kings, courtiers, and local elites on the one hand, and monks and their lay communities on the other.

One of the goals of this exercise is to subject all of these criteria to critical examination. The first move is to deny that the distinction between Jain and non-Jain applies to the entire tradition of Prakrit literature, or more precisely, that the meaning and significance of this distinction changes substantially over the course of history. This move simply serves to remind us that the distinction between Jain and non-Jain varieties of Prakrit is actually an artefact of European scholarship, associated with the work of Hermann Jacobi and Ernst Leumann. Indeed, by "Jain Prakrit," or "Jain Māhārāṣṭrī" as he called it, Jacobi actually meant the language of relatively late narrative literature, where the influence of Sanskrit was relatively more conspicuous than in the language of earlier court poetry. Since Jacobi's time, however, "Jain Prakrit" has come to be used rather loosely for any text by a Jain author written in any variety of Prakrit.[8] And in particular, it has come to be used of very early texts, such as *Taraṅgavatī* and *Wanderings of Vasudeva,* that Jacobi did not have access to until relatively late in his career. These works were written by Jain authors, but that does not mean that they belong to an exclusively Jain history, or that their authors' Jainism meaningfully accounts for the features of the text that would interest literary historians. The second move is to replace the retrospective of the present, and the two millennia of appropriation and exclusion that are bound up in it, with a prospective from the very beginnings of Prakrit literature: what would a history of Prakrit literature that is not already bifurcated into Jain and non-Jain traditions look like? This view has been hard to gain, because we seem to know so little about the earliest phases of Prakrit literature, but I believe that scholars have been overly skeptical: we in fact know a good deal, and what we do know undermines rather than supports the division of Prakrit into Jain and non-Jain histories.

PRAKRIT'S KINGS

Everyone knows that literature in India began with Vālmīki, the sage who transformed his grief (*śoka*) into metrical verse (*śloka*) and told the story of Rāma. Vālmīki is the first poet (*ādikavi*) and the *Rāmāyaṇa* is the first poem (*ādikāvya*).[9] What is this thing called "literature" that begins from the *Rāmāyaṇa?* Is it Sanskrit literature? Is Sanskrit already hidden inside the term "literature"? Was Prakrit contained within the tradition that began with Vālmīki, or does it have a beginning of its own?

Around 1600 CE, in a commentary to a work on vernacular meters called *Prakrit Piṅgala,* Lakṣmīnātha Bhaṭṭa suggested that if one countenances different beginnings for each literary language, there is space at the beginning for more than just Vālmīki. If Vālmīki was the "first poet" in Sanskrit, Piṅgala was the "first poet" of vernacular literature (*bhāṣā*). The first poet in Prakrit, according to Lakṣmīnātha, was Śālivāhana, the legendary king to whom *Seven Centuries*—the most popular, the most influential, and to all appearances the earliest work of Prakrit literature—is ascribed.[10] And although nobody else articulated his priority in precisely this way, as far as I am aware, this king was widely viewed as one of the key figures, if not the key figure, in the Prakrit tradition. Viśveśvara, who lived in the eighteenth century, praised the author of *Seven Centuries* by calling his work the "archetype" (*prakṛti*) of which all subsequent literature is an "ectype" (*vikṛti*)—including, most obviously, Viśveśvara's own *Seven Centuries,* where this verse appears.[11]

This king was known by several names. The forms Śālivāhana and Śālavāhana appear relatively late in the tradition. Early sources call him Sātavāhana or Hāla.[12] The former is the family name of the dynasty that ruled much of the Deccan between the early first century BCE and the early third century CE (see chapter 2). Later authors seem to use it primarily in reference to a single individual.[13] The name Hāla is included in the list of Sātavāhana kings found in the *purāṇas*.[14] This is no guarantee that there actually was a king named Hāla in the Sātavāhana line, given the occasional unreliability of the *purāṇas* and the complete absence of corroborating evidence from coins and inscriptions.[15] Inscriptional evidence, however, does confirm that Hāla was used as a personal name in this period, and hence the forced derivation of *Hāla* from *Sātavāhana* proposed by several scholars must be abandoned.[16] The names Hāla and Sātavāhana are used interchangeably in literary works, and lexicographers treat them as synonyms.[17]

There are many stories about Sātavāhana in Indian literature. Those I highlight here involve his patronage of Prakrit.[18] According to a well-known story, Sātavāhana was in despair after an embarrassing incident: as he was splashing one of his wives with water in the pool, she said, "Don't throw water on me!" (*modakaiḥ pūraya*), which the king interpreted as "Throw sweets at me!" When the tray of sweets came out, she berated him for not knowing the first thing about Sanskrit grammar. She told him that he should have analyzed *modakaiḥ* into *mā udakaiḥ*. The sources differ regarding what comes next, but as it's told in the *Twenty-four Prabandhas*—a collection of popular tales compiled by the Jain monk Rājaśekhara in 1349—Sātavāhana propitiated the goddess of language, Bhāratī, with a three-day fast, as a result of which he became a great poet and wrote hundreds of texts. Once he asked the goddess for the entire population of his city to become poets for an afternoon, and on that day a hundred million Prakrit verses were composed, which the king then compiled into the anthology called *Sātavāhanaka*.[19] A similar story is told in an anonymous commentary to *Seven Centuries*. There, Sātavāhana entreats the goddess Bhāratī to stay in his palace with him. She consents to do so only for two and a half days, during which time everyone associated with the palace spontaneously composes poetry and prose in the Prakrit language. It was these compositions that Sātavāhana then selected and arranged into seven hundred-verse groups, hence the name of the text.[20]

Both of these stories describe the composition of *Seven Centuries* as a supernatural event of collective effervescence.[21] Sātavāhana was instrumental in both bringing this event about and in transforming it into a textual artefact. We can read these stories along with another one, related by Merutuṅga in 1304, that brings the narrative closer to real-world practices of patronage. When Sātavāhana was told that he owed his good fortune in the present life to an act of selfless generosity in a previous life, he committed himself to giving away his wealth. He gathered all of the poets and scholars and offered forty million gold pieces for just four Prakrit verses, and then he arranged the verses that were produced on this occasion into a "an anthology seven centuries in extent and bearing the title *Sātavāhana*."[22] The patron, in all of these stories, creates an extraordinary circumstance by manipulating ordinary proportions in some way—either by paying an enormous amount for a small number of verses, or by having an enormous amount of verse generated in a short span of time—and the site of this manipulation is invariably the royal court.

These point of origin for all of these stories is *Seven Centuries* itself, one of whose first verses reads:

> Seven hundred ornate verses amid a crore
> were put together by Hāla, dear to poets.[23]

The most obvious meaning is that Hāla selected seven hundred verses out of a much greater number. But it also suggests a comparison between the verses of this anthology (*kośa*) and the contents of a royal treasury (also *kośa*), and thus the very equivalence between literary wealth and monetary wealth that Merutuṅga's story turns on.[24] Another verse in the anthology mentions the Sātavāhana king, comparing him to Śiva by reading the same word in two different meanings:

> There are only two who are capable of
> elevating the family of Pārvatī, or
> uplifting families fallen on hard times:
> Gaurī's beloved husband, and the Sātavāhana king.[25]

According to a unanimous literary tradition, *Seven Centuries* was a product of the royal court of the Sātavāhanas. This "courtliness" is the key to our knowledge and understanding of this text, and of the entire tradition that traces itself back to it. Its connection with the Sātavāhana court has, however, been subject to doubts. And although these doubts have little bearing on the courtly character of *Seven Centuries* in general—this is evident from a reading of the text itself—they do bear on the dating of the anthology and its role in literary history. Here I will review the principal arguments against an early date and explain why they are unconvincing.

One argument is based on the language of the text. The *Seven Centuries* exhibits lenition of intervocalic consonants to a greater degree than either inscriptions of the Sātavāhana period or the language of, for example, Aśvaghoṣa's dramas (early second century CE).[26] But the assumption that every language undergoes the same development at the same rate is demonstrably false, especially when we are talking about literary languages. Luigia Nitti-Dolci likened this argument to trying to figure out the date of Dante's works by comparing his Italian to the language of present-day Lithuanian peasants: we would probably say that Dante's language represents a "later stage of linguistic development," but that doesn't mean that Dante came later.[27] A more serious problem is the discrepancy between the languages of literature and the languages of inscription, which was itself highly literarized, in what I take to be the same political formation. But apart from the evident conservatism of the inscriptional language, it is likely that the language of *Seven Centuries* was meant to be distinctive, conforming more to the poetics of sweetness (see chapter 4) than the poetics of power (see chapter 2).[28]

The second type of argument, formulated first by D.R. Bhandarkar, has the following structure: if *Seven Centuries* were really as old as the ascription to Hāla would make it, then a whole slew of cultural references—the use of the seven-day week, skull-carrying ascetics, the romance of Rādhā and Kṛṣṇa, the Greek loan word *horā* and the Persian loan word *bandī*—would occur for the first time in this text, and that simply can't be the case. Nearly a century later, we know that some of these terms and concepts appear much earlier than Bhandarkar thought, but in any case his argument from silence is not at all probative.[29] We have every reason to expect *Seven Centuries* to be full of firsts, if it is in fact one of the first works of a new kind of literature. One argument of this type merits special consideration because it appeared to provide a definitive *terminus post quem*. Bhandarkar identified Vikramāditya, who is mentioned as a paragon of generosity in W464, with Candragupta II, who ruled in the late fourth and early fifth centuries. But a long and persistent tradition places the "first" Vikramāditya at 57 BCE, at the beginning of the era that bears his name. Bhandarkar's premise that no-one could have referred to Vikramāditya before Candragupta II raises more problems than it solves.[30] A first- or second-century date for *Seven Centuries* remains to be disproven.[31]

The fact that *Seven Centuries* is a collection has provided scholars with an escape clause for the problem of its date: whatever date we assign to "the anthology itself," and whatever we understand by that phrase, individual verses might come and go. V.V. Mirashi argued on several occasions that while the "core" of *Seven Centuries* dates to the age of the Sātavāhanas, it received additions until at least the eighth century.[32] Mirashi looked at the author names attached to individual verses by some commentaries on the text and sought to identify them with persons that are already known to us. But this project is flawed for several reasons. First, Mirashi identified the "core" of *Seven Centuries* with those verses found in all recensions of the text, which numbered 430 at the time of Weber's 1881 edition. But determining which verses are original is not simply a matter of checking whether a verse is present in all recensions; it requires us to have a convincing theory of its textual transmission, which neither Weber nor Mirashi had, and which we might never have. And given that the text itself proclaims its length, there is no way that we can equate the 430 shared verses with the 700-verse original. Secondly, Mirashi uses the attributions found in the commentaries uncritically, without venturing a theory of where these attributions come from and how they came to be associated with some but not all recensions of *Seven Centuries.* At risk of belaboring the point, Mirashi credits Pītāmbara's attribution of four verses to Vākpatirāja, whom he identifies with the eighth-century author of *Gauḍa's Demise,* and he assumes that these verses are later additions. But Bhuvanapāla and Ājaḍa attribute three of these verses to different authors. And two of these four verses, despite being eighth-century additions according to Mirashi, are found in the set of 430 verses common to all recensions which, also according to Mirashi, "may have formed the original kernel of the work."[33]

One of Mirashi's points, however, speaks to the courtliness of *Seven Centuries* in a different way. The lists of authors include a large number of names that end in *-rāja* or *-deva.* These lists thus suggest that many of the people who contributed to *Seven Centuries* were, or at least were later thought to be, members of royal families. Some corroboration can be found in the *Līlāvaī,* a novel in Prakrit verse, probably of the eighth century, in which Sātavāhana figures as the hero. Among Sātavāhana's ministers in that text are Kumārila and Poṭṭisa, who are both noted as authors of verses in the commentaries to *Seven Centuries.* It is impossible at this point to say whether the narrative of the *Līlāvaī* is based on the attributions of the commentarial tradition, or the other way around.[34] But combining them gives us a more specific, and in my view quite plausible, account of the double authorship of *Seven Centuries.* The authors whose verses comprise this text were participants in a literary culture that was centered on Hāla's court. Their verses are just not "courtly" in the thin sense of merely being composed at a court, but in the thick sense: their authors "discovered their collective consciousness in the experience of life at a court," and their verses are an expression of this consciousness. A poetic sensibility, style, and technique run throughout *Seven Centuries.*[35]

I want to emphasize here how new this way of producing literature was, and how new, in turn, the kind of literature it produced was. Previously, any texts that achieved the condition of "permanence," in Christian Novetzke's apposite term, were either religious in character, such as the Vedas or the canonical texts of the Jains and Buddhists, or belonged to a tradition of epic storytelling, such as the *Rāmāyaṇa* and *Mahābhārata.*[36] Later theorists of all persuasions categorically refused to bestow the status of "literature" (*kāvya*) on religious texts, however poetic the hymns of the *Ṛgveda* or the songs of Buddhist monks and nuns in the *Tripiṭaka* might seem to us.[37] The epics, by contrast, were often regarded as literary productions. But they were still regarded as products of mythical sages in time out of mind. But here, on the banks of the Godāvarī river, people who were interested and invested in literature gathered at the Sātavāhana court, and a set of social identities and cultural practices—those of the patron, the poet, the connoisseur, and the literary gathering (*goṣṭhī*)—thus converged around a new and decidedly this-worldly concept of "literature."[38]

This culture of *kāvya* coincided with and partook of the emergence of a culture of *kāma* in the prosperous Sātavāhana empire. Art of the period prominently features the pursuit of pleasure. Funerary reliefs from Sannati commonly depict the deceased in scenes of relaxation and revelry. Even in Buddhist meditation-halls, couples in love form an essential part of the decorative program. And scenes of the refined pleasures of courtly life—represented by barely clothed courtesans, luxury goods, and wine—unify the sculptural program at major Buddhist monuments. Indeed, this courtly aspect unifies the different subjects depicted at the *caitya* at Kanaganahalli, from scenes of the Buddha's life, to the story of Aśoka, to the depictions of the Sātavāhana rulers themselves.[39] And we should not forget that the *Kāma Sūtra,* which integrates literary pursuits into a more broadly aestheticized and eroticized lifestyle, was produced in the immediate aftermath of the Sātavāhana empire, around the middle of the third century CE.[40] With *Seven Centuries,* courtly culture produced for itself a textual artefact of a type that had previously been confined to the spheres—however loosely defined these are—of ritual, religion, and their associated forms of knowledge. But the Sātavāhana court was not unique. Around the same time, that is to say in the early second century CE, there was an explosion of literary activity at the court of the Kuṣāṇas further to the north, if legends connecting the Buddhist poets Aśvaghoṣa and Mātṛceṭa with this court have any basis in fact.[41] And although its chronology has been vigorously contested, the most recent research suggests that the Tamil *caṅkam* literature was contemporary with, and did not simply look back on, the Cēra, Cōḻa and Pāṇṭiya chiefs of the early centuries CE.[42] One way of looking at this phenomenon, in all of its occurrences, is as the transference of the figures (*alaṅkāra*s), characteristics (*lakṣaṇa*s), and qualities (*guṇa*s) that had served to amplify, strengthen, and beautify language into a new and independent domain of language use. Verse W3, discussed above, says that the verses of *Seven Centuries* have "figures" or "ornaments" (*sālaṃkārāṇa*), possibly suggesting a definition of literature per se. The emergence of literary discourse is closely linked to the literarization of discourse that we traced in inscriptions in the previous chapter. Literature suddenly became a thing that could be pointed at and named.

Seven Centuries itself tells us the name of this new discourse in a programmatic introductory verse:

> Prakrit poetry [*pāuakavvaṃ*] is nectar.
> Those who don't know how to recite it or listen to it
> make love into a science.
> How are they not ashamed?[43]

This verse is a declaration of independence, certainly of what it calls "Prakrit poetry," but also, I would argue, of poetry itself. The contrast here is not between Prakrit poetry and other kinds of poetry, or poetry in other languages, but between a literary and an analytic sensibility. Herman Tieken has pushed this contrast as far as possible, taking *Seven Centuries* and the *Kāma Sūtra* of Vātsyāyana as representatives of two diametrically opposed ways of thinking about love and sex. The *Kāma Sūtra*'s concern with classification and categorization ("fingernails are either long, short, or medium"), according to Tieken, is precisely what *Seven Centuries* ridicules and stakes a position against.[44] In my view the verse is more general. The literary enterprise it initiates is not simply a reaction to a science of erotics in Sanskrit, and Tieken's reading of *Seven Centuries* through the interpretive lens of the *Kāma Sūtra* reduces it to poetry of class-based condescension (as discussed below). Rather, this verse creates a space for learned discourse about love and pleasure by rejecting the models for such discourse currently on offer. The reading and exact significance of the word I have translated as "making love into a science" is unclear, but it seems to refer to the "obsession" (*tatti*) with "facts" (*tatta*) or "systems" (*taṃta*) that characterizes, not only the *Kāma Sūtra,* but almost every type of learned discourse prevalent in India around the turn of the first millennium CE.

The alternative model of learned discourse proposed here is "reciting and listening to" Prakrit poetry. There is no contradiction in foregrounding the performative quality of this literature at the beginning of a written text. Prakrit literature, as it is defined and modelled by *Seven Centuries,* consists of stable textual artefacts, above all, the single-verse *gāthā,* which are nevertheless only fully realized in their performance. And the ideal context of performance was the *goṣṭhī*. We learn first from the *Kāma Sūtra* that *goṣṭhī*s were gatherings in which men who were "peers in knowledge, intelligence, character, wealth, or age" sat with courtesans and discussed cultural subjects, including literature. One of the places where such gatherings could occur is the court (*sabhā*). The poet and theorist Rājaśekhara (ninth/tenth centuries) saw the organization of these gatherings as one of the key functions of royal power, and named Sātavāhana as an example in this respect.[45] The *goṣṭhī* is implied in the above verse as the site where "Prakrit poetry" is performed, and where "reciting and listening to" (*paḍhiuṃ souṃ ca*) includes all of the practices linked to this performance, such as evaluation, criticism, and discussion.

The history of courtly Prakrit begins with this collection, which is in fact a strange kind of beginning, and in the view of some scholars not really a beginning at all. If Hāla merely selected verses from a tradition that existed before him, then *Seven Centuries* is a *terminus ad quem,* rather than a *terminus a quo,* of the "Prakrit poetry" that it announces. For a generation of scholars that considered spontaneous beginnings improbable or impossible, *Seven Centuries* can only represent the culmination of a long tradition, over the course of which the Prakrit language was "built up" (*ausgebildet*) and made ever more suitable for literary expression. This is a period of what the medievalist Paul Zumthor called "formation," in contrast to the moment of "manifestation" in which a text first becomes visible to us in the historical record. In this kind of narrative, the texts that are actually written down and transmitted in manuscript form are like fossils of a living literary culture that was once much more widespread, and much richer in content, than it appears to us now.[46] Such a narrative also inflects Prakrit poetry itself as a more broadly based and popular phenomenon than the courtly productions, such as *Seven Centuries,* through which it is memorialized. The courtliness of this literature, according to this story, is an accident of transmission, whereas its popular character is its essence that the very name Prakrit—as in *prākṛtajana,* "the common man"—refers to. The "popular origins" narrative finds apparent confirmation in the content of *Seven Centuries* itself. As is well known, this collection is centrally concerned with village life, and its recurring characters are all "common people": the plowman, the village headman, the hunter, the bandit, and the women who pick flowers, grind grain, and watch the paddy fields.[47]

The "popular origins" narrative, besides serving as an account of where and how this literature developed, also serves as a way of reading and understanding it, according to which the verses depict the joys and hardships of village life from the inside. Take a verse such as the following (W169), which seems unambiguously sympathetic:

> Nothing remains to be done in the fields
> but the farmer doesn't come back home,
> avoiding the pain of a house made empty
> by the death of his dear wife.[48]

Immediately after Weber proposed the "popular origins" narrative, a number of scholars stepped up to propose a counternarrative of "courtly origins."[49] In recent years this counternarrative has been taken up, and taken to its furthest conclusions, by Herman Tieken. For Tieken, this literature is not "courtly" simply in the sense that it was compiled in proximity to a court. It is "courtly" in the further sense that it represents the perspective of the cultured, elite, urbane man—the *nāgaraka* described in the *Kāma Sūtra*—who looks upon village life with utter condescension. The premise of *Seven Centuries,* according to Tieken's reading, is the sophistication of courtly elites, which they demonstrate to each other by making jokes at the expense of common people. The key insight that Tieken has, which may be obvious to most readers but which runs counter to the "popular origins" narrative, is that this literature was not necessarily composed by the same kinds of people who figure in it as characters. It is "not a poetry *of* the village but . . . *about* the village."[50] Tieken thus reads the above verse (W169) with an implicit distancing of the speaking subject from the subject of the verse: whereas the farmer's wife was all he had, the courtly sophisticate has an endless supply of female companions in his multiple wives and courtesans.[51]

Both of these ways of reading Prakrit poetry turn on a series of diametrical oppositions: urban and rural, courtly and popular, elite and non-elite. They represent, accordingly, an "internal" and "external" hermeneutic, according to which the perspective of the speaker is either collapsed onto the perspective of those of whom he speaks, or is instead a total inversion of it. My own reading of these poems, and the way they have always been read within the Indian tradition, is based on a rather different premise. This literature is "courtly" in both the thin and thick sense, but the "thick" sense is not simply, as Tieken would have it, the haughty disdain of urban elites for the frustrations of village life. Rather, it is that the village was a topos, a fictionalized and conventionalized place, onto which the drama of courtly life was projected. This place served as a site of exploration: of rhetorical and descriptive possibilities, of social mores, and of emotional depths.[52] In the anonymous characters of Prakrit lyric poetry—and they are always anonymous—courtly elites could see reflections of themselves which were all the more striking precisely because of the enormous social differences that Tieken has highlighted.

What makes *Seven Centuries* a courtly text, what allows us to read it as one, is thus not only the circumstances of its composition, or even what its individual verses say, but rather the way in which they say it. "Clever speech," *chekokti,* is the current that runs throughout *Seven Centuries,* and which Bhuvanapāla enshrined in the title to his eleventh-century commentary on the text, the earliest available as of today.[53] The set of practices included within "clever speech" includes saying one thing while intending to convey the opposite, speaking two different messages to two different people using the same words, expressing the inexpressible through signs and gestures, and generally all manners of indirection, verbal and otherwise.

These consummately literary practices are also consummately courtly practices: "Savoir dissimuler," Cardinal Richelieu is said to have remarked, "est le savoir des rois."[54] For the poets of *Seven Centuries,* these practices were modelled in the most exemplary way by the inhabitants of the village (*gāma*), and even more so of the poor village (*kuggāma*). The interactions between a girl and her mother-in-law, between a lonely wife and a traveller, between two young lovers, between a young wife and her older co-wives, or between a girl and her friend-turned-messenger were no less complicated, and required no less skill in the manipulation of language, than the interactions that occurred at the royal court. Similarly, the village provided a model for the pursuit of sensual pleasure—arranging sexual encounters with each other is a full-time job for the characters in *Seven Centuries*—not only for the elites of the Sātavāhana court itself but for the merchants, traders, landowners, and officials who enjoyed unprecedented prosperity under Sātavāhana rule and who participated in the culture of *kāma.*[55]

Thinking of *Seven Centuries* as "pastoral" helps us avoid the literary-historical and interpretive faults that follow from thinking of it as "pure popular poetry" or its alleged opposite, "pure courtly poetry." It is courtly poetry about everyday life; it uses the village and its inhabitants and the natural world to fill out the repertoire of "clever speech." And as such it bears comparison with other pastoral genres that are, in some ways, much better known. Nobody believes that the goatherds of Theocritus or Virgil are true to life in any significant way, but neither are they objects of scorn or condescension on the part of these poets, who sought (and often received) the patronage of kings, emperors, and high-ranking officials; in their work "the reader is invited to embrace the beguilement of the song while remaining conscious that its spell is illusory."[56]

This reading of *Seven Centuries* is not new. It is borne out by the text itself and by the tradition that it began, and it was favored by some twentieth-century scholars.[57] In one pair of verses, someone is looking at the village "from the outside":

> Those people who live in a mountain village are really lucky.
> Nothing stops them from making love.
> The hedges grow thick
> and the reed thickets sway in the wind.[58]

> In the mountain villages of these parts
> the hedges blossom with *kadamba* flowers,
> the rock surfaces are clean,
> the peacocks are happy,
> the sounds of waterfalls echo—
> all so charming.[59]

We can distinguish three levels of meaning in these verses. The first is the text's meaning, which is what the words actually say. The second is the speaker's meaning, which arises on the understanding, or presupposition, that all of these verses are spoken by one person to another person. This is a meaning which the commentaries standardly supply. The tension between the text's meaning and the speaker's meaning, that is, between what is said (*vācya*) and what is suggested (*vyaṅgya*), would later fuel a debate about meaning in literature that would continue for centuries.[60]

The commentator Gaṅgādhara, for example, puts the first into the mouth of a woman who is arranging a tryst with her lover, and the second into the mouth of a messenger who is trying to induce her friend's lover to come to the village under description. The speaker's meaning elicits anything that is left unsaid in the text's meaning. In the first verse, of course, sex is mentioned explicitly, and the only question is how everything else in the verse relates to it. (The thick hedges hide the lovers from sight, and the wind provides cover for the lovers rustling the reeds in the thicket.) But in the second, the context of the verse—both its position after the first in the anthology and the dramatic context that the commentaries help us to supply—guides us to a meaning that remains implicit, which is again the suitability of mountain villages for illicit affairs.[61]

In both cases, there is a third meaning. We can call it the reader's meaning, in contrast to the previous two. These verses are meaningful for the reader, not because he is salaciously interested in the affairs of the fictional characters, but because something about the way these affairs are arranged and communicated has some interest or relevance to him. Because there are potentially an infinite number of such readers, this meaning is the most difficult to pin down. Yet the interest in obliquity, in indirection, in meaning without saying, is relatively constant. A key word in *Seven Centuries* is *vaṃka*, "crooked," which unites the graceful indirection of speech with the suggestiveness of glances and gestures.[62]

A verse worth mentioning in this connection, even though it is found in a much later collection, makes the alignment of these three meanings on the axis of "cleverness" a bit clearer. It is from Jineśvara's *Treasury of Gāthā-Jewels* (1194 CE):

> Where can you find speech that's crooked?
> Where do you find glances of half-closed eyes?
> Where sighs?
> In a village that's full of clever people.[63]

"Clever people" are the imagined speakers of the "crooked speech" (*vaṃkabhaṇiāi*) represented by Prakrit poetry. But they are also, necessarily, the poets who thought of these clever sayings in the first place and the readers who take such delight in thinking about them, deconstructing and reconstructing them, and imitating them. The worlds of the court and of the village converge in this category of "clever people" (*chaïlla, viaḍḍha*) and its defining practice of "crooked speech." And although this "hinge" between the rustic characters of *Seven Centuries* and its courtly readers is very often what the interpretation of its verses turns on, in a number of cases the hinge itself is foregrounded, such as the following:

> He looked at her, and she didn't look back.
> The simple girl wouldn't talk to him.
> She didn't even greet him properly.
> Just from this, clever people figured it out.[64]

We, as the readers of this verse, are asked to put ourselves in the position of the "clever people" in the village (*chaïlla*) and figure out what is going on between him and her. The commentators all agree that the girl is trying to hide her attraction, but nevertheless makes her efforts legible to certain kinds of readers.[65] Other verses thematize the difficulty of this kind of communication in the village, which contributes to its scarcity value.[66]

Another verse takes on a metaliterary significance by iconically collapsing the speaker's meaning into the reader's meaning:

> They are a pleasure to fondle,
> weighty, with hardly a gap in between them,

adorned by nothing but their natural marks—
whom do they not delight, these breasts
which are like poems,
a pleasure to analyze,
dense with meaning,
no extraneous words,
adorned with figures?[67]

This simile involves a number of other figures: "embrace" (*śleṣa*), where two separate meanings converge in a single expression, and "condensed expression" (*samāsokti*), where two separate subjects are discussed at once.[68] Pītāmbara says that the speaker is a woman who is indicating her friend's sexual availability by paying her breasts a compliment. In this case we see the critical function of distancing that the interpretive conventions perform: they offer "plausible deniability" to the readers of Prakrit poetry by confining its eroticism to an imagined world of speakers. Simultaneously, however, this distancing is undermined. The pleasures of literature and sexual pleasure are "embraced" so tightly that the reader cannot pull them apart—certainly not in this verse, but perhaps not in the rest of *Seven Centuries* either. Among the people who produced and perused *Seven Centuries,* sexual pleasure was not merely symbolic of the pleasures of literature; the two were mutually reinforcing components of a lifestyle that was organized around the pursuit and aestheticization of pleasure.

I will conclude this discussion of *Seven Centuries* by looking at two examples of its "crooked courtliness" and then at the implications that my reading has for literary history. The following is one of the few verses ostensibly addressed to a king. It uses "embrace" to compare a king's heart to the sky:

Who on earth could cover up something
so extensive, so pure, and so lofty
as your heart—or for that matter the sky—
apart from a cloud-breast?[69]

This is a standard example of royal eulogy (*praśasti*), which is one of the main modalities of later courtly literature in Sanskrit and Prakrit. We might imagine that it was composed by a member of the king's court and then included in this collection of because it happens to mention the word "breast" (*paoharaṃ*). This is how Bhuvanapāla understands the verse. But this is Prakrit poetry, the defining principle of which is that things are not what they seem. Gaṅgādhara tells us that we should imagine the verse as spoken, not by a poet, but by a procuress (*veśyāmātṛ*), who uses a clever compliment (*cāṭūkti*) to recommend a courtesan to the king. The fictional situation that Gaṅgādhara imagines has the effect of blocking our inference from the eulogistic content of the verse to the intention, on the part of the poet who actually composed the verse, to eulogize a king.

Similar is the following:

> Your heart is made out of pure nectar,
> your hands dispel longing,
> O moon-faced one,
> where can this fiery valor of yours,
> which consumes your enemies,
> possibly reside?[70]

The apparent contradiction (*virodha*) in this verse is between valor, which is always figured as fiery, and three cooling substances: nectar, water (implied in "your hands dispel longing," because royal donations were accompanied by pouring out a jug of water), and moonlight (emanating from the moon-like face). But whereas Ājaḍa thinks that the verse refers to a valorous king, Sādhāraṇadeva and the anonymous commentator of χ actually imagine that the verse refers to a woman, who is being flatteringly—and perhaps ironically—compared to a king. These verses certainly presuppose the court as the context against which their meanings emerge, even if they do not unambiguously point to it as the site of their own production. The text constitutes the court as a possible site of meaning in the same way that it does the village.

The tradition that looks back on *Seven Centuries* as one of its foundational texts was fascinated by its ability, first of all, to say two contradictory things at once. This "cleverness" or "indirection" of language (*chekokti, vakrokti*) was the essential principle of Prakrit poetry. But *Seven Centuries* was more than a collection of such sayings. It was a literary icon of this principle, a text that uniquely managed to be two contradictory things at once: rustic yet courtly, erotic yet sensitive, superficially simple but complex on further analysis, close to the language of everyday life yet unmistakably literary and refined. Bāṇabhaṭṭa thematizes this quality of *Seven Centuries* in his well-known praise of Sātavāhana at the beginning of the *Deeds of Harṣa* (seventh century):

> Sātavāhana has made an inexhaustible and urbane treasury
> of well-turned verses, all in the same meter,
> like jewels of proven quality.[71]

Bāṇa's readers would have known well that *Seven Centuries* is set in the village (*grāma*), so his description of the collection as "urbane" (*agrāmya*), which literally means "not of the village," must be taken as a reference to Sātavāhana's ability to transform what looks at first glance like village poetry into something that sophisticated connoisseurs of poetry, including King Harṣa's own court poet, can appreciate. The Jain monk Uddyotana, in his novel *Kuvalayamālā* (779 CE), refers to the same apparent contradiction in his own praise of Hāla: the king, like alcohol (*hālā*), was able to give the "playful eloquence of speech even to farmers."[72]

The "Prakrit poetry" that *Seven Centuries* announces is not just poetry in the Prakrit language, but it does mark one beginning—albeit not the only beginning, as we will see—of poetry in the Prakrit language. Like the poetry itself, the language is neither *grāmya* nor *agrāmya*, different both from the vernacular of common people and from the Sanskrit of learned discourse, as it was from the language of contemporary inscriptions. The dominant view regarding the literarization of this language is that it took place gradually and organically over a long period of time.[73] The alternative view is that Prakrit was engineered as a literary language specifically in order to serve as the medium for the new kind of literature represented by *Seven Centuries*. Herman Tieken ventured that this language is a mocking imitation of the speech of villagers, "as far removed from Sanskrit as possible."[74] While I differ radically from Tieken regarding the poetics of *Seven Centuries*, I agree that there is some interaction between its poetics and its language, although it is difficult to be precise about what it is. As I argue in chapter 5, Prakrit was conceived of as both the same as and the opposite of Sanskrit. It was the distinctive language of a new discourse that set itself against existing learned discourses in Sanskrit—and in order to be set against them, it had to have some kind of common ground with them—while remaining more or less intelligible to readers of Sanskrit. The pioneers of this literature perhaps found a suitable model in the language practices of the Jain community.

Rājaśekhara relates that Sātavāhana enjoined the use of Prakrit in his palace, just as Sāhasāṅka enjoined the use of Sanskrit. What kings do, Rājaśekhara intends us to understand from these examples, is fix the price of products in the marketplace of culture. Whatever Prakrit may have been and whatever it may have been called before Sātavāhana and his associates compiled their influential collection of lyrics in this language, it became something altogether different afterwards. It became a literary language whose special power—its seemingly innate eroticism and suggestiveness—was recognized and appreciated by people who cared about literature. And the class itself of "people who cared about literature" was virtually called into existence by *Seven Centuries*, which became the common property of, and a model for, a courtly literary culture.

The courtliness of *Seven Centuries* bears on the relationship between Prakrit and Tamil poetry. Since much of the scholarly discussion of *Seven Centuries* has been focused through this problem, it warrants a mention here, but since the issues are complex and beyond the scope of this study, it will be a very brief mention. George Hart argued that most of the distinctive features of Prakrit poetry, from its nature symbolism to its metrical forms, are adapted from Dravidian culture, and thus Prakrit poetry has a close genetic relationship with *caṅkam* poetry in Tamil that Hart dates to roughly the same period.[75] The parallels between Prakrit and Tamil poetry are indeed suggestive, but scholars remain divided over what exactly they are suggestive of, in large part because there has been no consensus regarding how to situate either Prakrit poetry or Tamil poetry in a coherent and convincing historical narrative.[76] The Tamil tradition, however, seems to have known *Seven Centuries,* if that is the text that Nakkīraṉār and Mayilainātar call *Cātavākaṉam* as an example of a poem named after its patron.[77]

One of the ways in which the Vākāṭaka kings of the Deccan followed in the footsteps of their immediate predecessors, the Sātavāhanas, was their encouragement of and participation in literary production. And as for the Sātavāhanas, literature for the Vākāṭakas meant Prakrit literature. Two of the classics of Prakrit literature are ascribed to Vākāṭaka kings. The earlier of these is *Hari's Victory* by Sarvasena, who ruled from Vatsagulma (modern Vāśim) around 330–350 CE.[78] Bhoja provides a few dozen quotations from this work, which is otherwise lost. Its subject is Kṛṣṇa's theft of the Pārijāta tree from Indra's heaven in order to give it to his wife Satyabhāmā. The later is *Rāvaṇa's Demise,* or as it is more widely known, *Building the Bridge,* by Pravarasena II. This king ruled first from Nandivardhana (modern Nagardhan), the traditional seat of the Vākāṭakas, and later from the eponymous Pravarapura (modern Mānsar) in the first half of the fifth century. Pravarasena II's regent in the early days of his reign was his mother Prabhāvatīguptā, herself the daughter of Candragupta II Vikramāditya. Their marital alliance with the Guptas seems to mark a turning-point not just in the political fortunes of the Vākāṭakas, but in their language practices as well. As noted in the previous chapter, Prabhāvatīguptā's numerous inscriptions, all composed in confident and relatively elaborate Sanskrit, represent a decisive shift away from Middle Indic. It is also significant that *Hari's Victory* and *Rāvaṇa's Demise* narrate the deeds of Viṣṇu, in his forms as Kṛṣṇa and Rāmacandra respectively. These works seemingly partake of the same devotion to Viṣṇu that animates the *purāṇas* compiled in roughly the same period, particularly the *Harivaṃśa Purāṇa* and the *Viṣṇu Purāṇa.* They also came to represent a literary style that later authors called Vaidarbhī (after Vidarbha, the heartland of the Vākāṭakas) or Vatsagulmī (after Sarvasena's capital).[79] In his influential discussion of the "ways" (*mārga*) of poetry in the first chapter of his *Mirror of Literature* (ca. 700 CE), Daṇḍin argued that it was the Vaidarbhī style, and not the contrasting Gauḍī style, that represented the height of literary beauty. And although Daṇḍin and his commentators usually give Sanskrit examples of this style—as they do for every topic in the *Mirror*—its identity and basic character were established by a group of Prakrit texts.

Pravarasena neatly summarizes the powers of literature toward the beginning of *Rāvaṇa's Demise*:

> Knowledge increases.
> Fame spreads.
> Virtues take hold.
> The deeds of great men are heard.

Is there anything about *kāvya*
that doesn't draw us in?[80]

This sentiment is so deeply ingrained in the tradition that it sounds cliché. Bhāmaha and Mammaṭa, just to take two prominent examples, start with it as one of the self-evident axioms of poetics. Yet a number of points bear emphasis here. First, Pravarasena is among the first to articulate these ideas. Secondly, in contrast to the limited scope that *Seven Centuries* announced for itself—*pāuakavva* was, as a counterpart to learned discourses on love, still in the end concerned with love—Pravarasena's *kavvālāvā* speaks directly and effectively to all domains of human life. Or those domains, at any rate, that most mattered to the publics to whom courtly literature was addressed: the cultivation of knowledge, the pursuit of public recognition, the fashioning of the self as an ethical subject, and the propagation of a set of ethical and cultural ideals. It seems fitting that this ambitious vision of the powers of literature frames a narrative of conquest. *Rāvaṇa's Demise* tells of the capture of Laṅkā and the defeat of Rāvaṇa by Rāma and his allies. It is not just a courtly poem, but an imperial one, composed during one of the high-water marks of empire in ancient India. Finally, Pravarasena enunciates this universalist vision of literature in Prakrit. Prakrit was by no means the universal language of literature in Pravarasena's day—he was, after all, the grandson of Candragupta II Vikramāditya, one of Sanskrit's legendary patrons—but it was, by this time, one of the two languages in which it was possible to imagine writing literature, ensconced in its long-term position as the only alternative to Sanskrit.

THREE MYTHS OF CONTINUITY

In the foregoing I have stressed the discontinuities of courtly Prakrit: it was a way of using language that had little historical precedent, and it helped to distinguish an emergent sphere of literature per se from the discourses that surrounded it. By contrast, the other history of Prakrit literature, that of Jain Prakrit, is usually told in a way that foregrounds its continuity along three dimensions, which tend to puncture whatever social, historical, and even linguistic boundaries we might draw around it. My purpose here is to explicitly lay out what these continuities are. But if it can be shown that they are myths—not in the sense that they are completely untrue, but in the sense that they represent a very particular and interested vision of the past—then like its courtly counterpart, Jain Prakrit might turn out to have had a historical beginning.

The works of Jain Prakrit are, first of all, represented as continuous with Jain teachings. The terms "canonical" and "post-canonical" reflect this continuity: they do not simply refer to texts composed at different historical times—in fact the historical position of many texts is very indeterminate—but texts that occupy a position within the particular temporality of the Jain tradition. This is a linear temporality marked out by the succession of teachers.

The *Wanderings of Vasudeva* (*Vasudevahiṇḍi*) provides an example of the work that this first concept of continuity does. This Prakrit text, composed by the monk Saṅghadāsa in the early centuries of the common era, is now well-known as an early and evidently faithful adaptation of Guṇāḍhya's *Great Story*, which was itself composed around the first century CE, and according to some traditions at the Sātavāhana court.[81] But in Saṅghadāsa's text, the adaptation of the *Great Story*—in which Vasudeva takes the place of Guṇāḍhya's hero Naravāhanadatta—is preceded by a section called "the origin of the story" (*kahuppattī*). There, Saṅghadāsa tells us that the story he is about to tell "has come down through the lineage of teachers." After narrating the stories of Jambūsvāmin and Prabhava, the leaders of Jainism in the generations after Mahāvīra, he comes to Mahāvīra himself, and it is through Mahāvīra that the story of Vasudeva is ultimately narrated.[82] Saṃghadāsa's historical vision leapfrogs over his principal source, Guṇāḍhya's *Great Story*, by several centuries.

The second kind of continuity is between Jain language practices and demotic, "everyday" language practices. Where the first refers to continuity over time, this is a synchronic continuity between different discursive spheres. Whereas other traditions create and maintain boundaries that separate the language of the tradition from the language of the surrounding world—the stereotype here is of the Brahmans jealously guarding the Sanskrit language like a secret—the Jains, according to this conceit, tended to dissolve those boundaries and to speak to the common people in a language they could comprehend.[83] It is true that a number of authors do emphasize the demotic character of Prakrit, but they do so at a time when this character was surely no more than notional, and in contexts that make it clear just how notional it was.

To critically examine this second kind of continuity, we can begin from a story that was told about Siddhasena Divākara, a Jain teacher widely believed to have been a contemporary of Candragupta II Vikramāditya (ca. 380–415 CE). His principal works marked the entry of Jain thought into a wider philosophical conversation between Buddhists and Brahmans.[84] But according to later hagiographic texts, Siddhasena was a Brahman who never quite shook his preference for Sanskrit. He was converted to Jainism when his formidable Sanskrit learning was defeated by the folk wisdom and popular appeal of the Jain monk Vṛddhavādin. Even after his conversion, however, he was embarrassed on behalf of the Jain community that their scriptures were written in Prakrit rather than in Sanskrit. So he offered to translate them into Sanskrit. The elders found this suggestion so reprehensible that Siddhasena was forced into exile from the community for twelve years. Siddhasena's suggestion amounted to a betrayal of the very ethos of populism and accessibility that had brought him over to Jainism in the first place. In this story, as

Phyllis Granoff has pointed out, Sanskrit stands for exclusivity and the privileges of birth, while Prakrit stands for inclusivity and the value of wisdom over mere learning.[85]

This is, in other words, a story about how Jains understood their own language practices. Within the story, the use of Prakrit is motivated by a fundamental commitment to making Jain doctrines accessible to the widest possible spectrum of people. But outside of the story, we have some reason to believe that it was actually the other way around: that later authors thought that Jainism was inclusive and "demotic" *because* its scriptures happened to be written in Prakrit. As far as I know, one of the earliest explicit statements about Prakrit's demotic character comes from Haribhadra Sūri, perhaps around the seventh or eighth century, in a widely quoted verse from his *Daśavaikālika Ṭīkā:*

> Those who know the truth
> have produced scriptures in Prakrit
> for the benefit of children, women,
>   the slow-witted, and the uneducated,
> and for men who strive after good conduct.[86]

Haribhadra is here reflecting on and trying to motivate the language that he has inherited through the Jain tradition—more than a millennium, of course, after the scriptural dispensation of which he speaks. But he was one of the first Jain teachers to use both Sanskrit and Prakrit extensively, and we might suspect that he was also one of the first to think of the choice between Sanskrit and Prakrit as a choice between two audiences, a learned elite and the unlettered masses. This dichotomy is a product of the representation of Sanskrit and Prakrit as complementary language practices, identical but opposed, which I will discuss in chapter 5. At the same time, Haribhadra's own use of Prakrit subverts this dichotomy. His Prakrit poetry, represented by *The Story of Samarāditya* for example, is no less learned, and I would venture to say no more accessible to the unlettered masses, than any of its Sanskrit counterparts. And consider the context of the verse. Assuming that we accept Haribhadra's claim that the *Daśavaikālika Sūtra,* and the other texts of the Jain canon, are actually in Prakrit—a claim that we will soon have reason to doubt—it should not be lost on us that Haribhadra's commentary on it is, in fact, largely in Sanskrit. On some level, he knew that Sanskrit would be more intelligible than Prakrit. There is, in other words, something slightly disingenuous about the claim that Prakrit is demotic in the context of Haribhadra's own literary production, even if it may be true—I emphasize *may*—that Prakrit was demotic to begin with.

Siddharṣi, a poet of the early tenth century, exemplifies how notional the demotic character of Prakrit was. At the beginning of his *Endless Stream of Likenesses and Births,* he notes that "Sanskrit and Prakrit are the two languages worthy of preeminence, and among them Sanskrit resides in the hearts of self-styled scholars, while Prakrit, beautiful to the ear, awakens true wisdom even in children." Why, then, has Siddharṣi written his large collection of stories in Sanskrit? "Nevertheless, the Prakrit language doesn't appeal to them. If you have the chance, you should please everyone: hence, by that principle, this work is composed in Sanskrit."[87]

A third of continuity is the underlying identity of Jain language practices, and their common identification as Prakrit. This is both a synchronic and a diachronic concept: the former because it organizes language taxonomically under the rubric of Prakrit, and the latter because this taxonomy encompasses the whole history of Jain language practices, at least for the first millennium of Jainism. The language of Mahāvīra's original teachings, collected in the canonical texts called *aṅga*s according to the Śvetāmbaras, but lost forever according to the Digambaras, was called Māgadhī or Ardhamāgadhī by the Jains themselves. Precisely at what point Jains came to regard this language, or indeed any other language, as Prakrit, or a variety of Prakrit, is very difficult to say. The late-canonical *Sthānāṅga Sūtra* and *Anuyogadvāra Sūtra* do mention a division of language into Sanskrit and Prakrit, but the context makes it clear that it applies to literary (or more precisely musical) practices rather than scripture.[88] In the twelfth century, the Śvetāmbara monk Hemacandra viewed the language of the canon as a Prakrit "of the sages" (*ārṣa*), and dedicated a surprisingly small portion of the rules of his Prakrit grammar to this variety.[89] Modern scholars have followed Haribhadra and Hemacandra in gathering all of the Middle Indic languages that Jains ever used under the category of Prakrit. According to the influential classification of Richard Pischel, the Jains employed three principal varieties of Prakrit: Ardhamāgadhī in the canonical texts of the Śvetāmbaras; Jain Śaurasenī in the doctrinal literature of the Digambaras; and Jain Māhārāṣṭrī in the commentarial and narrative literature of both sects.[90]

All three of these continuities are invoked in the proposition that the language of the Jain tradition is, and always was, Prakrit, and that the use of Prakrit is part of what characterizes Jainism as an inclusive and egalitarian religion in contrast to the Brahmanical traditions, which insisted on using the obscure and exclusive Sanskrit language.[91] No less a scholar than Ludwig Alsdorf described Jain literature as "an uninterrupted tradition on the soil of the motherland," organically developing from "anti-brahmanic, popular linguistic origins" and an "inclination to a popular tongue."[92] There are aspects of this representation that are plausible, if sentimental and indigenist. But it should be clear that such representations trade on a threefold continuity—between Jain literature and Jain religious teachings, between the various languages of Jainism, and between these languages and the languages of the everyday—which is hardly as obvious as Alsdorf takes it to be. There is little doubt that by the time that Jain communities were assembling, comparing, and commenting on their canonical scriptures in the fifth and sixth centuries, Sanskrit would have been equally if not more intelligible than the languages of Jain scripture and commentary, for the monastic and lay communities alike. The rationale for using Prakrit must therefore be sought in the history of Jain language practices.

PRAKRIT'S MONKS

I will focus in this section on some of the literature composed in "Jain Māhārāṣṭrī," given that the connections and divisions imposed on Prakrit literature by this name, first coined by Hermann Jacobi, constitute the forestructure through which we read and understand it.[93]

The name refers to a set of linguistic characteristics that, on the one hand, separate this language from Ardhamāgadhī.[94] These linguistic differences roughly correspond to differences of genre and, by the same token, chronological differences—but only roughly. Scholars have traced the influence of Ardhamāgadhī on the language of later Jain literature, as well as the influence of "Jain Māhārāṣṭrī" on the transmission of the Ardhamāgadhī scriptures.[95] The use of "Jain Māhārāṣṭrī" is thus associated with the cluster of texts that Ludwig Alsdorf called "late canonical and postcanonical verse literature," in contrast to "early canonical literature." One distinctive characteristic of this literature, according to Alsdorf, was its metrical form, the *gāthā,* which is all but absent from earlier literature. I argue in chapter 4 that the *gāthā* is indeed one of the diagnostic features of Prakrit literature, and the extensive use of this verse form in "Jain Māhārāṣṭrī" thus links it closely with non-Jain literature such as *Seven Centuries,* while distinguishing it from chronologically earlier layers of Jain texts.

On the other hand, the name "Jain Māhārāṣṭrī" establishes the language as parallel to, and therefore also distinct from, Māhārāṣṭrī pure and simple ("reine Māhārāṣṭrī," as Oskar von Hinüber revealingly calls it), the language of non-Jain Prakrit literature.[96] There is a double exclusion at work here: first and most obviously of non-Jains from "Jain Māhārāṣṭrī," which is by definition a language that can only be used by Jains to do things such as write commentaries on Jain canonical texts; secondly, however, it excludes Jains from the category of "Māhārāṣṭrī." This exclusion, which at first seems to concern a small and arcane field of textual production, turns out to have ramifications for Indian literary history as a whole. The texts that fall under the category of "Jain Māhārāṣṭrī" are typically considered in connection with the Jain scriptures and the non-canonical texts that either supplement them or stand in their place. They are not made to play any significant role in the history of "classical literature," or what the tradition itself called *kāvya,* and certainly not in its formative stages.[97]

One of the reasons for this separation is the Jains' "marked" status throughout Indian history. For the people who constructed the curriculums of literature in premodern India—most of whom, with a few late exceptions, were not themselves

Jains—Jain literature was usually Jain first and literature second. I think this markedness has more to do with the Jains being a religious minority than with any principled evaluation of the religious or ethical content of the texts under consideration. One would be hard-pressed to claim that Bhāravi's devotion to Śiva, for example, is more neutral or subdued than the Jainism of Uddyotana. Generally speaking, although Jain authors acknowledged the influence of non-Jain authors, non-Jain authors rarely returned the favor.[98] One example is the typology of stories that Ānandavardhana, a devotee of the Goddess, gives at the end of his *Light on Suggestion:* it is only from the adaptation of this passage at the hands of the Jain monk Hemacandra that we know that certain genres in Ānanda's typology are represented principally, if not exclusively, by Jain narratives, and indeed Ānanda's typology itself probably derives from the Jain poet Haribhadra.[99]

Corresponding to the "marked" status of Jain contributions to literary history is the "unmarked" status of authors of a broadly Hindu or Brahmanical persuasion whose works constitute something like a literary canon: Kālidāsa, Bhāravi, Māgha, Bāṇabhaṭṭa, Daṇḍin, Rājaśekhara, and so on. Indian literary culture was characterized by a tension between openness in principle and closedness in practice. Part of what made it such an attractive ideal was that it was, in principle, open to anyone who had the requisite knowledge, skills, and creativity, regardless of their religious persuasion. This ideal, however, bestowed legitimacy on actual practices that were often far less inclusive than the ideal would suggest: literary practices, for example, that enshrined the values of particular communities and their interests. This tension, in turn, was productive: not of a successive and inexorable broadening of literary culture in practice, as in Habermasian public spheres, but of a seemingly endless variety of cultural formations that hybridized the literary-cultural ideal with more or less substantive, and more or less rigid, religious and ethical commitments. When Jains wrote literature in Prakrit, they were not participating in a "shadow" literary culture entirely cut off from the mainstream, but neither were they recognized as full-fledged participants in the mainstream by the latter's own voices. They might be seen as creating a "counterpublic" to the mainstream literary public that Brahmanical authors presupposed.[100]

Early Jain literature often thematizes its marginalization from a mainstream literary tradition. I have already mentioned the founding myth, according to which the sage Vālmīki produced the *Rāmāyaṇa,* the first poem, by transforming his grief into verse. This was supposed to be the foundation, not merely of Brahmanical literature, but of literature as such. The Jain monk Vimala produced an alternative story, called *Deeds of Padma,* which directly challenged both the chronological priority and the truthfulness of Vālmīki's version.[101] The story of Rāma was in fact the story of Padma, which—like the story of Vasudeva for Saṅghadāsa—was transmitted by a line of Jain teachers that stretched all the way back to Mahāvīra himself.[102] Vimala's story is related through the mouth of

Mahāvīra's disciple Gautama, and it is occasioned by King Śreṇika's doubts about the version of the Rāma story with which he was familiar. How could the powerful Rāvaṇa be defeated by monkeys? Why would the compassionate Rāma shoot a golden deer, or for that matter kill Vālin? People who promote false teachings (*kusatthavādīhi*), the king infers, must have manipulated these stories for their own purposes.[103] Gautama confirms: it's all a lie that wicked poets (*kukaïṇo*) have told in their delusion.

Vimala lays claim to an authentic and unadulterated version of the Rāma story. Scholars, of course, were never convinced, and they have tended to argue the opposite: that Jains pilfered the narratives of other traditions—that is, the *Rāmāyaṇa*, the *Mahābhārata*, and the *Great Story*—to serve their own didactic ends.[104] I suggest viewing the Jain versions of these works not just as "Jain versions," but as attempts to lay the foundation stones for a new literary tradition. The language of this new tradition was Prakrit, in contrast to Vālmīki's Sanskrit. The authors had to have been conscious of this difference.[105] And this tradition, unlike Vālmīki's, would be not just open to Jain voices, but dominated by them. Sheldon Pollock has shown that the adaptation of the great epics was one of the key strategies by which new literary traditions both announced themselves and found their cultural-political orientation. In Pollock's account, this process is a component of vernacularization, and it begins—so far as we can tell—with Peruntēvaṉar's production of a Tamil *Mahābhārata* in the ninth century.[106] Against this theoretical background, Vimala's production of a Prakrit *Rāmāyaṇa* and a Prakrit *Lineage of Hari*, the latter now lost, as well as Saṅghadāsa's production of a Prakrit *Great Story* raise several important questions. Why transcreate at all? Why transcreate these texts? And what is the tradition in which these transcreations place themselves?

One important starting point for the tradition of "Jain Māhārāṣṭrī" is the tradition of commentary on the canonical texts of Jainism. These commentaries are among the earliest, and probably the most copious, productions in the Prakrit language. I say "the Prakrit language" advisedly, because their language is generally identical to the language of the literary works produced by Jains and non-Jains alike in the early centuries of the common era.[107] Any history of Prakrit literature must account for the striking connections between the discourses of commentary and literature. But none have, so far, for several reasons. First, the myths of continuity would have us believe that the commentarial discourses themselves do not have a beginning, that they represent processes of exegesis and diegesis that have been going on continuously since the days of Mahāvīra. Second, the dating of the commentarial discourse is extremely difficult, in part because there is no evidence whatsoever for its date apart from its association with particular Jain teachers, and their dates in turn are difficult to establish with any confidence, ranging from the third century BCE to the sixth century CE. And third, the dating of the literary discourse is just as uncertain. I think, however, that we can begin to connect some of these moving parts by relating them within a field of Prakrit textuality that appeared not much earlier and not much later than the first century CE.

The commentarial literature is notoriously complex, but its chronologically earliest layer is agreed to be a set of "explanations" (*niryukti*s) composed in Prakrit *gāthā*s and attributed to the teacher Bhadrabāhu. These are, more precisely, versified lists of topics for oral explanation.[108] One Bhadrabāhu, who is said to have led a group of Jain clerics to Śravaṇabeḷagoḷa in today's Karnataka when a famine threatened the Jain community in North India, is believed to have been a contemporary of Candragupta Maurya. But many scholars have resisted identifying this Bhadrabāhu, who would have lived in the early third century BCE, with the author of the *niryukti*s. The leading authorities on Jainism place Bhadrabāhu, the author of the *niryukti*s, in the first century CE.[109] Bhadrabāhu's explanations set into motion a process of commentary in Prakrit that continued for several centuries, and these centuries were decisive for Jainism as a religion: between the first and fifth century CE, the foundational texts were revised and expanded, Jainism split into two major sects, and the community attempted to constitute a stable canon of scripture through a series of councils. The common typology of commentary in Jainism distinguishes between the original "explanations" (*niryukti*s), the expanded "discussions" (*bhāṣya*s), also in Prakrit verse, and more "granular" commentaries (*cūrṇi*s) in Prakrit prose.

The readiest explanation for the use of Prakrit in this extensive commentarial discourse is simply that it was the spoken vernacular at the critical time and place in which this literature took shape. In composing, memorizing, reciting, and commenting upon texts in Prakrit, Jain monks were unknowingly laying the foundations for Prakrit textuality outside of the relatively narrow confines of their religious texts. Indeed, one of the reasons why there has been so little scholarly reflection on Vimala's or Saṅghadāsa's use of Prakrit as a literary language is that it seems a fait accompli: Prakrit was, in fact, the only language that Jain monks of this earlier period ever used.

But even if the use of Prakrit as a religious language was one of the preconditions for the subsequent use of Prakrit as a literary language, it was never a fait accompli that Prakrit would be used for literature. Sanskrit provides a useful parallel. It was used as a religious language for a thousand years before its sudden reinvention as a language of political power and imaginative literature; this reinvention did not simply entail Sanskrit's extension into new discursive spheres, but fundamental changes in the way the language was cultivated and deployed. This appears to be the case with Prakrit as well: rather than seeing the development of "Jain Māhārāṣṭrī" literature as slow and inevitable accumulation of religious material, we can discern a group of texts that employ the same language and verse forms as commentarial discourse, but for completely different purposes and with completely different results.

This group of texts includes *Wanderings of Vasudeva*, Vimala's *Deeds of Padma*, and Pālitta's *Taraṅgavatī*. These are texts that have just barely survived into the age of print, or in the case of the *Taraṅgavatī*, survived only in later abridgements. Many similar texts have been lost, including Vimala's *Lineage of Hari*. Nobody really knows when any of these texts were composed, but references in other texts place most of them before the middle of the first millennium CE.[110] Vimala's date is particularly controversial because he tells us that he completed the *Deeds of Padma* 530 years after Mahāvīra's death. Most reckonings would thus place him in the first century CE, which is as obvious to some scholars as it is impossible for others.[111] I see no reason to doubt that these texts are broadly contemporaneous with the efforts of Bhadrabāhu and later teachers to comment on the Jain scriptures, and also with the efforts of Hāla to stake out a role for Prakrit within literary discourse. They can thus be seen as a link between two textual cultures: one that saw itself as literary, and engaged in a dispute over the boundaries and definition of the literary, and one that employed textuality as a way of preserving and elaborating upon the doctrines of Jainism. For most of these texts, however, the specific connections to both of these cultures—to say nothing about the historical circumstances of their composition—remain obscure.

PĀLITTA'S *TARAṄGAVATĪ*

Pālitta's *Taraṅgavatī* is the missing piece that links the two histories of Prakrit literature to each other.[112] As noted above, this text only survives in later abridgements. Bhadreśvara included a synopsis of the story in 425 verses in his *Book of Stories* (twelfth century). Another, longer version (about 1640 verses) is called *Taraṅgalolā*. According to the final verse in the manuscript, a certain Yaśas copied it out for the monk Nemicandra, but whether it was he who abridged the original *Taraṅgavatī*, or whether he merely copied an existing manuscript of the abridged *Taraṅgalolā*, is unclear.[113] Whoever he was, the redactor notes his motivations at the beginning of the *Taraṅgalolā*:

> Pālitta composed a long story called *Taraṅgavatī*,
> full of regional words, intricate and extensive.
> In some places it has captivating groups of verses,
> in others closely bound couplets, and in still others
> longer runs that are difficult for others to understand.
> Nobody recites it, nobody asks for it to be recited, nobody tells it.
> It has become the special preserve of scholars.
> Nobody else can do anything with it.
> That's why I have collected the verses that Pālitta wrote
> and removed the regional words to create this abridged story,
> in the hope that it will not entirely disappear

from the hearts of other people.
I beg forgiveness from that monk.[114]

The "regional" words that, according to the author, got in the way of non-scholarly readers understanding the text are words that cannot easily be analyzed as deriving from Sanskrit. The use of such words was a distinctive feature of Prakrit in both its Jain and non-Jain varieties, and defining these words was the primary task of its associated forms of knowledge (see chapter 6).

Unlucky as the loss of Pālitta's original is, Harivallabh Bhayani has shown using parallel texts that *Taraṅgalolā* is a relatively faithful abridgement of *Taraṅgavatī.*[115] Pālitta was remembered as an important Jain teacher, and hence many stories about his life and career can be found in Jain narrative literature.[116] In fact, he was important enough for there to have been at least two of him, just as there were—at least according to some scholars—at least two Nāgārjunas, two Siddhasenas, and two Haribhadras. M. A. Dhaky argued convincingly that there were three: the existence of our Pālitta, the author of the *Taraṅgavatī,* is attested in late-canonical and post-canonical texts of the early first millennium CE; another adept, who was known by the Sanskrit name Pādalipta, was associated with the pilgrimage site of Śatruñjaya and probably lived in the early eighth century; yet another Pādalipta, the author of a Jain ritual manual, lived sometime after the eleventh century.[117] The stories about Pālitta aggregate details from a range of Jain sources about the various monks who had taken this name. As an example, Pālitta's teacher is usually said to be Āryanāgahastin of the Vidyādhara lineage. But the more recent narrative literature gives Maṇḍana and Saṅgrama as the monks who were charged by Āryanāgahastin with teaching him, and they are known to be the teacher and teacher's teacher respectively of the most recent (eleventh- or twelfth-century) Pālitta.[118] Some of the details related in the stories of Pālitta, however, point to an authentic tradition about events of the first century, such as the conflict between Sātavāhana and Nahapāna.[119]

The *Taraṅgavatī* is a novel in Prakrit verse, and specifically in the *gāthā* meter closely associated with Prakrit literature. It uses the strategy of emboxed narration that is common in the story literature of India, but in this case—as in later stories for which it served as a model, such as Uddyotana's *Kuvalayamālā* and perhaps also Daṇḍin's *Avantisundarī*—the stories span several human lifetimes. The recollection of past lives is the event that propels the narrative forward and, at the same time, backward. The central motif, which later authors usually mention in connection with *Taraṅgavatī,* is the pair of ruddy shelducks (*cakkāya*s) who are reborn as the lovers Taraṅgavatī and Padmadeva.[120]

The story takes place in Kauśāmbī, and later authors tell us that Pālitta himself was a native of Kośala, both in present-day Uttar Pradesh. But it was at the court of Sātavāhana in Pratiṣṭhāna, according to a unanimous tradition, that Pālitta achieved lasting literary fame. The Jain narrative literature relates that Pālitta already had worked in the courts of Muruṇḍa in Pāṭalīputra, of Bhīma in Oṃkāra, and finally of Kṛṣṇa in Mānakheṭa before he was summoned to the Sātavāhana court at Pratiṣṭhāna.[121] There Pālitta composed a "completely new work," the *Taraṅgavatī,* and explained it at court.[122] The work reportedly pleased the king but provoked criticism, jealousy, and accusations of plagiarism from other court poets and intellectuals. In response, Pālitta faked his own death, whereupon his rivals finally admitted that they had fabricated the charge of plagiarism.

It is significant that Uddyotana, in composing the eulogy of previous poets at the beginning of his novel *Kuvalayamālā,* begins with two verses that mention Pālitta and Sātavāhana together, and then one that focuses on Pālitta:

> The words of Pālitta, Sātavāhana, and the Chappaṇṇayas,[123]
> are like a lion's roar, and I'm like a young deer.
> How can I even *take a step / write one word?*
>
> Pālitta, whose mind was pure, whose virtues were deep,
> and who had the power to put the highest truths into writing,
> adorned Hāla in literary gatherings [*goṣṭhī*s] like a necklace,
> which had pure jewels, a strong cord,
> and was rich in gems of the highest quality.
>
> He is like the Himalaya, and his *Taraṅgavatī*
> is like the Ganges River that flows from it:
> pairs of ruddy shelducks make it beautiful,
> and it causes delight with the charm of its royal geese.[124]

Immediately afterwards, he praises Sātavāhana in a verse noted above. Abhinanda evoked the relationship between poet and patron in his *Deeds of Rāma* (ninth century):

> The excellent poet Śrīpālita was cherished
> by Hāla with the highest honor,
> the works of Kālidāsa achieved unparalleled fame
> through the enemy of the Śakas,
> Śrīharṣa brought to fruition the speech
> of the prose poet Bāṇa,
> and Śrīhāravarṣa has taken Abhinanda into his kind treatment
> constantly.[125]

In Pālitta the courtly and the Jain histories of Prakrit are crossed, or rather, they have not yet been separated from each other. Pālitta was a leading participant in the literary culture that was associated with Hāla's court. As Bhayani demonstrated, several verses of Pālitta's are included in *Seven Centuries,* and were likely excerpted or adapted from the *Taraṅgavatī*. Even if there is only a small number of verses shared between these texts, which are in any case incompletely preserved, they nevertheless point to a nexus of commonalities in form and content that are disguised by the distinct categories of "courtly poetry" and "Jain narrative literature." The language is similar: what sets the *Taraṅgavatī* slightly apart, both from *Seven Centuries* and from later literature in "Jain Māhārāṣṭrī," are its archaic features, which may also be regionalisms or colloquialisms. I note in chapter 6 that some of these features, which are typically associated with "archaic Jain Māhārāṣṭrī," are in fact described by the Prakrit grammarians, who are usually seen as describing a non-Jain literary language.[126] The *Taraṅgalolā* has several orthographic features that are typically associated with Jain texts, but I doubt both whether these features were present in the original *Taraṅgavatī* and whether they are diagnostic of a specifically Jain version of the language in any case.[127] The style is also very similar. It is self-consciously literary, and it abounds especially in figures of sense. The goal, even in Pālitta's narrative poem, is always to present a thought in a striking and elaborated way within the scope of a single verse. The metrical practice, too, seems to be more or less identical.

What's more, the *Taraṅgalolā* does not steer clear of eroticism—although it is hardly as frank as *Seven Centuries*—but rather channels it towards its own didactic ends. The opening scene of the novel, for example, has the nun Suvratā going out for alms with her students and captivating a neighboring housewife with her beauty, who says:

> Never in a dream, in a statue, in a painting, or in stories have I ever seen or heard of a woman as beautiful as this nun. What is she? A bouquet of loveliness put together by attractiveness? Or has the moonlight in all its beauty come down to earth? Could it be that creator has put the whole essence of youth into carefully making this slender girl, with all of her beauty and good qualities? If she looks so good with her head shaved, I can only imagine how stunning she was before! Her body is covered in dirt, and she wears no jewelry, but I can hardly take my eyes away from her. My gaze constantly wanders over every part of her body, eager to take it all in, stopping only to think how beautiful it is. Even the divine nymphs would feel an attraction to such a beauty, joined as it is with the nun's grace, and capable of lighting up one's heart, unlike anything else in the world. The goddess Lakṣmī herself has left her lotus pool, put on a nun's clothing, and come to my house, manifested by our generosity.[128]

There are faint echoes, or anticipations, of *Seven Centuries* in these verses.[129] Pālitta's specialty, to judge by quotations in later authors, was his striking descriptions of nature: the thunderous nights of the monsoon, the flight of a flock of parrots (a verse that appears in *Seven Centuries*), the rush of water buffalo into a lake, or the clear night sky.[130] Yet the above passage shows that the Jain monk was not aloof from the culture of *kāma* that surrounded him. Legend has it that he owes his name to this very inclination. The young monk, then named Nāgendra, was coming back from begging alms, and made up an alliterative verse as he was walking: "A mango from the red-eyed girl, a fig from the girl with flowerlike teeth, and fresh rice congree from the newly married girl: that's what I have in my pot."[131] On hearing this, his teacher Āryanāgahastin called him Ālitta, because his young student, who sought alms from the pretty girls, was "inflamed" (*ādīpta-*) by lust. Nāgendra said that he would prefer to be called Pālitta—which is to say, he wished that his teacher would consider him "illuminated" (*prādīpta-*) by virtue rather than "inflamed" by lust. The later versions of this story did not pick up on the subtle addition of a prefix, namely *pra-* in the sense of *prakarṣa* or "excellence," and instead connect the young monk's name with his reputed power of flight: he is said to have been "anointed on the feet" (*pādalipta*) with a magical preparation that allowed him to fly. I believe, however, that the power of flight and the name "Pādalipta" are both associated with a later teacher, and not with the first-century author of the *Taraṅgavatī*.

A. K. Warder acutely observed that the *Taraṅgavatī* was "a contrasting counterpart, as it were, to the lyrics collected by Sātavāhana, in the same new language."[132] Pālitta and Hāla were indeed the co-creators of Prakrit literature, each concerned with pushing the new discourse in a certain direction, but borrowing from and overlapping heavily with each other in the process. They were an odd couple. Hāla, if his opening verse is any indication, was a devotee of Śiva, but *Seven Centuries* wears its religion so lightly that some scholars have tried to read out of it, or into it, the philosophy of hedonistic materialism (Cārvāka or Lokāyata).[133] Pālitta was, of course, a Jain monk, and his novel concludes with Taraṅgavatī and Padmadeva accepting the Jain faith and becoming ascetics.

The storied relationship between Hāla and Pālitta, I think, was not one of mere contemporaneity or financial patronage: each partner brought unique resources to the literary enterprise they were jointly involved in. Pālitta, for his part, was well versed in Jain lore, which was at that very moment being collected and reformulated in the massive commentarial project of Bhadrabāhu: Pālitta and Bhadrabāhu share a language, Prakrit, and a metrical form, the *gāthā*, which they each employed in their own way to redefine the discursive parameters of Jainism. It is possible that Buddhist communities, who must have constituted a large portion of the population under Sātavāhana rule, also used Prakrit in similar ways, although we have very little evidence in this regard. The edifying stories of Jain preachers, however, did not in themselves count as literature, at least according to the new standards of literature that were emerging around the first century CE. It was only when Pālitta was pulled into Hāla's court, and made to "adorn his literary gatherings" (*goṣṭhīs*), that the old art of Jain storytelling was transformed into a new kind of literature. Just as subsequent poets looked back upon *Seven Centuries* as the prototype of the single-verse lyric (*muktaka*), subsequent poets looked upon *Taraṅgavatī* as the prototype of the romance (*kathā*). Even before the Pālitta and his *Taraṅgavatī* were known to scholarship, Rudolf Hoernle had suspected that Prakrit literature owes its origins to a process similar to what I have just described: "The Brahmanical opponents of the Jains . . . who employed the Sanskrit language for their religious and all higher literature, condescended to employ the literary Prákrit, created by the Jains, only for purposes of secular literature of a lower class (erotic and dramatic poetry, etc.) and, in doing so, subjected the language to a high degree of pedantic artificialization."[134] Leaving aside Hoernle's Victorian disdain for the pedantic and artificial, it does seem that courtly Prakrit owes much to the active involvement of Jain poets, and conversely, that Jain uses of Prakrit depended on the standard set by courtly literature for their wide dissemination and intelligibility.

CONCLUSIONS

This chapter has focused on the emergence of Prakrit literature, by which I mean *pāuakavvaṃ*, the conjuncture of both Prakrit and literature in their strict senses. I have traced this emergence from two different perspectives: the eroticized world of courtly lyric, and the didactic world of Jain narrative. My conclusion is that both camps cooperated in the production of this new discursive phenomenon. If we look at an author like Uddyotana, we see that he could look upon both Hāla and Pālitta equally as forebears. Yet the memory of literary culture came to be increasingly circumscribed by religious affiliation. Hāla was converted to Jainism centuries after his death, although it was primarily because of the high literary quality of *Seven Centuries* and not the alleged Jainism of its author that staid and celibate monks continued to read, copy, and imitate this extremely erotic text. Pālitta, for his part, was more or less erased from the memory of Hāla's court in Brahmanical sources. He is absent, for example, from the *Līlāvaī*, which makes Hāla and several of his co-authors characters in a fantastic romance. In this text, Hāla's closest advisor is Nāgārjuna. Although certainty is difficult on this point, I suspect that the *Līlāvaī* evokes the second-century Buddhist teacher, who was known to be an associated of a Sātavāhana king, rather than a later Nāgārjuna ("*siddha* Nāgārjuna") whom Jains identified as a student of Pālitta. Still, Pālitta's absence is striking.[135] He is also absent from the list of famous Prakrit poets that Rājaśekhara gives in his *Karpūramañjarī*.[136] Most of all, his *Taraṅgavatī* is now a permanent absence in Indian literary history.

I have zeroed in on a moment when Prakrit literature was given the form that it would take for more than a millennium afterwards. The still-dominant view is that Prakrit means "language of the common people." But when authors of the eighth, tenth, or twelfth centuries wrote Prakrit, they wrote in the specific literary language pioneered by Hāla and Pālitta around the first and second century CE. This was a crucial moment, not just for Prakrit, but for Indian literature as a whole.

It was the period in which the foundations of classical literature were established, from its figural vocabulary to its repertoire of genres to its linguistic parameters. Subsequent authors remembered Hāla and, to a lesser extent, Pālitta as important starting points of their traditions. And although they became legendary in their own right, they are among the earliest historical figures—as opposed to mythical sages—to appear in the genealogy of *kāvya* that poets provide.[137] *Seven Centuries* in particular was one of the most widely read and appreciated works of literature in India. Although much will of course remain obscure about the invention of Prakrit, there is also much that we can piece together from the available evidence. First, this invention took place in the Deccan around the first and second centuries CE. Second, it represents the convergence of the courtly culture of the Sātavāhanas with the discursive practices of the Jain community. No better example of this convergence exists than Pālitta himself, a Jain monk who attended Hāla's court and contributed verses to *Seven Centuries*. Third, the cultivation of Prakrit poetry at the Sātavāhana court is one of the earliest instances we can point to where literature was pursued for its own sake, where social identities attached to this new pursuit, and where political power took an active role in promoting this domain of culture.

Finally, I want to clarify what I mean by the "emergence," "invention" or "creation" of Prakrit literature, and of Prakrit as a literary language, since these terms are all likely to be misunderstood as implying a conscious effort to create something that did not exist before, like Esperanto. Literarization is the double movement by which a language is employed for expressive purposes and becomes invested with a literary expressivity. Part of literarization is the emergence of new discursive spheres, new genres and practices to occupy them, and new disciplines to regulate them. The languages of literature are constituted as such by this process. I would claim that a person can speak, recite, or sing in Prakrit only after a language called "Prakrit" has been identified and at least minimally characterized. It is possible that people used forms identical to Prakrit in their speech before the invention of Prakrit under the Sātavāhanas, just as it is possible that someone might have uttered the words "the time is out of joint" before *Hamlet* was composed. But just as knowingly quoting Shakespeare is different from serendipitously anticipating him, writing in Prakrit is different from writing forms that are similar or identical to Prakrit forms. Writing in Prakrit is a practice that has certain rules, procedures, norms, or models, whether they are defined implicitly or explicitly. Literarization as a process involves the building up of those models and the production of texts in accordance with them. This is why the discourse that literarization produces, *kāvya* or *kavva,* could be and often was described in terms of its norms (*lakṣaṇa*) and the texts that model them (*lakṣya*). Thus literarization is always accompanied by a rarification of discourse. What is elevated to the level of literature in this specific sense, through magnificent acts of generosity and miraculous acts of insight, is only a fraction of discourse, and what has survived in manuscript form is an even smaller fraction. This rarification applied to languages as well: the world was full of languages around the first century CE, but the practices of literature were keyed to a very small number of them. It was never inevitable that Prakrit would become one of them. But its successful use in the early centuries of the common era, under the patronage of Sātavāhana rulers and with the cooperation of Jain monks, ensured its position alongside Sanskrit as one of the primary languages of literature for roughly a thousand years.

4

The Forms of Prakrit Literature

How can we characterize Prakrit, as a language and as a literary tradition? The most straightforward answer might be to provide a systematic account of its differences from other languages, and specifically from Sanskrit. For Sanskrit and Prakrit are sister languages: we recognize one by contrast with the other. Prakrit was always represented and imagined through a "schema of co-figuration" with Sanskrit. From a very early period, a comparison between Sanskrit and Prakrit formed the basis of the systematic knowledge of the latter; the forms of the Prakrit language were almost always derived from corresponding Sanskrit forms. There is no doubt that Prakrit was, to a large degree, defined and characterized by contrast with Sanskrit—a contrast that formed the basis of the language order of premodern India. However, this picture is incomplete. It can lead us into thinking about Prakrit in purely structural terms, as if it were constituted entirely by its differences from Sanskrit.[1] If Prakrit was a position in the language order from which it was possible to compose literary texts, it was a position of a particular kind. We might say that it had a phenomenology and ask what it was *like* to occupy this position, to operate in the world of Prakrit textuality. Similarly, we might say that it had an aesthetics and ask what it was about Prakrit itself that contributed to the beauty, or strikingness, of Prakrit texts. Of course, the phenomenology and aesthetics of Prakrit emerge even more clearly when contrasted with those of Sanskrit, but in this chapter I want to examine them for what they are, rather than for what they are not. Similarly, Allison Busch has drawn attention to features of Braj Bhāṣā that made it not simply a vehicle for literary expression but an aesthetic object in its own right. Features of its grammar, its lexicon, and its metrical repertoire combined to give the language a particular "expressive range" that was highly valued in the literary culture of early modern North India.[2]

The idea that a language has an aesthetics is in some sense familiar from travelers' clichés. English speakers, for instance, have probably encountered the notion that German is "awful," angry-sounding, confusingly complex, hyperspecific in some particulars and frustratingly vague in others.[3] But I am not talking about a native speaker of one language discovering the "foreignness" of a foreign language, which is the central conceit of these clichés. I am referring to a situation that was common in premodernity but is almost unthinkable now, in which someone chooses to compose in a language not because it is his or her "native" language—for these languages were never anyone's "native" language—but because it offered specific expressive resources that he or she wanted to make use of. These resources are part of what an earlier generation of scholars meant by the German term *Ausbildung,* meaning both the historical process of making a language suitable for literary expression and the cumulative result of that process.[4]

The notion that languages have particular expressive resources is somewhat old-fashioned. Nowadays, one needs to be at least half joking to claim that one language is better than another in any respect. The old prejudices, for example, that one could only philosophize in Greek or in German, have been exposed as prejudices. The background assumption is rather that all languages are created equal, which is, of course, true in a certain sense. The problem occurs when we try to formulate a theory of literary language. Such a theory requires us to understand and explain what it was about a language that made people *choose* to compose literature in it, and often invest a significant amount of time and effort in mastering it. What they mastered was not "just" the language, but the modes of literary expression associated with it. I say "just" in scare quotes because these modes really were considered to be part of the language rather than external to it.

This is a different approach to literary language from the one literary theorists commonly take. They often take the distinction between "literary" and "non-literary" forms of a language as *given,* and describe the specific differences of one vis-à-vis the other. This is how Erich Auerbach arrived at his characterization of literary language as being "distinguished from the general language of daily life by its selectivity, homogeneity, and conservatism."[5] This approach, of course, presupposes that both of these forms are actually given. And perhaps it also presupposes a certain ontology of literary language in general, that it exists as a modification of the "general language of daily life." We might label this second presupposition "homoglossy," the idea that literary language forms a unity with a corresponding non-literary language. Precisely what kind of unity is meant is not always clear. If, however, we hold Auerbach's larger argument in mind—that a condition of a thriving literary culture is a literary language that forms a unity with the "mother language" of the community at large—then it becomes clear that homoglossy means that people write literature in a version of the language that they speak in their daily life.

I am very doubtful that either of these presuppositions is met in the case of Prakrit, or for that matter, in the case of many other literary languages. Consider Old Provençal, the language of the troubadours. What, exactly, is the "general language of daily life" that would correspond to it? Presumably a less selective, less homogeneous, and less conservative version of the language of troubadour poetry—a language that is not actually "given," in the sense of attested to by manuscripts, but postulated on the basis of troubadour poetry itself. But according to the authorities in this field, the Auerbachian presupposition of homoglossy is not met. The earliest troubadour whose works are extant, William of Aquitaine (late eleventh–early twelfth century), probably spoke Old French rather than Old Provençal in his daily life. In several of his poems he addresses a transregional public of troubadour poets, which became more and more transregional in successive generations. Within a century, the language of the troubadours was cultivated across southern France, in Catalonia, in North Italy, and in Sicily. By this point, as Pierre Swiggers has remarked, its public was largely "alloglossic." The geography of literary languages was clearly different, and bigger, than the geography of the "languages of daily life." One might insist that homoglossy is still a condition of the origin of literary languages, if not necessarily a condition of their continued use and popularity. Yet here, too, authorities on medieval literature would disagree. "The most recent work on the origin of the poetic languages of the Romance-speaking peoples," Paul Zumthor writes, "has established . . . that the languages in question were anything but direct emanations of a given natural dialect; from the very first they bear the mark of at least a potential unity and of artificiality; moreover, in relation to their spoken substrates they show some degree of abstraction."[6]

That is also true of Prakrit. Its existence as a literary language is not explained by the existence of another, similar, language of which we have no certain knowledge. Indeed, earlier generations of scholars considered its existence as a literary language to be a "veil" that separates us from its true origins, from the everyday forms of speech in which language "really" consists.[7] That is why, in this chapter, I focus on another type of explanation: the expressive resources that Prakrit was believed to offer. For utilizing these resources was, in part, what it meant to compose in Prakrit. I will discuss them on three levels: Prakrit's "sweet" texture on the level of its phonetics, its "quavering" rhythms on the level of its meter, and its "unbound" character on the level of its poetic compositions. I use quotation marks here to indicate that these are not my own judgments, but characterizations that ancient readers of Prakrit literature, and indeed authors of Prakrit literature, actually supplied.

SWEET SYLLABLES

In a verse from the *Brilliance of the Connoisseurs* that we have already encountered in the introduction, the poet Vairocana reflects on his chosen medium:

> Prakrit poetry is like a beautiful courtesan:
> erotic, alluring, full of *rasa,*
> delicate, provoking excitement and desire,
> it captivates your heart.[8]

Much of this verse can be explained by reference to the traditional subjects of Prakrit poetry. Ever since *Seven Centuries,* Prakrit had been the preferred medium for erotic lyrics. But in what respect is Prakrit "delicate"? We can turn to another reflection on Prakrit for a clue. This one comes from an anthology, called the *Vajjālagga,* compiled by one Jagadvallabha, which contains an entire section on the *gāthā,* the Prakrit poem, where the following verse is found:

> Interspersed with regional words,
> made of sweet syllables put into metrical form,
> playful, with meanings plain, powerful, and clear—
> Prakrit poetry is fully worth reciting.[9]

Here we find another set of characteristics, which don't quite match Vairocana's, but which are somewhat more specific: Prakrit poetry is "playful," but it is its meanings that are "plain, powerful, and clear," and its syllables that are "sweet."[10] These verses highlight a particular feature of how Prakrit sounds, of what we might call its phonic texture, continuing Vairocana's tactile metaphor, or following the *Vajjālagga*'s verse into a synesthetic realm, its phonic taste.

The oldest definition of literary "sweetness" relates not specifically to the sound or meaning of a text, but to the general capacity for enjoying it over and over again. The *Treatise on Theater* of the early centuries CE says that sweetness is "when a text has been heard many times, or spoken again and again, and does not cause annoyance." Herman Tieken has shown that such a concept was already available to King Aśoka, in the early third century BCE, who invokes it indirectly in his fourteenth Rock Edict.[11] This definition operates in the background of more precise and elaborated concepts of sweetness in literature. But I believe we can be more specific regarding what it was that caused people to recognize Prakrit's syllables as "sweet," beyond the fact that their repetition was a source of pleasure rather than annoyance. And I think that this quality, which was appreciated by Vairocana and Jagadvallabha, is related to a quality of which other readers of Prakrit were rather more critical.

In his *Comparative Grammar of the Modern Languages of India,* published in 1872, John Beames made a few observations about the language of *Seven Centuries.*

At the time it was one of the only texts written entirely in Prakrit that was available to European scholars, chiefly through the excerpts that Albrecht Weber had published in the course of preparing the edition of the text that would appear in 1881. Beames jumped to the conclusion that the Prakrit of *Seven Centuries* was "emasculated stuff": "the author ruthlessly massacres consonants and long vowels to suit his rhyme or rhythm, or to secure a more harmonious turn to his verse."[12] To Beames, Prakrit had too many "artificial sweeteners." It was made to sound a certain way by relying on arbitrary and capricious techniques. Prakrit's artificiality would become a refrain throughout the later nineteenth and early twentieth centuries. Beames connected it, albeit obliquely, with its femininity. I suspect that Prakrit's long-standing association with the feminine had preconditioned Beames's judgment, and specifically the fact that female characters were assigned varieties of Prakrit in stage plays, which by Beames's time had been known to European scholars for over a century, and perhaps also the fact that most of the verses in *Seven Centuries* were imagined to have been spoken by women, which would have been a more recent discovery. What about the Prakrit of *Seven Centuries* would have driven Beames to this assessment? And was he right?

Beames alluded to the modification of vowel length. There are certainly cases of shortening and lengthening, but I think these phenomena are hardly indicative of a "modification" of the language for poetic purposes. There are only a handful of words that are subject to these processes, and they seem to be conditioned by phonological factors. The adverbs corresponding to Sanskrit *yathā* and *tathā* are one example: each has two variants in Prakrit (*jahā/jaha* and *tahā/taha*), but the distribution in *Seven Centuries* shows that the long-vowel variant is usually conditioned by a preceding *ṇa*.[13] Similarly, almost all of the cases of vowel lengthening involve a preverb, for example, *pāaḍa*, from *prakaṭa*, in the above verse from the *Vajjālagga*. It is likely that the lengthening in such cases is a manifestation of accentual prominence. It does not matter whether Prakrit maintained the mobile accentual system of Vedic, as Richard Pischel maintained, or whether it had Latin-like accentuation rules that fixed the accent two or three syllables from the end of the word, as Hermann Jacobi argued.[14] Poets certainly took advantage of this kind of variation, but it is unlikely that they manipulated the length of vowels solely because of the exigencies of meter or rhyme.

What about the "massacre" of consonants? There are a number of phenomena to be noted here. First, Prakrit has a smaller inventory of consonants than Sanskrit as a result of the elimination of place-of-articulation contrasts. This was the most obvious difference between Sanskrit and Prakrit, and was often remarked upon in very early texts.[15] Thus there are three sibilants in Sanskrit (*ś*, *ṣ*, *s*), which are articulated in three different places: at the palate, at the palate with a curled tongue, and at the teeth, respectively. In Prakrit, there is only one sibilant (*s*), which does not contrast in its place of articulation with any other. Similarly, Sanskrit distinguishes dental and retroflex nasals (*n*, *ṇ*), even if their occurrence is largely determined by phonological context. In Prakrit, there is no significant contrast between the two.[16] Second, Prakrit does not permit combinations of heterorganic consonants, which are consonants articulated at different places in the mouth. This means that all such combinations become homorganic, or articulated at the same place, which includes double consonants (as in *uppala* from *utpala*) or combinations with a syllable-final nasal (as in *ciṃdha* from *cihna*). Third, single intervocalic consonants are subject to extensive lenition, literally, "softening," which it is tempting to gloss in this context as "sweetening." Aspirates are generally reduced to *h*, losing their place of articulation, and unaspirated stops are generally elided altogether. Cumulatively, these processes often produce forms which are mostly vowels with very few consonants: the word *prākṛta* itself, which becomes *pāua* (or *pāia* or *pāaa*), is one example.

Taken together, these processes result in two features that we might call musicality and indeterminacy. I don't mean musicality in the sense of tone or pitch—we know almost nothing about these features—but in the sense that Prakrit, with its high proportion of vowels to consonants, seems especially suitable for continuous and melismatic recitation. It is a phonetic characteristic, having to do with the way that Prakrit sounds, or perhaps even the way that it is pronounced. Prakrit's high proportion of vowels gives it a more "open" articulation. And the loss of place-of-articulation contrasts often means that the transition from one vowel-sound to another is "smoother," that is, there are fewer articulatory gestures involved. This quality is reflected especially in the "massacred" consonants that Beames referred to: *mṛga* "deer," *mṛta* "dead," and *mada* "lust" all become *maa*. And the same set of words serves as an example of indeterminacy, which is a semantic rather than a phonetic quality: a single Prakrit word, especially when it represents several different Sanskrit words, can have multiple meanings. Of course, polysemy is a basic fact of any language, and no human languages are completely "determinate" in this sense. Sanskrit, too, has its fair share of polysemous words.[17] But the phonology of Prakrit has greatly amplified its indeterminacy relative to Sanskrit.

Both musicality and indeterminacy might be imagined to be as useful in literature and song as they are useless, or even harmful, in other domains of language use: could people really have made themselves understood through forms such as *maa?* Yet the underlying phonological processes are so well attested across the spectrum of Middle Indic languages, from present-day Afghanistan to Sri Lanka, and are so common among the world's languages in general, that we should not suspect Prakrit authors of "faking" them. We should rather try to understand what contributions they might have made to Prakrit's literariness.

We can begin from the theory of alliteration (*anuprāsa*), the repetition of certain speech-sounds within a given unit of context. Indian literary theorists recognized varieties of alliteration that were distinguished by the character of the speech-sounds that were repeated. Perhaps the earliest such classification is that of Harivṛddha, who distinguished eight *bhaṇitis* or "modes of speech." Rudraṭa distinguished six varieties, and Bhoja distinguished twelve.[18] The musicality of Prakrit lends itself to some of these and not others: the defining characteristic of what Bhoja calls the "stiff" (*kaṭhora*), for example, is the combination of *r* and velar consonants (*k, kh, g, gh*), which is impossible in Prakrit. Prakrit does indeed lend itself to the varieties called the "sweet" (*madhura*) and the "delicate" (*komala*), the words with which Prakrit was described in the verses we examined at the beginning of this section. In Bhoja's system, these varieties are characterized by the use of a syllable-final nasal (*anusvāra*) and the use of *r* and *ṇ* respectively; Rudraṭa's "sweet" variety seems to combine both of these characteristics. Here I simply want to highlight Prakrit's suitability for these types of alliterative compositions.

I also want to draw attention to a type of alliteration that is common in Prakrit but impossible in Sanskrit, and which theorists who operated in Sanskrit seem to have struggled to define: the repetition of nothing. Because of the extensive lenition of intervocalic consonants, Prakrit often has nothing between vowels besides a hiatus, which Sanskrit tolerates in only a handful of rare words.[19] To illustrate a type of alliterative composition he called the "powerful" (*ojasvin*), Bhoja quoted a verse from *Rāvaṇa's Demise*, a Prakrit court epic composed by the Vākāṭaka king Pravarasena II around the early fifth century CE:

> *pattā a sībharāhaa-dhāu-silāala-ṇisaṇṇa-rāia-jalaaṃ* |
> *sajjhaṃ ojjhara-pahasia-dari-muha-ṇikkanta-vaüla-maïrāmoaṃ* ||

> They reached the Sahya mountain,
> where the clouds,
> resting on the exposed rocks,
> covered them in mist and took on their colors,
> and where the laughing of waterfalls
> and the wine-like smell of *bakura* flowers
> issued from the mouths of the caves.[20]

We can detect here a number of alliterative pairs (*sajjha/ojjhara*), which happen not to alliterate in Sanskrit (*sahya/nirjhara*), but only one instance of the doubling or repetition of retroflex consonants that Bhoja identifies as the characteristic of "powerful" alliteration.[21] This verse does exhibit the density of compound words that characterizes the "powerful" as a compositional quality (*guṇa*) rather than as a mode of alliteration, and it seems likely that this competing understanding of the "powerful" motivated Bhoja's choice of this example. But there is an alliterative quality to this verse which Bhoja surely perceived, namely, the density of hiatus, which is in fact only possible in Prakrit poetry.

The aural qualities that distinctively characterize Prakrit are all related to its musicality, the reduction of articulatory gestures and its tendency to openness. The fact that consonants had to combine with themselves or with a placeless nasal, and never with heterorganic consonants, gave it a kind of smoothness—one possible meaning of the key descriptor *komala.* And the elimination of consonants altogether in certain contexts brought vowels into contact with each other. These qualities, I contend, are what premodern authors had in mind—even if only at the back of their minds—when they described Prakrit poetry in general as sweet, soft, and tender. This feature of Prakrit's phonic texture or taste might have aligned particularly well with other types of musicality. For, as we will see below, its metrical patterns had their own kind of musicality. And there is some evidence that Prakrit verses were performed with particular melodies, at least in the context of the stage play, which would add another layer of musicality.[22]

Indeterminacy was put to use in poetry in a variety of ways. We have already encountered verses in *Seven Centuries* that depend on a single word being understood in two different meanings (e.g., W467, W428, and W364), and in other Prakrit texts there are "apparent contradictions" (*virodhābhāsa*s) that depend upon reading a word in two different senses. These features are of course common in Sanskrit as well. Prakrit merely increases the possibilities for "bitextual" techniques, in which the same sequence of phonemes is productive of different meanings.[23] But there are verses called *galitaka*s in which a certain type of "bitextuality" is a constitutive feature of the composition. Since *galitaka*s were only ever composed in Prakrit, these verses might help to make the case that the "sweet syllables" of Prakrit had specific literary purposes.

All of the known examples of *galitaka*s "in the wild" come from *Rāvaṇa's Demise.* Writers of metrical handbooks, such as Virahāṅka and Hemacandra, give a few additional varieties. We know that there were additional *galitaka* compositions in two Prakrit court epics that are now lost, *Hari's Victory* and *Rāvaṇa's Victory.*[24] These verses are characterized by a particular kind of end-rhyme: the exact same syllables are repeated, but each time they must mean something different. This feature, known as *yamaka,* or "twinning," is certainly difficult to realize—Daṇḍin discusses it in the "difficult" (*duṣkara*) chapter of his *Mirror on Literature*—but Prakrit has the advantage of relative indeterminacy. Here is one example from *Rāvaṇa's Demise:*

añjaṇa-rāaeṇa saï dhūsarantaāiṃ
gaṇḍa-alesu khalia-visamosarantaāiṃ |
sura-bandīṇa ṇaaṇa-galiāiṁ aṃsuāiṃ
kappa-laāṇa jattha maïlenti aṃsuāiṃ ||

Always dusky with lamp-black,
trickling down over their cheeks,

the tears from the eyes of the imprisoned nymphs
darkened the garments
on the branches of the *kalpa* trees.[25]

As often in these *galitaka* verses, Pravarasena utilizes the fact that a single Prakrit word, such as *aṃsua,* might have more than one meaning, corresponding in this case to *aśru* "tear" and *aṃśuka* "garment" in Sanskrit. Other strategies for making the rhyme work involve the manipulation of word-boundaries and the use of pleonastic suffixes such as we see in this verse: *dhūsarantaāiṃ, osarantaāiṃ,* and *aṃsuāiṃ* all involve the suffix that Sanskrit grammarians call *svārthe ka,* "pleonastic *ka,*" which in Prakrit might as well be called *svārthe a,* since the intervocalic -*k*- is always lost.

A comparison with Sanskrit offers, by way of a baseline, a convenient way of talking about what was distinctive about Prakrit in terms of the possibilities its musicality and indeterminacy opened up to poets. But these features do not in themselves depend on the comparison with Sanskrit: a word such as *aṃsua* will have the same semantic range regardless of whether we compare it with a set of corresponding Sanskrit words. This is important, because as much as a text such as *Rāvaṇa's Demise* seems to be mediated by Sanskrit—it was, and is, read through Sanskrit commentaries—the text itself does not *need* to be understood through a layer of Sanskrit meanings that lies underneath the Prakrit surface. Indeed the large number of *deśī* words, which do not obviously correspond to Sanskrit words, poses a problem for Sanskrit mediation, either as a theory of the text's composition (i.e., that Pravarasena composed it in Sanskrit and then "sweetened" it by transforming it into Prakrit) or as a theory of the text's reception (i.e., that readers could only understand it by translating it word-for-word into Sanskrit).[26]

Some of the representations of Prakrit in Indian literature as soft, delicate, tender, and so on might give us the impression that it was a specialized cant used exclusively for erotic poetry within the broader domain of Sanskrit textuality. This is the impression that scholars of the late nineteenth and twentieth centuries actually had. As we have seen, John Beames thought that Prakrit was an "emasculated" excuse for a language, providing the maximum possible scope to versification and song by suspending all of the rules of grammar. I think this is very far from the truth, but I also think that these critics were onto something. Prakrit does have certain phonic and semantic capacities that poets exploited effectively, capacities that I have been calling musicality and indeterminacy. Their exploitation did not amount to the creation of a language from scratch, but it did result in Prakrit being linked in the literary-cultural imaginary with the features of sweetness and delicacy, not just on the level of what Prakrit poetry was about, but on the level of how Prakrit poetry actually sounded. There was, of course, some interference between the evaluation of the style and content of the poetry—which was correspondingly lyrical, sensitive, and erotic in the main—and the evaluation of its phonic texture. But this is partly what I meant in framing this discussion around Prakrit's "expressive resources": the most fundamental features of the Prakrit language, such as its phonetics, become meaningful to its readers and contribute to its aesthetic power.

QUAVERING VERSES

Prakrit is a literature of *gāthās*. The word *gāthā* refers both to the most common and characteristic meter of Prakrit poetry and, by extension, to the Prakrit verses composed in that meter. This is clear from the verses in Prakrit anthologies that speak of the beauty of poetry, and in particular of Prakrit poetry: they generally refer to their subjects as *gāthās*.[27]

According to its derivation from the verbal root *gā*, "to sing," the word *gāthā* refers to a sung verse. This highlights one of the tensions inherent in Prakrit poetry. Sheldon Pollock has argued that "the realm of the oral, specifically, the sung" lies outside of "the sphere of literary culture."[28] Where are we to place Prakrit *gāthās*? Are they closer to the songs that one might sing to pass time at the grinding stone, or to the literate productions of professional poets? I have argued in the previous chapter that Prakrit texts helped to establish "the sphere of literary culture" where works of literary art, *kāvya*, were produced. They are some of the earliest texts to identify themselves as *kāvya*, and form a crucial part of the genealogy of *kāvya*. The *gāthā*, like Prakrit itself, thus seems to stand between two categories that have been essential for conceptualizing and historicizing cultural practices in India: on the one hand, the oral, musical, and sung; on the other, the literate, textual, and recited. In this section I describe what is distinctive about Prakrit versification, and I venture a number of claims about the role of Prakrit versification practices and metrical knowledge in the history of literature and textuality more broadly in India.

Gāthā is an old Indo-European word. Its Avestan cognate (*gāϑā*), which is probably more widely known, refers to the songs ascribed to Zarathushtra that constitute the oldest and most sacred texts of Zoroastrianism. The earliest attested uses of the word *gāthā* in India are unsurprisingly connected with the chanting of Vedic hymns. Later Vedic texts cite a number of verses—referred to as *ślokas* and *gāthās*—that are unattached to any particular tradition of Vedic recitation.[29]

None of these earlier traditions exhibit the unique metrical structure that characterizes the Prakrit *gāthā*. Avestan and Vedic verse are syllable-counting, and it appears that particular forms of syllable-counting verse are an Indo-European inheritance.[30] The Prakrit *gāthā*, however, belongs to a class of verse forms that is regulated by *gaṇa*s rather than by syllables. A *gaṇa* is a "group" of moras, and a mora is a prosodic unit: it is what a light syllable (⏑) has one of, and what a heavy syllable (–) has two of. Light syllables, for our purposes, are those that contain a short vowel and no final consonants; all other syllables are heavy. On top of a given framework of *gaṇa*s may be overlaid a seemingly endless variety of "surface forms," consisting of particular syllabic configuration. The basic rule of *gaṇa*-counting verse is that a heavy syllable, which consists of two moras, must never cross a boundary between *gaṇa*s. These meters, which the tradition generally called *jāti*s, are hence very flexible.[31] Fundamental to the entire system of *gaṇa*-counting verse is the metrical equivalence of two light syllables and one heavy syllable—an underlying prosodic structure that linguists call the moraic trochee. With a few exceptions, this system is absent from earlier traditions of versification in India.

The mora, although it is defined prosodically, could serve as unit of time as well. It is thus a unit of rhythmic equivalence: a *gaṇa* of four moras, for example, should have the same duration regardless of the particular configuration of syllables in which it is realized. Hence *gaṇa*-counting meters, in contrast to syllable-counting meters, can be thought of as having an inherent "beat." A meter that consists of a sequence of four-mora *gaṇa*s can be recited in "common time."

Most *gaṇa*-counting meters, and above all the Prakrit *gāthā*, exhibit additional forms of rhythmic regulation. A *gaṇa* might be realized with a syncopated or unsyncopated rhythm, that is, with a prominence on the second or first mora of the *gaṇa*. At this finer level of analysis, "rhythm" does not simply arise from the way light and heavy syllables are strung together, but from the way that syllables are parsed into prosodic feet. The parsing of syllables into prosodic feet is a phonological procedure that Prakrit verse has incorporated into its metrical grammar, and the details of this procedure need not concern us here.[32] The upshot of foot-parsing is that word boundaries play an important role in characterizing the rhythm of a *gaṇa* as syncopated or unsyncopated: thus, for example, the shape ⏑|⏑⏑⏑ patterns with the "syncopated" shape ⏑–⏑, while ⏑⏑|⏑⏑ patterns with the "unsyncopated" shape ––.

The alternation of rhythms is built into the deep structure of the Prakrit *gāthā:* the odd *gaṇa*s must be unsyncopated, and some but not all of the even *gaṇa*s must be syncopated. But writers on metrics recognized a particular type of *gāthā* in which this rhythmic alternation appears on the surface. This is the *capalā*, a "quavering" or "modulating" verse that realizes all of the even *gaṇa*s with the syncopated shape ⏑–⏑, surrounded on either side by a heavy syllable to reinforce the contrast. Writers distinguished variants that were "front-modulating" (*mukhacapalā*) and "back-modulating" (*jaghanacapalā*), depending on whether the first or second line exhibited this pattern. Their primarily motive in doing so, however, seems to have been to elicit a pair of double meanings: among the cast of characters in Prakrit erotic poetry are the woman who says just a little too much (*mukhacapalā*) and the woman who moves her hips just a little too much (*jaghanacapalā*) to be above suspicion.[33] The Prakrit *gāthā* ends with another built-in syncopation—a single light syllable toward the end of its second line—which is what allows us to recognize the two-line verse as a discrete metrical unit.

To see how this type of versification works, we can take an example from a *gāthā* about *gāthās* in Vairocana's *Brilliance of the Connoisseurs:*

ekkā vi ittha vivihā samaa-visesena vaṇṇa-bheeṇa |
dīsaï ṇaḍi vva gāhā bhiṇṇa-rasā bhiṇṇa-bhāvā a ||

Though one, it is manifold.
Like an actress
who wears different face paint at different times,
the *gāthā*,
with different ways of reading its syllables,
expresses different emotional states.[34]

Determining the weight of each syllable gives us the following pattern:

–– ◡–◡ ◡◡– ◡◡◡◡ –– ◡–◡ –– ◡
–◡◡ ◡–◡ –– –◡◡ –– ◡ –– ◡

And grouping these syllables into *gaṇas* gives the following pattern:

––, ◡–◡, ◡◡–, ◡◡◡◡, ––, ◡–◡,––, ◡
–◡◡, ◡–◡, ––, –◡◡, ––, ◡, ––, ◡

Note the alternation of syncopated *gaṇas* (in gray) and unsyncopated *gaṇas*. Note, too, that the *gāthā* is a "catalectic" meter, which means that both lines leave off the last syllable of the final metrical unit. As noted above, the second line has a shortened sixth *gaṇa* that syncopates the whole rest of the line, signaling the end of the verse.

These quavering verses, with their endless variety of syllabic patterns and their subtle alternations playing out over a stable rhythmic framework of *gaṇas*, are the mainstay of Prakrit literature. *Gaṇa*-counting meters are found in other literatures, and other metrical forms are found in Prakrit. But they are "Prakrit meters" in a sense that goes beyond the fact that they are common in Prakrit. To write in Prakrit was, to a very large extent, to write in *gāthās* or related *gaṇa*-counting meters. Less appreciated, but perhaps more historically significant, is the converse: to write in *gāthās* was to write in Prakrit.

It is well known that there are no traces of *gaṇa*-counting verse in Vedic literature, or indeed in any Sanskrit texts prior to Patañjali's *Great Commentary* (around the second century BCE). These meters occur for the first time in the canonical literature of the Buddhists and the Jains, and hence in the "Middle Indic" languages we call Pali and Ardhamāgadhī. Both canons, however, represent texts that were transmitted orally for centuries before being "committed" to writing. The scare quotes are necessary because, far from fixing the text in a determinate and inalterable shape, the technology of writing introduced completely new possibilities of revision, expansion, and interpolation. Thus, despite containing material that may well go back, in some form, to the time of Buddha and Mahāvīra, and hence to the sixth and fifth centuries BCE, the texts as we have them are products of the early centuries CE. In the case of the Pali canon, an ambitious commentarial enterprise led by the Sri Lankan monk Buddhaghosa represents a snapshot of the textual tradition in the fifth century. And in the case of the Ardhamāgadhī canon, the council of Valabhī, also in the fifth century, represented the end of a long and highly disputed process of canon formation.

Both sets of texts have an internal chronology in which the use of *gaṇa*-counting meters is centrally implicated. Ludwig Alsdorf has shown that the oldest layers of these texts use the "old *āryā*," an archaic version of the *gāthā* discovered by Hermann Jacobi in 1884. The use of the *gāthā* in its classical form is limited to chronologically later layers.[35] According to the picture sketched by Alsdorf, we have in both canons an "early" layer in which just one *gaṇa*-counting meter, the old *āryā*, is used sporadically alongside the more frequent syllable-counting meters such as *anuṣṭubh* and *triṣṭubh,* and a "later" layer in which the classical *gāthā* is found. The classical *gāthā* is thus a sign of lateness. On this basis, Alsdorf suggested that the "later" layer of the Jain canon, where the *gāthā* is the preferred verse form, was later than the "later" layer of the Pali canon, where the *gāthā* is still relatively rare. The Pali canon, he argued, was constituted at a time before the *gāthā* had become "the metrical fashion of the epoch." Roy Norman has argued, equivalently, that the Buddhist community ultimately responsible for putting the Pali canon together had moved to South India right around the time when the *gāthā* was gaining popularity in the North.[36]

What is the significance of the use of the *gāthā* in the later portions of the Pali and Ardhamāgadhī canons? The very limited scholarly discussion on this question frames it within the two processes of "development" (or "borrowing") and "popularization."[37] The first refers to the transformation of existing verse forms into new ones; it is the historical process that "metrical etymology" traverses. According to Hermann Jacobi, and most scholars after him, the *gāthā* developed from the syllable-counting meters of an earlier metrical repertoire by according greater and greater scope to the techniques of contraction (replacing two light syllables with a single heavy syllable) and resolution (replacing a single heavy syllable with two light syllables) until we can no longer call the meters "syllable-counting" at all. The evidence for such a process comes from "transitional forms" that are partly syllable-counting and partly mora-counting. These include the late Vedic and early Pali/Ardhamāgadhī *triṣṭubh,* which sometimes employs contraction and resolution; the *vaitālīya* and *aupacchandasika,* which are mora-counting at the beginning of the line and syllable-counting at the end of the line; and finally the old *āryā*, which is mostly mora- or *gaṇa*-counting but more strictly regulated than the classical *gāthā* as to its alternating rhythm. According to an alternative hypothesis of George Hart, the *gāthā* did not develop from the syllable-counting meters we encounter in earlier Sanskrit texts, but was borrowed from a Dravidian tradition of versification. This tradition would have to be old enough for the "early" portions of the Pali and Ardhamāgadhī canons to borrow from it, and thus it would have to be much earlier than the existing corpus of Tamil literature.

These accounts do not explicitly tell us how, much less why, this process of development or borrowing got started. Was there a period of experimentation? Were there influences from other traditions, Dravidian or otherwise, and if so, what was their nature? Or should we assume that traditions are always developing, generating new verse forms and sloughing off old ones? Some of this explanatory work is done, albeit implicitly, by the second process of "popularization." But this term requires some caution. Being popular in the sense of being frequent within a corpus of texts is very easy to conflate with being popular in the sense of being demotic or current among the common people. There is thus a temptation, most clearly visible in A. K. Warder's account, to explain *gaṇa*-counting versification as a popular-demotic movement. And if it is the canonical texts of Buddhism and Jainism where the *gāthā* and related meters first occur, then that may be because of the willingness of these religions to speak the language of, and sing the songs of, the common man. I think this is highly sentimental. We would, however, expect different systems of versification to be correlated with different forms of life, and perhaps the "Magadhan" culture that lies in the background of Buddhism and Jainism is part of the story of *gaṇa*-counting versification.[38]

I would like to offer a different way of thinking about the changes in versification practice from the earlier to the later layers of the Pali and Ardhamāgadhī canons. These traditions were Prakritized. It has long been known that the Pali canon, in particular, was "Sanskritized" over the course of its transmission, and by this word we understand the replacement of earlier Middle Indic forms, whether morphemes such as *-ttā* or lexemes such as *bambhaṇa,* with their Sanskrit equivalents (*-tvā* and *brāhmaṇa*).[39] These replacements indicate that the textual tradition that would later be identified as "Pali" came under the influence of a Sanskrit textual tradition. Although "influence" is a slippery term, we have a close parallel in the tradition that we have come to identify as "Buddhist Hybrid Sanskrit": texts like the *Divine Stories* and *Extensive Play of the Bodhisattva* employ a Middle Indic language that has been Sanskritized to an even greater degree than the Pali canon.[40]

By Prakritization I mean the transformation of a textual tradition through the language, versification, and aesthetics of Prakrit literature. This process is somewhat more difficult to put into evidence than Sanskritization, but only because our eyes have been trained to the superficially obvious differences between Sanskrit and *all* varieties of Middle Indic. What if we trained our eyes to the more subtle differences between Prakrit and other kinds of Middle Indic? We have already seen that a distinctively Prakrit kind of versification enters into the Pali and Ardhamāgadhī traditions at some point in their history. We might also see that if they can be assigned a date at all, the texts that prominently feature *gaṇa*-counting meters date from around the first century CE or later.[41]

The Jain tradition, at least, provides relatively clear evidence for this sea change in versification practices. Although the new *gaṇa*-counting meters like the *gāthā* appear in some canonical texts, most of these texts are rather late (after the first century), and as noted above, Alsdorf showed that the vast majority of *gāthā* verses in texts such as the *Uttarādhyāyana Sūtra* that are considered to be earlier are interpolations. But of what period specifically?

The Jain canon is embedded in an extensive exegetical literature, one layer of which—called "explanations" (*niryuktis*)—is composed entirely in Prakrit *gāthās*. As we saw in chapter 3, these "explanations" reflect an expansion and transformation of the Jain scriptural tradition associated with the teacher Bhadrabāhu, and dates to around the first century CE. A comparison between the Āvaśyaka *Niryukti* of the Śvetāmbara Jains, and the *Mūlācāra* of the Digambaras, two collections of religious stories, shows how this transformation happened: while the two texts contain much material in common, the *Mūlācāra,* which according to Nalini Balbir is the older version, presents it in *anuṣṭubh* verses, and the *Niryukti* presents it in *gāthās*.[42]

What else, besides a new kind of versification, betokens the Prakritization of these traditions? The "explanations" are well known to be linguistically distinct from the texts they purport to explain, although the habit of referring to both languages as "Prakrit," as well as extensive mutual influences over the course of their transmission, have rendered this difference much less conspicuous. Dalsukh Malvania has noted in passing that manuscripts of the Jain scriptures without commentaries look more like Ardhamāgadhī, and manuscripts with commentaries look more like Prakrit ("Jain Mahārāṣṭrī").[43] We may therefore even speak of a double Prakritization. The first phase is the commentarial elaboration of the Jain canon in the language and meters of Prakrit literature, associated with the efforts of Bhadrabāhu. The second is the subsequent conceptual and, to a lesser degree, linguistic redetermination of the canonical texts themselves as Prakrit texts.

We do not encounter such linguistically distinct layers in the Pali canon. But once again, if we look closely, we can see that the use of the *gāthā* indexes other differences. Take the example of the *Songs of the Buddhist Nuns.* This is a collection of verses attributed to the first few generations of Buddhist nuns, which has been considered a "precursor" to the Prakrit poetry of *Seven Centuries* and to the entire tradition of *kāvya.*[44] It is not just a coincidence that the two longest and most expressive poems, those of Isidāsī and Sumedhā, are the only ones to utilize the *gāthā.* The new verse form betokens a new way of using language, one that is aware of and attentive to its expressive powers. The closest intertext of these poems is not, to my mind, *Seven Centuries*, but rather Pālitta's *Taraṅgavatī*, in which the title character tells the story of her conversion in expressive Prakrit *gāthās*. The chronological priority of the Buddhist *Songs* to Pālitta's *Taraṅgavatī* is not entirely self-evident; I do not take it for granted, as some scholars do, that the entire Pāli canon was fixed by the second century BCE. But even if no certainty can be reached on this specific point, the later portions of the Pali canon seem to draw from a wider literary discourse in Prakrit that was taking shape around the first century CE.[45]

The claim that the textual traditions of Buddhism and Jainism were "Prakritized" before they reached their final form does stand in need of further research. It would imply, however, that traditions of versification, just like the languages in which they subsist, do not grow and wither like plants; and that instead of connecting the use of the *gāthā* in Pali and Ardhamāgadhī texts with a completely hypothetical practice of demotic versification, we might connect it with the actually existing practices of Prakrit literature—which, as I have emphasized at several points, are not necessarily demotic practices. Prakritization is not popularization. My claim here is that the *gāthā* is not only common in Prakrit texts, but distinctively characterizes Prakrit as a discursive formation. Of course, the *gāthā* does not exclusively occur in Prakrit, or even "Prakritized" texts: it has a long history of use in technical Sanskrit, from *śloka-kārikās* in Patañjali's *Great Commentary* (second century BCE), to the argumentative verse of Nāgārjuna's *Dispeller of Disputes* (second century CE) and Īśvarakṛṣṇa's *Verses on Sāṃkhya* (ca. third century CE). In Sanskrit, however, it was a convenience: its flexibility allowed it to accommodate technical terms, as Helmer Smith argued. In Prakrit, by contrast, it was the default meter.[46]

The *gāthā* is the only meter to have entire works written about it: the first, although its date remains uncertain, is the *Definition of the Gāthā* (*Gāthālakṣaṇa*) by Nanditāḍhya.[47] But other works on metrics—above all Virahāṅka's *Collection of Mora- and Syllable-Counting Meters* (ca. eighth century) and Svayambhū's *Meters* (ninth century)—provide a glimpse onto a lost world of Prakrit versification that was much more varied than its Sanskrit counterpart. As the title of Virahāṅka's work suggests, the repertoire included both the syllable-counting meters (*vṛttas*) that were typically used in Sanskrit literature as well as the mora-counting meters (*jātis*) that were more often used in Prakrit literature. The most popular of the mora-counting meters, besides the *gāthā*, was an "acatalectic" variant called the *skandhaka*, which did not omit the final syllable from the last *gaṇa* of each line. The *skandhaka* was employed in Prakrit court epics, such as *Hari's Victory* and *Rāvaṇa's Demise*. But the category of *jāti* also included various kinds of rhymed verse, including the *galitakas* we encountered above and *khañjakas* we'll see below. These works defined a large number of strophic forms in which simple verse forms were combined.

These strophic compositions take us back to the theme with which this section began: Prakrit's dual status as a language of literate textuality of a high order, as well as a language closely associated with musical performance. The few surviving examples of strophic compositions, which come from stage plays, exemplify the ambiguity of this position. Before considering them, it helps to bear in mind a similar ambiguity in the case of stage plays from ancient Greece. These plays were typically performed with choral odes. In earlier plays, such as those of Aristophanes, the text of the odes was transmitted along with the dialogue in manuscripts. In later plays, such as those of Menander, odes were generally not transmitted with the dialogue, although it is usually assumed that they were part of the performance. There is no question that these odes belonged to "the realm of the oral, specifically, the sung," but the decision of whether they also belong to "the domain of literary culture"—whether they constitute an essential part of the literary work—has been made for us by the manuscript tradition. We might ask whether Prakrit songs, like these choral odes, belong to the play-as-performance or to the play-as-literature.

The Prakrit and Apabhramsha songs that appear in some manuscripts of the fourth act of Kālidāsa's *Urvaśī Won by Valor* brings the question into focus. Are they Kālidāsa's own compositions—which would make them, in the early fifth century CE, the earliest examples of Apabhramsha verse available to us—or were they added in the course of time?[48] The stage directions associated with these songs make them out to be *dhruvā*s, a kind of "mood music" that directors may choose to include in their staging of a play. We have plenty of evidence, including from the *Treatise on Theater*, that Prakrit and Apabhramsha songs were often employed in the play-as-performance, without necessarily constituting part of the play-as-literature. But as the fourth act of *Urvaśī Won by Valor* shows, the dividing line is not always clear.

The question becomes even more complicated when these Prakrit songs enter into the mimetic world of the stage play. I am referring to situations where characters are represented as singing, or listening to, Prakrit songs. One example could be the verse from the *Recognition of Śakuntalā* that Śakuntalā intends to send to Duśyanta in a love letter, discussed in the introduction. But let us look at another example, a rare strophic composition found at the beginning of Harṣa's *Ratnāvalī:*

kusumāuhapiadūaaṃ maülāvaṃto cūaaṃ |
siḍhiliamāṇaggahaṇao pāaï dāhiṇapavaṇao ||
viasiavaülāsoao icchiapiaamamelao |
palivālaṇaasamatthao tammaï juaīsatthao ||
  ia paḍhamaṃ mahumāso jaṇassa hiaāiṁ kuṇaï maüāiṃ |
  pacchā viṃdhaï kāmo laddhappasarehiṁ kusumabāṇehiṃ ||

The southern breeze is here, bringing buds to
the mango, the dear messenger of the God of Love,
slackening anger and quarrels,

making the *bakula* and *aśoka* trees blossom,
bringing pining lovers together,
while groups of young girls gasp for air,
incapable of waiting any longer.
Thus does the spring month first soften people's hearts,
then, when his flower-arrows find an opening,
the God of Love pierces them.[49]

This is a Prakrit song, which Svayambhū identifies for us as a *śīrṣaka* or strophic composition. It has two parts, and hence is called a *dvipadī-khaṇḍa.* The first part is a *khañjaka,* a generic term for a "piece" of a larger strophic composition, which in this case is a *avalambaka:* two verses made up of quarters of thirteen moras each, with the rhythm ⏓⏓⏑– at the end, and end-rhyme between successive quarters. The second part is a *gīti,* a verse form very similar to the *gāthā* but with two lines of equal length, rather than a shortened second line. Both parts exhibit end-rhyme, which is a characteristic of Prakrit *khañjaka*s, and of most Apabhramsha meters, but very rarely figures in the Sanskrit and Prakrit that survives in written form. In this case, the rhyme enhances the musicality of the language, for example in the repetition of the consonant-less sequence *-ūaaṃ* in the first line, which must have been further enhanced by its musical setting.

We must not forget, however, that this is not just a Prakrit song, but a dramatic representation of a Prakrit song. At this point in the *Ratnāvalī,* King Udayana comes out to watch the Holi celebrations with his friend Vasantaka, and he sees the two servant girls Madanikā and Cūtalatikā dancing and singing the song quoted above. The king is impressed, and he has Vasantaka go and try to learn it from them. But Vasantaka is a bit clueless, and he mistakes their song for a *carcarī,* another type of song and dance that was performed at the spring festival. Madanikā tells him that the song was not a *carcarī,* but a *dvipadī-khaṇḍa.* By including a dramatization of the spring festival in his play, Harṣa has made the performance of a Prakrit song part of the play-as-literature.

INEXHAUSTIBLE COLLECTIONS

Prakrit is a literature of *gāthā*s, but this latter word does not simply refer to the language's most popular and most characteristic metrical form. The *gāthā* is the poem, syntactically and semantically complete on its own, that takes this form: the whole world of the poem must be contained in its two lines. A verse incorporated in the *Anuyogadvāra Sūtra,* compiled sometime before the fifth century, says that "a soldier is known from his armor, a woman from her outfit, a pot of rice by a grain, and a poet from a single *gāthā.*"[50] The earliest and most influential work of Prakrit literature, *Seven Centuries,* is made up of such single-verse poems. And it was principally through anthologies such as *Seven Centuries* that Prakrit literature was known and studied, both in the premodern and the modern world. There were, of course, many other genres. Jain narrative literature in Prakrit, which flourished between the eighth and twelfth centuries, far exceeds anthologies in sheer volume. But the anthology always retained a special connection with Prakrit in the literary imagination.

The anthology is the only Prakrit genre represented by Hindu, Buddhist, and Jain authors. But the sectarian affiliation of the compiler has very little to do with the actual content of the anthology, which is often taken from other poets in any case. The *Treasury of Gāthā-Jewels* (1194 CE) is a case in point: Jineśvara begins the collection with verses in praise of the Jina, Brahma, Viṣṇu, Śiva, and Sarasvatī taken from earlier literature. This additive and syncretic character is one of the anthology's key features. We see, in the first few pages of Jineśvara anthology, verses from the *Seven Centuries,* from Vākpatirāja's *Gauḍa's Demise* (eighth century), from the *Vajjālagga,* and remarkably, because the original text is completely lost, from Guṇāḍhya's *Great Story* (*Bṛhatkathā*). The anthology is central to Prakrit literature because it defines and presents "Prakrit literature" as a field of intertextuality.

A collection was called a "treasury" (*kośa*), and the verses contained therein were often likened to gold and jewels.[51] Daṇḍin distinguished the "treasury" from "aggregation" (*saṅghāta*), but it is difficult to tell whether he is following an older tradition.[52] The distinction, according to both Ratnaśrījñāna and Vādijaṅghāla (both in the tenth century), is that the treasury features verses on various themes while the aggregation presents verses on a single theme. Vādijaṅghāla offers the *Constellation* (*Tārāgaṇa*) of Bappabhaṭṭi, discussed below, as an example of a treasury (along with the *Treasury of Gāthā*s, which likely refers to *Seven Centuries,* and an otherwise-unknown *Spotted Antelope*), and the Tamil anthologies (*draviḍasaṅghāta*) as examples of aggregations.[53] According to Taruṇavācaspati, however, the treasury differs from the aggregation in that it contains verses from various authors, and Bhoja also uses the authorship criterion to distinguish the two genres in his *Illumination of the Erotic.*[54]

Daṇḍin's remarks, or rather the various interpretations of his unusually cryptic categorization, raise what I consider to be the two primary issues in the study of anthologies as a genre: their formal organization and their authorship. The history of the genre is another important issue, but it will suffice to note here that the anthology is present from the very beginnings of Prakrit literature—and also of Tamil literature—and that Hari Ram Acharya has traced the influence of the *Seven Centuries* on later anthologies in Sanskrit.[55] This is a major point of difference between Sanskrit and Prakrit as literary traditions. As a literature of *gāthā*s, Prakrit is and always has been a literature of anthologies, many of which precede the earliest anthologies of Sanskrit literature by centuries. When it comes to single-author collections, there are outstanding Sanskrit examples from the middle of the first millennium, such as Bhartṛhari's *Three Centuries,* Amaru's *Century,* and Ravigupta's *Treasury of Āryās.* Or rather, these are traditionally considered to be single-author collections. Daniel Ingalls has judged that Amaru's *Century* is actually the work of several poets, and probably carried ascriptions of individual verses to particular poets in the early stages of its manuscript transmission.[56] There are a number of single-author collections in Prakrit from roughly the same period, including Bappabhaṭṭi's *Constellation* and Vairocana's *Brilliance of the Connoisseurs.*

Regarding multiple-author "treasuries," however, most of the early examples are in Prakrit. Besides *Seven Centuries,* several collections of Prakrit verse were compiled by Jain monks and laymen. The earliest example—before 1337 CE, and sometime after Vākpatirāja's composition of *Gauḍa's Demise* in the eighth century—is evidently Jagadvallabha's *Vajjālagga.* Other examples include Jineśvara's *Treasury of Gāthā-Jewels* (1194 CE) and the collections printed with it (*Subhāsiyagāhāsaṃgaha* and *Subhāsiyapajjasaṃgaha*). The *Verses of the Chappaṇṇayas* should be included in this category, too, although the text that survives under this name is almost certainly not the text that authors such as Daṇḍin, Uddyotana, and Abhinavagupta knew. The latter seems to have been the work of a poetic collective, somewhere between the single-author and multiple-author models. From Daṇḍin's reference to them in the beginning of his *Avantisundarī,* we know that their *Verses* were in circulation around the year 700, but I suspect that they, like *Seven Centuries,* belong to the period of Sātavāhana rule in the first or second century CE.[57] And, of course, as Vādijaṅghāla reminds us, the Tamil anthologies (*draviḍasaṅghāta*) were also in circulation, if only in Tamil Nadu, by the middle of the first millennium. By contrast, the earliest surviving multiple-author "treasury" in Sanskrit, if we do not count Amaru, is the *Treasury of Subhāṣita-Jewels* (*Subhāṣitaratnakośa*), compiled just before the twelfth century.

Extent is the most obvious way of characterizing an anthology that has no overall thematic organization, and this is how *Seven Centuries* received its name. But why are its verses counted in groups of a hundred, and why are there seven of them? S. V. Sohoni suggested that the model was the *Bhagavadgītā,* which also contains around 700 verses, and that Hāla actually intended it as an anti-*Bhagavadgītā.* But there is little evidence for this interpretation. Equally unconvincing is Acharya's suggestion that the phrase "seven centuries" (*sattasaī*) simply sounds better in Prakrit than other candidates.[58] If the element *sāta* in the names Sātavāhana and Sātakarṇi does in fact derive from *sapta* "seven," as S. A. Joglekar has suggested, then the *Seven Centuries* might be an oblique reference to the name of the patron or his dynasty, but I remain doubtful.[59]

The commentators on *Seven Centuries* knew that verses in the anthology sometimes cluster around a given theme or word. Herman Tieken elaborated on this "linking" as an organizational feature, but it is not nearly as systematic as that found, for example, in Kālidāsa's *Cloud Messenger,* where almost every verse is linked to the preceding verse by a repetition of a word.[60] The verses of each century are, for the most part, "unbound" (*anibaddha*), as Bhāmaha would call literature of this type.[61] They are thus vulnerable to rearrangement. This appears to have happened often in the history of *Seven Centuries.* Not only are chunks of verses found in different places in different versions of the anthology, but several versions exhibit a complete rearrangement of the verses according to their topic. These topically organized versions include Sādhāraṇadeva's recension and the "First Telinga Recension," both studied by Albrecht Weber for his edition of the text, and the *Gāthāmuktāvalī* described by H. C. Bhayani. The topics are generally referred to by the Prakrit word *vajjā,* which is etymologically identical to the *paryāya*s mentioned by Ānandavardhana and Abhinavagupta, or by the Sanskrit word *paddhati.* Compilers such as Jagadvallabha and Jineśvara would employ this formal device in their *Vajjālagga* and *Treasury of Gāthā-Jewels* respectively.[62]

The arrangement into *vajjā*s seems to be a formalization of a looser thematic grouping evident in earlier collections of verses. Vairocana's *Brilliance of the Connoisseurs,* the date of which remains unknown, moves from topic to topic in a natural but not formally explicit sequence: from a reflection on the qualities of good readers, for example, to a reflection on the qualities of good lovers. Bappabhaṭṭi's *Constellation,* of the later eighth century, exhibits a similar arrangement. The *Constellation* was compiled by Bappabhaṭṭi's friend Śaṅkuka, who composed "index-verses." Each index-verse names two to five verses by a keyword in each. Often, but not always, Śaṅkuka mentions the theme or topic according to which he has arranged the verses. Here is one example:

> Vādin! How can we praise you?
> You are the one who praises,
> as shown by these five verses:
> *susiyattaṇa, bahulakkhaya, sirīsa,*
> *jaladugga,* and *vāraṇārī.*[63]

The five verses whose keywords are mentioned in the index-verse are all eulogies of a king. But the index-verse also serves another important function: it maintains the attribution of the verse to its author.[64] The practice of composing index-verses (*dvāra-gāthā*s) is as old as Prakrit textuality itself. In composing their "explanations" (*niryukti*s) and "discussions" (*bhāṣya*s) on canonical texts, Jain commentators enumerated topics for discussion in index-verses. This practice was redeployed to strengthen the fragile bond of authorship in Prakrit literary culture. Unbound verses, which collectively represent a great deal of Prakrit literature, are not just unbound from larger structures of meaning, but from the formal and material structures that often served as the locus of attribution. We can think of the anthology not only as a site of collection, where these unbound verses could be integrated into such a structure, but as a site of dispersion: being anthologized in one work or in one manuscript—and it is often impossible to distinguish between the two—was simply a temporary stopover in the life of a Prakrit *gāthā*.

On this topic, there is a pair of *gāthā*s in the *Brilliance of the Connoisseurs* that sets out two modes of existence for Prakrit poetry:

> *suviārasahā vimuhī aṇṇāṇa aṇaṇṇagoarā dāṇi* |
> *kulavālia vva lukkaï gehe ṇiasāmiraṃjiṇī gāhā* ||
>
> A *gāthā* that is very thoughtful
> and kept to oneself, away from others,
> pleases the one who possesses it,
> as a woman in the confines of the family,
> prudent, uninterested in and inaccessible to others,
> pleases her husband.
>
> *kittivaaṃsā vimalā maṇoharā bahuviāraüjjaliā* |
> *aïkkaṃtapiālāvā gāhā savvattha bhamaï vesa vva* ||
>
> The more attention is lavished on it,
> the more it shines, pure and captivating,
> garlanded by wide renown:
> the *gāthā* that goes beyond lovers' conversations
> is to be found everywhere
> like a courtesan.[65]

The first verse seems to recommend the private enjoyment of Prakrit poetry, but this is tempered by the second verse, which recommends, instead, its public circulation. We can note, briefly, that this is how Prakrit *gāthā*s work in general: although they are self-contained and "unbound," their profusion of meanings depends on a network of prior texts. It is as if every *gāthā* presupposes every other, each forming a node in a vast intertextual network. Appearing "everywhere" means appearing in an infinitude of contexts, of anthological or performative settings, and hence of new possibilities of contextual meaning. In this case, the meanings of the two verses are not quite complementary but not quite contradictory either; as an ethos of reading, they commend both intimacy and, with a wink, promiscuity.

We are used to distinguishing between a literary work itself and its reception or afterlife, or between an original "meaning" and a "significance" for later readers. But Prakrit *gāthā*s exist entirely in their reception: *esse est legeri*. The recognition of this fact motivated Śaṅkuka to preserve his friend's *gāthā*s by anthologizing them, fitting them out with index-verses, and writing them down in manuscript form—by transforming them into structure, we might say, to borrow a phrase of Gadamer's.[66]

One example will serve to illustrate the processes of constant recontextualization in which the life of a *gāthā* consists. The *Mirror for Poets* is a Prakrit text on metrics of the thirteenth century. In exemplifying some varieties of the *gāthā*, a commentator on this text, probably not far removed from the time of the *Mirror*, distinguished the *brāhmaṇī* variety as having the maximum number of heavy syllables (27). He adduced the following verse:

gajjaṃte khe mehā phullā nīvā paṇacciyā morā |
naṭṭho caṃdulloo vāsāratto halā patto ||

The clouds are thundering in the sky.
The *kadamba* is in bloom.
The peacocks are dancing.
The moonlight is gone.
The first night of the monsoon is here, my friend.[67]

This is one of the only verses that the commentator ascribes to a specific author, and that author is Pālitta. Not too long before it was cited in the *Mirror*, the learned Jain monk Hemacandra cited the first few words of this verse as an illustration of two grammatical rules in his *Siddhahemacandra* (mid-twelfth century).[68] Hemacandra, however, does not identify the author. Neither does Bhoja, one of Hemacandra's principal sources, who cites the verse on two occasions. First, as an example of the "inferential" kind of reason (*jñāpaka-hetu*) in his *Illumination of the Erotic*, and second, as a variety of the "forward-and-backward-looking" kind of inference (*sāmānyataḥ*) in his *Necklace of Sarasvatī* (both early eleventh century).[69] Here we have three authors citing the same verse: one for its metrical features, one for its grammatical features, and one for its logical features. Yet the verse itself is found in no extant work of Prakrit literature. Where did these authors encounter this verse, and how did the anonymous commentator of the *Mirror for Poets* know that Pālitta was its author?

I think it is possible that these authors all cited the verse from Pālitta's now-lost *Taraṅgavatī*. But if this verse managed to escape oblivion, it is because it was cited; and if it was cited, it is because it was citable. The survival of Pālitta's poetry, as well as the survival of its attribution to Pālitta, has taken several courses. First, and most obviously, there is the tradition of *Taraṅgavatī* (including later retellings), to which Pālitta's name is attached as an author. Yet even here it might be recalled that Pālitta, according to Jain legend, was accused of plagiarizing *Taraṅgavatī* from one of his colleagues at the Sātavāhana court.[70] But there is also the anthology tradition, and further, there are the indirect traditions of "accidental anthologies": those texts like the *Mirror for Poets* and Svayambhū's *Meters* that, in the course of exemplifying a set of metrical or grammatical phenomena, end up assembling an anthology of verses. Another example is the *Explanation of the Suggestion Verses* of Ratnākara, which assembles and revises Abhinavagupta's commentary on the Prakrit verses cited in Ānandavardhana's *Light on Suggestion*.

We know very little about the way that anthologies, especially Prakrit anthologies, were produced. The seminal text of this tradition is of course *Seven Centuries*, but this is a typically problematic case: with our earliest direct witness, the commentator Bhuvanapāla (ca. eleventh century), we intercept the tradition nearly a thousand years into its history. By this time, authors had for hundreds of years been citing verses "from *Seven Centuries*," which is to say, verses that are also found in later manuscripts of *Seven Centuries*. In fact, nobody actually attributes these verses to this work; if the verses are attributed at all, they are attributed to a particular author. Svayambhū's metrical handbook provides an example: a verse that he attributes to Pālitta is identical to W75 in *Seven Centuries*, which the commentators on that text likewise attribute to Pālitta. While I do not share the skepticism of earlier scholars regarding these attributions ("worthless" according to A. B. Keith), no serious research has been done on them, and it is not at all clear where they come from.[71] Take, as another example, verse W394: "In the spring, the peacock cranes its neck to drink a drop of water from the tip of a blade of grass, as if it were a pearl pierced by an emerald thread."[72] This is a rare case of agreement between the commentators regarding the authorship of the verse: Bhuvanapāla, Ājaḍa, and Pītāmbara all assign it to Pālitta. But how do they know? I speculate that *Seven Centuries* probably was the source of many of these citations, but that it once circulated with a large complement of intertexts and paratexts—including a list of authors and perhaps collections of the works of individual authors—that has been substantially winnowed over the course of its transmission.

In closing, I would like to return to the larger structures of meaning from which Prakrit *gāthā*s are "unbound." The great literary theorist Abhinavagupta maintained in the late tenth century that there was a qualitative difference between a large-scale work, in which all of the narrative elements are presented to the reader before his very eyes, and a small-scale work like the single-verse poem, which presents the reader with few or no narrative elements. We aren't given to know, for example, who is speaking, who is being spoken to, and what has happened prior to the verse being spoken. In order to understand the verse—in other words, to give meaning to it—we must conjecture all of these elements. And while the verse itself might give us some clues, Abhinavagupta makes it clear that only readers who are practiced in the conventions of the relevant kind of poetry can successfully make those conjectures. Such readers can picture the narrative situation as if it were before their very eyes, despite or perhaps due to the fact that they have had to imagine it.[73]

One difference between the large-scale and the small-scale work thus pertains to reading practices, and indeed to practice in the more common sense: readers of a small-scale work, in the absence of explicit narrative development, need to turn to past experience, to prior texts, which collectively provide the reader with conditions of meaning and interpretation. I know of no better example of this kind of reading practice than Abhinavagupta's own interpretation of a Prakrit verse (W886) in his commentary on Ānandavardhana's *Light on Suggestion*, where he conjectures not one, not two, but *eight* possible narrative contexts, each with a slightly different meaning.[74] In this way, although the Prakrit *gāthā* is formally "unbound," it is always reintegrated into a larger structure of meaning—for Abhinavagupta these are primarily *narrative* structures, but we could also consider figurative or affective structures—that itself depends on a potentially boundless number of intertexts. It is noteworthy that the very narrative elements that Abhinavagupta says the reader must supply, the verse's "points of attachment" to a structure of narrative meaning such as the speaker and addressee, are usually supplied by the commentaries to *Seven Centuries:* "a woman says this to her friend," "a woman says this to her messenger," and so on. These short introductions serve as paratexts that aid in the understanding of the text. They are strikingly similar to the *kiḷavi*s that are transmitted as paratexts to the Tamil *caṅkam* poems, which likewise set out the speaker and addressee in certain conventional roles.[75]

Prakrit *gāthā*s live in the complexities of collection and dispersion, of citation and recontextualization, skipping over and across the transmission histories of individual texts. Within Indian literary culture, their "unbound" character was prized and celebrated, since it allowed individual verses to speak to different purposes from within different texts—but it was also a liability, since it made over to future generations the responsibility of transmitting verses faithfully and preserving their attribution. We might even think of all Prakrit *gāthā*s as fragments: not just the stray verses of now-forgotten poets such as Abhimānacihna that have been preserved in accidental anthologies such as Syavambhū's *Meter,* but the verses that are transmitted to us in intentional anthologies as well. For fragments present a shard of meaning that can only be appreciated against a background of intertexts, but this background changes. The conventions that emerge for reading *gāthā*s in one context might change as we move over to another: consider, in this connection, the divergent interpretations of the commentators on *Seven Centuries.* Prakrit *gāthā*s were characterized by their appearance, and continual reappearance, in various contexts—in performance or in a manuscript, in a topically arranged anthology or cited in a grammatical textbook, introduced by an "index-verse" or by the definition of a poetic figure. This promiscuity was a conspicuous feature of Prakrit's phenomenology and aesthetics, of what it was like and what attracted people to it.

This chapter has surveyed three kinds of distinctiveness about Prakrit literature: the sweetness of its syllables, which I understood in relation to phonetic characteristics that made the language smooth, open, and musical; the quavering rhythms of its verse, which refers to the special kind of versification associated with Prakrit poetry, which allowed enormous variation over a regular beat with syncopation permitted on the off-beat; and the prevalence of single-verse poems, which is connected with certain forms of textual organization, like the anthology, particular reading practices, and above all with an open-ended "ontology" that not only allowed but positively encouraged poems to circulate promiscuously, to appear in diverse contexts, to mean different things to different people. These features can be said to characterize Prakrit internally, since they are the resources internal to the language and to the tradition that Prakrit poets made conscious use of. In the next chapter, we will turn to the ways in which Prakrit is characterized externally, that is, under a series of contrasts that differentially established its place in the language order of India.

5

Figuring Prakrit

The unity of a language is represented always in relation to another unity.
—NAOKI SAKAI, "*HOW DO WE COUNT A LANGUAGE?*"[1]

Equivalence in difference is the cardinal problem of language . . .
—ROMAN JAKOBSON, "*ON LINGUISTIC ASPECTS OF TRANSLATION*"[2]

INTRODUCTION

The most straightforward way to determine what Prakrit was is to look at how it was represented, that is, how it appeared from within the literary and intellectual culture of premodern India. Chapters 2 and 3 offered a largely diachronic account of Prakrit's invention as a literary language. This chapter provides an analysis of Prakrit's synchronic position within the order of literary languages. It follows an ongoing attempt to "figure out," by representing it in figures, Prakrit's relation to other languages. What is remarkable is that no one seems ever to have thought that such an analysis was even necessary: scholars have focused their explanations, as reductive as they tend to be, on why certain kinds of people used Prakrit, or were represented as using Prakrit, rather than why Prakrit was available for such uses in the first place.

In what follows, I adopt Naoki Sakai's idea of a "schema"—itself adopted from Kant—to characterize the language order of premodern India. My idea of a schema is historicist and constructivist, like Sakai's but completely unlike Kant's. The problem Sakai addressed with this idea is the "unity" of a language.[3]

On the one hand, it is second nature for us to count languages, that is, to represent them as unified objects that can be enumerated in a series. Sanskrit and Prakrit do not differ in this respect from English, Japanese, Russian, and French. Language's discrete character is essential to almost everything that we can think to do with it. "Narrating, reciting, listening, reading, writing and translating" are all performed in a way that presupposes and reproduces the differences between languages.[4] For any given language, the unity of that language, and thus its ability to be counted alongside other languages, is given as well. On the other hand, it is still *second* nature. We would like to believe that our representations of language "cut nature at the joints," but the closer we look, the further we get from finding any.[5] We find, instead, that what holds a language together, and what categorically separates it from others, is not any intrinsic property, but effective fictions, of which we are collectively the authors.

A schema is, in Kant's words, "the representation of a general procedure by which the imagination supplies its image to the concept" of which it is the schema.[6] It is a "mediating representation" (*vermittelnde Vorstellung*) that allows us to bring the messy and gradient language practices as we encounter them in "the real world" under discrete and ordered categories.[7] Schemas perform the work of figuration, classification, and categorization that enable us to think of languages as objects. It is through the representational work of schemas that Prakrit became a language: an internally homogeneous and discrete object, differentiated from other such objects—and above all from Sanskrit—as a species of a genus. But the effects that schemas have thus go far beyond the representational work that they do. They provide us with concepts with which we can reflect upon, evaluate, and regulate our own uses of language, as well as the range of social practices that intersect with language use. This results in a feedback loop: concepts are based on practices, practices are based on concepts, and thus the objects and relations that a schema posits come to form part of the world that the schema is meant to represent. A schema can thus be seen as a blueprint for, rather than merely a picture of, a language order.

Schematism, the capacity or even requirement to produce schemas, may be "an art hidden in the depths of the human soul," but a schema itself is a historical artifact.[8] It belongs to those deeply embedded patterns of reasoning and representation so deeply in a culture that we generally call "common sense," and hence it underlies the particular ways of speaking about and using language that are prevalent within that culture. The closest Sanskrit equivalent of the kind of schema I have in mind is *vyavasthā*, something that sets a number of other things in their place relative to one another, a single figure that encompasses and imposes order on an enormous diversity of practices.

The approach adopted in this chapter differs radically from the method by which Indological scholarship has traditionally attempted to understand "language talk" in premodern India, namely, by invoking the paradigm of sociolinguistics and reading the sources as proxies for attitudes toward and beliefs about language in the various segments of premodern Indian society. Among the many methodological and epistemological liabilities in this approach is the tendency to view language as a "dependent variable" and social distinctions as the "independent variable." On this view, language is a reflection of more fundamental patterns in social organization. Given that religion is still thought of as the most important source of social distinctions in premodern India, this view often has the effect of reducing language to religious identity, and thus of producing facile equations between Brahmans and Sanskrit, or between Jains and Prakrit. The tendency to treat Sanskrit and Prakrit as transhistorical categories is another liability that makes it difficult to see when and how people began thinking of and representing language in these terms.[9] This tendency is explained in part by Hermann Jacobi's intentional conflation of the emic terms "Sanskrit" and "Prakrit" with the etic terms "Old Indic" and "Middle Indic," discussed in chapter 1.

My approach differs less radically from the one developed by Sheldon Pollock, and shares with it the goal of denaturalizing such familiar concepts as Sanskrit and Prakrit by tracing out their history.[10] But where Pollock minimizes the differences between Sanskrit and the other members of the "closed set" of literary languages, I am interested in the logic of internal differentiation within this set. And where Pollock assigns a nomothetic function to many of the representations discussed here, I assign them a schematic function. Precisely what this function is will become clear over the course of this chapter, but to begin with, I mean that representations of language do not simply list languages that already exist—they do not gather together languages that meet a certain criterion, such as "their availability across region, ethnie, sect, and time" as Pollock suggests—but stake out discursive positions that languages occupy vis-à-vis each other. They are as much ways of making sense of language practices, of "figuring them out," as they are rules regarding their use.

This chapter departs from earlier scholarship in one other significant respect. Just as the preceding chapters enabled us to challenge the historical priority of Sanskrit by considering alternative points of origin for the "poetry of polity" (*praśasti*) and high literature in general (*kāvya*), this chapter enables us to challenge the conceptual priority of Sanskrit by focusing on the relational figures through which languages were represented. According to the schemas reconstructed here, Sanskrit and Prakrit defined each other, contrasted with each other, and complemented each other. This approach ties in with the slightly revisionist history of Prakrit, as well as Sanskrit, offered in this book: rather than naming timeless categories of speech, Sanskrit and Prakrit came into use as names of languages around the first century CE, when the language order they jointly constituted came into being.

THE ARCHETYPAL SCHEMA

The archetypal schema here is the underlying framework of the language practices of "classical India"—the literary and intellectual culture of India from the first to the twelfth centuries CE, in which Sanskrit and Prakrit jointly served as the parameters of textual production. This characterization closely resembles Pollock's characterization of the "Sanskrit cosmopolis." One reason I have adhered to the older term is simply to avoid confusion: the "Sanskrit cosmopolis" is really a metonym, based on the importance of Sanskrit to the entire cultural order, but in this chapter I am interested precisely in Sanskrit's others.

The representations that the archetypal schema provides procedures for constructing are the statements in which participants in literary and intellectual culture articulated an understanding of their own language practices. Many of these texts are "classical" in the further sense that they are foundational within their respective discourses. They reflect an understanding of language that has a long history of effects. This is why I call the schema presented here archetypal: other ways of understanding language in India, up to the present day, presuppose it as a template.

The most common formulation of this schema is the *bhāṣātraya,* "the three languages": Sanskrit, Prakrit, and Apabhramsha. This is the figure that Bhāmaha and Daṇḍin present in the two foundational works in the discourse of poetics, the *Ornament of Literature* and the *Mirror of Literature.* This is just one form of the schema—not everyone who has attempted to make sense of the language practices of this literary and intellectual culture enumerates precisely three languages—but I take it to be representative of a broad consensus regarding the number of languages, their identity, and their relationship to one another. Its archetypal status is easily illustrated by the fact that the fourfold and sixfold schemas that begin to emerge in the ninth century incorporate and expand upon the threefold schema.

Four important features characterize this archetypal schema: the opposition between Sanskrit and Prakrit; the identity of Sanskrit and Prakrit; the totality of the practices the schema represents; and the iterability of its distinctions. Together these give the language order of classical India its unique shape: the central dichotomy of Sanskrit and Prakrit, the asymmetrical relation between the two, and the peripheral position of Apabhramsha. The role and status of a language within a language order are the result of a complex configuration of factors on the level of schematic representation. "Cosmopolitan" and "vernacular" are two of the roles that may be available, but they do not exhaust all of the possibilities—Prakrit does not easily fit into either category—and it would be a mistake to understand them as universal categories that classical Indian culture just happens to instantiate.

OPPOSITION

At the core of the basic schema lies a binary opposition between Sanskrit and Prakrit. Generally, one can speak of opposing two things that already exist, or of an opposition that creates two things that did not exist before. It is the latter sense that I intend here. Sanskrit and Prakrit exist in a "schema of co-figuration," where the representation of one determines the representation of the other.[11] There are two aspects of the schema of co-figuration that I would like to emphasize at the outset, because they lead to an understanding of the relationship between Sanskrit and Prakrit that differs from what one commonly encounters in scholarship.

One aspect is the prior indeterminacy of the objects under co-figuration. The schema does not simply apply contrasting attributes to each member of the pair—although this is one of its important functions—but rather defines what each member of the pair is. Although we tend to see the opposition between Sanskrit and Prakrit as an opposition between two languages, it is only as a result of a schematic representation that we can oppose Sanskrit and Prakrit as languages in the first place. This claim opens up the possibility that Sanskrit and Prakrit were not always what they currently seem to be. For example, Sanskrit and Prakrit are figured in the *Treatise on Theater* not as languages, for which other terms are used, but as two distinct types of actors' lines.

The second aspect is the lack of a prior independent existence for each of the objects under co-figuration. Co-figuration implies that the emergence of Sanskrit and Prakrit as objects of representation was more or less simultaneous. Of course there is a sense in which Sanskrit existed prior to the Sanskrit–Prakrit dichotomy. But this type of Sanskrit, the language of Vedic texts, was quite different from that which we commonly call "classical"—the language that the archetypal schema delineates—and in fact there is no evidence that it was even called "Sanskrit" much before the first and second centuries CE. Exactly the same can be said of Prakrit. Co-figuration replaces the question of whether Sanskrit or Prakrit came first—the answer to which depends entirely on one's chosen definitions—with an answerable question about what phenomena the words "Sanskrit" and "Prakrit" were applied to.

One kind of opposition is built into the words Sanskrit and Prakrit themselves. The words form, as George Grierson noted, a "naturally correlated pair."[12] The word *saṃskṛta,* from the verb √*saṃ-s-kṛ,* means in the broadest terms "what has been elaborated."[13] The word *prākṛta* means what exists in, or has come from, the source (*prakṛti*).[14] In contrast to Sanskrit, it refers to the original state of something prior to elaboration. Hence Grierson contrasted them as "artificial" and "unartificial."

The words *saṃskṛta* and *prākṛta* did not start out as designations for languages. It seems likely that they were employed for this purpose in order to represent the practices they designated as opposites. This interpretation is consistent with the ritual connotations of *saṃskṛta,* according to which Sanskrit is speech that has been "purified" for ritual use. This term, as Sheldon Pollock argues, forges an association between Sanskrit and the sphere of Vedic ritual, where the language was used both in actual ritual practice, in the form of hymns and prayers, as well as to talk about those rituals and the forms of knowledge that they presupposed. But it is important to note that "Sanskrit," as a designation for a language, is used only after the "prestige economy" of this language had expanded far beyond the sphere of ritual alone.[15] One of the earliest known uses of the word *saṃskṛta* to refer to a language occurs in the *Rāmāyaṇa.* In the *Sundarakāṇḍa,* Hanumān considers how he should address Sītā, and says: "If I present a *saṃskṛtā* speech, like a twice-born, she will mistake me for Rāvaṇa and get scared. I must address her with a human [*māṇuṣaṃ*] speech, full of meaning."[16] This passage contrasts Sanskrit as the language of twice-born Brahmans, such as Rāvaṇa, with the language of humankind as a whole. We can view this passage, as Pollock does, as a reflection of the social and discursive limitations that applied to the use of Sanskrit in the centuries preceding the *Rāmāyaṇa*'s composition. But we can also view it as a reflection of a set of circumstances that did not exist long before this passage itself was composed. The first circumstance is an increased distance between languages, in Heinz Kloss's sense of *Abstand*, or at least an increased awareness of this distance, relative to Patañjali's time. As is well known, Patañjali represented incorrect words as local deviations from the corresponding correct words rather than systemic deviations that might possess a logic and structure of their own.[17] This distance allowed people to think of languages as distinct systems, rather than as a single system that included arbitrary variation within it. The second circumstance, closely linked to the first, is choice. The necessity of choosing a language, and the awareness of doing so, is a special feature of literature, and radiates from literature into other discourses. Pollock is right to connect the *Rāmāyaṇa*'s consciousness of its own language with its self-declared status as the first work in an entirely new type of expressive literature.[18] Hanumān's dilemma of what language to frame his speech in is the same as that of Vālmīki, the author of the *Rāmāyaṇa*. Whenever language is an object of choice, we require a schema to tell us what the choices actually are.

We don't know when the *Rāmāyaṇa* was composed, but it was likely in the first century BCE. Around this time, and continuing into the early centuries of the common era, Jain monks were collecting, revising, and expanding a body of canonical literature. In a long discussion of music that several canonical texts share, it is observed that the language of song can be either Sanskrit or Prakrit.[19] This rather accidental passage reveals to us both the circumstances in which language is an object of choice, and what the choices were in such circumstances. Just as the Vedic scriptures never proclaim that they are composed in Sanskrit, the Jain scriptures never proclaim that they are composed in Prakrit, and only mention Sanskrit and Prakrit in a passage that clearly concerns the practices of a different cultural realm: that of literature and music.

The most compelling illustration of co-figuration occurs in a passage from Kālidāsa's *Birth of Kumāra* (early fifth century CE). During the celebration of Śiva and Pārvatī's wedding, Sarasvatī congratulates the couple:

> Sarasvatī praised the couple with a speech
> that she delivered in two ways:
> one purified by *saṃskāra* to the excellent groom,
> and one that could easily be understood to the bride.[20]

Kālidāsa here imagines the speech of Sarasvatī, the goddess of language and literature, in accordance with the same schema that distinguished Sanskrit and Prakrit as literary languages. In the literary culture that Kālidāsa inhabited, Sarasvatī did in fact speak two languages. Kālidāsa composed the *Birth of Kumāra* in Sanskrit within generations of Sarvasena composing another court epic, *Hari's Victory*, in Prakrit. The earliest available commentary on this passage of the *Birth of Kumāra*, Vallabhadeva's, explicitly identifies Sarasvatī's "speech delivered in two ways" with Sanskrit and Prakrit.[21] This passage is therefore a self-conscious reflection, from one of the foundational figures of *kāvya*, on the language practices of *kāvya* itself. Its wording even anticipates the wording of later works of poetics that sought to divide up the sphere of "textuality" (*vāṅmaya*) on the basis of language.

Kālidāsa's image shows us not just the dichotomization of literary language into Sanskrit and Prakrit, but some of the specific contrasts that create this dichotomy. One contrast etymologically defines Sanskrit as the language that is "purified by *saṃskāra*"; Prakrit's lack of *saṃskāra* is implicit here, but is explicitly stated in other texts.[22] It has proven difficult to say what *saṃskāra* means here because the word originally referred to the consecration of ritual objects and only by extension to language. There were many ways in which a language might be thought to possess *saṃskāra:* it could be consecrated for ritual use; it could be endowed with a certain kind of power or prestige; it could be validated by the teachings of grammarians; it could be produced by people who have been instructed in these teachings; it could be produced with care and attention; or it could be all of these things. In this context, *saṃskāra* likely refers in the first place to the rules enunciated by Pāṇini, around the fourth century BCE, that defined Sanskrit as a discrete, unitary language—without, however, using the name "Sanskrit" in reference to it. Co-figuration implies that Prakrit is projected as the opposite of Sanskrit across all of these senses.

A verse from Vākpatirāja's *Gauḍa's Demise* (early eighth century) provides a further example of these contrasts: "The loveliness of Sanskrit words unfolds through the beauty of Prakrit, and the splendor of Prakrit through the excellence of Sanskrit's *saṃskāra*."[23] What Prakrit uniquely contributes to a work is "beauty," whereas Sanskrit's unique contribution is *saṃskāra*, which in this context might mean grammatical perspicuity—the quality that enables Vākpati's work to be appreciated in a court where the preferred medium is Sanskrit. For Vākpatirāja, Prakrit can possess *saṃskāra*, but only by borrowing it from Sanskrit.

Another contrast that emerges from Kālidāsa's verse is that Prakrit is simple and Sanskrit is difficult. A Sanskrit sentence is conceived as an elaborate complex of discrete grammatical elements; it was defined by this complexity, a literal "putting-together" or *saṃskāra*. Thus a topos in Prakrit literature is that Prakrit is easier than Sanskrit because it does not require the in-depth grammatical knowledge that Sanskrit does.[24] Earlier we encountered a similar representation of Prakrit among Jain writers. They wished to depict their scriptures, which they claimed were composed in Prakrit, as inherently more accessible to the unlettered masses than the scriptures of other religious traditions. "Those who know the truth," Haribhadra wrote around the seventh century, "have produced scriptures in Prakrit for the benefit of children, women, the slow-witted and the uneducated, and for men who strive after good conduct." I argued in chapter 3 that such representations depend on and reinforce a myth of continuity between Prakrit and demotic language practices. It will be clear from the following chapter that for nearly the entire period with which we are concerned here, Prakrit was no less of a learned language than Sanskrit was, and Prakrit had grammars and lexicons just as Sanskrit did. And difficulty and complexity are, of course, relative concepts: there were no doubt people for whom Sanskrit was more easily intelligible than Prakrit and vice versa. The important point here, however, is that Prakrit was consistently represented as essentially different from Sanskrit in this respect, from its first literary monuments onward.

The ways in which the earliest Prakrit literature explicitly positioned itself against Sanskrit—representing itself as a discourse that was about, if not exactly for and by, common people (*prākṛta-jana*), rather than scholars and ritual specialists—are discussed in chapter 3, citing the following programmatic verse from *Seven Centuries*:

> Prakrit poetry is nectar.
> Those who don't know how to recite it or listen to it
> make love into a science.
> How are they not ashamed?[25]

This passage is among the earliest examples of the word *prākṛta* (*pāua*) used in connection with a language, and hence complements the earliest use of the word *saṃskṛta* in the passage from the *Rāmāyaṇa* discussed above. This verse turns on a contrast that illuminates what "Prakrit poetry" is. On the one side stand those who exercise themselves in scholarly disputes. On the other side stand those who compose and appreciate "Prakrit poetry," a phrase that could imply the poetry of common people in contrast to scholars, or common poetry in contrast to sophisticated scholarly discourse, besides poetry in the Prakrit language.[26] Prakrit and its other, Sanskrit, thus align onto the discourses of *kāvya* and *śāstra* and the personas stereotypically associated with them: sensitive litterateurs and fastidious, fault-finding scholars. This verse hints at the possibility that these two languages can complement each other and inhabit the same social space.

The most extensive early discussion of this shared social space, jointly inhabited by Sanskrit and its others, is Vātsyāyana's *Kāma Sūtra* (late third to early fourth century). In the course of describing the day-to-day activities of the urbane man (*nāgaraka*), Vātsyāyana has him attend a *goṣṭhī*, which is "when men of equal knowledge, intelligence, character, wealth and age, accompanied by courtesans, sit down together to discuss suitable matters, either in a courtesan's house, the court, or one of their own houses." What takes place there is "critical discussion of literature and fine arts," followed by the appreciation of beautiful women.[27] Later on, Vātsyāyana cites a few verses concerning *goṣṭhī*s from an older source. One of them claims that "one who participates in discussions in *goṣṭhī*s, neither exclusively in Sanskrit (*saṃskṛtena*) nor exclusively in the regional language (*deśabhāṣayā*), will become highly esteemed in the world."[28] This verse is another early use of the word *saṃskṛta* in reference to a language. The opposition is between the "regional language" (*deśabhāṣā*) and Sanskrit, which is figured as transregional in contrast. Prakrit is not explicitly mentioned here, although I consider it likely that the term "regional language" here refers to Prakrit, which is the only Indian language besides Sanskrit and probably Tamil for which we have evidence of literary production in the early first millennium.

This verse commends a "middle way" between the exclusive use of Sanskrit and the exclusive use of the regional language. This might mean that Sanskrit should be used in some contexts and that the regional language should be used in others, or it might mean that both Sanskrit and the regional language should be employed in similar contexts.[29] In either case, this verse locates both of them in the same social space, namely, the *goṣṭhī*, and in the same social actor, namely, the *nāgaraka*. The fact that Sanskrit and Prakrit were figured as opposites does not mean that they were relegated to entirely different social and discursive spheres.

The literary culture that Prakrit partially constituted was overwhelmingly dominated by men, as Vātsyāyana's descriptions of *goṣṭhī*s show. But Prakrit was represented as being more understandable to women and more open to women's participation than Sanskrit, and for these reasons preferred by women to Sanskrit, as we see in the verse from the *Birth of Kumāra*. Sanskrit and Prakrit conform to a pattern in which the social exclusivity of high culture generates parallel traditions purporting to offer the same kind of content but with fewer restrictions. Sanskrit was "high," and accessible only to people of a certain social status, while Prakrit was "not quite so high" and in principle open to everyone.

The comparative accessibility of Prakrit is a commonplace in Prakrit literature. A verse from the *Vajjālagga*, a collection of Prakrit poetry compiled near the end of the first millennium, says: "Prakrit poetry is playful and has sweet syllables; it is adored by young women and is erotic. So who is going to recite Sanskrit?"[30] The effect, as in the other programmatic passages we have seen so far, is to claim the territory of poetry for Prakrit, and especially poetry that has love as its central theme. Prakrit poetry is a discourse that notionally includes men and women; it is a poetry that not only speaks *about* women, but a poetry in which women speak and are spoken to.

Prakrit was not just favored by young women, according to these representations, but figured as a young woman. Some manuscripts of Rājaśekhara's *Karpūramañjarī*, a stage play of the early tenth century, read a verse in the prologue that claims that "Sanskrit compositions are harsh, but a Prakrit composition is soft; the difference between these two is as great as between a man and a woman."[31] A verse from Jayasiṃha Sūri's *Explanation of the Garland of Advice* (860 CE) uses an impressive triple entendre to imagine the Prakrit language—here called "the language of Maharashtra," *marahaṭṭhayabhāsā*—as a beautiful woman:

> Teeming with charming words,
> manifesting the theme of love,
> and bejeweled with lovely sounds,
> the language of Mahārāṣṭra is like a woman—
> walking attractively,
> revealing her intentions,
> and decked with gold and jewels,
> and like a forest—
> laced with lovely paths,
> where you can see mynah birds,
> and clothed in beautiful leaves.[32]

Prakrit is here, as in the verse just quoted from the *Vajjālagga*, figured as "soft," referring to its characteristic lenition ("softening") of intervocalic consonants (see chapter 4). But the comparanda that Jayasiṃha Sūri chooses are motivated by the content of Prakrit poetry just as much by its form: *Seven Centuries* is full of women arranging meetings with their lovers in the forest.

It is the nature of "not quite so high" culture that there is something higher than it. What Prakrit gained in being represented as more broadly accessible than Sanskrit (whether or not it actually was more accessible), it lost in exclusivity and thus prestige. Prakrit authors attempt to close the prestige gap by presenting the differences between Sanskrit and Prakrit as superficial and irrelevant to the meaning that the text itself conveys. One verse from the *Vajjālagga* figures Sanskrit and Prakrit as two equivalent options for expressing a given sense: "Sanskrit or other than Sanskrit, depending on who has come to listen, it is the meaning that produces a special kind of *rasa*, never before experienced. Isn't it amazing?"[33] The form of the binary here, Sanskrit and non-Sanskrit, has two implications. One is that the Sanskrit–Prakrit binary becomes a merism for all language: there is nothing not encompassed by either "Sanskrit" or "non-Sanskrit." The second is that Sanskrit is the unmarked member of the Sanskrit–Prakrit pair. This asymmetry comes out of an older view, represented, for example, by the grammarian Patañjali, that makes the language that Pāṇini described language as such without any further specification. For the entire classical period, composing a text in Sanskrit required no apology or explanation, whereas composing a text in Prakrit often did. This is one symptom of Sanskrit's discursive dominance, and of its superposition within the language order that Pollock has referred to as "hyperglossia."[34]

One Sanskrit work that does comment on its own choice of language is Govardhana's *Seven Centuries of* Āryās, a collection of lyrics in Sanskrit produced in eastern India around 1200 CE. But this is because Govardhana conceived his work as a Sanskrit response to Hāla's *Seven Centuries:*

> It took *force*
> to turn this poetry, whose *rasa* is most suited to Prakrit,
> toward Sanskrit,
> just as it took *Balarāma*
> to turn the Yamunā, whose water naturally flows down,
> toward heaven.[35]

This comparison may carry a suggestion that Sanskrit represents a diversion from the "natural" course of language represented by Prakrit, or it may simply have served to situate Sanskrit, the "language of the gods," in its rightful heavenly place. The purpose of the comparison, however, is to emphasize the difficulty in transforming the kind of "speech" (*vāṇī*) for which Prakrit had long been thought appropriate or even obligatory—namely, stand-alone verses of a predominantly erotic character in the *gāthā* meter—into Sanskrit.

Most of the above passages that help us recover the representations of Prakrit current in the language order of classical India come from literary texts. But the opposition of Sanskrit and Prakrit is not limited to these sources. When I describe the schema as "archetypal," part of what I mean is that it supplies a general framework for thinking about and talking about language within all of the domains of culture. One particularly important domain, besides the literary, is systematic thought about language. The discussion that I highlight here comes from Bhartṛhati's *On Sentence and Word,* a seminal work on the philosophy of language from around the fifth century CE.

Bhartṛhari implicitly juxtaposes Sanskrit and Prakrit by presenting two opposing views about what is correct and what is incorrect in language use:

> "The language of the gods was brought into confusion by incompetent speakers."—
> but on this point, people who hold it to be non-eternal have the opposite opinion.[36]

The prose commentary on this slightly obscure verse seems to get Bhartṛhari's intention right. The first half represents a view according to which Sanskrit, the "divine language," was once pure, but over time became corrupted by the accumulated mistakes of careless speakers. This view places Sanskrit at the root of all current language practices, and also accounts for the deviation (*apabhraṃśa*) of those language practices from each other and, of course, from Sanskrit. The "opposite" view referred to in the second half sees Sanskrit, not as the root of all language practices, but as a secondary elaboration and codification of preexisting language practices. Proponents of this view call these originary practices "Prakrit," which can be analyzed as meaning "existing in the original." Bhartṛhari also alludes to this position in his *Light* on the *Great Commentary*, an incomplete gloss on Patañjali's treatise.[37] In this view, words are correct, not because their use leads to merit (*dharma*), as Patanjali had argued when trying to establish the purposes of grammar, but only because they accord with conventions. Accordingly, it is the "original" Prakrit words that are correct, while Sanskrit words represent an unsuccessful attempt to "dress up" language.[38] It is nearly certain that the "others" to whom Bhartṛhari refers are Jains who employed Prakrit for literary, religious, and philosophical texts and who defended their language practices with arguments similar to those summarized in the prose commentary to *On Sentence and Word*.[39] It is because Prakrit had become an important counterweight to Sanskrit in Jain intellectual circles, as well as in literary circles beyond Jainism, that Bhartṛhari can represent an argument for its originary status. Bhartṛhari's Prakrit, in other words, is not just any language that deviates from Sanskrit, but the specific language or languages that Jains defended as legitimate for religious and philosophical use.[40]

The co-figuration of Sanskrit and Prakrit is one of the key features of the archetypal schema of language in classical India. Sanskrit and Prakrit are two discrete objects, and objects of broadly the same type, but they contrast across multiple dimensions. The dimensions highlighted in this brief survey include the social (the comparative accessibility, however notional, of Sanskrit and Prakrit to women), the aesthetic (the harshness of Sanskrit and the softness of Prakrit), the discursive (the affinity of Prakrit for *kāvya* and of Sanskrit for *śāstra*), the grammatical (the presence of absence of *saṃskāra*). Sanskrit was figured as "the language of the gods," and at this stage, Prakrit was contrastively figured as "the language of men." These differences render them complementary rather than incomparable; they constitute the twin parameters of discourse.

IDENTITY

The archetypal schema also represents Sanskrit and Prakrit in a particular and at first glance paradoxical relationship that I call "identity-in-difference." All schemas represent languages as identical in the minimal sense in that they are species of a genus. But a more substantive kind of identity obtains between Sanskrit and Prakrit, which are considered to be made out of the same linguistic stuff.

The strongest case for the identity of Sanskrit and Prakrit was made by the tenth-century poet Rājaśekhara in the prologue to his Prakrit play, *Karpūramañjarī:*

> The particular meanings are the same,
> and the words are the same—
> even if they undergo some change.
> A literary work is a special kind of composition,
> whatever language it happens to be in.[41]

The conclusion of this verse might lead us to think that the poet can choose whatever language he wishes, since every language has words and meanings that can be combined to make literature. But that is not the argument that Rājaśekhara makes, nor is it an argument that he would make. For Rājaśekhara makes very clear in his other works his opinion that literature could only be composed in four languages—Sanskrit, Prakrit, Apabhramsha, and Paishachi (see below)—and this verse is a defense, in Prakrit, of writing a play in Prakrit.[42] The argument is rather that if the definition of literature applies to a work in Sanskrit, then it should apply equally to a work in Prakrit. It is not simply that Prakrit is capable of conveying the same meanings as Sanskrit, or that Prakrit words differ only superficially from the corresponding Sanskrit words, but that Prakrit shares with Sanskrit the particular (*visesa*) words and meanings in which their literariness consists. Their underlying identity ensures that Sanskrit can be "transformed" (*pariṇamantā*) into Prakrit, in the way that milk, and only milk, can be transformed into curd.

Transforming Sanskrit into Prakrit is precisely what the discourse of Prakrit grammar accomplishes: it explicitly figures Sanskrit as an archetype (*prakṛti*) that can be systematically modified to produce Prakrit as an ectype (*vikṛti*), although the domain of such relations included only a part of the Prakrit language. I will limit my discussion here to one text which includes the earliest available Prakrit grammar, the *Treatise on Theater* ascribed to Bharata; chapter 6 will discuss other texts in this tradition.

The *Treatise on Theater* is a compilation of knowledge related to theater probably produced between the third and fourth century CE. It offers one of the earliest systematic accounts of literary language in India. Language was a primary concern to the compilers because "verbal representation" (*vācikābhinaya*) was essential to all ten major forms of theatrical performance, and was thus considered to be "the body of theater."[43] The *Treatise on Theater* is the earliest text to clearly and systematically distinguish between Sanskrit and Prakrit, and it is the text that most clearly presents the relationship of "identity-in-difference" of Sanskrit and Prakrit.[44]

The discussion of language occupies the first sixty-two verses of the *Treatise*'s seventeenth chapter. In this section, "Sanskrit" and "Prakrit" are terms used as modifiers, not of language (*bhāṣā*), but of *pāṭhya,* the actors' lines. Abhinavagupta's detailed eleventh-century commentary makes it clear that *pāṭhya* is not just the text of a play, something the *Treatise on Theater* generally calls *kāvya*, but the precise way in which the text is realized on the stage.[45]

There are exactly two kinds of lines, Sanskrit and Prakrit.[46] The *Treatise* defines Prakrit as follows:

> A Prakrit line is exactly the same as Sanskrit, but reversed:
> it is devoid of the quality of *saṃskāra*.
> It consists of various intermediate grades.[47]

Prakrit is, paradoxically, both "the same as" and the "reverse of" Sanskrit. What distinguishes them, as we saw above, is the presence or absence of *saṃskāra*, which Abhinavagupta plausibly understands in this context to be the "care" that results in the "maintenance" of the language in an identical state. Abhinavagupta explains that Sanskrit and Prakrit have an identical linguistic substratum (*prakṛti*), but Prakrit "comes from" that substratum "in the form that it takes without *saṃskāra*"—invoking the standard analysis of *prākṛta* as "what has come from the *prakṛti*."[48]

The *Treatise on Theater*'s definition of Prakrit involves a further paradox. If Prakrit lacks the very quality of *saṃskāra* that provides language with stability, it must be a "deviation" (*apabhraṃśa*), a practice that is characterized by the absence of those regularities (*niyama*) by which a language is constituted as a unity. And if this is the case, then any attempt to explicitly formulate the regularities of this practice—as the *Treatise on Theater* set out to do—is doomed to fail. Abhinavagupta poses the problem succinctly: "what regularity can a 'deviation' possibly have?" He answers with a creative interpretation of the last quarter of the verse. Prakrit owes its regularity to its conventional acceptance (*prasiddhi*) within specific regions (*deśaviśeṣa*), in contrast to Sanskrit, whose regularity is prior to its conventional acceptance in any particular place.[49]

The *Treatise on Theater*'s definition of Prakrit raises the question of how can we think about regularity outside of the paradigmatic regularity of Sanskrit. There was, however, no need for its compilers to reinvent the wheel. To answer this question, they availed themselves of existing literature about the definition and analysis of Prakrit. First, the *Treatise on Theater* presents the standard threefold classification of Prakrit words that was also presented in early grammars of the language that are now lost (see the discussion in chapter 6): Sanskrit-identical (*samānaśabdaṃ*), Sanskrit-derived (*vibhraṣṭaṃ*), and regional (*deśīgatam*).[50] Then it quotes from and adapts some of these lost grammars to produce a "mini-grammar" of Prakrit in two complementary sections.[51]

In connection with *Treatise on Theater*, it is worth noting one other important passage in which Prakrit furnished an example, or rather *the* example, for thinking about regularity outside of Sanskrit. That is Kumārila Bhaṭṭa's discussion of the language of Buddhist scriptures in his *Explanation of the System* (ca. seventh century). He claims that the authority of the Buddhist scriptures must be rejected because they fall under the *Mīmāṃsā Sūtras'* category of "illegitimate compositions." They are illegitimate, he claims, because they are "not even Prakrit." "Those texts are composed in mostly incorrect words from the Māgadha and Dākṣiṇātya languages and their degraded forms," he says, and after quoting a verse in a Middle Indic language, he complains that it is "more degraded than the degraded regional languages with which we are familiar." The examples that he gives show his familiarity with literary Prakrit and Apabhramsha. One of these examples is the word *saṃskṛta-*, which appears in the degraded language of the Buddhists as *saṃkaḍa-*. He says that the "correct incorrect" form, as familiar from Prakrit and Apabhramsha, should be *sakkaa-*.[52] Prakrit provided Kumārila with a model of how words could be correct in the sense of conforming to some standard while at the same time being incorrect in the sense of deviating from Sanskrit.

To return to the *Treatise on Theater*, we have almost no evidence as to what languages were in fact used on stage before this text was compiled. A few fragments of Aśvaghoṣa's otherwise-lost plays from the early second century seem to use a more archaic version of the languages we find in later plays.[53] The *Treatise on Theater* itself provides many examples of *dhruvā* songs in the thirty-second chapter that are composed in what also appears to be a rather archaic language.[54] It is difficult to speak with confidence about these texts—one on account of its fragmentariness, the other on account of its corruption—but it certainly appears that their language does not agree in all of its particulars with the language that the *Treatise* describes in the seventeenth chapter, as Luigia Nitti-Dolci was among the first to note.[55] I do not think that this difference can support detailed claims about the historical development of the Prakrit language, or languages, such as Manomohan Ghosh's argument that Śaurasenī is merely an older form of Prakrit than Mahārāṣṭrī, the standard literary language. Rather, it appears that the compilers of the *Treatise on Theater* had defined one kind of "Prakrit" by reference to another. Their goal must have been to categorize and describe the languages that were used in stage plays, including Sanskrit and its others. But the world in which the *Treatise on Theater* took shape was one in which Prakrit was already a literary language of some standing. Its compilers appeared to borrow the name, as well as the basics of a grammatical description, from the discourses of "literature heard" (*śravyakāvya*)—Prakrit lyric and courtly epic—in order to characterize the language practices of the stage play, or "literature seen" (*dṛśyakāvya*). As Abhinavagupta tells us, Bharata's purpose is not to describe the languages of the stage in very precise detail, but simply to give a general indication of how they sounded. For this purpose, the rules formulated by other texts and integrated into the seventeenth chapter served that purpose adequately.[56] The use of "real" Prakrit—that is to say, the language of *Seven Centuries* and *Rāvaṇa's Demise*—in plays is commonly thought to be a later innovation, found in Kālidāsa and later playwrights. The evidence for earlier practices, however, is very slight, essentially limited to the fragments of Aśvaghoṣa's plays and the difficult-to-date *Little Clay Cart* by Śūdraka.

The next sections map the distinction between Sanskrit and Prakrit onto the plurality of language practices of the theater. Scholars usually take for granted a model that organizes these language practices into two sets: Sanskrit, which contains only itself, and "the Prakrits," which contains all of the languages besides Sanskrit, such as Śaurasenī, Māgadhī, and so on.[57] This model has come to dominate modern scholarship in part because it came to dominate premodern thinking about language. For this reason it is important to note that it is completely absent from the *Treatise on Theater* itself. The work instead offers two *alternative* models, one for relating the specific language economy of the theater to the dichotomy of Sanskrit and Prakrit in the literary-cultural sphere, and one for relating it to the messy world of regional languages beyond it.[58]

The first model involves a fourfold classification of language (*bhāṣā*) which supervenes upon, rather than replaces, the twofold classification of lines into Sanskrit and Prakrit.[59] This relates to a distinctive feature of theater vis-à-vis other kinds of literature: it alone has "speakers" (*vaktṛ*) who pronounce its "text."[60] The four types are "superlanguage" (*atibhāṣā*), "noble language" (*āryabhāṣā*), "birth language" (*jātibhāṣā*), and "other-origin" (*yonyantarī*). The first two types are identified with Sanskrit.[61] The last type is spoken by animals; all that is said about it is that it "rests upon theatrical convention" (*nāṭyadharmīpratiṣṭhitā*). The third type, "birth language," is spoken by human beings, and it is said to be "twofold," involving both Sanskrit and Prakrit. The following verses specify the "birth language" by assigning either Sanskrit or Prakrit to human speakers. These assignments are well-known and do not need to be reviewed here.[62]

The *Treatise* then presents a second model that does not involve the categories of Sanskrit and Prakrit at all: "Alternatively, if they so choose, producers may employ the regional languages, for the text [*kāvyam*] of a play arises in various regions."[63] The category of "regional languages" includes seven "languages" (*bhāṣā:* Māgadhī, Āvantī, Prācyā, Śaurasenī, Ardhamāgadhī, Bāhlikā, and Dākṣiṇātyā) and seven "sublanguages" (*vibhāṣā:* Śakārī, Ābhīrī, Cāṇḍālī, Śābarī, Drāmiḍī, Āndhrī, and Vānaukasī). The names of the languages refer to regions, but it is important to keep in mind that "regions" in this sense are constituted by people rather than places: Māgadhī is the language of the Magadhas, not of Magadha. The names of the sublanguages refer to groups of people who are either not associated with a particular region, or associated with regions outside of a core cultural area. This model has its own rules of language assignment, but they refer to theatrical rather than social roles: leading men, leading ladies, rogues, jesters, and so on. The default language of this model appears to be Śaurasenī.[64]

These two models might represent different traditions of theatrical practice. But whatever their origins, it is only by combining them into one that we can produce the familiar model in which a unitary Sanskrit is set over a plurality of Prakrits. Dhanañjaya, a scholar of dramaturgy of the tenth century, is perhaps the first to make this combined model explicit. He understands "Prakrit" and "regional language" as synonyms—making Śaurasenī and Māgadhī varieties of Prakrit—and says that "Prakrit, particularly Śaurasenī, is used by women and low-status men," in contrast to high-status men, who use Sanskrit. As one moves from the top to the bottom of the social hierarchy, the language practices become less unified and more regionalized: "low characters speak the language of the region to which they belong."[65]

The *Treatise on Theater*'s discussions of language raise important questions about representation: how a schematic model can represent the language practices of a literary form, and how these language practices themselves represent the world outside. This section ends with a recommendation to "take from the world whatever is not spoken of here," and most scholars have assumed that the languages the *Treatise* describes are "literary versions of the actual languages."[66] But imitating is not the only way of representing, and it seems impossible to regard the literary languages as "versions of" the spoken vernaculars for which they are named in any significant sense.[67] The *Treatise on Theater* gives us to know that certain characters are entitled to use a transregional language, as Sanskrit is unambiguously characterized by its contrast with the regional languages. At the same time, they give us to know that other characters are not entitled to use this language; we must therefore imagine them as speaking the language of the region to which they belong. But it does not follow that these characters must actually speak some form of the language of the region to which they belong. A commitment to linguistic realism of this kind would entail enormous practical problems: everyone, from the author of the play to the actors to the audience, would be required to master an impossibly broad variety of language practices. Abhinavagupta gestures towards this explanation when he remarks that the limitation of "languages" and "sublanguages" to seven each serves to exclude the infinite variety of spoken dialects.[68]

In my view, the models presented by the *Treatise on Theater* offer a compromise solution to this problem. Sanskrit and Prakrit would become the principal languages employed in the theater. This maneuver brought the language practices of the theater into conformity with those of the wider literary culture to which the theater now belonged, where Sanskrit and Prakrit had long since been established as the primary languages of expressive textuality. As noted above, the languages considered to be "Prakrit" in the theater were not exactly the same as literary Prakrit. These languages were named for regions and represented the speech of those regions according to theatrical conventions. The differences between them, however, as well as the differences between them and the literary Prakrit that served their archetype, were carefully constrained so as not to transgress the limits of intelligibility. The language practices of the theater were thus limited by the principle of identity-in-difference: the different languages were minor modifications of the same linguistic substratum. Nowhere is this clearer than in Bhavabhūti's *Mālatī and Mādhava*, where the Sanskrit-speaking hero Mādhava, impersonating Mālatī's Prakrit-speaking friend Lavaṅgikā, pronounces a verse that can be understood in both languages simultaneously.[69]

The last section of the discussion of language in the *Treatise on Theater* is concerned to reintroduce regional characteristics that otherwise would not find expression in a theater, which primarily employed the standardized and increasingly transregional languages of Sanskrit and Prakrit. This section begins with a proscription on the representation of the languages of certain groups (*jātis*): "in theatrical productions, the text should not be made to reflect the language in the case of groups such as Barbaras, Kirātas, Āndhras, and Dramilas."[70] What these groups may have in common is their outsider status, at least in the social imaginary of Sanskrit drama. But it is naïve to read this statement as evidence of a sociolinguistic attitude according to which the language practices of these despised groups were denigrated and avoided. It simply states that the languages of these groups—including at least a few Dravidian languages—are too distant from Sanskrit and Prakrit to share a stage with them: it enforces the principle of identity-in-difference. Regional languages that differed less radically from Sanskrit and Prakrit could be represented, but only according to certain conventions that simplified their bewildering diversity and multiplicity into a small number of diagnostic differences. These conventions would allow a listener to recognize, for example, the word *māṇavaü* as "northern," *māṇavao* as "western," and *māṇavae* as "eastern," like similar shibboleths in English ("y'all" indicating the American south, "yous guys" Philadelphia, "yinz" Pittsburg, and so on).

The *Treatise on Theater* gives an exhaustive account of what it means for Sanskrit and Prakrit to be "the same" and yet "opposite" each other. Its redactors used Sanskrit and Prakrit to anchor a continuum of literary language practices. Given that verbal representation was the "body of theater," the continuity of language practices was essential to maintaining theater's bodily integrity. This continuity can be seen as a space of translation, in the etymological sense of moving back and forth, across the divisions instituted by the schema. This kind of translation, however, forecloses the possibility of translation in the sense familiar to us: precisely because Sanskrit and Prakrit are figured as an underlying unity under different kinds of transformation, there was no need to actually translate a Prakrit text into Sanskrit or vice versa. And in fact the earliest translations from Prakrit into Sanskrit—never the reverse—known to me date from the eleventh century, when the language order begun to shift in such a way as to marginalize Prakrit.[71]

TOTALITY

Another basic feature of the schema under consideration here is the totality of the practices it schematizes. The space constituted by Sanskrit and Prakrit expands to fill the entirety of literary language; any languages that are not encompassed within this space are not literary. Or, as a verse anthologized in the *Verses of the Chappaṇṇayas* states: "The person who knows how to speak neither Sanskrit nor the purest kind of Prakrit has one refuge: silence."[72]

There are different ways of representing this totality, for example, the merism "Sanskrit and non-Sanskrit."[73] By far the most important representation is what I call the "enumerative totality," which expands the binary structure of Sanskrit and Prakrit into an *n*-ary structure. The earliest and most influential example of such an enumerative totality is the "three languages"—Sanskrit, Prakrit, and Apabhramsha—espoused, if not formulated, by the founding fathers of the discourse of poetics, Bhāmaha and Daṇḍin, before the beginning of the eighth century.[74]

Bhāmaha was perhaps the first to claim that literature as a whole (*kāvya*) can be exhaustively divided up into Sanskrit, Prakrit, and Apabhramsha.[75] Daṇḍin invoked a metaphor to make the status of this division clear: it is the "body of literature" (*śarīraṃ kāvyānāṃ*) that can be analyzed in terms of language, in contrast to "ornaments" (*alaṅkāraḥ*), the term under which the tradition had gathered figures of sound and sense and which supplied the title of Bhāmaha's work.[76] The body of literature was textuality itself, "what was made of language" (*vāṅmayam*), which in Daṇḍin's schema was "Sanskrit, Prakrit, or Apabhramsha, or mixed."[77]

The "body of literature" was a metaphor of substance as opposed to accident: a text without figuration was plain, and perhaps not even literature, but a text without language was impossible. It was also a metaphor of unity. So long as "the whole of literature" is conceived of as an "organic unity of the highest order"—a unity that the discourse of poetics presupposed and sought to theorize—then the languages in which literature subsists can be thought to constitute an "organic unity" as well.[78] Rājaśekhara's famous image of "literature man" (*kāvyapuruṣa*) is a reinterpretation of Daṇḍin's metaphor that makes the "four languages" (Daṇḍin's three with the addition of Paishachi) into actual body parts: Sanskrit is the face, Prakrit the arms, Apabhramsha the groin, and Paishachi the feet.[79]

The "three languages" served as a top-level classification of literature. The word *bhūyaḥ* in Daṇḍin's formulation does not mean that literary works may rarely be composed in other languages ("primarily"), but, as the commentator Ratnaśrījñāna notes, simply serves to introduce a new classification ("moreover"). Alternatively, we could take it as referring to the fact that every single literary work is either predominantly composed in one of the three languages—which Pollock has therefore called "primary languages"—or, in the case of stage plays, involves a tightly constrained "mixture" of languages.[80] Bhāmaha implicitly and Daṇḍin explicitly map these languages onto literary genres.[81]

To enumerate is to exclude, as any speaker of Sanskrit would recognize.[82] Sanskrit, Prakrit, and Apabhramsha never fully comprehended the domain of language practices, even textual language practices, at any point in Indian history. We can make sense of this apparent disconnect between theory and practice by highlighting two related features of enumerative totalities in general.

First, they are totalizing representations rather than representations of a totality. Take, for example, the story of Guṇāḍhya's renunciation of the "three languages" related in the *Ocean of the Rivers of Story*, a twelfth-century collection of tales in the tradition of the *Great Story* attributed to Guṇāḍhya. In the *Ocean*, Guṇāḍhya is said to lose a bet with his colleague Śarvavarman about how long it will take to teach Sanskrit grammar to King Sātavāhana, and in consequence he gives up "Sanskrit, Prakrit, and the regional language, the three languages that are possible for human beings."[83] This leads him to learn "the fourth language," that of inhuman ghouls called Piśācas, while living with them in the forest (see below).[84] This story uses the rhetoric of *n*-ary structures to make the "three languages" representative of human culture as a whole, in contrast to the "fourth" language, which represents its very opposite.[85] Despite the claim that they represent all of human culture, the figure of the "three languages" foregrounds Sanskrit and Prakrit and thus represents human culture from a privileged, educated, and courtly perspective. His story transforms the languages of the Sātavāhana court into the languages of literary culture and then into the languages of human civilization.

Rājaśekhara makes the same point even more clearly:

> The language of the gods is worth hearing,
> and the Prakrit languages are naturally sweet.
> Apabhramsha is very pleasant,
> and there are choice works in the language of the ghouls.
> There are different paths,
> but these are the ones that are preferred.
> The one who writes in all of these is indeed a master poet.[86]

There are more languages than those enumerated in the schema, but these four are the only ones that matter. Nor do all four matter equally. Rājaśekhara called himself "skilled in all languages," but he did not write any significant works in Apabhramsha or Paishachi.[87] He advanced his claim to total expertise on the basis of his Prakrit compositions: for many poets could write in Sanskrit, but few—perhaps even none—had attempted to write an entire play in Prakrit, as Rājaśekhara did. Sanskrit and Prakrit metonymically represented the totality of literary languages, and even if Sanskrit remained Rājaśekhara's preferred medium, Prakrit represented for him the seldom-gained summit of literary expertise.

Second, the enumerative totality is an integrated unity. Daṇḍin was more concerned than Bhāmaha to demonstrate that the languages of the schema were internally related. Perhaps this is because, as a resident of Kāñcīpuram in the Tamil country around 700 CE, he was exposed to different literary cultures that each had their own linguistic parameters. In contrast to Bhāmaha, Daṇḍin offers the standard threefold classification that systematically relates Prakrit to Sanskrit. He also proposed a solution to the slight disjuncture between what Prakrit meant in the context of "literature heard" and what it meant in the context of "literature seen." He noted that it is the former that Prakrit was primarily associated with: this kind of Prakrit was, after all, the language in which "were composed works such as the *Building of the Bridge*, an ocean full of jewels of beautiful sayings." But he added something to this characterization of the language, namely, that it was based in the region of Maharashtra.[88] As we will see in chapter 6, this is also a relatively conventional description of the literary language (see the verse of Jayasiṃha above), and true to its historical origins in the western Deccan. But in the context of Daṇḍin's discussion, this remark gave Prakrit a "regional" character that distinguished it from Sanskrit and brought it closer to another set of languages: namely, the theatrical languages notionally derived from Prakrit and given names that associate them, just as notionally, with particular regions. Daṇḍin says that Śaurasenī, Gauḍī, and Lāṭī—respectively associated with the northern midlands, the Ganges plain in the east, and present-day Gujarat in the west—can also be considered Prakrit in the context of representing conversations (*vyavahāreṣu*) in stage plays.[89] He includes "other languages similar to them" (*tādṛśī*) in this set, reinforcing the *Treatise on Theater*'s constraint that the languages employed on the stage need to be more or less mutually intelligible. Daṇḍin's discussion, especially compared to Bhāmaha's relatively brief remarks, significantly expands the rubric of "Prakrit" and the languages it encompasses, but at the same time insists on the internal relationships between the languages that belong to this category: firstly, in terms of the preeminent position of the literary Prakrit, now increasingly regionalized as "Mahārāṣṭrī," and, secondly, in terms of the criterion of similarity that applies to the languages of stage plays.

Within the literary culture whose practices it schematizes, the figure of the "three languages" was widely understood to be total in these senses. Uddyotana's Prakrit romance *Kuvalayamālā* (778 CE) furnishes an important example in which Sanskrit, Prakrit, and Apabhramsha represent all of the languages that are "possible among human beings." Dhanadeva is a merchant who has been shipwrecked in a distant land, and finally finds a quiet place in the forest to rest, after escaping cannibals and man-eating birds. He falls asleep under a tree, but immediately wakes up to the chattering of the ghouls (*piśāca*s) who inhabit the forest. It takes him some time to identify the language that he hears, because he needs to compare it to Sanskrit, Prakrit, and Apabhramsha before finally deciding that it must be the "the fourth one, the language of the ghouls" (*caütthā bhāsā pesāyā*):

> He listened and thought: "Wait a minute. What is this language that I hear being spoken? Hmm. Well, it can't be Sanskrit, because that is harsh like the heart of a wicked person, difficult to understand with its hundreds of horrible options for forming all of the different words, compounds, indeclinables, prefixes, case endings, and genders. And this isn't like that. So could it be Prakrit? Hmm, that's not it, either, because that is pleasant like the words of good people, made up of the nectar that streams forth when great men churn the ocean of life that constantly surges with the waves of all learning, with compositions of various types that perfectly join their sounds and words together. And this certainly isn't like that. So might it be Apabhramsha, then? Hmm, it's not that either, because that is a mountain stream that gushes with floodwaters from the downpours of the first springtime clouds, rolling and swelling with the steady and unsteady waves that are the words of Sanskrit and Prakrit both pure and combined, alluringly harsh and gentle like the words of a lover in playful anger. And this isn't like that at all . . . "[90]

The basic principle of this representation is the opposition between Sanskrit and Prakrit. Sanskrit is the sum of its grammatical parts much in the way that Latin was an assemblage of third-person passives and ablative plurals to generations of British schoolchildren, and associated with the tedium and terror of learning those distinctions. Prakrit, the language in which Uddyotana composed the *Kuvalayamālā,* is not necessarily natural and spontaneous, but it is figured as more closely aligned with lived experience, and thus more pleasant and more appropriate to literary compositions. There is an ethical difference, too: Sanskrit is aligned with wicked people—perhaps the sanctimonious and hypocritical Brahmans that Uddyotana's teacher, Haribhadra Sūri, lampooned in his *Rogue Stories*—while Prakrit is cultivated by good people, preeminent among whom are Jain monks like Uddyotana himself.[91] Apabhramsha is not represented as an entirely distinct third language but as a recombination of Sanskrit and Prakrit.

Uddyotana is well aware that other kinds of languages exist; he even represents a number of "regional languages" in a market scene later on in the novel.[92] But the "three languages" are the languages of the court—as the description of the court of Dṛḍhavarman shows—and the languages of the literary culture that Uddyotana himself, and the protagonists of his novel, participated in.[93]

Svayambhū offers another compelling metaphor of totality in the introduction to his *Deeds of Padma* (ninth century). There, he compares the Rāma story to a great river that has flowed throughout the generations, and he compares the two banks of the river to Sanskrit and Prakrit. This is likely a reference to his predecessors, Vimala's *Deeds of Padma* in Prakrit and Raviṣeṇa's *Legend of Padma* in Sanskrit: the literary tradition prior to Svayambhū is divided into just two languages in the same way that a river has just two banks.[94]

A final example of what the enumerative totality represents can be drawn from a passage in Bilhaṇa's *Deeds of King Vikramāṅka,* composed in eleventh-century Karnataka, but looking back in the following excerpt on the poet's home town in Kashmir:

> What can I say about Pravarapura?
> It's a source of wonder,
> filling the ears with the nectar of so many marvelous stories,
> where the Sanskrit and Prakrit languages
> resound in every single house
> as if they were the mother languages
> even of women, to say nothing else.[95]

Here Sanskrit and Prakrit form a binary structure that contrasts with the *janmabhāṣās*, literally, "birth languages," that one might have expected housewives to speak. This binary represents "culture" with all of the tensions and aspirations of the English word: the "works and practices" in general that define us as members of a group, and those of intellectual and artistic creativity in particular.[96]

ITERABILITY

The distinctions that operate over a schema as a whole can be reinscribed onto its constituent parts. This process of iteration results in fractal representations, rather than the *n*-ary representations we have surveyed in the preceding section. In contrast to the diachronic expansion of a schema through the introduction of new distinctions, the iteration of existing distinctions is synchronic. The representations produced by iteration run parallel to each other, while those produced by expansion follow upon each other in history.

Apabhramsha furnishes the major example of iteration within the language order of classical India. The term "Apabhramsha" itself, meaning "deviation," has a longer history than either "Sanskrit" or "Prakrit" in Indian discourses on language. Patañjali used it as a synonym for incorrect words, and his usage was recognized by Daṇḍin: "with reference to scientific works, anything other than Sanskrit is called Apabhramsha."[97]

The qualification is necessary because, by Daṇḍin's time, Apabhramsha had acquired a more specific meaning. It referred to a literary language besides Sanskrit and Prakrit, and thus Daṇḍin defines Apabhramsha, with reference to literary works, as "the language of people such as the Ābhīras." The Ābhīras were a group who came to political prominence in the Deccan in the twilight of the Sātavāhana empire, around the middle of the third century, but Daṇḍin's statement provides nearly all we know about their association with Apabhramsha as a literary language.[98] It is significant that this newcomer to the field of literary languages was given the very name that was formerly used to denominate all non-Sanskrit language practices. Prakrit was Apabhramsha, in this basic sense of a "deviation," before Apabhramsha was Apabhramsha. In other words, Apabhramsha slid into the position in the language order occupied by Prakrit. Not only that, but it was imagined and represented in very much the same way as Prakrit was. Daṇḍin's tenth-century commentator Ratnaśrījñāna mentions a tradition that analyzed Apabhramsha into exactly the same four categories into which earlier teachers had divided Prakrit.[99]

Apabhramsha is thus seen as the result of a kind of mitosis of Prakrit. This representation aligns with the relationship between Prakrit and Apabhramsha in practice, for these languages often occupy the same discursive space: works in Apabhramsha include prologues in Prakrit (such as the *Message Poem* of ʿAbd ur-Raḥmān); Prakrit anthologies include verses in Apabhramsha (such as the *Verses of the Chappaṇṇayas*); Apabhramsha verse forms were used occasionally in Prakrit, Prakrit verse forms were used abundantly in Apabhramsha; the same authors composed works in both languages. ʿAbd ur-Raḥmān expressly represents himself as a Prakrit poet, and for good reason: not only does the *Message Poem* include several Prakrit *gāthās*, but it engages with Prakrit intertexts at nearly every turn.[100] It is with some justice, then, that Herman Tieken has sought to see Apabhramsha as "a Prakrit," by which he means that Apabhramsha literature is essentially Prakrit literature written in a different language.[101]

Another clear example of iteration comes from the way that Abhinavagupta understood the categories of language laid out in the *Treatise on Theater.* What Bharata calls a "language" (*bhāṣā*) is a deviation (*apabhraṃśaḥ*) from Sanskrit, and what Bharata calls a "sublanguage" (*vibhāṣā*) is a deviation (*apabhraṃśaḥ*) from a language.[102] Another example might be drawn from the use of the concept in Prakrit grammar. In this discourse, Sanskrit figured as the archetype (*prakṛtiḥ*) and Prakrit as the ectype (*vikṛtiḥ*): Prakrit words were derived from Sanskrit words by a set of transformational rules. When Prakrit grammar grew to encompass the languages of the theater, Śaurasenī and Māgadhī occupied the position of ectypes in relation to Prakrit, which was repositioned as an archetype. Just as in the *Treatise on Theater*'s typology, a procedure of derivation connects Sanskrit to Prakrit, and the same procedure connects Prakrit to Śaurasenī and Māgadhī. In the influential grammar composed by Hemacandra in the middle of the twelfth century, the *Siddhahemacandra,* the final stop on this itinerary is Apabhramsha. Iteration within this schema comes to an end with Apabhramsha, perhaps because Apabhramsha—whatever specific practices this term referred to—is always axiomatically configured as the furthest stop away from the starting point that is Sanskrit. The same logic operates in the eastern Prakrit grammars, for example in Mārkaṇḍeya's *Sum-Total of Prakrit,* although here it is the *paiśācika* languages that are the last stop, after *bhāṣās*, *vibhāṣās*, and *apabhraṃśas*.

The scope of Bhoja's discussion of language in his *Illumination of the Erotic*, like the *Siddhahemacandra* modeled on it, is the totality of literary culture.[103] But whereas Hemacandra represents each successive language as a transformation of the preceding, Bhoja proceeds by iterative divisions. The "three languages," each of which has three further subdivisions, and each of those has two varieties, are his starting point. Regarding Apabhramsha, Bhoja arranges six notionally regional varieties under the three subdivisions of "high," "middle," and "low." Regarding Prakrit, Bhoja synthesizes two existing classifications, one that recognized a number of "regional" varieties of Prakrit (Śaurasenī, Māgadhī, etc.), and one that classified Prakrit words on the basis of their derivational distance from Sanskrit (*tatsama, tadbhava, deśya;* see the following chapter). Bhoja's "Prakrit" is divided into "natural" (*sahajam*), "derived" (*lakṣitam*), and "distorted" (śliṣṭam). The first category alludes to a kind of language that is independent of grammar, either because it is identical to Sanskrit (*saṃskṛta-samam*) or because it has no relationship to Sanskrit at all (*deśyam*); the second includes the main varieties of Prakrit that are grammatically derived from Sanskrit, *mahārāṣṭram* and *śaurasenam*; the third includes languages that are more distant from Sanskrit (such as *māgadham*) or at least more obscure to the grammarian (such as *paiśācam*); the latter are similar in status to the *Treatise on Theater*'s "sublanguages," in that they are second-order deviations.

The principle of iteration explains why the representations of language we encounter in Indian texts, although they do differ from each other, differ in systematic and tightly constrained ways. We can formulate for them a set of "implicational universals," a term that linguists use to describe the necessary occurrence of one feature given another feature. If a representation distinguishes two languages, then one of them must be Sanskrit. If it distinguishes three, then Sanskrit and Prakrit must be two of the three. And if it distinguishes more than three, then it must include Sanskrit, Prakrit, and Apabhramsha. These implications build in some latitude, since there is always at least one indeterminate slot, but the other slots are determined by the schema under analysis here.

THE HALF-LANGUAGE

To say that the schema described above is archetypal is, in the first place, to recognize its primacy in ordering language practices over a vast domain of textual production. In fact, the large-scale formation that has been described as "classical India," and more recently as the "Sanskrit cosmopolis," can be reframed in terms of these ordered language practices: it is the world in which textuality is governed by the schema of co-figuration of Sanskrit and Prakrit. It is not simply the world in which these specific languages are employed, but the world in which the use of these languages is essentially linked to the exercise and maintenance of culture-power. As Sheldon Pollock has argued at length, this was not only, and perhaps not even primarily, due to military conquest, colonization, trade, or the spread of religious ideas.[104] Absolutely essential to the determination of Sanskrit and Prakrit as languages of culture power were schematic representations such as those we have seen in this chapter.

Prakrit has generally been omitted from this story, as the very phrase "Sanskrit cosmopolis" suggests. But once we recognize that languages are constituted as what they are only within larger structures that I call language orders, we must recognize also that Sanskrit depends on Prakrit and vice versa, both historically and conceptually. As I have tried to show, the names "Sanskrit" and "Prakrit" only come to be used to designate language practices in around the first century CE, and are used to designate them contrastively within a new sphere of textuality whose limits they jointly define. Apabhramsha appears somewhat later, but when it does, it appears within the framework already established by the opposition, identity, and totality of Sanskrit and Prakrit. Textuality in the Sanskrit cosmopolis was never simply Sanskrit textuality, but it was configured by the identity-in-difference of Sanskrit, Prakrit, and Apabhramsha.

This schema is archetypal in the further sense that it admits of modifications. Arguably, the language order it describes was only uprooted and replaced by European colonialism. This leaves more than fifteen hundred years of language practices that were subsumed under a wide variety of schemas that can generally be seen as ectypal modifications of the archetypal schema presented above, as well as language practices that remained more or less outside of the unified language order or constituted a kind of counterpart to it. Śrīnātha, the fourteenth- and fifteenth-century Telugu poet, can serve as a good example of both. In composing literature in Telugu at all, he was certainly breaking away from the model of the "three languages." He was, however, not rejecting it but extending it. He styled himself a "lord among poets in the eight languages." The following sections will explain how the schema was extended from three to eight, but for the moment it will suffice to note that Śrīnātha includes Sanskrit, Prakrit, and Apabhramsha among these languages. Despite this expansion, a number of important language practices remained unintegrated in his schema, above all those introduced by the Bahmani sultans just to the west: Arabic, Persian, and Turkish. Śrīnātha is well aware of these languages, and praises one of his patrons for his mastery of them, but does not—and perhaps cannot—integrate them into a single representational schema with the "eight languages."[105]

These concluding sections will examine just two modifications of the archetypal schema: the addition of Paishachi as a "half-language," and later as a full language, alongside Sanskrit, Prakrit, and Apabhramsha; and the expansion of this schema of three and a half or four languages into the enduring schema of six languages. I focus on these modifications in particular because the first illustrates the power of the schema to conjure an entire language from nothing, as it were, and the second represents a major redetermination of Prakrit as a concept and as a category.[106]

An inscription in far-off Cambodia around 900 CE described King Yaśovarman I as "a Guṇāḍhya who hates Prakrit" (*guṇāḍhyaḥ prākṛtāpriyaḥ*), an apparent contradiction, which resolves to "rich in virtues and no lover of what is base."[107] Guṇāḍhya was the author of the *Great Story*, which has been called one of the three streams of Sarasvatī alongside the *Mahābhārata* and the *Rāmāyaṇa*.[108] The *Great Story* itself, however, is lost: all we have are retellings in Sanskrit, Prakrit, and Tamil.[109] It seems to be always already translated, for the earliest mention of it in the sources available to us is an inscription in which the Gaṅga king Durvinīta claims to have rendered it into Sanskrit.[110] Yaśovarman's reference to Guṇāḍhya might lead us to think that the *Great Story* was composed in Prakrit. But Daṇḍin seems to have considered it an exception to the rules of textuality he himself enunciated. Stories (*kathā*), he tells us in the *Mirror of Literature*, are composed in all languages, but most commonly in Sanskrit. The exception is "the wondrous *Great Story*, which is composed in *bhūtabhāṣā*."[111]

There has been an enormous amount of discussion about what this *bhūtabhāṣā* was and what its characteristics were. Scholars have attempted to identify this language with the spoken vernacular of one or another group. The crucial maneuver has been the identification of Daṇḍin's *bhūtabhāṣā* with the language that ghouls (*piśācas*) are imagined to speak and are, on a few occasions, represented as speaking. The identification with *bhūtabhāṣā* with Paishachi, as this imaginary language was so called, rests on the interpretation of the compound as a "language of the dead." But I believe that Daṇḍin meant to describe the language of the *Great Story* as a "dead language": a language of the literary past. This *bhūtabhāṣā* was neither Sanskrit nor Prakrit nor Apabhramsha. It was incompatible, for reasons that are lost to us, with the principles of textuality that governed the classical language order, and that is why the only text ever known to have been composed in this language, the *Great Story*, seems to have always been known through translations.

The earliest surviving Kannada text, the *Way of the Poet-King* (ninth century), faithfully represents the circumstance of co-figuration described earlier in this chapter: besides Kannada, which the text endeavors to theorize, the only languages mentioned are Sanskrit and Prakrit, which are represented as the only languages in which high literature may be composed.[112] But in the tenth century, a number of authors started to speak of "three and a half languages," where the half was Paishachi.[113] It is "half" a language precisely in the sense that Daṇḍin suggests: important literature has been composed in it, but unlike the "three languages," no new literature could be composed in it. But does their use of the name "Paishachi" suggest that it was really thought of as the language of ghouls?

I have argued that the appearance of Paishachi within schemas of language after Daṇḍin's time was the result of a literary joke gone wrong—or perhaps gone right.

Uddyotana tells us that he included some passages in languages other than Prakrit in the *Kuvalayamālā* "for fun" (*koūhaleṇa*).[114] In a scene I've already mentioned, the merchant Dhanadeva finds himself surrounded on a desert island by a horde of ghouls (*pisāyas*) who speak ghoulish (*pesāyā*). The language of this scene might plausibly be modeled on that of the *Great Story,* as a dead language that Uddyotana cleverly repurposed as the language of the undead. The Kashmiri retellings of the *Great Story* in the eleventh century say that Guṇāḍhya composed the work in ghoulish, precisely because he took a vow that prevented him from using the three languages current among men, but significantly this detail is absent in all of the earlier retellings of the story. In my view, this detail reflects a retrospective identification of the dead language in which the work was composed as the language that Uddyotana calls Paishachi. Whatever the truth is, Paishachi went from being a non-language in the enumerative schemas of the seventh and eighth centuries to being a half-language, and later on a full language, in subsequent representations. It is not that new literature was written in this language. On the contrary, fewer and fewer people seemed to have had direct access to the *Great Story* as time went on. What was new was simply that it had been included in the schemas from which it had earlier been excluded. This made it available, in principle, for literary composition, although the lack of literary models made composition in the language difficult in practice. In fact, apart from fragments of the *Great Story,* nearly the only writing in Paishachi we have are literary experiments like Uddyotana's. A very similar scene to the one in the *Kuvalayamālā* would be included by Jineśvara in his *Story of Nirvāṇa and Līlāvatī* (1036), and Hemacandra in the twelfth century would write a short section in Paishachi to illustrate the grammatical rules that he collected in the *Siddhahemacandra* and probably culled from experiments like Uddyotana's.

THE SIX LANGUAGES

The transformation of Paishachi from non-language to language is just one part of an important refiguring of language practices that took place shortly before the ninth century: the threefold schema of Sanskrit, Prakrit, and Apabhramsha was replaced by a sixfold schema that added Śaurasenī, Māgadhī, and Paishachi. The earliest text to exhibit this refiguration is Rudraṭa's *Ornament of Literature,* composed in Kashmir in the early ninth century.[115] Śaurasenī and Māgadhī, as we saw above, were used exclusively in the theater, which had in the generations before Rudraṭa become the analytical focus of Kashmiri theorists of Sanskrit literature. As is well known, during the reign of Jayāpīḍa (779–813), Bhaṭṭa Udbhaṭa began a tradition of studying and commenting upon the *Treatise on Theater* in Kashmir. The shift in focus to "literature seen" (*dṛśyakāvya*), as opposed to "literature heard" (*śravyakāvya*), entailed a shift of focus from monoglossic to polyglossic genres. In the theater, language was not predetermined by genre, but could be an object of choice and purposeful manipulation.

One of the techniques of language manipulation is *bhāṣāśleṣa,* in which a verse is spoken in two or more languages at the same time, either with the same meaning or with different meanings.[116] This provides a way of manipulating the language assignments in a play—for instance, a character who is "supposed" to speak Sanskrit may speak Prakrit and vice versa—as well as a clever way of saying two different things to two notionally different groups of people.[117] But it also provides a way of surreptitiously modifying the language of a composition in "literature heard," which otherwise does not admit of such changes. Hence we find *bhāṣāśleṣa* sections in works such as Bhaṭṭi's *Poem* and Śivasvāmi's *Rise of Kapphiṇa.* Bhoja's discussion of the "type" of language (*jāti*) in his *Necklace of Sarasvatī* reflects this new theoretical orientation according to which language is an object of choice, and therefore something about which judgments of propriety (*aucitya*) can be rendered. This represents a major departure from Bhāmaha and Daṇḍin. For Rudraṭa and Bhoja, language does not just constitute the "body" of literature but could itself become an "adornment."

Rudraṭa's "six languages" provided the basis for a new kind of linguistic knowledge that was textualized in the form of the multilingual grammar. The earliest datable text that might be called a multilingual grammar is in fact Namisādhu's commentary on the *Ornament,* completed in 1069. While commenting on Rudraṭa's exposition of the "six languages," Namisādhu provides a short description of each of them, referring to rules that he has either taken from earlier grammars (perhaps Harivṛddha's lost grammar, which he quotes elsewhere) or inferred from actual texts (such as Uddyotana's *Kuvalayamālā* in the case of Paishachi). Other multilingual grammars from around this time include the "expanded" version of the *Light on Prakrit,* with chapters on Śaurasenī, Māgadhī, and Paishachi (see chapter 6), and Kramadīśvara's *Distilled Essence.* The most complete and most influential grammar of this type was Hemacandra's *Siddhahemacandra,* which adopts Rudraṭa's "six languages" as its organizing principle and defines Sanskrit, Prakrit, Śaurasenī, Māgadhī, Paishachi, and Apabhramsha in turn. For most authors after Hemacandra, that there were six languages was common knowledge.[118]

CONCLUSIONS

The schema that I have presented in this chapter underlies the representation of language in classical India. It supplies the basic categories—including the languages themselves—and calibrates a complex set of relations, constituting a framework within which language can be thought. The overall picture that emerges from this schema should now be clear. Sanskrit and Prakrit are mutually constitutive languages, closely related to each other but contrasted across a number of dimensions.

Even further from Sanskrit in the direction of Prakrit is Apabhramsha. These three languages form a coherent unity. They are the only languages in which literature can be composed, and they thus represent the linguistic parameters of a literary culture.

This picture closely matches the actual practices of literature from the second to the ninth century, from Kashmir to the Kaveri river. This picture has two particularities, in comparison with later imaginations of language in South Asia, that I will simply note here; many other particularities could be discerned if the comparative lens were turned to literary cultures outside of South Asia. The first is that language is imagined as monocentric. It does not matter whether Sanskrit or Prakrit is taken to be the center, since they are imagined to be identical at a deeper level in any case. The name "Prakrit" itself suggests a relationship to a single "source" (*prakṛti*). On this model, all languages are related to each other through the central source. There is no possibility of a polycentric language order of the kind that the Pāṇṭiya rulers of the area around Maturai in Tamil Nadu fashioned in the ninth century, in which Sanskrit and Tamil were accorded something approaching equal status and authority.[119] The second particularity is that vernacular textuality is not just absent but unthinkable within this schema. There is plenty of evidence that Prakrit and especially Apabhramsha were thought of as regional languages (*deśabhāṣā*s). This does necessarily imply that regional languages as we understand them were in turn thought of as Prakrit or Apabhramsha: as the following two chapters show, regional languages were indeed represented as Prakrit and Apabhramsha, but this was part of the process of vernacular literarization that took place centuries after the foundations of the Sanskrit cosmopolis, including the archetypal schema of its language order, had been laid.[120] For much of the first millennium, the regional was not conceived as a source of authority or legitimacy in itself, but was rather defined negatively, as a site of difference from transregional Sanskrit.

The classical schema made Prakrit an object of imagination, representation, and knowledge. The following chapter will examine in detail the systems of knowledge that Prakrit was the object of, grammar and lexicography, and the concepts and strategies that were developed in these systems. One of these concepts is "the regional" (*deśya*), which links the classical language order to the vernacular language orders that followed it.

6

Knowing Prakrit

PRAKRIT KNOWLEDGE

The history of Prakrit is closely bound up with the history of knowledge about Prakrit. In this chapter I examine the discourses in which this knowledge was systematically articulated. To see precisely how these discourses constituted Prakrit as a stable and coherent object of knowledge, we need to look at them at two different resolutions. At a lower resolution, what we see are texts that are situated in traditions, and the important question is how the traditions of Prakrit grammar, metrics, and lexicography develop in tandem with Prakrit literary traditions. At a higher resolution, what we see are conceptual strands that run throughout these texts, structuring them and tying them into larger discursive configurations. The extension of concepts formulated in order to account for Prakrit into new domains of textuality was crucial to the process of vernacularization, although modern scholarship has ignored or minimized the provenance of these concepts.

Just what was systematic knowledge of Prakrit? In the middle of the twelfth century, the Jain monk Hemacandra composed a number of works in which he sought to synthesize the knowledge that was necessary to participate fully in literary culture.[1] This knowledge was organized into the four domains of grammar, lexicography, metrics, and poetics, each the subject of separate works by Hemacandra himself. There is much that is new in this configuration, but it exhibits two features that characterize systematic knowledge of Prakrit over its long history: first, it is dispersed over interlocking domains; second, it is a literary-cultural knowledge, which is clear enough in the case of metrics and poetics, but must be emphasized in the case of grammar and lexicography. The "contexts of use" (*prayoga*) with which grammarians and lexicographers were concerned were always literary contexts. To illustrate his own rules, Hemacandra very often quotes verses from literary works such as *Seven Centuries* and *Rāvaṇa's Demise,* and very rarely from the Jain scriptures, and he never quotes examples from the language of everyday life.

Prakrit knowledge was thus philological. For this characterization I invoke a heuristic distinction between philology, which is oriented toward texts, and linguistics, which is oriented toward language—"heuristic," of course, because texts are made out of language, and language, for most of human history, can only be accessed through texts.[2] Although the primary object of Prakrit knowledge was language, it was never language per se, but language that either was, or could be, deployed in literary texts. Prakrit knowledge was not a "model of" a linguistic reality with an independent existence, but a "model for" the continuous recreation—through reading, commenting, anthologizing, recombining, and composing anew—of literary traditions. We risk misconstruing the enterprise entirely if we conceive of it on the model of linguistics, either in its Pāṇinian or modern incarnations.[3]

The central component of this configuration was grammar. The "centripetalizing" force of grammatical discourse in the modern world—its ability to determine or redetermine language as a single object with a single source of authority—has long been recognized. It has been particularly important in shaping the national languages which modern subjects have identified with and cathected upon.[4]

But grammar is not an invention of modernity. In this chapter I adopt a two-pronged strategy for recovering what Prakrit grammar was, and, more important, what it did, in premodern India.

On the one hand, I argue that Prakrit grammar was just like any other grammatical discourse. These discourses do not simply list, or provide the rules for generating, forms of a given language. They teach people to think of the language under description, of language in general, and of culture more broadly, through a certain set of models, concepts, and relations.[5] Since Prakrit grammar is seen as a tiny, obscure subject, lacking both the sophistication and dynamism of Sanskrit grammar, and hence hardly studied at all, I want to emphasize this point: anyone in premodern India who thought in any depth about the relationships between different languages, or between cultural practices delimited by language—in a word, about polyglossia—used concepts that originated in Prakrit grammar.

On the other hand, I argue that Prakrit grammar was different. We can think about these differences using the terms that grammatical discourse in India itself provides. It consists of a set of rules, called a *lakṣaṇa* ("that which defines"), which serves to characterize a set of linguistic phenomena, called a *lakṣya* ("that which is defined"). With regard to the former, Prakrit grammar is very closely related to Sanskrit grammar, but because it needs to define one language in terms of another—because it is interlingual rather than intralingual—it has certain concepts, strategies, and techniques of its own.[6] With regard to the latter, Prakrit grammar describes a very different kind of language from Sanskrit or the regional vernaculars, not to speak of modern national languages. There were never, to our knowledge, any communities that defined themselves by their use of Prakrit, no "Prakritikas" comparable to Kannadigas or Tamilians, nor did Prakrit ever approach Sanskrit's broad acceptance as a language of learning that cut across such communities. It was, for most of its history, an exclusively literary language, and the enterprise of Prakrit grammar could not but reflect the fact that the language belonged to an elective subculture of experts and connoisseurs, if it belonged to anyone.

This approach requires going behind the descriptive–prescriptive dichotomy, and by that I mean examining the complex relationships between *lakṣya* and *lakṣaṇa,* and between grammar and its uses and effects, that are preprocessed and flattened out by the terms "descriptive" and "prescriptive." The descriptive–prescriptive distinction was never explicitly made in Indian grammatical traditions, and it dissolves upon closer analysis even in the twentieth-century projects that explicitly identify with one or the other modality.[7] Yet it retains a heuristic value. Conceiving of Prakrit grammar as a "descriptive" enterprise would require us to identify the specific forms of language that it sought to describe at various points in its history; conceiving of it as "prescriptive" would require us to identify its specific practical applications. But because these conceptions are only heuristic, we should not expect to find, in the first case, a stable object language represented by a fixed corpus of texts, and in the second, a coherent regulative agenda. Ultimately these tasks will take us back to the ontology of the languages for which Prakrit grammar serves as an epistemology: where, when, for whom, in what contexts, and given what preconditions did they exist?

AN ARCHAEOLOGY OF PRAKRIT KNOWLEDGE

Our history of Prakrit knowledge starts in the middle of *its* history. The earliest contributions to Prakrit grammar and lexicography that we can reliably locate in time were composed in the tenth and eleventh centuries, long after these discourses first took shape. These include the *Prakrit Lakṣmī* of Dhanapāla (972) and Namisādhu's commentary (1069) on Rudraṭa's *Ornament of Literature.* Earlier texts survive in the discourse of Prakrit metrics, but these too carry indications of a longer prehistory that is lost to us. The scarcity of surviving works is probably due to the "Hemacandra bottleneck." Hemacandra's writings became the primary reference point for the systematic knowledge of Prakrit almost as soon as the ink was dry, and consequently earlier works were no longer studied and transmitted. Much has been lost, and much that survives cannot be dated with certainty. An example of the latter is Caṇḍa's grammar, which has circulated in various forms and under various names, and has been assigned to the last centuries BCE (by Hoernle) and the early second millennium CE (by Bloch) and various times in between.[8]

What I offer in the following pages is an archaeology of Prakrit knowledge, although more in the spirit of Cuvier than of Foucault. It is an attempt to construct a historical narrative on the basis of texts that resist it: lost texts, fragmentary texts, poorly preserved texts, corrupt texts, authorless texts, imaginary texts, mythical texts. The fact that we cannot always link these texts to names, places, and dates does not mean that they lie outside of history. Nor is the history of Prakrit knowledge as a discourse identical with the chronology of the individual texts that constitute it. My archaeology attempts to recover the overarching goals of these texts, their scope and analytical techniques, their principal intertexts, and the changes that the discourse underwent.

The materials that do survive suggest that Prakrit knowledge began at the court of the Sātavāhana kings in the early centuries of the first millennium CE. This should come as no surprise after seeing in chapter 3 the leading role that Sātavāhanas played in inventing and patronizing Prakrit literature. It also appears that the earliest works of Prakrit literature presuppose a body of systematic literary knowledge. *Seven Centuries*, for example, is strikingly unified in metrical form and language. There are scattered indications that the very people responsible for giving *Seven Centuries* its final shape—above all the author-editor known to tradition as Sātavāhana—were also responsible for theorizing the grammatical, lexical, and metrical forms of which Prakrit literature consisted.[9]

On seven occasions in his Prakrit lexicon, Hemacandra refers to Sātavāhana's Sanskrit definitions of Prakrit words. The words cannot be traced in *Seven Centuries*, so Hemacandra must be either paraphrasing or quoting another work. The latter seems more likely, given that most of the references can be read as parts of an *anuṣṭubh* verse, although Hemacandra may be using an intermediate source.[10] Virahāṅka and Svayambhū, writing around the eighth and ninth centuries respectively, also refer to Sātavāhana in the context of Prakrit metrical forms, and notably forms that do not occur in *Seven Centuries*.[11] Ghanaśyāma, an author of the eighteenth century, refers to "Śālivāhana" as a lexical and grammatical authority who wrote a work called *Moonlight of Prakrit* (*Prākṛtacandrikā*). Some, but not all, of these references involve a Prakrit word being defined with a Sanskrit synonym in an *anuṣṭubh* verse (or a reference that can plausibly be reconstructed as such), and it is possible—although by no means certain—that Ghanaśyāma was quoting from the same work as Hemacandra.[12] This work seems to have been a practical handbook to Prakrit composition, covering the basic points of grammar as well as points of usage and vocabulary.[13]

Another author only known to us from fragments is Harivṛddha. He is often mentioned in the same breath as Sātavāhana, and it seems likely that he was his contemporary. A few of his verses are quoted by Ratnaśrījñāna (tenth century) and

Namisādhu (eleventh century). What is notable about these verses is that they are written in Prakrit, using the *gāthā* verse form typical of Prakrit literature. Similar verses are quoted without attribution in other works, including the *Dhavalā* and *Jayadhavalā* of Vīrasena and Jinasena (ninth-century Karnataka), the *Treatise on Theater,* Nanditāḍhya's *Definition of the Gāthā,* and Caṇḍa's *Definition of Prakrit.* Together they show that knowledge about Prakrit was articulated, and probably was first articulated, in Prakrit. The grammatical fragments provide a broad characterization of Prakrit phonology and morphology rather than concise transformational rules in the style of either Pāṇini's grammar of Sanskrit or later grammars of Prakrit.[14]

The most important, and to all appearances the most influential, idea in Harivṛddha's fragments is the "metagrammatical" classification of Prakrit itself, which I discuss later. These verses also show, however, that knowledge of Prakrit was never limited to knowledge of the forms of the Prakrit language, but was always oriented toward literary practice. One verse of Harivṛddha enumerates eight varieties of speech (*bhaṇiti*s), which largely coincide with what later authors would call alliterative styles (*anuprāsavṛtti*s).

Luigia Nitti-Dolci saw in the grammatical fragments an abortive attempt, on the part of Jain scholars, to describe the language in which the texts of their tradition were composed, in contrast to the language of secular and courtly texts. She saw Caṇḍa's *Definition of Prakrit* as a synthesis of this material, which was "neither abundant nor properly classified."[15] As I argued in chapter 3, however, separating Jain and non-Jain varieties of Prakrit—what scholars now call Jain Māhārāṣṭrī and Māhārāṣṭrī—would have made little sense to the people who actually wrote in these languages. Nor it is clear that the authors of these Prakrit verses were themselves Jains. What will become clear, however, is that Harivṛddha saw himself as defining a field of Prakrit literature rather than a field of Jain literature that happened to be written in Prakrit.

At least one text, *Mirror of Figures* (*Alaṃkāradappaṇa*), testifies to the existence of a discourse on poetics in Prakrit. Although it tells us little that we didn't know from Sanskrit sources, it may well be earlier than most of those Sanskrit sources. I believe that this text represents the discourse on poetics prior to Bhāmaha (prior to 700 CE), a period concerning which we otherwise have only fragmentary evidence.[16] For the moment, however, the position in the history of poetics of *Mirror of Figures*—and works of systematic knowledge in Prakrit more generally—must remain an open question.

We are on more solid ground when it comes to metrics. We have two major treatises on metrics written in Prakrit, Virahāṅka's *Collection of Mora- and Syllable-Counting Meters* and Svayambhū's *Meters,* and both refer to a handful of earlier authors. Svayambhū lived in the later ninth century; he wrote Apabhramsha epics about Rāma (*Deeds of Padma*) and Ariṣṭanemi (*Deeds of Ariṣṭanemi*). The identity of Virahāṅka remains a mystery. Velankar located him between the sixth and eighth centuries.[17] Although I cannot prove it, I suspect that Virahāṅka's *Collection* is an early work of the brilliant eighth-century poet, doxographer, and philosopher Haribhadra before his conversion to Jainism. The name Virahāṅka refers to his use of the word *viraha* as a "signature" (*aṅka, cihna,* or *lāñchana*) that poets worked into the concluding verses of their works. The only author I know to have used this signature is Haribhadra, but the signature *viraha* ("separation," usually of two lovers) is slightly odd for a Jain monk, and explanations of it in Jain sources seem forced. Haribhadra might thus have used the signature *viraha,* "separation," when he was young, and after his conversion to Jainism, reinterpreted it as *bhavaviraha,* "separation from worldly existence."[18] A possible corroborating instance is the *Prakrit Lakṣmī,* written in 972 CE by Dhanapāla, who would later convert to Jainism and write *Tilakamañjarī* and *Fifty Verses for Ṛṣabha.*[19]

Prakrit metrics is not just Sanskrit metrics in Prakrit. Although it defines and exemplifies all of the syllable-counting meters used in Sanskrit literature, called *vṛtta*s, its real focus is on the mora-counting meters that distinctively characterize Prakrit literature, called *jāti*s; this dual aspect is referenced in Virahāṅka's title. Prakrit metrics defines many more of these *jāti*s than Sanskrit metrics does, and in fact many more than are actually attested in the surviving literature. Svayambhū in particular gives us some insight into the richness of Prakrit literature at his time, quoting from authors such as Jīvadeva and Śuddhasvabhāva whose works are otherwise completely lost.

A number of other early authors are merely mentioned, or briefly quoted, in later works. Unsurprisingly, many of those who made contributions to lexicography and metrics were themselves poets, as we know from the fact that other authors have quoted their verses or from the fact that they are identified by literary noms de plume. One author whom Svayambhū quotes is Abhimānacihna ("the poet who used the signature 'pride'"), the author of a lexicon in Prakrit cited frequently by Hemacandra. These quotations confirm the impression that the systematic knowledge of Prakrit developed alongside Prakrit literary practice throughout the first millennium CE.

As the distance from its original circumstances of composition grew, and as it was rearranged, integrated into other texts, and lost, this earlier material was imagined to belong to "time out of mind," and was accordingly reattributed to sages of the mythical past.[20] Sometimes such reattribution occurred even in the absence of temporal distance, for reasons that are still difficult to determine. The best-known case is that of the *Vālmīki Sūtras,* a grammar of Prakrit that was, as the name implies, thought to have been composed by the semi-mythical author of the *Rāmāyaṇa.* A. N. Upadhye has argued convincingly that these *Vālmīki Sūtras* are none other than the *sūtras* composed by the Jain monk Trivikramadeva in the thirteenth century, which were reattributed to Vālmīki by later Hindu authors.[21]

Another example is Pāṇini. Starting, it seems, with Bhoja in the eleventh century, a number of authors believed that the most influential Sanskrit grammarian had also written a grammar of Prakrit. The few quotations from this alleged grammar make it hard to believe that its author was Pāṇini, who in any case lived several centuries before people began thinking about Prakrit as a language.[22]

The attributions to Pāṇini and Vālmīki locate the origins of Prakrit knowledge in the founding figures of the Sanskrit grammatical and literary traditions respectively, and thus affirm the prevalent understanding of Sanskrit and Prakrit by making them literally cognate traditions. The "eastern grammarians" (Puruṣottamadeva, Laṅkeśvara, Rāmaśarman, Mārkaṇḍeya) likewise refer to several mythical sages—Śākalya, Bharata, Kohala, and Kapila—under whose names various systems of knowledge circulated, of which only the *Treatise on Theater* ascribed to Bharata survives.[23]

It might be argued that the ascription of works of Prakrit lexicography and metrics to Sātavāhana is parallel to the ascription of Prakrit grammars to Vālmīki and Pāṇini, in that the author's celebrity precedes and occasions the ascription. The reason I credit the former and not the latter is that Prakrit literature was the basis for Sātavāhana's celebrity, whereas the others were known first and foremost for their contributions to Sanskrit literature and its forms of knowledge and were only associated with Prakrit much later. Further, there are deep connections between the literary productions of the Sātavāhana court and Prakrit forms of knowledge that either did not exist, or can easily be explained otherwise, in the other cases.

The earliest Prakrit grammar that survives in its entirety—or, as we will see, in more than its entirety—is *Light on Prakrit,* ascribed to the legendary figure Vararuci. The earliest and most widespread traditions about Vararuci make him one of the ministers of King Nanda, who ruled the Gangetic plain just prior to Alexander the Great's forays into India. He is, however, also counted among the "nine jewels" of the court of Candragupta II Vikramāditya. Several texts besides *Light* circulate under his name, most notably a one-act play called *Both Go to Meet* and a collection of one hundred gnomic verses. A verse commentary on *Light,* called *A Cluster of Blossoms of Prakrit,* gives Vararuci the family name Kātyāyana, which evokes—if it does not identify him with—the famous author of a set of critical notes (*vārttikas*) on Pāṇini's *Aṣṭādhyāyī. Cluster* is hardly the first text to identify Vararuci with Kātyāyana.[24]

From one perspective, then, the authorship of the earliest and most important grammar of Prakrit is thus beset with philological difficulties. The fragile originary connection between a man and his work, moving forward through time, collides against the will to remember otherwise—to reach back into the past and overwrite it, to reassign identities, to constantly reauthorize the text. From another perspective, the solution to this problem is ultimately not a judgment about the historicity, or lack thereof, of these crisscrossed traditions, but an understanding of the motivations, logics, and mechanisms of attribution. For these we have a parallel in the oldest extant grammar of Pali, which is likewise attributed to Kātyāyana (Kaccāyana in Pali). Centuries after the historical Kātyāyana composed his *vārttika*s on the *Aṣṭādhyāyī*, his name—and that of Vararuci, with whom he was identified—was attached to projects that sought to apply the principles and techniques of Sanskrit grammar to Middle Indic languages.

These projects can be seen as part of a broader movement to "liberate" these techniques, so to speak, from the tradition of the *Aṣṭādhyāyī*, with the goal of bringing to order a wider variety of language practices.[25] This movement, which propelled Sanskrit beyond its ritual confines into its new role as a language of power, started with *Kaumāralāta* and *Kātantra*, both composed in the early centuries of the common era.[26] *Light on Prakrit*'s debts to the tradition of *Kātantra* have been overlooked, perhaps because they are obvious. Besides some overlap in their technical terminology, the *sūtra*s of both works, unlike those of *Aṣṭādhyāyī*, are arranged topically. *Light* also puts its very brief treatment of nominal suffixes at the end of a chapter on "miscellaneous rules," and the section on nominal suffixes in *Kātantra* is believed to be a secondary addition by none other than Vararuci-Kātyāyana. Perhaps because of what many perceived to be his critical attitude toward Pāṇini in his *vārttika*s, Vararuci-Kātyāyana was the go-to sage for authorizing additions and interventions in these new non-Pāṇinian systems.[27]

The *Light* that Vararuci, as we may continue to call him, shone on Prakrit came from the Sanskrit grammatical tradition. His use of Sanskrit as a metalanguage, of concise transformational rules, and of technical terms and abbreviations sets *Light* far apart from the general descriptions of Prakrit contained in the floating Prakrit verses discussed above. It became the most popular and most widely circulated grammar of Prakrit, used directly or indirectly as a source by every single subsequent grammar.[28]

What did *Light* shine on exactly? It has repeatedly and rightly been emphasized that *Light* is not a grammar of Prakrit in the broad sense of "Middle Indic." The language it defines, as scholars were quick to notice, is substantially similar to the language of the Prakrit literary tradition, represented above all by *Seven Centuries*. Nitti-Dolci in particular insisted that *Light* is not general or extensive enough to serve as a grammar of a language, but must instead be seen as a grammar of a text. She speculated that Vararuci sought to describe the language of an anthology that was similar to, but not identical with, *Seven Centuries* as it has been transmitted to us. Its purpose, she claimed, was to assist people who already knew Sanskrit to compose verses in Prakrit like those found in that anthology.[29]

Light is a grammar of a literary language, but the crucial question, which Nitti-Dolci glosses over with her assumption of a text "similar to but different from" *Seven Centuries*, is: exactly what literature was composed in the language that *Light* describes? Against the common equation of "literary Prakrit" with "grammatical

Prakrit," there stands the fact that many forms either directly mentioned in or presupposed by *Light* are not attested in the extant classics of Prakrit literature such as *Seven Centuries.* This in itself is not surprising, because much of this literature has been lost. More striking is the fact that some forms taught by Vararuci have turned up only in quite early Jain texts. The best example is the past tense in *-īa,* which appears in *Light* but which was not noted in any literary texts prior to 1936, when Ludwig Alsdorf found it in *Wanderings of Vasudeva.*[30] Another example is the locative singular form of the first-person pronoun *mae,* which is likewise mentioned in *Light,* but which Anna Aurelia Esposito has only recently spotted "in the wild"—again, in *Wanderings of Vasudeva.*[31]

It seems very plausible to me that *Light on Prakrit* was composed with such texts in mind—not just *Wanderings of Vasudeva,* but romances in verse like *Taraṅgavatī.* It has often been remarked (starting with Hermann Jacobi) that Jain texts in Prakrit deviate from the rules established by grammars like Vararuci's, and this deviation licenses us to speak of "Jain Prakrit" (or "Jain Mahārāṣṭrī") as distinct from the language Vararuci sought to describe.[32] This label, which Jacobi originally based on Sanskritizing features of relatively late Jain commentaries and narrative literature, has since been applied to any form of Prakrit written by Jains. But as I noted in chapter 3, we need to be careful of overstating the continuities within the use of Prakrit by Jains and understating its continuities with its use by non-Jains. Forms taught by Vararuci that occur in Jain literature and nowhere else have greater weight in regard to the question of the grammar's target language than forms occurring in Jain literature and nowhere else that are not taught by Vararuci. It may even be possible that *Light on Prakrit* was composed by a Jain author in a Jain literary milieu, and like Trivikrama's transformation into Vālmīki, non-Jain authors found it necessary to reattribute the text to Vararuci-Kātyāyana.

Little can be said with certainty about *Light*'s textual history. Nitti-Dolci died soon after publishing her study, and her call for a "critical edition of Vararuci based on all the commentators and all the grammarians who have drawn materials from his work" has gone unheeded.[33] I doubt very much that Bhāmaha, the author of the popular *Manoramā* commentary on *Light,* is identical to the scholar who wrote *Ornament of Literature.* Vīrasena and Jinasena in the ninth century do not seem to have been aware of *Light.* Abhinavagupta, in the eleventh century, does refer to *Light* in a little-known passage where he glosses "half-Sanskrit" by mentioning the opinion of others that it refers to "Prakrit itself, defined in accordance with the rules pronounced by Vararuci and so on, and distinct from the regional languages such as Śaurasenī."[34] This is, to my knowledge, the earliest datable reference to the text, along with quotations of *Light* in the commentaries of Bhuvanapāla on *Seven Centuries* and Harṣapāla on *Rāvaṇa's Demise* (both eleventh century). Despite his reference to Vararuci, Abhinavagupta himself seems to have been more familiar with a lost work called *Illustration of Prakrit* (*Prākṛtadīpikā*) and Utpaladeva's commentary thereon, which he recommends to his readers. One might have expected Abhinavagupta to have known the *Manoramā* commentary on *Light* if it was really composed by the well-known scholar of poetics.[35]

One event in *Light*'s textual history, however, is worth remarking upon, since it signals a fundamental shift in the orientation of Prakrit knowledge. As Nitti-Dolci demonstrated, the "Prakrit" that Vararuci's *Light* originally illuminated was singular. At some point, however, chapters were added to describe Paiśācī, Māgadhī, and Śaurasenī. These additional chapters represent a pluralization of the category of "Prakrit." Previously, knowledge of Prakrit meant knowledge of the grammar, lexicon, and metrical forms of Prakrit literature. This was "literature heard" (*śravyakāvya*), poetry such as *Seven Centuries* and *Rāvaṇa's Demise.* The languages used on the stage, of "literature seen" (*dṛśyakāvya*), were similar enough to this unitary kind of Prakrit to have been considered variants or ectypes of it, and hence they never formed the primary object of systematic knowledge in contradistinction to the Prakrit of "literature heard." At first, we might interpret Daṇḍin's declaration that the languages of the stage should be considered Prakrits (discussed in chapter 5) as an affirmation a centuries-old approach that awarded conceptual and analytic primacy to Prakrit as the language of "literature heard," and in which the languages of the stage were somewhat of an afterthought. But we can also see it as his idiosyncratic solution to the problem of whether literary Prakrit, used in "literature heard," could be identified in some sense with the languages of "literature seen," and thus whether Prakrit was a species or a genus. The difference is that genera do not have specific characteristics, and in this case, they do not have grammars. The redactors of *Light on Prakrit* clearly considered it a genus. What had earlier been "Prakrit" was reconfigured, in accordance with the logic of regional specificity that governed the languages of the stage, as the species "Mahārāṣṭrī": crucially, the word appears in the expanded version of Vararuci's *Light,* but not the older version. Pluralization meant that Prakrit, now Mahārāṣṭrī, no longer stood above the other languages, but alongside them.

The languages added to *Light* confirm that the pluralization of Prakrit implied thereby is the exact same pluralization evident in Rudraṭa's expansion of the archetypal schema from three to six languages, which, as noted in chapter 5, attends a shift in analytical focus from monoglossic to polyglossic forms. From this point on, knowledge of Prakrit had a very different shape. It was, first of all, knowledge of "the Prakrits"; second, it was primarily but not exclusively oriented toward the theater; third, it formed part of an increasingly large and interconnected body of literary-cultural knowledge, at the apex of which was poetics (*alaṅkāraśāstra*).

It was in this context that Hemacandra compiled his grammar of the "six languages" around the middle of the twelfth century. To understand Hemacandra's position in the history of Prakrit grammar, it is useful to pair him with another twelfth-century scholar, Puruṣottamadeva. Hemacandra was a Śvetāmbara Jain monk who spent most of his career at the Cāḷukya court of Aṇahilavāda, in the north of today's Gujarat, patronized first by Jayasiṃha and then by Kumārapāla. His works span, and in many ways define the boundaries of, the totality of literary-cultural knowledge; he is known as *kalikālasarvajña,* "an omniscient of the Kali age." And he was, according to George Grierson, the founding figure of the "Western School" of Prakrit grammar. Puruṣottamadeva represents the "Eastern School," which Grierson traces back to Vararuci. He was a Buddhist from eastern India. Besides his *Grammar of Prakrit,* he wrote a large number of Sanskrit lexicons and a commentary on Pāṇini's *Aṣṭādhyāyī.*[36]

For both Hemacandra and Puruṣottamadeva, the care of Prakrit was part of the care of language, and this care in turn had much stronger links to a cosmopolitan literary and intellectual culture than it did to the particular religious traditions with which Hemacandra and Puruṣottama were affiliated. Hemacandra offers only a few comments about the specific features of the language of Jain scriptures—*ārṣa* Prakrit, as he calls it—in comparison to the language of poetry, which he quotes in abundance.[37]

Scholars have justly criticized Grierson's idea that there existed two separate "schools" of Prakrit grammar, one prevalent in the east and one in the west.[38] The curious persistence of Grierson's historiography warrants a longer critique, but three main problems can be summarized here. The first is the very idea of a "school." If it means a fixed set of core doctrines that are elaborated and defended by its members, and if belonging to a school means self-consciously identifying with it to the exclusion of other schools, then there have never been "schools" of Prakrit grammar. Grierson's "schools" are made up of authors who tend to rely on common sources, and thus a more appropriate term—although still problematic for reasons discussed below—is "traditions." The second is the idea that these schools were regional. For Grierson, the regionality of these schools was not simply a question of where their authors are located on a map, but a promise, which turned out to be false, that these schools would address the linguistic particularities of their respective regions. Besides this false equivalence between an author's regionality and the regionality of the language he describes, Grierson also constructed a false equivalence between the regionality of a tradition and the regionality of its sources. There are authors whose works are transmitted only in eastern India, among them Puruṣottama, Rāmaśarman, and Mārkaṇḍeya. But this does not imply that their principal source, Vararuci, came from eastern India as well, since his work was known everywhere from Kashmir to Kerala. The final problem is use of the figure of "two schools" to structure the history of Prakrit grammar. This figure creates the false impression that two schools developed in parallel and in isolation from each other. But all of the "western" grammarians discussed by Grierson relied directly or indirectly upon the "eastern" *Light on Prakrit,* and "eastern" writers like Mārkaṇḍeya relied heavily on the "western" Hemacandra. The differences between the "western" Hemacandra and the "eastern" Puruṣottama, for example, largely reflect differences in how this source material has been refashioned; they do not do not amount to a radically different theories of Prakrit or radically different descriptions of the language.

In defense of Grierson's theory, however, it must be admitted that Puruṣottama, Rāmaśarman, and Mārkaṇḍeya constitute a somewhat separate and localized tradition. They were much more concerned with the languages used on the stage, and although they incorporate Vararuci's grammar in its entirety, they appear to have utilized a larger body of early material on this subject than Hemacandra or his followers had access to. All of them operate with a top-level classification of *bhāṣās*, *vibhāṣās*, *apabhraṃśas*, and *paiśācikas* that appears to be an elaboration (by Kohala?) of the schema we find in Bharata's *Treatise on Theater.* But they also refer to authors, foremost among whom is Śākalya or Śākalya-Māṇḍavya, whose account was closely related to the one given in *Treatise on Theater.*[39]

The history I have reconstructed for the systematic knowledge of Prakrit prior to Hemacandra can be articulated into three phases. In the final phase, Prakrit and Sanskrit are both objects of the same systematic knowledge. Prakrit needs to be accessed through Sanskrit: in the case of Hemacandra's grammar, this literally meant getting through seven books of Sanskrit grammar for the treatment of Prakrit in the eighth. In this phase Prakrit is a container and template for a multiplicity of languages that occur in the domain of theater or "literature seen," where these languages co-occur with Sanskrit.

In the preceding phase, Prakrit and Sanskrit exist in their respective traditions of "literature heard," and they are each objects of separate discourses of knowledge. These discourses themselves, however, are articulated in Sanskrit through the conventions of the Sanskrit grammatical tradition. This is the phase in which Sanskrit forms of knowledge are deployed in order to fully account for Prakrit difference, and it is best represented by the original version of *Light on Prakrit.*

In the earliest recoverable phase, knowledge of Prakrit is articulated in Prakrit and without much reference to Sanskrit forms of knowledge. As an example, sometimes the same metrical forms that are used in Sanskrit and treated in Sanskrit metrical treatises are defined somewhat differently in Prakrit metrical treatises. It was in this phase that Prakrit difference was first enunciated under the category of "the regional" (*deśī*), and knowledge of Prakrit was thus articulated under this name (*deśīśāstra*). A fitting representative of this phase is Harivṛddha, but it encompasses almost the entire discourse of metrics (Virahāṅka, Svayambhū) and lexicography (Dhanapāla) prior to Hemacandra.

These phases do not, of course, divide the history of Prakrit knowledge into discrete and non-overlapping segments. Instead they represent different ways of constituting Prakrit as an object of knowledge. The logic of one phase can, and often does, continue into subsequent phases: this is exemplified by the chapters added to *Light on Prakrit,* or by the stray rules in Caṇḍa's *Definition of Prakrit* that brusquely characterize other varieties of Prakrit. These "phases" might even be differentiated more by audience than by time: as Nitti-Dolci emphasized, works like *Light* were intended for an audience whose knowledge of Prakrit was mediated by Sanskrit, whereas the works that I assign to the first phase were largely intended for people who read and engaged with Prakrit literature without the mediation of Sanskrit. By describing them as "phases," I mean to evoke a model of additive development, in which knowledge is received, revised, and reenunciated, rather than the Griersonian model of spontaneous generation, in which the entirety of a tradition's content and principles are present at the moment of its foundation.[40] An important feature of my additive model is that the concepts of the earlier phase are foundational concepts upon which the whole subsequent history of the discourse depends.

GRAMMAR, METAGRAMMAR AND THE REGIONAL

One of these foundational concepts is the division of Prakrit into three categories. The earliest discussions of such a division occur in Bharata's *Treatise on Theater* and in Daṇḍin's *Mirror of Literature,* and luckily Daṇḍin's tenth-century commentator Ratnaśrījñāna quotes several passages from Harivṛddha on the subject.[41] All of these discussions imply what Ratnaśrījñāna makes explicit: under this analysis, Sanskrit is singular, and Prakrit is plural. Its plurality, however, does not consist in the plurality of Prakrit languages such as Śaurasenī and Māgadhī, but in the plurality of its "modes" (*prakāra*), the aspects in which Prakrit appears in relation to Sanskrit. This point bears emphasis, because it might at first appear that Prakrit's plurality makes it an open-ended category for an endless variety of language practices, whereas in my view it has the exact opposite effect: it is a precondition for its precise grammatical description.[42] "Sanskrit-identical" Prakrit (Daṇḍin's *tatsama*) appears identical to Sanskrit. "Sanskrit-derived" Prakrit (Daṇḍin's *tadbhava*) can be understood as a systematic modification of Sanskrit. Finally, "Regional" Prakrit (Daṇḍin's *deśī*), has no perceptible relation to Sanskrit at all.[43]

These three categories refer, in all of these discussions, to the Prakrit language. Ratnaśrījñāna reproduces Harivṛddha's examples: *hari-* "Viṣṇu," *hara-* "Śiva," and *kamalā-* "Lakṣmī" are identical in both Sanskrit and Prakrit, allowing for some differences in their case-endings; *mahinda-* "Indra," *sindhava-* "of Sindh," and *bahira-* "deaf" can be thought of as "derived" from the corresponding Sanskrit forms (*mahendra-*, *saindhava-*, and *badhira-*); *bokkaṇa-* "crow," *kaṃkelli-* "Aśoka tree," *ciriḍḍihilla-* "curds," and *sitthā-* "bow-string" have no apparent relation to the Sanskrit words that are current in those meanings. These categories, however, are not limited to the analysis of lexical units. In principle, they apply to "all aspects of the structure" of the language.[44] I would press this point further: the paradigmatic status of language meant that the categories developed for language could apply to a wide range of other practices, and the threefold analytic could—and in limited ways did—function as a general analytic of culture.

A closer look at these categories shows how they are indebted to the analysis of language but not confined to it. One function that they perform is comparing two forms and converting the difference between them into one of three values. Crucially, however, the differences between individual forms are a function of the global differences between the domains from which these forms are drawn. They are structural. In Harivṛddha's examples, the different phonological systems of Sanskrit and Prakrit are what generate the particular differences between selected lexical forms. This analysis is exhaustive and non-overlapping: every single Prakrit word can be brought under one, and only one, of these three categories. The analysis can therefore be thought of as a way of characterizing the relation between a given Sanskrit "input" and a desired Prakrit "output," provided that exactly the same rules—in this case the rules of Prakrit phonology—apply equally to all inputs. "Sanskrit-identical" are forms to which the rules apply vacuously. "Sanskrit-derived" are forms in which the input and output differ, but in which those differences can be brought under a regular description. "Regional" are forms in which the input–output relation is opaque.

The three categories thus serve as what I call a metagrammar: a figure that simultaneously delineates the domains in which the rules can apply non-vacuously and characterizes the rules themselves as derivational.[45] A metagrammar presents something to us as an object of grammatical knowledge and tells us, in very broad terms, what that knowledge consists of and how it is to be applied. In the case of Prakrit, this tripartite figure programmatically lays out the shape that knowledge of Prakrit in fact took. Whatever was "Sanskrit-identical" was to be passed over, since it was already targeted by other knowledge systems. The goals of grammar and lexicography were to relate Prakrit forms to Sanskrit forms in those cases where the relation was not already transparent.

The original metagrammatical usage of these categories is very different from the merely descriptive usage that George Grierson and his students introduced in the late nineteenth century. Grierson used *tatsama* to refer to any word, in any early modern or modern Indian language, that had more or less the same form as the Sanskrit word, and *tadbhava* to refer to those words that had undergone some kind of phonological transformation. Because of the continuous reintroduction and retransformation of Sanskrit words, however, new categories such as semi-*tatsama* and semi-*tadbhava* had to be invented. The same language—indeed the same speaker—could use a *tatsama* form such as *bhakt,* a *tadbhava* form such as *bhāt,* and a semi-*tadbhava* form such as *bhagat,* each with a specialized semantic value.[46] In Harivṛddha's system, however, the rules apply without exception, and the only possible "output" in Prakrit of the Sanskrit word *bhakta-* would be the "Sanskrit-derived" form *bhatta-*.

The role of history is another important difference between the premodern and modern use of these terms. For Grierson, a *tadbhava* word was one that had undergone change with respect to its Sanskrit original, and this kind of change took place in history. The process that transformed *bhakta-* into *bhatta-* and then *bhāt* is the inexorable progression of the Indic languages from "Old" to "Middle" to "New." For the Prakrit grammarians, however, the three categories of course constituted a single synchronic system. The "derivation" of Prakrit forms from Sanskrit forms, too, was primarily thought of as an analytic procedure, with absolutely no reference to the historicity of either Sanskrit or Prakrit: these were emphatically not historical forms of knowledge.[47] The decision to make Sanskrit the fixed point of reference for the analysis of Prakrit had nothing to do with the priority, either in historical or axiological terms, of the former to the latter. It seems to have been motivated, instead, by the very grammatical principle of *lāghava*, or economy: if 50, or 90, or 95 percent of the derivation of a word can be accomplished by referring to knowledge systems that already exist, why duplicate the effort?

This is not to say that premodern Indians were incapable of thinking about their language practices in historical terms, as some have argued.[48] In a famous passage, Namisādhu declares that Prakrit is *prāk-kṛta*, "fashioned first," and that the *prakṛti* or "original" from which it derives is not Sanskrit but "the innate faculty of speech of all living beings without being refined by grammar and so on."[49] Hemacandra, too, refers to Prakrit as "without a beginning."[50] Yet both authors happily define Prakrit and its subvarieties in reference to Sanskrit.[51] Hemacandra makes it clear that his analysis of Prakrit starts from Sanskrit at the beginning of the Prakrit section of his grammar:[52]

> The original [*prakṛti*] is Sanskrit, and Prakrit is so called because it either "originates in" or "comes from" Sanskrit.[53] Prakrit is introduced as a topic immediately after Sanskrit. And providing rules for Prakrit immediately after Sanskrit has the purpose of indicating that the rules given here pertain only to Prakrit that has its origin [*yoni*] in Sanskrit words, which are either fully formed or not, and not to Regional Prakrit. Sanskrit-identical Prakrit, however, is already known from the rules on Sanskrit. Further, the stems, affixes, genders, case assignments, ways of forming compounds, technical terms, and so on are the same for Prakrit as they are for Sanskrit.

Hemacandra saw no contradiction between his belief in the eternality of Prakrit and his use of metagrammatical categories that made Sanskrit the standard of comparison. These categories allowed him to systematically divide up the realm of Prakrit knowledge more than any previous author had. He treats of "Sanskrit-derived" words in his grammar and generally defines "Regional" words in a separate lexicon, the *Garland of Regional Nouns.*

Such an approach requires comparison between two linguistic domains, but one of them, the "original," is named in the very categories, while the other, Prakrit, is merely implied. But the metagrammatical categories did serve to characterize

Prakrit as a language, insofar as it was distinguished from Sanskrit both by its transformational rules and by the mysterious category of the "regional." Prakrit knowledge, too, was distinctively constituted by its concern with regional practices. An important rule of Vararuci's *Light on Prakrit* introduces certain words as whole-cloth substitutes for Sanskrit words. When commenting on this rule, Vasantarāja notes an alternative classification of Prakrit words into "imitations" (*anukārin*) and "transformations" (*vikārin*) of the corresponding Sanskrit words, which roughly map onto the categories of "Sanskrit-identical" and "Sanskrit-derived." Vasantarāja rejects this classification precisely because it fails to account for those words which are "known with utter certainty to be Prakrit" but are neither identical with nor derived from Sanskrit words.[54]

The regional came to characterize Prakrit and its forms of knowledge in two different ways, to the mild confusion and frustration of modern scholars.[55]

On the one hand, "the regional" is a purely negative concept: it is what is left over when the Sanskrit-identical and Sanskrit-derived portions of the lexicon are sifted out. This is the concept that underlies Hemacandra's *Garland of Regional Nouns* (*Deśīnāmamālā*), which organizes and defines the words that are left over (*avaśiṣyante*) because they cannot be properly formed by the rules enunciated in his grammar.[56] This does not mean that all of the words collected in Hemacandra's lexicon cannot, in principle or in practice, be derived from Sanskrit words. The lexicography of the regional was emphatically not etymology, in the modern sense of tracing words to their historical roots. There are many words in Hemacandra's lexicon that can easily be traced to an Old Indic root.[57] What matters to Hemacandra is whether the corresponding word actually exists in Sanskrit as he knew it, and further, whether it is current in the same sense in which the Prakrit word is used. Further, many words have been excluded from Hemacandra's lexicon simply because he chose to include them in his grammar instead.[58] The significance of the regional as a negative concept for Hemacandra was precisely that the words included under this category were excluded from the positive space occupied by Sanskrit and Sanskrit-derived Prakrit.

On the other hand, "the regional" is a positive concept. It refers to the practices of a region, regardless of or prior to the analysis of those practices in relation to others. "The regional is defined," according to a verse attributed to Bhoja by Mārkaṇḍeya, "by what occurs in each particular region of kings and peoples."[59] This positive sense is more expansive, in that it should include forms that are identical to or derived from Sanskrit forms, since after all these forms too have their place in the practices of a region. Prakrit knowledge was knowledge of the regional, and it seems to have been the first branch of knowledge that defined itself by and concerned itself with regional practices.[60] Hemacandra refers to earlier works on Prakrit as *deśīśāstra*s, and his predecessor Dhanapāla referred to his own Prakrit lexicon as a *deśī;* similarly Pṛthvīdhara refers to a work called

Light on the Regional (*Deśīprakāśa*) when commenting on the Prakrit of *Little Clay Cart.*[61]

With what particular region was "the regional," as the distinctive element of Prakrit and its forms of knowledge, associated? All early authorities agree that it was Mahārāṣṭra that gave content to the regional as a category: "the regional is defined," Harivṛddha said, "by those words whose meanings are conventionally known in the region of Mahārāṣṭra."[62] On this vision, which very likely represents the way that the pioneers of Prakrit literature thought about their own practices, the regionality of Prakrit refers to its connection with Mahārāṣṭra in particular, and not to a general connection with one of any number of regions. This vision did not recognize parallel "dialects" of Prakrit, each associated with its own region. Or rather—as we will see below—it recognized such dialects but did not place them on the same level with Prakrit properly speaking. As we see from Harivṛddha's definition, the regional is defined by the conventional acceptance of words, or potentially any kind of practice, within that region.[63] Regional knowledge, in other words, has a distinct modality: it works by convention (*prasiddhi*), whereas Sanskrit knowledge works by derivation (*siddhi*). That is, rather than locating forms within a derivational matrix that lies outside of space and time, it locates them within a temporally and geographically bounded field of practice.

Prakrit is often called Māhārāṣṭrī in modern scholarship, and it is widely and mostly correctly thought of as a linguistic precursor to Marathi.[64] The territorial limits of Mahārāṣṭra as a "region" in premodern India were no doubt different, and of a different nature, than the limits of the modern state of Mahārāṣṭra. But even if we accept that Prakrit and Marathi are associated with the same region, the nature of that association is different. It does not seem possible to think of Prakrit and Marathi as situated on a single historical continuum. One of the unique aspects of Prakrit, which at the same time makes it difficult to fit into existing typologies of language, is that it was regional without being vernacular.

There are two senses of "vernacular" which it helps to distinguish here, and neither of them apply to Prakrit.[65] The first is a language practice that has an exclusive connection with a regional imaginary, which in turn serves as the basis for a cultural, social, or political identity. This way of thinking about the regional is deeply ingrained in the discourse of language in modern India, but it is almost completely absent throughout the period in which Prakrit literature first took shape. And it is particularly absent from Mahārāṣṭra, which was a cover-term for a number of smaller regions such as Vidarbha, Ṛṣika, Aśmaka, and Kuntala that had long been more salient, culturally and politically, than the macroregion that they constituted. Although the Cāḷukya king Pulakeśin II, in the early seventh century, could be described as "king of the Mahārāṣṭras," it was not until the Yādavas in the twelfth and thirteenth centuries that Mahārāṣṭra formed the basis of a vernacular polity in this sense.[66] The Sātavāhanas, who presided over the political integration of this region, never used the term Mahārāṣṭra, although the title *mahāraṭṭhi* in Sātavāhana-era inscriptions refers to a high-ranking official who administered a relatively large region on behalf of the Sātavāhanas, and this arrangement of shared sovereignty was probably the precursor to the territorial notion of Mahārāṣṭra or "the Mahārāṣṭras" that we encounter later on. But as far as I can tell, Prakrit was never thought of as a marker of identity, regional or otherwise, and hence it does not have the element of political salience that is so important to modern vernacular languages.

This, of course, raises the question of why Prakrit was defined in relation to Mahārāṣṭra in the first place, especially if this relation conferred no obvious benefits or consequences. I can only guess that, around the time when Prakrit was theorized, Mahārāṣṭra was one of those spaces—like the "Northern Cities" of the United States—which is defined in the present by shared linguistic phenomena that are presumably explained by shared social, cultural, or economic determinants in the past. The linguistic landscape of the Deccan must have been very diverse in the first few centuries CE, but the space between the Vindhyas and the Bhīma river might have formed a linguistic area with sufficiently self-similar patterns of speech, at least among people of a particular social background—let us say, suggestively, the *mahāraṭṭhi* elite that are so well represented in inscriptions.

The etymology of "vernacular" furnishes a second sense: the untutored language of the household slave, and thus a language practice that is natural, common, and prior to grammatical discipline. Clearly Prakrit, as the language of courtly literature and the object of an appreciable body of articulated knowledge, does not fit very well into this category. Many scholars, however, follow Namisādhu in arguing that Prakrit must once have been a "vernacular" in this sense, before courtly literature and its forms of knowledge arrested its natural development. In the introduction I stated my insistence on viewing Prakrit as a cultural practice rather than as a natural phenomenon, and here I can add a further argument for distinguishing Prakrit from the natural phenomenon of vernacular speech. The first person (so far as we know) to theorize Prakrit's regionality, Harivṛddha, clearly maintained that this regionality did not make it into a "common" language, since that was a different category of language use altogether.

To the standard three categories of analysis—Sanskrit-identical, Sanskrit-derived, and Regional—Harivṛddha added a fourth, which he called "common" (*sāmaṇṇa*).[67] A "common" language, on this schema, is the language of everyday conversation. This, at any rate, is what Bhuvanapāla means when he explains a word in *Seven Centuries* "by recourse to the Common," since he appeals to the practices of everyday people.[68] The idea seems to have been that the first three categories constituted "Prakrit" within a single system of literary practice, whereas the fourth category could be called "Prakrit" only within a different system. Consonant with Harivṛddha's distinction is Daṇḍin's statement that certain languages are considered Prakrit when they are used to represent conversation in plays.[69]

The implication is that conversational language is not considered Prakrit outside the confines of this genre. Within the tradition constituted by *Seven Centuries* and *Rāvaṇa's Demise*, Prakrit is not a "common" language that represents conversation, but the primary language of the literary work. This interpretation is corroborated by the fact that several vernacular grammars that adapt the classification of Prakrit include alongside the traditional three categories a fourth category of *grāmya*, meaning vulgar or unsophisticated, which seems to reflect the earlier category of "common" (see below).

The regionality of Prakrit is thus quite different from the regionality of a vernacular, either in the sense of a vehicle of regional identity or in the sense of a common language of conversation. It can be seen as a kind of regionality that is self-undermining for the following reason. The regionality of Prakrit is a site of impermeability to a general approach by which language practices are understood in relation to a given model: what you cannot understand by comparison with a model based on Sanskrit is, by definition, regional. This very impermeability, however, is the raison d'être of the systematic knowledge of Prakrit. Making regional forms an object of systematic knowledge, however, renders them intelligible outside of the region in which they are "conventionally recognized" (*saṃketita, prasiddha*). If Prakrit was in any sense based on the regional language of Mahārāṣṭra in the first few centuries CE, the literature and its forms of knowledge quickly became almost as transregional as Sanskrit itself. *Light on Prakrit* exemplifies this point, both in its distribution (it was studied throughout the entire subcontinent) and in the purposes that it serves: namely, to allow people to read, understand, and compose Prakrit literature, whether or not they were familiar with the regional language practices of Mahārāṣṭra.

This sketch of the tripartite and quadripartite divisions of Prakrit helps to explain the shape that knowledge of Prakrit actually took. The objects of systematic knowledge of the regional (*deśīśāstra*s) were the Sanskrit-derived and Regional aspects of Prakrit. Less obvious, but no less important, is the fundamentally supplemental, practical, and instrumental character of this knowledge. When Trivikrama began his influential grammar in the thirteenth century with the principle that "the formation of Prakrit should also be known from actual practice," he was simply making explicit a principle that had guided the enterprise of Prakrit grammar from its beginnings. "Actual practice," as Appayya Dīkṣita III would later make clear in his commentary on Trivikrama's grammar, did not mean the language of casual conversation, but "the usage of literary authorities."[70]

The "founding of grammatical norms on literary practices" in Prakrit knowledge, as Sheldon Pollock has noted in connection with vernacular knowledge, is the very opposite of the priority of theory to practice in Sanskrit literary culture.[71] This empirical approach, as well as the categories that Prakrit grammar provided, would have profound effects on the self-theorization of vernacular literary culture.

But in order to understand these effects, we need to understand what motivated the theorists of Prakrit to give priority to literary practice, and what the theoretical implications of this commitment were for the knowledge which they were giving shape to.

Early attempts to articulate knowledge of Prakrit were wildly unsystematic, including such rules as "vowels are sometimes substituted for other vowels." Even Vararuci's *Light on Prakrit,* despite its thematic organization, is more or less a list of Prakrit equivalents for Sanskrit forms. Nitti-Dolci hesitated even to call it a "grammar," since, in contrast to Sanskrit grammars such as the *Aṣṭādhyāyī* or even the *Kātantra,* it did not build up a coherent system from general principles: it outsourced the general principles to Sanskrit grammar ("the rest comes from Sanskrit" is the last rule of *Light on Prakrit*) and confined itself to a sketch of Prakrit's deviations.[72]

The rules that Prakrit grammar did provide were, of course, thought to be correct and authoritative—otherwise there would be no point in enunciating them—as shown by Mārkaṇḍeya's corrections to the text of Rājaśekhara's *Karpūramañjarī,* and Ghanaśyāma's tireless criticism of alleged mistakes in Kālidāsa's Prakrit, both on the basis of Prakrit grammar.[73] But the rules were not exhaustive. The conjuring word of Prakrit grammar is *bahulam,* "variously," which allows forms not otherwise derived by the grammar to be admitted as correct. Hemacandra begins his discussion of Prakrit with this word. In Vararuci's *Light on Prakrit,* it appears in a list of substitutes. Although in principle many of these words could be derived from a corresponding Sanskrit word (e.g., *dāḍhā* from *daṃṣṭra*), in practice it would have been tedious—even by the standards of Prakrit grammar—to do so. The eighteenth-century commentator Rāma Pāṇivāda remarkably proposes to split the rule into two, a trick of the Sanskrit grammatical tradition called *yogavibhāga,* and produces a rule that simply reads *bahulam.* He is quite upfront about the implications of this strategy:

> How then is the following usage possible: "then the Pauravas listened to Nārāyaṇa, who was standing nearby"?—Our answer: because the rule has exceptions.—You keep shouting "exceptions! exceptions!" for every rule. I don't know what your authority is for that.—That's true. But later we will see the rule *dāḍhādayo bahulam,* and there I will split up the rule, with the result that that the rule "with exceptions" [*bahulam*] is construed with every single operation. Taking usage as our guide, we can understand the words "with exceptions," and the grammar can derive anything that we want it to.[74]

The status of Prakrit grammar can be summarized as follows. It sketched out the basic forms which one was likely to encounter in Prakrit literature, even if "Prakrit literature" was somewhat of a moving target, and was "empirical" to the extent that it followed literary practice (*prayogānusāreṇa*). It could be used in a regulative capacity, to show that certain forms were incorrect, or to correct a transmitted text. It was not, however, held to characterize all of the forms that could possibly be encountered in literature exhaustively. Thus its regulative authority was founded on that of the literature on which it was putatively based. The resulting form of knowledge suffered, in comparison to Sanskrit grammar, from a "lack of rigor," as scholars were eager to note. But the comparison is misplaced, since Sanskrit and Prakrit grammar were different enterprises—*vyākaraṇa*, or "language analysis," almost never being used to describe Prakrit grammar—that were motivated in very different ways and sought to define very different fields of language use.[75]

PRAKRIT IN THE VERNACULAR

As I argue in the following chapter, Prakrit receded into the background over the course of the second millennium, and its obsolescence is directly related to the emergence of vernacular textuality. We can say that the regional vernaculars occupied much of the same space in the language order that Prakrit had previously occupied. There are perhaps functional reasons for this replacement: if Prakrit had executed some of the functions of a vernacular within the classical language order—as a counterpractice to Sanskrit, for example—then true vernaculars, once literized and literarized, could perform those functions just as well or better. But such an approach to the problem would need a much more detailed account of the functions that the languages performed, and even then I doubt it would be entirely convincing. What I will focus on here, instead, are the genealogical reasons, that is, the influence that Prakrit forms of knowledge had on the self-theorization of vernacular literary culture. This influence was profound, and it has gone almost entirely unrecognized.

To put the argument in a stronger way: the concepts provided by Prakrit forms of knowledge, and the particular relationship to literary practice embodied in it, were some of the conceptual conditions for the emergence of vernacular literature in South Asia. It is not that vernacular literature would never have existed without Prakrit—indeed an argument could be made that Prakrit delayed the emergence of vernacular literature by several centuries—but that Prakrit provided the conceptual foundations for these new literary practices, including the concept of "the regional" itself.

There are three general types of relationship that emergent vernacular literatures had to Prakrit. These relationships seem to depend both on the region and the linguistic distance, in Heinz Kloss's sense of *Abstand*, between Prakrit and the vernacular in question. The first relationship obtained in North India, where vernacular languages were more or less closely related to Prakrit and Apabhramsha. Here, the vernaculars were largely thought of as a further iteration of Apabhramsha, which was itself conceived of as a kind of iteration of Prakrit. The early history of literary vernaculars in North India is a very complex topic, in part because these vernaculars do not identify themselves in the way that makes them easily recognizable as "early" forms of modern vernacular languages. As is well known, this literature generally identifies its language either as a form of Apabhramsha (*avahaṭṭha*), or simply as vernacular speech (*bhāṣā*), or, particularly but not exclusively among Muslim authors, as "Indian" speech (*hiṃdavī*).[76] Making these literary languages into protoforms of languages that came to be known, named, taught, classified and described under the epistemic regimes of European colonialism has quite a few liabilities.[77] I will only mention one: this project puts a lot of emphasis on the "forward" connections, and very little on the "backward" connections. Thus Apabhramsha works are sometimes taken to represent "Old Hindi," whereas the vernacular poems of Vidyāpati are often claimed for "Old Bengali" or "Old Maithili," and the *rāso*s of Rajasthan and Gujarat are variously identified as "Old Rajasthani" or "Old Gujarati."[78]

Useful as these identifications may be for some purposes, they obscure the "backward" connections that these literatures make, often explicitly and deliberately, to foregoing traditions of literature in Prakrit and Apabhramsha. They also obscure the connections across these literatures, not only through their Prakrit and Apabhramsha models, but in terms of the circulation of textual material across linguistic boundaries. Within the region of North India, where Apabhramsha and early vernacular literatures shade into each other, Prakrit was available as a model of literary language distinct from Sanskrit, but this model was never invoked to produce grammars of the literary vernaculars. The only precolonial grammar of a North Indian literary vernacular is Mīrzā Khān's grammar of Braj Bhāṣā, written in Persian in 1676, with which this book began.

By contrast, the South Indian literary vernaculars—Tamil, Kannada, Telugu, and Malayalam—were described in grammars from a very early period. This difference may be due in part to the influence of the Tamil grammatical tradition, represented above all by the *Tolkāppiyam*. But in the case of the earliest grammars of Kannada and Telugu, the model was not Tamil grammar but Prakrit grammar. The categories of Prakrit grammar provided a way of organizing knowledge about languages like Kannada and Telugu that had come to incorporate a large number of Sanskrit lexemes but still included elements that were not derived from Sanskrit. We will see how vernacular grammars redeployed these categories. In the South, the vernaculars did not represent themselves as continuous with Prakrit, as in the North, but in place of Prakrit: the "regional" (*deśī*) was no longer a category of Prakrit knowledge, but of vernacular knowledge.

The third region was Southeast Asia, where, much as in South India, the regional vernaculars were completely unrelated to Sanskrit and Prakrit in terms of their structure, but had incorporated a large amount of their vocabularies. Here I will confine my observations to Java, since this is the only part of the region where we have some idea of the kind of cultural work that Prakrit, or rather the idea of Prakrit, performed. As in North India, no precolonial grammars of Javanese, or any other regional vernacular in Southeast Asia, were ever produced. But we know that Prakrit provided a general model of a literary language that was not Sanskrit. And it is relatively clear that Javanese poets thought of their literary language as a kind of Prakrit. They describe the translation of a text from Sanskrit into Old Javanese as both Javanization and Prakritization. Both occur in the preface to the *Virāṭaparvan,* which was performed in 996 CE at the court of Dharmavaṃśa Təguḥ: the king "partook of the auspicious beginnings of Javanizing the work of Vyāsa," which was also the "auspicious beginnings of composing the Prakrit version of the present story of the *Virāṭaparvan.*"[79] The use of the word "Prakrit" to refer to Old Javanese is relatively widespread. One text, in outlining the norms of poetic composition, states axiomatically that "language is Sanskrit and Prakrit," where the latter clearly refers to Old Javanese.[80]

One other region that was undoubtedly transformed by the culture of reading and writing in Sanskrit was the land to the north of India, including modern Tibet and China's Xinjiang province. I will skip over a discussion of how, if at all, Prakrit might have affected the course of vernacularization in this area, but of course vernacularization did proceed very differently here than in the other three regions noted above.

In the remainder of this chapter we can examine more closely the ways in which Prakrit forms of knowledge provided a model for understanding the emergent literary vernaculars. These forms of knowledge first of all addressed the foundational question of how regularity, systematicity, and grammaticality can exist outside of the paradigm of Sanskrit. We saw in chapter 5 that Abhinavagupta's pointed question "What regularity can a degraded practice have?" was answered in the context of the *Treatise on Theater* by a short overview of Prakrit grammar. And there we also saw that Kumārila Bhaṭṭa was able to criticize the Buddhist scriptures as "not even Prakrit" because Prakrit provided the model for a practice that was regular in its own way despite its deviation from Sanskrit. Secondly, Prakrit forms of knowledge supplied an analytic for the systematic comparison of Sanskrit and its others. Vernacular languages had no choice but to retrace these two major theoretical steps, and retrace them—rather than blaze a new theoretical trail—is precisely what they did.[81]

Vernacular knowledge takes its major categories of analysis from Prakrit knowledge: Sanskrit-identical, Sanskrit-derived, Regional, and in some cases, Common. As I have argued above, these categories are not simply descriptive. Just as in the case of Prakrit, they simultaneously define the domains and the character of vernacular knowledge. In Prakrit grammar, in an important sense, these domains were "given": a word's belonging to one or another of them was a brute fact, not a parameter that could be manipulated. In vernacular grammars, however, the differentiation of these domains had consequences for literary practice, in that an author could choose a word from one category rather than another in order to achieve certain goals.

One of the best examples for the reuse of these categories comes from *Jewel-Mirror of Language* of Keśava, composed in 1260 CE. The only two languages under discussion are Sanskrit and Kannada. Kannada can be mixed with Sanskrit, or it can be "pure Kannada" (*accagannaḍaṃ*). The latter can be analyzed, however, into Sanskrit-identical (*tatsamaṃ*), Sanskrit-derived (*tadbhavaṃ*), and Regional (*dēśīyaṃ*) components, an analysis that clearly demonstrates the "absent presence" of Prakrit grammar. Just as in Prakrit grammar, Sanskrit-identical words are a small subset of Sanskrit words to which the rules of "pure Kannada" apply vacuously, and Sanskrit-derived are those that can be related to corresponding Sanskrit words by means of transformational rules. Regional are those words that modern linguists would classify as having "Dravidian" rather than "Indic" roots; in any case they cannot be derived in a stepwise fashion from Sanskrit words. Keśava's discussion of these three categories relates to the conditions under which Sanskrit and Kannada words can co-occur. *Jewel-Mirror* notes that Sanskrit and Kannada words generally cannot join to form compound words.[82] These restrictions are not new in Keśava; similar guidelines can be found in earlier works of Kannada literary theory, including *Way of the Poet-King* and *Analysis of Literature*.[83]

Such restrictions were not based on a proto-nationalist ideology of linguistic purism, but on the recognition that the phonological systems of Sanskrit and Kannada are different. The underlying principle is that the same phonological constraints should apply throughout a word, including throughout each constituent of a compound word. Otherwise, the compound is "contradictory" (*viruddhaṃ*); it is, in other words, a constraint against word-level macaronism. But this constraint only applies to "unmodified Sanskrit" stems (*samasaṃskṛtaṃ*). If a stem is either Sanskrit-identical or Sanskrit-derived, it can be used freely with Regional words. In effect, a poet can use any Sanskrit word he wishes, so long as he follows Keśava's guidance, in the seventh chapter of *Jewel-Mirror*, in transforming them into words of "pure Kannada."[84] This chapter provides rules that are similar to, and must have been modeled on, the rules of Prakrit grammar that take Sanskrit forms as input and yield Prakrit forms as output.[85] Using such procedures, authors could mix Sanskrit and Kannada in a way that was validated by general linguistic and aesthetic principles. In order to constitute Kannada as a language categorically distinct from Sanskrit, but at the same time capable of absorbing its lexical resources, Keśava theorized it in exactly the same way that earlier scholars had theorized Prakrit.

Prakrit served Keśava and other vernacular intellectuals as a model of a counterpractice to Sanskrit: one that basically mirrored Sanskrit practices, but at the same time transmuted them into something different, and included within this difference sites of analytical impermeability or resistance that were gathered under the category of the regional. This final category, which constituted the exceptions to the rules in Prakrit grammar, became the principal target of the rules in vernacular grammars. Keśava's discussion of Sanskrit-identical and Sanskrit-derived words in the seventh chapter of *Jewel-Mirror* makes it clear that he understands the rest of the vocabulary of "pure Kannada" to be regional.

Around the same time as Keśava, Ketana produced *Ornament of the Āndhra Language*, likely the earliest grammar of Telugu.[86] Ketana invokes the same three categories, with the addition of a fourth, the Vulgar or Common (*grāmya*). His examples make it clear that Common words are not "obscene" words, as some scholars have maintained, but rather colloquial forms not preferred in poetry. The category is thus parallel to Harivṛddha's "common" (*sāmaṇṇa*). It is quite possible that Ketana actually took this classification from Prakrit grammars now lost to us, since he refers to such works—albeit vaguely—in his introduction.[87] Whereas Keśava's "pure Kannada" (*accagannaḍaṃ*) is a cover term for Sanskrit-identical, Sanskrit-derived, and Regional words, Ketana numbers "pure Telugu" (*accatenugu*) as a fifth category alongside the inherited four—but only to include the other categories, "excluding Sanskrit-identical words," under "pure Telugu" as a larger category.[88] And although Ketana gives examples of "pure Telugu" words separately from the other categories, it is unclear exactly what makes these words different from "Regional" words.[89]

Ketana appears to have understood by "Sanskrit-identical" any Sanskrit words not accommodated into the phonological system of Telugu; he collapses the distinction that Keśava had observed between "Sanskrit-identical" (*tatsama*), referring to small class of Sanskrit words that already conform to the phonology of Kannada and therefore do not require further transformation, and "Sanskrit" plain and simple (*samasaṃskṛta*). Whereas Keśava's "pure Kannada" includes "Sanskrit-identical" words, Ketana's "pure Telugu" does not. *The Wishing-Stone of the Āndhra Language*, ascribed to the eleventh-century poet Nannaya, but only "rediscovered" by Appakavi in the mid-seventeenth century, also uses the fourfold distinction between Sanskrit-identical, Sanskrit-derived, Regional, and Vulgar words. On the basis of this text, Appakavi defines "pure Telugu" (*accatelugu*) as consisting of Sanskrit-derived and Regional words without any mixture of Sanskrit words. For him, the regional is defined by what the Āndhra people actually speak, and can thus be further divided into two categories: "pure Āndhra words" (*śuddhāndhram*), presumably those spoken in Āndhra itself, and "Āndhra words of foreign origin" (*anyadeśajāndhram*), presumably words of other regional vernaculars that had taken hold in Āndhra.[90]

The strategy of reappropriating existing categories to create new spaces for analysis would not work for vernacular metrics. Vernacular metrics defined itself against a single but bifurcated tradition: Nāgavarman's tenth-century *Ocean of Meters* begins with the meters of "the two languages," Sanskrit and Prakrit, which are used "in all regions," before discussing the meters used "in the language of the region of Karnataka."[91] In fact the division is not as neat as Nāgavarman makes it out to be. The last section involves a completely different system of prosody, and consequently some of the meters that are particular to Kannada literature but nevertheless use the same system of prosody as Sanskrit and Prakrit meters—such as the *ragaḷe*—are treated in the earlier section. Nāgavarman's combination of two prosodic theories in one treatise is iconic of the "cosmopolitan vernacular" he is concerned to theorize, which combines the literary resources of both traditions.[92]

But there were certain features of the discourse of Sanskrit and Prakrit metrics that were conducive to Nāgavarman's intervention. It was modular from the beginning, in the sense that it accommodated two different systems of prosody, one that counted by syllables (*vṛtta*) and one that counted by moras (*jāti*). Although syllable-counting meters were widely associated with Sanskrit, and mora-counting meters with Prakrit, both types occur in both languages, and treatises on metrics in Sanskrit and Prakrit differ primarily with regard to the detail they go into for each class.[93] Nāgavarman seems to have considered the Kannada meters, which consist of "blocks" (*aṃśa*s) that count moras but in a different way than Prakrit *jāti*s, as a subclass of *jāti* meters.

There is, moreover, a close relationship—perhaps but not self-evidently one of influence or descent from a common ancestor—between the *jāti* meters of Prakrit and the *jāti* meters of the Dravidian languages.[94] These meters, in contrast to Sanskrit *vṛtta*s, are typically composed of underlying rhythmic structures that can each be realized by any number of combinations of light and heavy syllables. The internal structure of these structures in Prakrit and Kannada is very similar, and the major difference between them is just that the former and not the latter have a fixed number of moras. In view of these similarities, the opposition between Kannada, on the one hand, and Sanskrit and Prakrit, on the other, has much more to do with the regionality or transregionality of their respective literatures, as Nāgavarman himself makes clear, than with the underlying principles of verse construction. But if we were to categorize meters according to their underlying principles, we would probably see a larger category of "regional" versification that includes Prakrit, the original and archetypal *deśī* tradition, alongside a range of vernaculars. This category would owe its existence, first of all, to the structural similarities between Middle Indic and Dravidian prosody, as well as to historical processes of "Prakritization" in the early phases of vernacular textuality. The *kanda*, the most popular meter of early Kannada literature, is an example of the latter, as it derives transparently from the Prakrit *skandhaka*. The *ragaḷe*, strongly reminiscent of Apabhramsha meters, may be an example of the first, unless it is actually derived from Apabhramsha models.

By way of summary, we may say that the metagrammatical categories so widely invoked in the enterprise of vernacular self-theorization were borrowed from

Prakrit, and that this borrowing is one of the most important ways in which the Prakrit tradition, as a *tertium quid*, mediated between an established Sanskrit tradition and an emergent vernacular tradition. Since my primary goal in this chapter is a history of effects of Prakrit forms of knowledge, my focus has been on the conceptual relations between these traditions; much more could be said about the historical processes by which these concepts were transmitted.

What does it mean for vernacular knowledge to be mediated by Prakrit knowledge? It is not simply that the latter was a condition of historical possibility for the former, but that vernacular knowledge is essentially defined by a mediation between Sanskrit and vernacular forms. The primary site of this mediation is the domain called "pure Kannada," or "pure Telugu." The concept of purity is bound up in the modern world with concepts of genealogical descent that are not only absent from these domains but fundamentally incompatible with them: both "pure Kannada" and "pure Telugu," according to their earliest definitions, admitted words originating in Sanskrit, namely, Sanskrit-identical and Sanskrit-derived. Their "purity" consisted, rather, in the fact that they were brought under a single linguistic description. Words of any origin could be integrated into a "pure" vernacular through the mediation of a transformational grammar. Prakrit, I have argued, provided the model for this mediation, but Prakrit was not itself a participant in it: it served as a catalyst, and then receded into the background.

Prakrit's absent presence in vernacular forms of knowledge has become a simple absence in modern scholarship. One example is Lisa Mitchell's sketch of premodern grammarians of Telugu against the background of what she calls "the Sanskrit *vyākaraṇa* tradition." By this latter term, however, she really means "the Prakrit grammatical tradition," since the categories she describes are the three categories discussed above that constitutively and contrastively define the field of Prakrit grammatical knowledge and never had anything to do with the analysis of Sanskrit or the discourse of *vyākaraṇa* in which that analysis was undertaken. Sheldon Pollock similarly classed Prakrit with Sanskrit as part of a "cosmopolitan" tradition, in dialectical opposition to which vernacular forms of knowledge developed. And it is very true that Sanskrit forms of knowledge were much more important to this process than Prakrit forms of knowledge. The concepts and terminology borrowed from Sanskrit grammar in Keśava, Ketana, and Appakavi are all much conspicuous than those borrowed from Prakrit grammar.[95] But the specific connections between Prakrit and vernacular forms of knowledge have dropped out, and as a result, the latter are invested with a somewhat illusory newness. And while Prakrit was, in many relevant senses, "cosmopolitan," it also provided a template—one that was followed again and again—for constructing systematic knowledge of regional practices (*deśīśāstra*s).

The metagrammatical categories, and particularly that of the regional, were crucially important to the self-theorization of vernacular literature in Kannada and Telugu. But the effects of Prakrit knowledge on vernacularization were hardly limited to these categories. The notion of a mixed language was important to several vernacular traditions, above all Malayalam.[96] To all appearances, the earliest actual practice of composing in a mixed language in South Asia, and certainly the earliest theoretical reflection on the practice, is the combination of Sanskrit and Prakrit in Jain commentarial culture of the mid-first millennium CE. Jinasena describes the mixture of Sanskrit and Prakrit in his *Jayadhavalā* commentary (completed in 837 CE) as *maṇipravāla,* a mixture of rubies and red coral.[97] In explaining the word "half-Sanskrit" (*ardhasaṃskṛta*) in *Treatise on Theater,* Abhinavagupta suggests that it is a combination of Sanskrit with a regional language and refers to "*maṇipravāla* in the South" and "*śāṭakuta* in Kashmir," and in the same breath mentions the possibility that it is simply Prakrit.[98]

The case of *maṇipravāḷa* is a straightforward instance, but not the only one, of Prakrit creating a space that vernacular languages would fill, thus seemingly creating the conditions for its own obsolescence. This has led, in the scholarly world as well as in popular narratives, to the erasure of Prakrit from the history of language in South Asia, which is commonly told through the oppositional categories of Sanskrit and regional language, cosmopolitan and vernacular. What I have tried to show in this chapter is that Prakrit forms of knowledge formed the background for vernacular forms of knowledge. Similarly, Prakrit grammar has long been seen as a half-baked and flawed enterprise, falling far short of the theoretical economy and sophistication of Sanskrit grammar. I have argued here that many of its perceived failures can be explained by the purposes it served, its relation to other discourses, and the way in which it was elaborated over the centuries. Further, these theoretical and methodological deviations from Sanskrit grammar are precisely where Prakrit grammar, along with Prakrit metrics and lexicography, had the longest and most important history of effects: its concern with practice, its orientation toward existing bodies of literature, and the concepts devised for shuttling between Sanskrit universality and Prakrit particularity.

7

Forgetting Prakrit

sakkaya vānī buhaana bhāvaï
pāua rasa ko mamma na pāvaï |
desila vayanā saba jana miṭṭhā
teṃ taisana jaṃpaü avahaṭṭhā ||

—VIDYĀPATI, *VINE OF GLORY (KĪRTILATĀ)*[1]

SUMMARY

The previous chapters have examined Prakrit's position in the language order of India. I argued that Prakrit was not the endless stream of popular language: it referred to a specific set of language practices the beginnings of which we can locate, more or less, to the first century CE. It was around this time that a new kind of textuality emerged—*kāvya* or *kavva*—which was self-consciously expressive, in which the way something was said mattered just as much as what was said. This was a centuries-long process rather than a single historical event, and the impossibility of producing a precise time line has frustrated attempts to find a single "beginning" for the massive and diverse tradition of *kāvya*. Nevertheless, as chapters 2 and 3 have argued, the language practices of the Sātavāhana court had an enormous impact on the history of *kāvya* and on the shape of the classical language order. The inscriptions of the Sātavāhanas show that they created a language of power and were subsequently engaged in a long contest over what languages in particular would fulfill that role. They consistently, although not without exception, represented themselves in an expressive Middle Indic, and this language defined their cultural politics for centuries, even after their empire came to an end.

The literarization of political discourse we see in the inscriptions of the Sātavāhana era is contemporaneous with the emergence of a literary culture organized around the production and appreciation of *kāvya*. Although the connections between the two spheres remain elusive, the preferential use of one variety of Middle Indic in political discourse corresponds to the preferential use of another variety, Prakrit, in literary discourse. The Sātavāhana court had a major role in establishing Prakrit as *the* language of this new type of literature, at least within the macroregion of the "Southern Path" that they laid claim to. And Prakrit, in turn, helped to establish *kāvya,* or *kavva,* as an independent domain of language use by demarcating it from learned discourse in other languages. Of course, we typically think of Sanskrit as the preeminent language of *kāvya,* even in its earliest days. I maintain, however, that we should think of Sanskrit as entering a discursive sphere that was already constituted by practices in other languages, foremost among them Prakrit. As a result of its entry into this new sphere, it was both for the first time in its already-long history defined as "Sanskrit" in opposition to Prakrit and transformed into a language of expressive literature that was not necessarily linked to a particular religious tradition—a language, in other words, like Prakrit.

My argument in chapters 2 and 3 is that the "literarization" of various forms of discourse that took place around the first century CE—a process that many scholars have noticed, although Sheldon Pollock is one of the few to have named it and suggested an explanation for it—is inextricable from their "Prakritization." I do not mean that preexisting discourses were "translated" into Prakrit. On the contrary: the forms of textuality that emerged in this period were largely Prakrit forms to begin with. When Bhadrabāhu composes versified notes to the Jain canon, he uses Prakrit *gāthā*s, and he is one of the first in the Jain tradition to do so. When Nāgārjuna, who is reputed to have enjoyed the patronage of the Sātavāhanas, composes Buddhist philosophical works in Sanskrit *āryās,* he is using a verse form that originated in Prakrit literature. And above all, it is Prakrit literature that defines a large part—although certainly not the whole—of what it means for *kavva/kāvya* to be "courtly" literature: not simply produced at the court, but embodying a refined courtly aesthetic and operating through indirection, obliquity, and suggestion. The positive features of Prakrit literature—what it meant, on the level of phonemes, verse forms, and compositional forms, for a text to be a Prakrit text—have been explored in chapter 4.

Seven Centuries, a product of the Sātavāhana court, is rightly seen as one of the foundational texts of this literary tradition. I argued in chapter 3 that previously overlooked Jain texts like Pālitta's *Taraṅgavatī* are just as critical for understanding its history. The texts that survive are sufficient to establish that Jain authors made contributions to the burgeoning literary culture of the early centuries CE that were no less significant than the cultivation of Sanskrit literary forms by Buddhist authors such as Aśvaghoṣa and Kumāralāta. And although these texts are often shunted off into a separate tradition of "Jain Prakrit" or "Jain Māhārāṣṭrī," we would do better to think of a wider field of textuality that accommodates them alongside their Sanskrit and Prakrit intertexts. In chapter 6, against the common conception that views Jain Prakrit as an exception to the grammatical norms of Prakrit, I suggested that Jain texts may actually have been the grammatical norm.

The dichotomy of Sanskrit and Prakrit is one of the focal points of chapter 5, which surveys the various ways in which Prakrit was figured. I argue there that the representations of Prakrit should be seen as schemas, in the technical sense that they bring a variety of literary language practices to order by determining their relative position in an overarching system of representations. Sanskrit and Prakrit, which come to be used as names of complementary language practices at around the same time, are figured as identical but opposite, and co-constitutive of the whole of textuality. These representations determine Prakrit as a completely different kind of language than we are used to. It is like Sanskrit, in that it is effectively transregional, the primary language of a tradition of sophisticated and courtly literature, and cultivated by Hindus, Buddhists, and Jains alike; it is nevertheless regional in some significant sense, the language in which low and uneducated people are represented as speaking, and relatively circumscribed and minor in relation to Sanskrit. But this very minority makes it a useful indicator of the structures in which it is embedded: Prakrit poets, for example, almost always reflect on their choice of language in a way that Sanskrit poets rarely do. And insofar as it reveals the structures on which literary languages depend for their being and for their being-known—regimes of representation, of systematic knowledge, of discipline and practice—Prakrit gives us a crucial starting point for thinking about literary languages in general, in India and elsewhere.

Chapter 6 examines some of the forms of systematic knowledge that constituted Prakrit in greater conceptual and historical detail. Prakrit grammar is often treated as though it were an unsophisticated adaptation of Sanskrit grammar, but such an approach overlooks the important cultural work that Prakrit grammar performed, which was qualitatively different from the work of Sanskrit grammar. I offer a reading of the organizing concepts of Prakrit grammar and lexicography, and to a lesser extent Prakrit metrics, as the instruments of an unprecedented project of large-scale comparison between language practices. These forms of knowledge help us to understand what it meant for Prakrit to be "regional." It is the remainder of this comparison, but also its principal object; the regional is what knowledge of Prakrit is really knowledge of. With the first fully articulated theory of the regional in India, Prakrit discourses give regional-language discourses a way of understanding themselves in relation to Sanskrit, as we have seen in the case of the earliest grammars of Kannada and Telugu.

REORDERING LANGUAGE

"Those who know how to recite Prakrit poetry," says a verse that appears for the first time around the twelfth century, "are as rare as those who know how to make garlands of *kubja* flowers, or how to pacify a woman's wrath."[2] This verse harkens back to Prakrit's "declaration of independence" (W2, discussed in chapter 3) about a thousand years prior, but at the same time registers a new sense of Prakrit's rarity: not just of the practice of reciting it, but of the knowledge that skilled recitation depends on. This chapter will examine the transformations that Prakrit underwent that might underlie this sense of rarity. For something must have changed. Prakrit was an essential component of literary culture in the first millennium, with a corpus of texts that poets actively contributed to and that theorists actively engaged with. Over the course of the second millennium, however, textual production in Prakrit seems to decrease, the language becomes increasingly confined to Jain scholars, and generally Prakrit was much less important for thinking about the literary than it had been previously.

A contraction in three areas—textual production in the language, its public, and its significance—appears to diagnose a "decline." But that is not exactly the story I want to tell in this chapter. Decline narratives are always susceptible to a number of criticisms. One is their evidentiary basis. Especially in the case of Prakrit literary practices, with so many texts lost and quite a few still awaiting publication, it might seem imprudent and arbitrary to compare what is known of one period to what is known of another. A second criticism relates to interpretation. Does *Rāma pāṇivāda's* production of two long poems in Prakrit in the early eighteenth century constitute an exception to a general pattern of decline, for example, or should it prevent us from speaking of decline in the first place? And how in principle should we decide between these options? These questions involve a third criticism, which is teleology. The teleology might be on the level of historical narration, where phenomena are selected and organized according to their eventual decline, or it might be on the level of explanation, where phenomena are said to already contain in themselves the seeds of their inevitable decline. Although both kinds are defensible, defending them requires a commitment to a model of historiography or to a theory of history that we might not be prepared to make. We might wonder, instead, whether there are other ways of narrating what happened to Prakrit over the course of the second millennium than through the motif of decline.

There are additional liabilities in attempting to fit Prakrit into a narrative of decline. Decline might be gauged by the rarity, obscurity, or marginality of a phenomenon that was once abundant, prominent, and central. But Prakrit was always a "minor" literature in comparison to Sanskrit, and this difference was not accidental but constitutive. Even authors who treated Prakrit as a popular and widely accessible language nevertheless tended to present it as being faute de mieux for readers who lacked Sanskrit—and even those authors, as we have seen, usually went on to compose in Sanskrit anyway.[3]

Applying a decline narrative to Prakrit might thus lead to the self-contradictory view that it was *always* in decline. Yet this is precisely how the history of Prakrit is often narrated. Decline narratives force us to think about languages and literary traditions in vitalist terms, namely, as "dead" or "alive." As naturalized as these terms may be for us, their original use—and still their most common use—is to denigrate older literary traditions in favor of newer ones.[4] The vitalist metaphor also underwrites a certain historiography of Prakrit that I discussed in the introduction: the whole history of Prakrit textuality, on this view, is merely the afterlife—or perhaps the long-drawn-out death—following a hypothetical period of vitality that predates our textual sources. In the beginning was Prakrit storytelling and song, and writing turned it into a dead letter, a game for over-educated elites.[5]

The historiography of death and decline thus may not be the best way to come to terms with what actually happened to Prakrit over the course of the second millennium. In what follows, I will attempt to relate these changes—for they were indeed changes—to a reconfiguration of the language order: the transregional language order of which Prakrit formed a critical part, and which extended all over South Asia, but was succeeded by regional language orders in which Prakrit was replaced, redetermined, or otherwise pushed to the margins. Prakrit did remain an essential component of the literary-cultural knowledge that educated people were expected to master, but the purposes and actual uses of this knowledge were much different in what Sheldon Pollock has called the "vernacular millennium" than they had been previously.[6]

Thus I will be arguing that Prakrit was deeply affected by the regionalization of culture and politics that occurred at the beginning of the "vernacular millennium," that is, between the ninth and thirteenth centuries. Because the history of Prakrit is the history of the language order in which it is contained, I find the ecological metaphor developed by Shantanu Phukan more compelling than the metaphors of language life and death. We cannot say that Prakrit occupied the same "niche" that the vernacular languages would later occupy. The ecological metaphor allows us, however, to go beyond the functionalism according to which already-existing languages are matched with already-existing purposes, toward a model in which the languages and purposes themselves depend on a larger configuration of literary practices—the "intricate inter-dependencies and rivalries . . . of literary communities," as Phukan says.[7]

Since Prakrit was both notionally regional and effectively transregional, it is at first unclear what we should expect the effects of the regionalization of culture on it to have been. And in fact, there were a wide variety of such effects—not all of which can be unambiguously characterized as "decline"—and this variety ultimately resulted in the concept of "Prakrit" losing much of its definition and coherence. Probably in response to these "centrifugal" energies, a considerable number of grammars and commentaries were composed between the fifteenth and eighteenth centuries that synthesize, reorganize, and rearticulate what was known of Prakrit.

This chapter will first chart the ways in which Prakrit was edged out of the language order even while it retained, at least in some places, a notional place among the "six languages." The different processes of displacement provide a valuable perspective on the different processes of transculturation that are now often lumped together under the term "vernacularization." It is well known that Dravidian-speaking South India vernacularized much differently than the Indic-speaking North, and I argue that Prakrit must play a crucial role in explaining this difference.[8] The chapter will then examine the "centripetal" forces that reconstituted Prakrit as an object of knowledge, or rather as an object of locally differentiated knowledges: for in a very few cases, knowledge of Prakrit remained crucially important to the continuation of local traditions of devotion or performance; in other cases, it symbolized one's total mastery over the field of linguistic science; in most cases, it was the arcane science of a mostly forgotten literary past. The last section of the chapter returns to the theme of displacement and examines the transformation of Prakrit into the language of the snakes.

DISPLACEMENT

Prakrit once had a "place" in the language order of classical India. In the schemas that defined and regulated language practices, and especially literary language practices, Prakrit was situated alongside Sanskrit and Apabhramsha. Prakrit also had a "place" in the language practices themselves, populating the discursive worlds that these schemas brought to order. When I speak of "displacement," then, I mean Prakrit's displacement from a position of importance both in actual practices and in the conceptual ordering of these practices. I also mean to imply that Prakrit's place was taken by something else: some of Prakrit's functions were taken over by Sanskrit, while others were taken over by vernacular languages.

An example of Prakrit's placement will help us to understand what exactly it means for Prakrit to have been displaced. Around the beginning of the eleventh century CE, the Paramāra king Bhoja had a pair of poems in Prakrit, each about a hundred verses long, inscribed on the walls of a building that would later be known as the Bhojaśālā in his capital of Dhārā in today's Madhya Pradesh.[9] The first poem praises Kūrma, the tortoise that supports the earth on its shell. The second praises Bhoja for outdoing Kūrma in the task of supporting the earth. In these inscriptions we have, uniquely, the clear expression of a political vision in Prakrit poetry that is about and attributed to a reigning king. These poems, mediocre as their editor judged them to be, demonstrate the highly visible "place" of Prakrit in one of the most powerful and most storied courts of India. Prakrit was accorded this place by virtue of its status as a literary language—indeed, as an exclusively literary language—and not by virtue of its notional connection with any particular region, community, or religious tradition. And hence these poems also demonstrate the prominent role that literature and its practices were accorded in imagining the political. The prominent place of Prakrit in the physical space of Bhoja's capital merely confirms what is obvious from reading the king's literary-critical works, *Necklace of Sarasvatī* and *Illumination of the Erotic*, which together quote about two thousand Prakrit verses.[10]

The pair of poems at Dhārā is one of the very few instances of inscribed Prakrit poetry—as distinct from the Middle Indic that the Sātavāhanas employed in their inscribed poetry of politics—and most of the other examples are also from Dhārā.[11] Bhoja is also one of the last kings to patronize Prakrit poets, or perhaps one of the last kings for whom there were any Prakrit poets to patronize.[12] As a rule Prakrit, which entered history as a language of courtly literature and retained that status until Bhoja's time, was exiled from royal courts throughout the second millennium. There are exceptions, but as I will suggest below, these exceptions make the use of Prakrit part of a fantasy of a literary past.

The classical schema of "six languages," which Bhoja himself had adopted in his *Illumination of the Erotic*, remained the primary way in which authors and theorists crystallized the unending variety of language into a conceptually ordered set of literary possibilities. But as noted in chapter 5, underlying any such representation is a schema of co-figuration that defines languages in contrast to each other. For the classical language order, Sanskrit and Prakrit were the basic terms of co-figuration; Apabhramsha was a further iteration of Prakrit's differences, and Māgadhī and Śaurasenī were dramatic ectypes of Prakrit. Even an Apabhramsha poet such as Svayambhū (ninth century), when reflecting on the great river that is the story of Rāma, observed that Sanskrit and Prakrit were its two banks.

THE NEW DUALITY

Vernacularization fundamentally changed the schema of co-figuration. In region after region of southern Asia, starting in the ninth century, the dichotomy of Sanskrit and Prakrit was replaced by the dichotomy of Sanskrit and the regional vernacular. As shown in chapter 5, Prakrit provided the concepts through which vernacular language practices were theorized: lexemes could be Sanskrit-identical, Sanskrit-derived, or regional. Prakrit's two systems of versification, syllable-counting and mora-counting, likewise set a precedent for the introduction of regional versification practices into the higher forms of literary culture. I do not mean that the study of Prakrit literature somehow "inspired" vernacularization, but that when the will to "literarize" the regional languages appeared, Prakrit provided some of the key theoretical tools for doing so.

This model sheds some light on the difficult question of how the agents of vernacularization understood their own language practices. Sheldon Pollock has argued that the vernaculars were never (with a handful of exceptions) considered "Prakrits," since Prakrit was essentially a component of the cosmopolitan culture in contrast to which the vernaculars defined themselves; Herman Tieken has argued, in contrast, that "Prakrits" are precisely what the vernaculars were understood to be, since Prakrit was essentially a representation of local speech in a literary register.[13] Under the schema of co-figuration, however, a language might be thought of as "Prakrit" not because it was functionally (or still less grammatically) similar to Prakrit, but just because it was Sanskrit's other.

The examples of the vernacular being called Prakrit that Tieken has extracted from Pollock's book are important, but not for the reasons Tieken thinks. The first example is an inscription of 699 CE, which contains a date in Sanskrit and presents the details of a grant in Kannada, and notes in the Sanskrit portion that the Kannada portion is "in the Prakrit language."[14] Second, there is the widespread use of the word *prākṛta* in Java to refer to the language we would call Old Javanese, a usage that seems as old as Old Javanese literature itself (see chapter 6). Lastly, there is the statement of the seventeenth-century poet Ākho that "Sanskrit is of no use without Prakrit," by which he means his own Gujarati language.[15] These examples hardly suffice to establish that the vernaculars were, as a rule, thought of as Prakrit, although this was probably the case in Java. More important, they all involve a contrast with Sanskrit. Thus they attest to an idea of "Prakrit" as a counterpart to Sanskrit that was much more deeply entrenched than the actual practices of Prakrit literature. Not coincidentally, these practices are nowhere in evidence in any of these examples, which suggests that in them the vernacular is not figured as one "Prakrit" among many, but as the only possible alternative to Sanskrit within the textual cultures in which they were produced.

As I noted above, we need to be sensitive to the very different trajectories of vernacularization in different regions of South Asia, and we can use the representation of Prakrit to trace some of these differences. Kannada and Telugu literature, to begin with, have a topos of the "both-poet." In a passage from the later tenth-century *Ocean of Meters*, discussed in chapter 6, Nāgavarman refers to metrical forms found "in all domains" of "both languages" (*ubhayabhāṣā*), evidently meaning Sanskrit and Prakrit, since Nāgavarman contrasts them with the Kannada language and its particular metrical forms. But in several other examples, "both" refers to Sanskrit and Kannada. The poet Ponna, famous for composing the *Legend of Śāntinātha* in Kannada, was given the title "emperor among both-poets" (*ubhaya-kavi-cakravartin*) by the Rāṣṭrakūṭa king Kṛṣṇa III (r. 939–968), which the poet explicitly tells us was for his skill in both Sanskrit and Kannada. Ranna, author of the *Legend of Ajitanātha* in Kannada who worked under the Cālukya king Tailapa II (r. 973–997), would also style himself a "both-poet" (*ubhayakavi*). One further example comes from Telugu literature. The second of the "trinity" of poets who rendered the *Mahābhārata* into Telugu is the thirteenth-century poet Tikkana, who is described by his contemporary Ketana in the latter's *Ornament of the Āndhra Language* as a "friend of both-poets" (*ubhayakavimitru*).[16] In fact, none of these poets composed any works in Sanskrit that we know of. Yet the title "both-poet" refers to the capacity to compose in Sanskrit and in the vernacular, or at least the capacity to compose in the vernacular in a highly Sanskritic style. None of these poets wrote a word of Prakrit as far as we know.

From the later history of Kannada and Telugu, one could hardly figure out that a language called Prakrit even existed. The Vīraśaiva movement presented itself, and its language practices, as radically opposite to Sanskrit. Pālkuriki Somanātha, for example, opposes Sanskrit to Telugu as coconut to honey.[17] Peddana's *Deeds of Manu* begins with a praise of earlier poets, with the Sanskrit poets in one group and the Telugu poets in another.[18] The cultural logic is similar to that of inscriptional discourse in the first century CE (chapter 2): being recognized as a language means being recognized as different from another language, and as a result language practices tend to cluster around binary oppositions.

Whereas vernacular traditions of the South replaced Prakrit with the regional language in the schemas that ordered their literary practices, those of the North generally continued to employ the three-way contrast between Sanskrit, Prakrit, and Apabhramsha. Bhoja knew of a *Bhīma Kāvya* that he described as composed in a "vulgar language" (*grāmyabhāṣā*); tellingly, Hemacandra recasts this phrase as "vulgar Apabhramsha" (*grāmyāpabhraṃśa*), a phrase that simultaneously identifies the language with Apabhramsha and also registers some differences from it.[19] As noted in chapters 5 and 6, Apabhramsha was configured as the last stop on a derivational path that started from Sanskrit, and over the centuries, regional varieties of Apabhramsha began to develop and shade into what we think of as modern vernaculars.[20]

What I want to emphasize here is that as Apabhramsha was pulled closer to the vernacular practices of the North, its distance from Prakrit increased. For some poets, of course, Prakrit and Apabhramsha—even this newer, regionalized Apabhramsha—remained mutually constitutive. This was true of ʿAbd ur-Raḥmān, the thirteenth-century author of a *Message Poem* in Apabhramsha, who identified himself as a Prakrit poet. But the verse of Vidyāpati (fourteenth/fifteenth-century Mithilā) quoted at the beginning of this chapter marks an ongoing and intentional displacement of Prakrit from the practices of literature. R. S. McGregor translated Vidyāpati's *pāua rasa ko mamma na pāvaï* as "who does not grasp and relish natural speech?"[21] On this interpretation, Vidyāpati may be associating his language, Avahaṭṭha, with "natural speech" as signified by the word "Prakrit" (*pāua*). I prefer another translation, suggested by Tsuyoshi Nara: "nobody can understand the complexities of the *rasa* of Prakrit."[22] Vidyāpati recognizes Prakrit but assigns it no sphere of practice: the learned prefer Sanskrit, he says, and everyone enjoys the vernacular, which his own "Avahaṭṭha" approximates; the mysteries of Prakrit, however, are known to no one.[23]

TRANSLATION AND ABRIDGMENT

The Kannada poet Ponna claimed in the tenth century that the "poets who professed to write in the three and a half languages" stole all of their material from other poets.[24] After Ponna's time, however, poets in South India largely gave up whatever pretense they had of writing in Prakrit. If poets were concerned with Prakrit literature at all, rather than adding to it, they were concerned to adapt it to the new conditions of the vernacular millennium.

Two complementary examples of this kind of adaptation come from the Reḍḍi court of coastal Andhra around the turn of the fifteenth century. Pedakomaṭi Vema Reḍḍi or Vema Bhūpāla (r. 1403–1420) produced an *Essence of the Seven Centuries*, a selection of around one hundred verses from the original *Seven Centuries* of Hāla, with Vema's own commentary, featuring a word-for-word rendering of each verse into Sanskrit (a *chāyā* or "shadow").[25] Vema might have gotten the idea of abridging and translating *Seven Centuries* from one of the poets in his court. The famously learned and productive Śrīnātha is said to have translated *Seven Centuries* into Telugu toward the beginning of his career, but the text is now lost.[26]

In both cases, it was important to the authors to appropriate the courtly aesthetic of *Seven Centuries*, but doing so required transposing it into either Sanskrit or Telugu. Vema tells us, at the beginning of the *Essence*, that "he is that very Hāla."[27] Let us take up his invitation and compare the two kings. Vema's *Essence* is an abridgment of an earlier anthology; none of the poems in it—with the possible but unlikely exception of a handful of verses not found in other recensions of *Seven Centuries*—were composed by Vema or any of his court poets. Vema did live up to Hāla's ideal by generously supporting poets and scholars like Śrīnātha. But not a single one of these poets wrote in Prakrit.

These transcreations of *Seven Centuries* at the Reḍḍi court invite comparison with Govardhana's *Seven Centuries of Āryās*, produced at the court of Lakṣmaṇasena around 1200 CE. Govardhana's explicit goal was to "turn poetry whose *rasa* is most appropriate for Prakrit into Sanskrit," as the verse quoted in chapter 5 says. Although Govardhana's anthology is much more learned, allusive, and sophisticated than Hāla's, its playfulness and frankness—the *rasa* of Prakrit poetry—represent a departure from earlier traditions of lyric poetry in Sanskrit. Prakrit served a purpose in the Sena court, but as in the Reḍḍi court, that purpose was to supply an aesthetic ideal that could be creatively appropriated by poets working in other languages, and who would indeed redefine what it meant to write courtly literature in Sanskrit (in the case of Govardhana) or Telugu (in the case of Śrīnātha).

Even within the community of Jain monks, who took a special interest in Prakrit because of the vast religious literature in it, translation was one of the conditions for its survival in the vernacular millennium. Up until the turn of the thirteenth century, the Jain communities of North India produced an incredible volume of narrative literature in Prakrit, which remains largely unstudied to this day. After the first few decades of the thirteenth century, however, there is a precipitous decline in textual production in Prakrit and Apabhramsha.[28] The downturn is very nearly contemporaneous with the appearance of a rich literature in what scholars call "Old Gujarati" or "Mārū-Gūrjar," the earliest surviving examples of which are the tales of the battle between Bharateśvara and Bāhubali composed by the Jain monks Vajrasena Sūri (ca. 1170) and Śālibhadra Sūri (1185).[29]

The downturn in original writing in Prakrit also coincides with a remarkable effort to translate the important works of Prakrit literature into Sanskrit. There is a pattern in thirteenth-century literary production that strongly suggests that the stream of Prakrit was being systematically diverted into Sanskrit, on the one hand, and a rapidly regionalizing variety of Apabhramsha, on the other.

John Cort has drawn on Mahopadhyāya Vinayasāgara's research to sketch a "writer's workshop" in the Kharatara Gaccha centered around Jineśvara Sūri and his students, who revised and corrected each others' work.[30] Jineśvara Sūri himself (1189–1275) produced works in Sanskrit, Prakrit, Apabhramsha, and the vernacular, but it seems significant that he added a Sanskrit autocommentary to his biography of Candraprabha in Prakrit prose. His students rarely wrote in Prakrit, and Cort notes that this sets Jineśvara's circle apart from earlier literary circles. One of his students was Jinaratna Sūri, who wrote exclusively in Sanskrit. His first major work was a history of the four "self-enlightened" Jinas (1255), which probably takes its starting point from Śrītilaka Sūri's Prakrit work on the same subject (1205). His last work, completed in 1285, is an abridgment and translation into Sanskrit of a long narrative called *A Story of Liberation and Līlāvatī* (*Nivvāṇalīlāvaī*, now lost), which was in turn composed by the "first" Jineśvara Sūri, founder of the Kharatara Gaccha, in 1036. In the introduction to the text he claims to be producing his epitome for reasons of spiritual advancement, and that some people will be interested in "just the story" (*kathāmātra*) without the literary embellishment of the original. Jinaratna justifies his decision to epitomize an earlier text by referring to "epitomes of the *Tilakamañjarī* and so on."[31] The reference to Dhanapāla's *Tilakamañjarī*, which was written in Sanskrit, obscures the fact that Jinaratna's text, besides being an abridgment, is a translation.

Exactly at the same time that Jinaratna was reworking *A Story of Liberation and Līlāvatī* into Sanskrit, a number of monks belonging to the Candra Gaccha were doing the same to other works of Prakrit literature. In the middle of the thirteenth century, Ratnaprabha Sūri made a Sanskrit *campū* out of Uddyotana Sūri's Prakrit *Kuvalayamālā*. In 1265, Munideva created a Sanskrit epitome of

Devacandra's Prakrit *Deeds of Śāntinātha.* And in 1268, Pradyumna Sūri created a Sanskrit epitome of Haribhadra Sūri's *Story of Samarāditya.* Pradyumna had actually edited Ratnaprabha's and Munideva's epitomes, and made corrections to some Prakrit manuscripts currently kept in Jaisalmer. This activity even more clearly represents a program of translation and abridgment, and as Christine Chojnacki has pointed out, the formal features these works share (e.g., the reduction of the text to about a third of its original extent) suggest that the authors were following a rubric.[32] And although Sanskrit works were also epitomized as part of this program—Dhanapāla's *Tilakamañjarī,* which Jinaratna mentioned, and Siddharṣi's *Endless Stream of Likenesses and Births*—the goal was evidently to make the important literary works of the past available to a thirteenth-century readership whose interest was primarily in spiritual edification, and whose knowledge of Prakrit was limited at best. The project continued into the fourteenth century, when Dharmacandra made a Sanskrit epitome of the Prakrit *Story of Malayavatī.*[33]

Similar to these transcreations, but probably somewhat earlier, is the abridgment of Pālitta's *Taraṅgavatī* into *Taraṅgalolā.* As we saw in chapter 3, the redactor acknowledges the difficulty that most people experienced in reading Prakrit texts—especially in understanding their regional vocabulary—as the primary reason for creating *Taraṅgalolā.*

This selection from the domain of literature is more or less representative of textual production as a whole. Nemicandra's *Essence for Gommaṭa,* composed for the Gaṅga minister Cāmuṇḍa Rāya in the later tenth century, is one of the last major works of Digambara Jain doctrine to be written in Prakrit. Cāmuṇḍa Rāya was himself a writer of Kannada, and patronized such eminent Kannada authors as Ranna and Nāgavarman. In subsequent centuries, most of the important Prakrit works of the Digambara Jains, including *Essence for Gommaṭa,* would be translated into Sanskrit and Kannada, or have Sanskrit and Kannada commentaries written on them. And this process was by no means limited to South India: John Cort has shown how Digambara communities in North India, and above all in eighteenth-century Agra, made an industry out of vernacularizing doctrinal works that were originally composed in Prakrit.[34]

These diverse processes of displacement, abridgment and translation all point to the precarious position that Prakrit had going into the twelfth and thirteenth centuries. Although nearly everyone continued to enumerate Prakrit among the three, four, six, or eight languages of Indian literary culture, its existence was increasingly notional. Literary production shifted from Prakrit to Sanskrit and the vernaculars: evidence for this comes from the Sanskritization or vernacularization of Prakrit texts, first of all, but also from the relative paucity of Prakrit texts after the thirteenth century. These new patterns of literary production corroborate a conceptual realignment: over the course of the vernacular millennium, the organizing dichotomy of the language order was increasingly not Sanskrit/Prakrit but Sanskrit/Vernacular, as attested by the topos of the "both-poet."

Yet knowledge of Prakrit, which Rājaśekhara considered a *conditio sine qua non* for poets in the early tenth century, cannot be said to have unequivocally gone into decline. Although some eleventh-century authors like Bhoja seem to have taken it for granted that their readers would be able to understand Prakrit, others—notably Abhinavagupta and his student Kṣemendra—consistently did their readers the favor of providing a Sanskrit gloss of Prakrit verses in their literary-critical works.[35] The translation efforts of Pradyumna Sūri and his circle suggest that there was a small and probably shrinking group of Prakrit experts in the thirteenth century who wrote for an educated public of Jain monks who could hardly understand Prakrit at all. And over the next several centuries, Prakrit knowledge would become expert knowledge even more than it had been in the past.

RESUSCITATION

One of the most careful and comprehensive works of Prakrit grammar is a commentary on Vararuci's *Light on Prakrit* by Vasantarāja, which was probably composed in the later eleventh century.[36] Vasantarāja named his commentary *Resuscitation of Prakrit* (*Prākṛtasaṃjīvanī*), tacitly recognizing that Prakrit was being displaced from the language order of India. But just what did Vasantarāja aim to resuscitate? Over the remaining course of the vernacular millennium, that is, from the twelfth century to the early eighteenth, we find a profusion of texts like the *Resuscitation* which reorganize, refashion, and explain the rules of Prakrit grammar as they were formulated by Vararuci and Hemacandra. Many of these texts were produced at important centers of political and intellectual power, and some were produced by the most learned scholars of their age.

Let us look at four examples. Lakṣmīdhara composed *Moonlight of the Six Languages* around the middle of the sixteenth century. He seems to have enjoyed some support from the kings of Vijayanagara, the most powerful polity in South India at the time.[37] *Moonlight* is simply a rearrangement of the Prakrit grammar of Trivikrama. And Trivikrama's grammar itself, composed in the early thirteenth century, is largely a rearrangement and expansion of Hemacandra's definitive grammar of Prakrit, presented in the last chapter of his *Siddhahemacandra*. The same applies to *Exposition of the Six Languages* by Bālasarasvatī, a Telugu scholar who lived at the turn of the seventeenth century, which also rearranges the grammar of Trivikrama. The third example is Śeṣa Kṛṣṇa, a Vārāṇasī-based intellectual active in the latter half of the sixteenth century. Śeṣa was the foremost grammarian of his time, and he is best known today as the teacher of the famous grammarian Bhaṭṭoji Dīkṣita.[38] He is the author of *Moonlight of Prakrit*, which is largely a versification of Trivikrama's and Hemacandra's rules (the commentary borrows wholesale from these two authors) but includes a number of other citations indicative of his wide reading. Śeṣa wrote it after his *Moonlight of Words,* a versified grammar of Sanskrit.[39] With the final example, we return from Vārāṇasī back to South India, and specifically to the Nāyaka kingdom of seventeenth-century Maturai. There Appayya Dīkṣita III, the grand-nephew of his famous namesake, produced a work titled *Jewel-Lamp of Prakrit.*[40] Appayya refers to Hemacandra, Trivikrama, and Lakṣmīdhara, among others, but his *Jewel-Lamp* is essentially an abridgment of Trivikrama's grammar. Appayya's text was evidently meant to be used alongside Trivikrama's, since his abridgments render the grammar incoherent on its own.

All of these three authors, living within about a century of each other, produced Prakrit grammars, but did so by rearranging, versifying, or abridging previous grammars. The only one to actually write Prakrit that we know of is Śeṣa Kṛṣṇa, who uses it as a secondary language in plays such as *Kaṃsa's Demise.* These authors all avow that their goal is to make Prakrit easier for students to learn. But why was it important for students to learn Prakrit in the vernacular millennium anyway, when the sphere of Prakrit literature had basically contracted to the women's parts in Sanskrit plays?

Prakrit seems to have taken on a symbolic significance as the capstone of cosmopolitan language practices that was only enhanced by its late-medieval rarity and marginality. Although regional literary cultures were increasingly oriented toward "the two languages," some intellectuals held themselves to the higher standard of proficiency in "all languages," which includes Prakrit in all of its theatrical varieties. Prakrit, even if it was used only occasionally, was still indispensable for writing plays on the model of Kālidāsa, Bhavabhūti, and Rājaśekhara. And it was, of course, equally indispensable for reading the classical works of Sanskrit drama.

There were several ways of demonstrating this proficiency. Two authors of Kerala, Līlāśuka and Rāma Pāṇivāda, composed devotional poems in Prakrit about Kṛṣṇa. Līlāśuka's *Poem of Cihna,* composed around 1300, is a *śāstra-kāvya,* exemplifying Vararuci's rules for Prakrit much as Bhaṭṭi exemplified Pāṇini's rules for Sanskrit. Rāma Pāṇivāda's two epic poems, *Kaṃsa's Demise* and *Uṣā and Aniruddha,* written in the eighteenth century, are not explicitly *śāstra-kāvya*s. But Rāma Pāṇivāda did write a commentary to Vararuci's grammar, and his two Prakrit poems can easily be seen as an attempt to put this grammatical knowledge to use.

Other authors demonstrated their proficiency in "all languages" by vying with Rājaśekhara, the dramatist who was one of the first poets to claim to be "omnilingual" and to hold this forth as an ideal for other poets. Rājaśekhara employed Prakrit extensively in his play *The Pierced Statue,* but later decided that he would go one step further and produce a play entirely in Prakrit. This play was

Karpūramañjarī, which is the earliest surviving representative, if not the earliest work altogether, of the genre of *saṭṭaka.* The *saṭṭaka* is a romantic comedy in which all of the characters speak Prakrit; it is filled with song, dance, witty repartee, and soft-core eroticism.

A handful of poets tried to outdo, or at least redo, *Karpūramañjarī* with *saṭṭaka*s of their own. These plays, and the specifics of their debt to *Karpūramañjarī,* are well known and need not be discussed here at length.[41] The earliest is the fifteenth-century *Rambhāmañjarī* of Nayacandra Sūri, a Jain monk whose other major work, the *Poem of Hammīra,* narrates the battle between the Cāhamāna prince Hammīra and ʿAlāʾuddīn Khilji in 1301. *Rambhāmañjarī* is also set in the heroic past, and its hero, Jaitracandra, is clearly modeled on the Gāhaḍavāla king Jayacandra of Vārāṇasī, fabled enemy of Pṛthvīrāja Cāhamāna (later twelfth century).[42] *Rambhāmañjarī* is about the king's infatuation with the young Rambhā; since their marriage is secured already in the first act, the second and third acts are entirely given over to love games and love songs. There is no hint that Jaitracandra will be betrayed by his wife and end up dead in the Yamunā river, as other sources tell us.

Rudradāsa wrote a *saṭṭaka* called *Candralekhā* for Mānaveda II of Calicut (ca. 1660), which its editor, A. N. Upadhye, did not appreciate very highly.[43] Around the same time, in the court of Mukuṇḍadeva of Orissa, Mārkaṇḍeya wrote a *saṭṭaka* called *Vilāsavatī,* which he referred to in his Prakrit grammar (*Sum-Total of Prakrit*), but which is now lost. In the early eighteenth century, Viśveśvara of Almora produced a large number of literary works, among them a *saṭṭaka* called *Śṛṅgāramañjarī.* The last *saṭṭaka* is the *Ānandasundarī* of Ghanaśyāma, the minister of Tukkojī of Tañcāvūr (r. 1729–1735).

Ghanaśyāma's *Ānandasundarī* makes it clear that the whole enterprise of producing *saṭṭaka*s is a form of applied philology. The composition of a *saṭṭaka* is an ostentatious performance of a certain kind of philological knowledge, namely, the knowledge of literary Prakrit, which had become rare, and hence valuable, over the course of the vernacular millennium. Ghanaśyāma's commentaries on the plays of Kālidāsa and Rājaśekhara reveal him to be an overbearing pedant, constantly correcting classical authors for failing to follow the rules of Prakrit grammar as he understood them from Vararuci.[44] It is a great shame that his commentary on *Seven Centuries* seems to be lost. His *saṭṭaka* gives him the opportunity to put his knowledge of Prakrit to use, and he does so with remarkable aplomb: one of the recurring characters is the poet Pārijāta, a stand-in for Ghanaśyāma himself, who enacts Prakrit plays (*garbhanāṭaka*s, plays within the play) and composes sophisticated Prakrit poetry on the spot. He enhances the *deśya* lexicon inherited from Rājaśekhara by "Prakritizing" Marathi words.[45] And the play is full of witty ripostes, ribald jokes, and puns. When the *vidūṣaka* asks whether so learned a poet as Ghanaśyāma is ashamed to stage a play in Prakrit—the same question put to the director in Rājaśekhara's *Karpūramañjarī* (chapter 5)—the director responds as follows:

> A heretic can't stand a sacrifice,
> an adulterer can't stand good conduct,
> and an idiot can't stand knowledge.
> A person stubbornly finds fault with whatever is hard for him.
> All those who are known for just one language
> are halfway poets:
> the one who is a poet in all languages
> shines in the world as a full-on poet.[46]

Composing in Prakrit is how Ghanaśyāma can demonstrate his philological expertise and, closely bound up with it, his poetic skill. It is not as if the vernacular millennium passed these authors by: Nayacandra includes Marathi in his *Rambhāmañjarī*, Rāma pāṇivāda wrote extensively in Malayalam, and Ghanaśyāma refers constantly to Marathi and Tamil idioms. Rather, they saw Prakrit as a vital component of the cosmopolitan literary tradition. They seem to be reacting to the process whereby cosmopolitan was collapsed into Sanskrit and Sanskrit alone. They resisted this process by attempting to resuscitate Prakrit. Whether or not they were successful, this "resuscitated" Prakrit was quite different from Prakrit in the first millennium. First of all, it was all the more deeply embedded in, and dependent upon, the traditional forms of Sanskrit literary culture: there simply was no Prakrit outside of a handful of theatrical genres (the *nāṭaka, nāṭikā,* and *saṭṭaka*) and the occasional epic (*mahākāvya*). Indeed, apart from the Kerala-based authors Līlāśuka and Rāma Pāṇivāda, Prakrit was exclusively a language of stage plays, and was hence even more strongly associated with the speech of women, children, and fools. Second, the use of Prakrit was entirely dependent upon grammars and model texts, and hence composing in Prakrit was a classicizing and even perhaps even archaizing exercise. The editors of these latter-day Prakrit plays have often remarked that they appear to have been composed in Sanskrit and "translated" into Prakrit, in the manner of an exercise-book.[47] Thus, as Ghanaśyāma's comment indicates, however much Prakrit is denigrated within the world of the play, within the world of the poet it indicates a commitment to a cosmopolitan ideal of literature.

We can understand the production of Prakrit grammar and of the competitively learned *saṭṭaka* as complementary tendencies in the later history of Prakrit. These are "centripetal" tendencies, as they respond to the dispersion and marginalization of Prakrit in the vernacular millennium by linking it ever more closely with a more central cultural phenomenon: namely, Sanskrit grammar and Sanskrit literature. They are also "centripetal" in that they produce a more condensed version of Prakrit, one with a very specific grammatical shape and with a very specific discursive role. We can see a related tendency in the production of commentaries on classical Prakrit texts.

Here we will consider just one example: the commentaries on *Rāvaṇa's Demise* by Pravarasena.[48] The tradition of commenting on this work goes back to the late tenth or early eleventh centuries, not too long after the first complete commentaries on any literary texts were composed (Prakāśavarṣa's commentary on Bhāravi's *Arjuna and the Hunter,* late ninth or early tenth centuries). The most striking feature of this commentarial tradition, however, is the number of kings who participated in it. The tradition begins with none other than Bhojadeva's father, the Paramāra king Sindhurāja (r. 995–1010 CE), otherwise known as Sāhasāṅka, whose work is now lost. Another early commentator (late eleventh century) is Harṣapāla, the king of Kāmarūpa. The best-known commentary is that of Rāmadāsa, a prince of the Kacchavāha family. Rāmadāsa wrote this commentary at the request of Jalāluddīn Akbar in 1595 CE.[49] The attraction that this text in particular held for kings and emperors is beyond the scope of this discussion, but as noted in chapter 3, it is not just courtly but imperial: it imagines the territorial expansion of political power through Rāma's conquest of Laṅkā.

The production of commentaries on *Rāvaṇa's Demise* was often a joint effort. Harṣapāla refers to the "experts in Prakrit" who helped him prepare his commentary.[50] But the anonymous commentary known as *Moonlight of the Truth of the Bridge* (*Setutattvacandrikā*) deserves special notice. This commentary refers to the interpretations of at least five other commentators by name: Sāhasāṅka and Harṣapāla, the otherwise-unknown Śrīnivāsa and Lokanātha, and above all Kulanātha. Merely collecting all of these manuscripts must have required a sustained effort in the late sixteenth century. *Moonlight* seems to represent an attempt, on the part of a group of scholars in Bengal, to produce a conspectus edition of the text—unlike most other commentaries on *Rāvaṇa's Demise,* it includes the text and a Sanskrit translation—and a commentary that reflects all of the interpretations that were then available. This is not so different a project from Nīlakaṇṭha Caturdhara's hunt for manuscripts of the *Mahābhārata* for his own commentary in the late seventeenth century.[51] The stakes of the project, however, were different: without a commentary that rendered it intelligible to a Sanskrit reading public, *Rāvaṇa's Demise* would never have been read at all in the vernacular millennium, and it might have suffered the same fate as *Hari's Victory* by Sarvasena, another Vākāṭaka court epic that is now lost.

THE LANGUAGE OF THE SNAKES

I began this book with Mīrzā Khān's statement that Sanskrit, Prakrit, and the vernacular (*bhāṣā*) were the three main languages used for literary purposes in India. Although we can now recognize that this statement belongs to a discourse on language and a realm of practice that is more than a millennium in the making, his description of Prakrit as "the language of the snakes" nevertheless seems to diverge sharply from earlier traditions. For neither the classical works of Prakrit literature nor the literary theorists who read these works closely contain such a characterization. Prakrit was represented as erotic, suggestive, sweet, and popularly accessible. But serpentine?

This transformation is one of the ways in which the story of Prakrit is brought to a kind of conclusion. For understanding Prakrit as "the language of the snakes," as we will see, identifies the language with a textual tradition quite different from the one we have been examining so far. And in reidentifying Prakrit, it replaces the older language order constituted by the opposition between Sanskrit and Prakrit with an early modern order in which Sanskrit and especially Prakrit are subordinated to vernacular language practices.

Ths story of Prakrit's redetermination begins in the middle of another story, which is still quite contested: the beginnings of vernacular literature in North India. Around the year 1315, a text took shape that posterity has known as *Prakrit Piṅgala*. It is ostensibly a metrical handbook, and the title implies that it was meant to do for Prakrit what Piṅgala, the author of the *Chandaḥ Sūtra,* had done for Sanskrit: namely, define all of the metrical forms that were in common use. Almost all of these definitions, however, are drawn from a long-standing tradition of metrical analysis in Prakrit and Apabhramsha, the key representatives of which (Virahāṅka, Svayambhū, and Hemacandra) were discussed in chapter 6. The examples in *Prakrit Piṅgala,* too, seem to be largely drawn from existing literature, and particularly from martial poetry of the thirteenth and fourteenth centuries. We encounter, for example, verses in praise of Hammīra, whose last stand against ʿAlāʿuddīn Khilji at Raṇasthambhapura in 1301 was related in Sanskrit and Persian narratives.[52] This contemporary poetry, however, is mostly not in Prakrit. Nor is it in the kind of Apabhramsha that Hemacandra influentially described in his grammar. Scholars generally call it Avahaṭṭha, a regionalized variety of Apabhraṃśa, taking their cue from authors such as Vidyāpati whose vernacularization of Apabhramsha was touched on above.[53]

Who wrote *Prakrit Piṅgala*? Piṅgala presides over the text, insofar as he was the "founder" of the discourse that the text transcreates. The discourse of metrics is what makes the sea of textuality navigable—this metaphor is at least as old as Daṇḍin—and hence the very first verse of the text praises Piṅgala as "the first boat of *bhāṣā.*"[54] But with this verse the text secures *for itself* the status of the "first poem" in this emergent literary tradition, and the status of "first poet" for Piṅgala, who is imagined to be at the helm of the ship. Piṅgala is also "marked" as the author by a *chāp,* or poetic signature, in many of its verses.[55] This, indeed, is how Lakṣmīnātha (1601) and Keśavadāsa (1602) have read this text: not just as a transposition of the discourse of metrics into a new tradition of poetry, but a first attempt to encompass, define, and exemplify this tradition through its metrical forms. Wherever we locate the beginnings of vernacular literature in North India, and whatever we mean by this phrase, *Prakrit Piṅgala* is at least an important and understudied part of this story.[56] *Prakrit Piṅgala* gets its moorings from Prakrit literature and the Prakrit discourse on metrics, and it cites a couple verses from classics such as *Seven Centuries* and *Rāvaṇa's Demise*. But at the end of the day, it represents a literary practice distinct from Prakrit, to which it has given its name: *piṅgala*, one of the two main literary vernaculars of the Rajput kingdoms.

A long-standing tradition considered Piṅgala, the author of the *Chandaḥ Sūtra*, to be a *nāga*. Lakṣmīnātha is more specific: the Brahman Piṅgala was the incarnation of the serpent-king Śeṣa.[57] For those authors who knew Prakrit principally from *Prakrit Piṅgala*, Prakrit was indeed the language of the snakes—or more precisely, of *the snake*, Piṅgala. This explanation, which to my knowledge was first proposed by Namvar Singh, also accounts for the fact that this particular representation of Prakrit is limited to authors who came within *Prakrit Piṅgala*'s sphere of influence, or equivalently, authors who wrote in or about Braj Bhāṣā: Keśavadāsa, Bhikhārīdāsa, and Mīrzā Khān. I have not traced the representation of Prakrit as the "language of the snakes" in any author before the seventeenth century or outside of what came to be known as the "Braj Maṇḍal" of North India.[58]

The identification of Prakrit as the "language of the snakes" depended upon the confluence of a number of processes that I have traced in this chapter. One is the role that learned discourses, and in this case the discourse of metrics, played in preserving Prakrit as an object of knowledge. Another is the displacement of Prakrit by vernacular languages in the space of literary possibilities, and the attendant rise of vernacular textuality and decline of Prakrit textuality. Taken together, however, these processes attached the name "Prakrit" to the vernacular language practices that were collected and theorized in *Prakrit Piṅgala*, but these practices were in fact quite different from the older language practices that Prakrit had originally designated. The language of the snakes was Prakrit, but a notional, mythological Prakrit.

The representations of the vernacular millennium have had an enormous influence on how people inside and outside of India view India's literary past even today. The duality of the language of the gods and the language of men leaves no place for Prakrit except in the subterranean world of the serpents, and all of its modern parallels—the duality of learned and popular, or even cosmopolitan and vernacular—similarly fail to accommodate this language comfortably. Yet these representations are themselves the result of a process of transculturation that fundamentally rearranged the language order in which Prakrit was embedded. The qualities that were Prakrit's strengths throughout the first millennium of its existence—its alterity to Sanskrit, its transregional circulation, its existence within the sphere of literary discourse alone—became its liabilities. What was once a "both-and" language become a "neither-nor" language.

APPENDIX A

Time Line of the Sātavāhanas and Their Successors

The standard nomenclature of the Sātavāhana kings, evident in their inscriptions, but not in the *purāṇas*, is tripartite: (1) a metronymic (Sātavāhana kings almost exclusively belong to the Vasiṣṭha or Gotama *gotra* on their mothers' sides); (2) a theonym (often Śrī, but sometimes including other Śaiva elements); (3) a personal name (almost always either Sātakarṇi or Puḷumāvi). V. V. Mirashi's argument (1975) that Śrī and the like are "prefixes" that can be added or changed at will should be abandoned.

For the genealogy of the *purāṇas*, see Pargiter 1913, whose sigla I refer to in the notes (generally Mt = *Matysapurāṇa*, Vā = *Vāyupurāṇa*, Vṣ = *Viṣṇupurāṇa*, Bḍ = *Brahmāṇḍapurāṇa*, Bh = *Bhāgavatapurāṇa*).

TABLE 2 Time line of Sātavāhana kings

Name	Approx. date	Inscriptions
Vāsiṣṭhīputra Śrī Chimuka Sātavāhana[1]	120–96 BCE?[2]	1
Kṛṣṇa	96–88 BCE?[3]	2, 3
Śrī Sātakarṇi[4]	88–42 BCE?[5]	4, 5, 6, 7
Śakti[6]	HIATUS	
Mantalaka[7]		
Sundara[8]		
Gautamīputra Śiva Sātakarṇi[9]	?–60 CE[10]	—
Gautamīputra Śrī Sātakarṇi[11]	60–84 CE[12]	8, 9, 10
Vāsiṣṭhīputra Śrī Puḷumāvi	84–119 CE[13]	11, 12, 13, 14, 15, 16, 17, 18, 19, 20, 21, 22, 23, 24
Vāsiṣṭhīputra Śrī Sātakarṇi[14]	119–148 CE[15]	25, 26, 27, 28
Vāsiṣṭhīputra Śivaśrī Puḷumāvi	148–156 CE[16]	29, 30
Vāsiṣṭhīputra Śrīskanda Sātakarṇi	156–170 CE[17]	31

Continued

TABLE 2 *Continued*

Name	Approx. date	Inscriptions
Gautamīputra Śrīyajña Sātakarṇi[18]	171–199 CE[19]	32, 33, 34, 35, 36, 37, 38
Gautamīputra Śrīvijaya Sātakarṇi	200–205 CE[20]	39
Vāsiṣṭhīputra Śrīcaṇḍa Sātakarṇi[21]	206–220 CE[22]	40, 41
Māṭharīputra Śrī Puḷumāvi	220–230 CE[23]	42

[1]The name is variously spelled (Simuka and Chimuka are the only variants in inscriptions, but the *purāṇas* include a range of corruptions and Sanskritizations: Śiśuka, Śiśruka, Śiśurka, Śikhuka [Mt], Śipraka [Vṣ], Sindhuka, Chismaka [Vā]). His metronymic is known from an inscription at Kanaganahalli [1] as well as a coin from Nevāsā-Paiṭhaṇ (Bhandare 1999: 186). Coins found recently at Kanaganahalli (Poonacha 2013) confirm that prior to becoming a king, he was a *mahāraṭṭhi*.

[2]Twenty-three years (Mt, Vā, Bḍ). His only inscription is dated to year 16.

[3]Ten years (Vā), eighteen years (Mt).

[4]The *purāṇas* refer to two early kings of this name. The first, who succeeds Kṛṣṇa, is spelled Śātakarṇi (Vā), Śāntakarṇi (Bḍ, Vṣ), Śāntakarṇa (Bh), Mallakarṇi (Mt). The second, who succeeds kings named Pūrṇotsaṅga and Skanda-stambhi (see Pargiter for details), is called Śātakarṇi in all accounts. The successors of the second are Lambodara, Āpīlaka (with many variants), and Meghasvāti. Scholars now tend to accept the existence of only one early king of this name (cf. Bhandare 1999: 191).

[5]The first Śātakarṇi is assigned ten years; the second, fifty years. The only dated inscription of this king [4] is dated to year 30.

[6]A king named Svāti (Āti Vā) is reported to follow Meghasvāti. Śakti and Svāti could easily derive from the same Middle Indic form (Satti or Sāti). This king is assigned eighteen (Mt) or twelve (Vā) years. After him the *purāṇas* give Skandasvāti. After Skandasvāti, Mt and *e*Vā give Mṛgendra Svātikarṇa, Kuntala Svātikarṇa, and Svātivarṇa. Then the *purāṇas* join again to give Pulomāvi (with many variants) and Ariṣṭakarṇa (with many variants).

[7]After Ariṣṭakarṇa, and before Mantalaka, the *purāṇas* give a king named Hāla, who ruled for five years (Mt) or one year (Vā, Bḍ). Mantalaka's existence is corroborated by the reliefs at Kanaganahalli [25]. The purāṇas assign him a rule offive years. After Mantalaka, the *purāṇas* give a king named Purīndrasena (Mt) or Purikaṣeṇa (Vā, Bḍ).

[8]This king, called Sundara Śātakarṇi only in Mt and *e*Vā (just Śātakarṇi elsewhere), ruled for one year. His existence is corroborated by the reliefs at Kanaganahalli [25]. He was succeeded by a Cakora Śātakarṇi (Mt, *e*Vā, Bh) or Cakāra (Vā, Vṣ).

[9]Called Śivasāti in most *purāṇas*, but Śivasvāmi in a few manuscripts of Vā, and Arindama in Bh.

[10]Eighteen years according to the *purāṇas*.

[11]From Gautamīputra (referred to as such in the *purāṇas*) onward, the *purāṇas* generally agree in their sequence, although not in their dates, with numismatic and epigraphic evidence.

[12]Given twenty-one years by the *purāṇas*, but his latest extant inscription is dated to year 24.

[13]Given twenty-eight years by the *purāṇas*. His latest inscription [21] is dated to year 35.

[14] The existence of this king is noted only by one manuscript of the *Vāyupurāṇa* (*e*Vā).

[15]Twenty-nine years, according to *e*Vā.

[16]Seven years, or four (*e*Vā).

[17]No number of years is given in the *purāṇas*. The inscription that possibly bears his name at Nāṇeghāṭ is dated to year 13.

[18]In the *purāṇas* he is always called Yajñaśrī, but inscriptions call him Śrīyajña.

[19]Twenty-nine years (Mt), twenty (*j*Mt), nine (*bceln*Mt), nineteen (Vā, Bḍ), or twenty-seven (*k*Vā). Inscriptions dated to his twenty-seventh year.

[20]Six years, or ten (*fgj*Mt). Inscriptions up to year 6.

[21]Called Caṇḍaśrī (cf. the note on Śrīyajña above) in Mt, and Daṇḍaśrī in Vā, Bḍ.

[22]Ten years according to the *purāṇas*, but two inscriptions are dated to year 11, confirming Bhandare's guess of around fifteen years.

[23]Seven years according to the *purāṇas*, but his Kanaganahalli inscription is dated to year 10.

TABLE 3 Time line of Mahāmeghavāhana kings

Name	Approx. date	Inscriptions
Khāravela[1]	Mid first century BCE	46, 47
Siri Sada	c. 20 BCE–10 CE	48
Mahā Sada	c. 10–30 CE	49
Vijaya Sada	c. 30–40 CE	
Asaka Sada	c. 40–65 CE	
Siva Sada	c. 65–75 CE	
Sivamaka Sada	c. 75–100 CE	50

[1]The dating reflected in this table derives from Bhandare 2016: 41.

TABLE 4 Time line of Ikṣvāku kings

Name	Approx. date	Inscriptions
Śrī Cāntamūla	225–240 CE[1]	53, 54
Vīrapuruṣadatta	240–265 CE	55, 56, 57, 58, 59, 60, 61, 62
Ehuvula Cāntamūla	265–290 CE	63, 64, 65, 66, 67, 68, 69, 70, 71, 72, 73
Rudrapuruṣadatta	290–315 CE	74, 75, 76, 77

[1]The dates of the Ikṣvāku kings given here follow Rosen Stone 1994.

APPENDIX B

Sātavāhana Inscriptions

This appendix lists the inscriptions that have been discussed or referred to in the book (principally in chapter 2), along with other inscriptions that are relevant for establishing the chronology of the Sātavāhanas, their contemporaries, and their immediate successors. They are arranged by dynasty, then by ruler. The dates assigned to the inscriptions vary widely; the dates given here accord with the chronology adopted in the book (see appendix A). For the locations of most of these inscriptions, see the map in figure 6.

The references are limited to editions of the inscriptions and a small selection of recent scholarly discussion (for older discussion see the references in *Sircar* and *LL*). I have, in addition, given each inscription a unique identifier for purposes of reference within the book.

ABBREVIATIONS

Andhra = B. S. L. Hanumantha Rao, N. S. Ramachandra Murthy, B. Subrahmanyam, and E. Sivanagi Reddy, *Buddhist Inscriptions of Andhradesa.* Secundarabad: Ananda Buddha Vihara Trust, 1998.

ASWI-N = G. Bühler, "The Nânâghât Inscriptions," in *Archaeological Survey of Western India* 5, ed. J. A. S. Burgess (London, 1883), pp. 59–74.

ASWI-K = G. Bühler, "Kānheri Inscriptions," in *Archaeological Survey of Western India* 5, ed. J. A. S. Burgess (London, 1883), pp. 74–87.

Bhilsa = A. Cunningham, *The Bhilsa Topes; or, Buddhist Monuments of Central India.* London: Smith, Elder. , 1854.

EK = K. P. Poonacha, *Excavations at Kanaganahalli.* Delhi: Archaeological Survey of India, 2013.

Gai = G. S. Gai, *Inscriptions of the Early Kadambas.* Delhi: Indian Council of Historical Research, 1996.

Gokhale = S. Gokhale, *Kanheri Inscriptions.* Pune: Deccan College Post Graduate and Research Institute, 1991.

ICN = E. Senart, "Inscriptions in the Caves at Nasik," *Epigraphia Indica* 8 (1905–1906): 59–96.

ICK = E. Senart, "Inscriptions in the Caves at Kârlê," *Epigraphia Indica* 7 (1902–1903): 46–74.

ICTWI = J. A. S. Burgess and B. Indraji. *Inscriptions from the Cave-Temples of Western India.* Bombay: Government Central Press, 1881.

Ikṣvākus = P. R. Srinivasan and S. Sankaranarayanan, *Inscriptions of the Ikshvaku Period.* Hyderabad: Government of Andhra Pradesh, 1979.

Jag = J. A. S. Burgess, *The Buddhist Stupas of Amaravati and Jaggayyapeta.* Varanasi [Benares]: Indological Book House, 1970 (reprint of 1887 edition).

Junnar = J. A. S. Burgess and B. Indraji, "Junnar Caves and Inscriptions," in *Inscriptions from the Cave-Temples of Western India,* pp. 41–55. Bombay: Government Central Press, 1883.

KI = Maiko Nakanishi and Oskar von Hinüber, *Kanaganahalli Inscriptions* (supplement to the *Annual Report of the International Research Institute for Advanced Buddhology at Soka University* for the Academic Year 2013, vol. 17). Tokyo: International Research Institute for Advanced Buddhology, Soka University, 2014.

LL = "Lüders's List" = H. Lüders, *Appendix to Epigraphia Indica and Record of the Archaeological Survey of India, Vol. X: A List of Brahmi Inscriptions from the Earliest Times to about A. D. 400 with the Exception of Those of Asoka.* Calcutta: Superintendent Government Printing, 1912.

Mirashi = V. V. Mirashi, *The History and Inscriptions of the Sātavāhanas and the Western Kshatrapas.* Bombay: Maharashtra State Board for Literature and Culture, 1981.

San = I. K. Sarma and J. Varaprasada Rao, *Early Brāhmī Inscriptions from Sannati.* New Delhi: Harman Publishing House, 1993.

Sircar = D. C. Sircar, *Select Inscriptions.* 2nd ed. Calcutta: University of Calcutta, 1965.

Tsu. = Keisho Tsukamoto, *A Comprehensive Study of the Indian Buddhist Inscriptions.* Kyoto: Heirakuji Shoten, 1996.

INSCRIPTIONS OF THE SĀTAVĀHANAS

Vāsiṣṭhīputra Śrī Chimuka Sātavāhana (ca. 120–96 BCE?)

1. *Kanaganahalli inscription of the time of Vāsiṣṭhīputra Śrī Chimuka Sātavāhana, year 16. EK* A. 101; *KI* I. 3. On a slab of the upper drum (*medhi*) of the *mahāstūpa*. Ca. 110 BCE.

Kṛṣṇa (ca. 96–88 BCE?)

2. *Nāsik inscription of the time of Kṛṣṇa. LL* 1144; *ICN* 22; Sircar 75; Mirashi 1; Tsu.Nasi.23. Inscription of Śramaṇa, *mahāmāta* (*mahāmātra*) in the reign of "King Kṛṣṇa of the Sātavāhana family" (*sādavāhanakule kanhe rājini samaṇena mahāmāteṇa leṇa kārita*. Ca. 90 BCE.
3. *Ivory seal of Kṛṣṇa from Nevāsā.* Sankalia 1960: 202–203. Reads *kanhasa*. Ca. 90 BCE.

Śrī Sātakarṇi (ca. 88–42 BCE?)

4. *Candankheḍā seal of Sātakarṇi, year 30.* Falk 2009. Ca. 60 BCE.
5. *Sāñcī inscription of the time of Sātakarṇi. LL* 346; *Bhilsa* 190; Mirashi 2; Tsu.Sanc.384. Records the donation of the south gate (*toraṇa*) at Sāñcī by Vāsiṣṭhīputra Ānanda, the foreman of artists for King Śrī Sātakarṇi (*rāño sirisātakaṇisa āvesanisa vāsiṭhiputasa ānaṃdasa dānaṃ*). Ca. 60 BCE.
6. *Nāṇeghāṭ inscription of Nāganikā. LL* 1112; *ASWI-N* 1–2; Sircar 75; Mirashi 3; Tsu.Nana.1; Gupta 1975; Mirashi 1977; Gokhale 2004–2006. Ca. 40 BCE.
7. *Nāṇeghāṭ statue-gallery label inscriptions. LL* 1113–1118; *ASWI-N* 3–8; Sircar 76–81; Mirashi 4–9; Tsu. Nana.2–7. Reading: *rāyā simuka sātavāhano sirimāto, devi-nāyanikāya raño ca siri-sātakanino, kumāro bhāya* . . . [gap], *mahāraṭhi tranakayiro, kumāro hakusiri, kumāro sātavāhano*. Ca. 40 BCE.

Gautamīputra Śrī Sātakarṇi (ca. 60–84 CE)

8. *Kārle inscription of Gautamīputra Śrī Sātakarṇi (?), year 18 (?). LL* 1105; *ICK* 19; Mirashi 12; Tsu.Karl.32. Grant of the village Karajaka to the Mahāsaṃghika monks at Valūraka (Kārle). Ca. 78 CE.
9. *Nāsik inscription of Gautamīputra Śrī Sātakarṇi, year 18. LL* 1125; *ICN* 4; Sircar 83; Mirashi 11; Tsu.Nasi.2. Regranting of a village once owned by Uṣavadāta to the monks at Triraśmi (Pāṇḍuleṇa). Ca. 78 CE.
10. *Nāsik inscription of Gautamīputra Śrī Sātakarṇi, year 24. LL* 1126; *ICN* 5; Sircar 84; Mirashi 13; Tsu.Nasi.3. Instead of the village granted in [9], which did not generate any income, the monks at Tiraṇhu (Pāṇḍuleṇa) are granted a new piece of land. Issued jointly with Gautamīputra Sātakarṇi's mother, Gautamī Balaśrī. Ca. 84 CE.

Vāsiṣṭhīputra Śrī Puḷumāvi (ca. 84–119 CE)

11. *Sannati* praśasti *of Gautamīputra Śrī Sātakarṇi. San* A. 1; *KI* A. Below a frieze of a grieving scene. Probably earlier than the Nāsik *praśasti* [18]. Reading: [*s*]*iri sātakaṇisa samuditabalavāhanasa abhagavāhanasa sātavāhanasa beṇākaṭa-vidabha-uparigirāparānta-asaka-mūḍakasa jayavi-cakora-vala-raṭha-dakhina*[*path* . . . *su*]*sūsakasa pitu-satu-vera-niyātakasa aneka-sa*(*ṃ*)*gāma-vijita-vijayasa khakharata-kula-ghātakasa aneka-rāja-mathaka-patigahitasa padana-sāsanasa ekakusasa eka-dhanudha*[*dharasa*]. " *KI* restores the metronymic of the king as *vāseṭhi*, although I would expect *gotami*. Ca. 85–100 CE.
12. *Sannati* praśasti [*of Gautamīputra Śrī Sātakarṇi*]. Varaprasada Rao 1995. This inscription is in Sanskrit and in the *vasantatilaka* meter. Probably belongs with the preceding inscription [11]. Ca. 85–100 CE.

13. *Nāsik inscription of the time of Vāsiṣṭhīputra Śrī Puḷumāvi, year 2. LL* 1147; *ICN* 25; Mirashi 36; Tsu.Nasi.26. Records a private donation. Note the title *raño vāsiṭhiputasa sāmisiripulumāisa.* Ca. 86 CE.
14. *Kārle inscription of the time of Vāsiṣṭhīputra Śrī Puḷumāvi (?), year 5. LL* 1107; *ICK* 21; Mirashi 15. Records a private donation. Ca. 88 CE.
15. *Nāsik inscription of Vāsiṣṭhīputra Śrī Puḷumāvi, year 6. LL* 1122; *ICN* 1; Mirashi 16; Tsu.Nasi.1. Ca. 89 CE.
16. *Myākadoni inscription of [Vāsiṣṭhīputra] Śrī Puḷumāvi, year 6.* Sukthankar 1917–1918; Sircar 90; Mirashi 34. Sharma 1975–76 corrects Sukthankar's reading from year 8 to year 6 and ascribes this inscription to the last ruler named Puḷumāvi, but Sarma 1993: 79–80 and Bhandare 1999: 319 affirm its attribution to the successor of Gautamīputra Śrī Sātakarṇi. See also the Vāsana inscription below [23]. Excavation of a tank by Samba in a locale called *sātavāhanihāra.* Note that the king is called *raño sātavāhanānaṃ [si]-ripuḷum[ā]visa.* Ca. 90 CE.
17. *Kārle inscription of the time of Vāsiṣṭhīputra Śrī Puḷumāvi, year 7. LL* 1100; *ICK* 14; Sircar 85; Mirashi 17; Tsu.Karl.27. Records the donation of a village to the monks at Valūraka (Kārle) by Mahāraṭṭhi Vāsiṣṭhīputra Somadeva, son of Mahāraṭṭhi Kauśikīputra Mitradeva. Ca. 91 CE.
18. *Nāsik inscription of Vāsiṣṭhīputra Śrī Puḷumāvi, year 19 = Gautamī Balaśrī's* praśasti *of Gautamīputra Śrī Sātakarṇi. LL* 1123; *ICN* 2; Sircar 1965; Mirashi 18; Tsu.Nasi.4. Ca. 103 CE.
19. *Nāsik inscription of Vāsiṣṭhīputra Śrī Puḷumāvi, years 19 and 22. LL* 1124; *ICN* 3; Sircar 87; Mirashi 19; Tsu.Nasi.5. Ca. 97–100 CE. Grant of another village for the upkeep of the Queen's Cave, in place of the village mentioned in [18]. Ca. 103 and 106 CE.
20. *Kārle inscription of the time of Vāsiṣṭhīputra Śrī Puḷumāvi, year 24. LL* 1106; *ICK* 20; Sircar 88; Mirashi 20; Tsu.Karl.33. Private donation; the donors have Iranian names (Harapharaṇa and Setapharaṇa). Ca. 108 CE.
21. *Kanaganahalli inscription of the time of Vāsiṣṭhīputra Śrī Puḷumāvi, year 35.* Falk 2009; *EK* A75; *KI* I. 8. Records a private donation. Ca. 119 CE.
22. *Dharanikoṭa inscription of the time of [Vāsiṣṭhīputra Śrī Puḷumāvi], [year 35].* Seshadri Sastri (1937–1938), Tsu.Dhar.1. The date is effaced, but the editor suggests restoring *panatrisa.* Ca. 119 CE.
23. *Vāsana inscription of Vāsiṣṭhīputra Śrī Puḷumāvi.* Sharma 1975–1976. Refers to (a temple of?) Mahādeva Caṇḍaśiva. Sharma identifies the ruler with the last king of the dynasty, but this has been disputed by Sarma 1993: 79–80 and Bhandare 1999: 319, who identify him with the successor of Gautamīputra Śrī Sātakarṇi. Ca. 84–119 CE.
24. *Amarāvati inscription of the time of Vāsiṣṭhīputra Śrī Puḷumāvi. LL* 1248; Mirashi 21; *Andhra,* p. 50; Tsu.Amar.12. Private donation. The king is referred to with the Śaka title *svāmi* (*ra[ño] vā[siṭhi]puta[sa] [sā]mi-siri-puḷumāvisa*). This is among the earliest of the Sātavāhana inscriptions from coastal Andhra. Ca. 84–119 CE.

Vāsiṣṭhīputra Śrī Sātakarṇi (ca. 119–148 CE)

25. *Kanaganahalli label inscriptions.* The historical kings mentioned are Aśoka (*rāyā asoko: KI* I. 1 and I. 2; *EK* A95 and A97); Chimuka Sātavāhana (*rājā siri chimuka sādavāhano: KI* I. 4; *EK* A96); Sātakarṇi (*rāyā sātakaṇ[i mahāce]-(t)[i]yasa r(u)pāmayāni payumāni oṇ(o)yeti* "King Sātakarṇi donates silver lotus flowers to the Great Caitya": *KI* I. 7; *EK* A102); Mantalaka (*rāya matalako: KI* I. 5; *EK* A94); Sundara Sātakarṇi (*rāyā sudara sātakani: KI* I. 6; *EK* A240); Puḷumāvi (*rāya puḷumāvi ajayatasa ujeni deti: KI* I. 9; *EK* A99). These are all inscribed on the upper drum (*medhi*), which was first encased during the reign of Chimuka Sātavāhana (see [1]) and renovated during the reign of Vāsiṣṭhīputra Śrī Sātakarṇi. Ca. 120 CE.
26. *Kanaganahalli inscription of the time of Vāsiṣṭhīputra Śrī Sātakarṇi, year 6. EK* A15; *KI* I. 10. Records a donation by a caravan trader. Ca. 124 CE.
27. *Sannati inscription of the time of Vāsiṣṭhīputra Śrī Sātakarṇi.* Nagaraja Rao 1985: 1; *San* A2. Ca. 119–148 CE.
28. *Kānherī inscription of Vāsiṣṭhīputra Śrī Sātakarṇi. LL* 994; *ASWI-K* 11; Mirashi 25; Gokhale 16; Tsu.Kanh.16. This is one of the only Sanskrit inscriptions of the Sātavāhanas (see also [12]), and records the donation of a cistern by a minister of the queen of Vāsiṣṭhīputra Śrī Sātakarṇi, who is also the daughter of the Mahākṣatrapa Ru[dradāman]. Since Rudradāman bears the title Mahākṣatrapa, this must date to after 141 (when Rudradāman still had the lower title Kṣatrapa). Ca. 141–148 CE.

Vāsiṣṭhīputra Śivaśrī Puḷumāvi (ca. 148–156 CE)

29. *Sannati inscription of the time of Vāsiṣṭhīputra Śivaśrī Puḷumāvi. San* A3. Ca. 148–156 CE.
30. *Banavāsi inscription of Vāsiṣṭhīputra Śivaśrī Puḷumāvi.* Mirashi 22 Narasimha Murthy and Bhatt 1975. This is a memorial stone (*chaā-pattharo*) to the chief queen of Vāsiṣṭhīputra Śivaśrī Puḷumāvi (*raño vāsiṭhīputasa sivasiri-puḷumāvisa mahādeviya*). Murthy and Bhat identified this king with Śivaśrī of the *purāṇas*; Mirashi thought that Śivaśrī was merely an honorific and identified this king with the successor of Gautamīputra Śrī Sātakarṇi. Ca. 160 CE.

Vāsiṣṭhīputra Śrīskanda Sātakarṇi (ca. 156–170 CE)

31. *Nāṇeghāṭ inscription of Vāsiṣṭhīputra Śriskanda Sātakarṇi, year 13. LL* 1120; Mirashi 23; Gupta 1992. Bhagavanlal read the name as *Chatarapana;* Mirashi suggests *Sirikhada* instead (coins of Skanda Sātakarṇi are known). Gupta suggests (unconvincingly) restoring *arahaṇa.* Ca. 169 CE.

Gautamīputra Śrīyajña Sātakarṇi (ca. 171–199 CE)

32. *Nāsik inscription of the time of Gautamīputra Śrīyajña Sātakarṇi, year 7. LL* 1146; *ICN* 24; Sircar 89; *Mirashi* 26; Tsu.Nasi.25. Donation of a cave begun by a monk Bopaki and completed by the Mahāsenāpatinī Vāsu. Ca. 178 CE.

33. *Kanaganahalli inscription of the time of Gautamīputra Śrīyajña Sātakarṇi, year 10–19. KI* I. 11. Ca. 181–190 CE.
34. *Kanaganahalli inscription of the time of Gautamīputra Śrīyajña Sātakarṇi, year 11. EK* A143; *KI* I. 12. Ca. 182 CE.
35. *Kānherī inscription of the time of Gautamīputra Śrīyajña Sātakarṇi, year 16. LL* 1025; *ASWI-K* 15, Mirashi 27; Gokhale 25; Tsu.Kanh.25. Donation and endowment of a cave by a merchant layman. Ca. 187 CE.
36. *Cinagañjāṃ inscription of Gautamīputra Śrīyajña Sātakarṇi, year 27. LL* 1340; Bühler 1892*a*; Mirashi 29; *Andhra*, p. 128; Tsu.Chin.1. The king is called *raño gotamiputasa araka-siri-yaña-sātakaṇisa*, perhaps employing the Tamil *aracaṉ* as the equivalent of Sanskrit *svāmi*. Ca. 198 CE.
37. *Amarāvati inscription of the time of Gautamīputra Śrīyajña Sātakarṇi*. Sarkar 1971; Mirashi 62A; *Andhra*, p. 59. This is one of the very few Sanskrit inscriptions from within the Sātavāhana empire. Donation by Jayila, a lay follower from Ujjayinī, to the *mahācaitya*. Ca. 171–199 CE.
38. *Kānherī inscription of the time of Gautamīputra Śrīyajña Sātakarṇi. LL* 987; *ASWI-K* 4; Mirashi 28; Gokhale 5; Tsu.Kanh.5. Donation of a cave. Uses the title *sāmi-siri-yaña*. Ca. 171–199 CE.

Gautamīputra Śrīvijaya Sātakarṇi (ca. 200–205 CE)

39. *Nāgārjunakoṇḍa inscription of the time of Gautamīputra Śrīvijaya Sātakarṇi, year 6*. Sarkar 1965–1966; Mirashi 32; *Andhra*, p. 136; Tsu.Naga.69. This is one of the earliest instances of writing double consonants (*sātakaṇṇisa*). Ca. 205 CE.

Vāsiṣṭhīputra Śrīcaṇḍa Sātakarṇi (ca. 206–220 CE)

40. *Kanaganahalli inscription of the time of Vāsiṣṭhīputra Caṇḍa Sātakarṇi, year 11. EK* A68; *KI* I. 13. The editors of *EK* identify the king (*vāsiṭhiputasa saḍasatakanisa*) with Vāsiṣṭhīputra Śrī Sātakarṇi rather than Vāsiṣṭhīputra Caṇḍa Sātakarṇi, and read the year as 2 rather than 11; I follow *KI*. Ca. 216 CE.
41. *Koḍavali inscription of the time of Vāsiṣṭhīputra Śrīcaṇḍa Svāti, year 11* (?). *LL* 1341 Krishna Shastri 1925–1926; Mirashi 33. Donation of a minister. The reading of the inscription is very doubtful. Ca. 216 CE.

Māṭharīputra Śrī Puḷumāvi (ca. 220–230 CE)

42. *Kanaganahalli inscription of the time of Māṭharīputra Śrī Puḷumāvi, year 10. EK* A150; *KI* I. 14. Ca. 230 CE.

Other Inscriptions

43. *Nāsik inscription of Mahāhakusiri. LL* 1141; *ICN* 19; Mirashi 10; Tsu.Nasi.20. Records the construction of a *caitya* by Bhaṭṭapālikā, daughter of the the royal minister Arahalaya from Calisīla (*rāyāmaca-arahalayasa calisīlaṇakasa duhutuya*), granddaughter of Mahāhakusiri, and wife of the royal minister and treasurer Aggiyatta[?] (*rāyāmacaya agiyataṇakasa bhaṃdākārikayasa bhāriyāya*). Ca. 20 CE.

44. *Kānherī inscription of [?], year [9]. LL* 1021; Mirashi 36; Gokhale 39; Tsu. Kanh.39. Rapson 1908 [1967]: liii and Mirashi think that the donor of this inscription and the Banavāsi inscription of Hāritīputra Viṇhukaḍḍa Cuṭukulānanda Sātakarṇi [52] are the same. But the identification is impossible; see Bhandare 1999: 338. The donor is Nāgamulanikā, the daughter of a Mahārāja (perhaps the one named in the inscription, now effaced), the mother of the Mahāraṭṭhi Skandanāgasātaka, and the sister of the Mahābhoja [Ahija].
45. *Kuḍā inscription of Goyammā, daughter of the royal minister Hāla. ICTWI* no. 18 (Kuḍā); *LL* 1053. *rājāmacasa hālasa* [*duhu*]*tāya goyaṃmāya* [*leṇaṃ*].

INSCRIPTIONS OF OTHER DYNASTIES

Mahāmeghavāhanas

46. *Hāthīgumphā inscription of Khāravela. LL* 1345; Sircar 91; Barua 1929: 7–30; Jayaswal 1929–1930. Mid-first century BCE.
47. *Mañchapurī inscription of Khāravela's queen. LL* 1346; Sircar 92 Barua 1929: 55–56. Mid-first century BCE.
48. *Guṇṭupalli inscription of Mahāmeghavāhana Siri Sada.* Sircar 1969–1970; Sarma 1978; *Andhra,* p. 109; Tsu.Gunt.1–4. Four nearly identical pillar inscriptions, recording the donation of a writer (*lekhaka*) for the king (*mahārājasa kaligamahisakādhipatisa mahāmekhavāhanasa siri-sadasa*). Beginning of first century. CE.
49. *Velpūru inscription of Mahā Sada.* Sircar 1957–1958; Shastri 1993, 1996*a*; Tsu. Velp.1. Donation of a *maṇḍapa* by a lamp bearer (*disi-dhārikā*) of the king, who is called *aira* and *hāritiputa.* Shastri contends that this king is the same as the king mentioned in the Guṇṭupaḷḷi inscription; Bhandare 2016 disagrees. Ca. 10–30 CE.
50. *Amarāvati inscription of Sivamaka Sada. LL* 1279; Mirashi 24; *Andhra,* p. 53; Tsu.Amar.75. End of first century. CE.

Banavāsi Branch

51. *Maḷavaḷḷi inscription of Hāritīputra Viṇhukaḍḍa Cuṭukulānanda Sātakarṇi, year 1. LL* 1195; *Epigraphia Carnatica* 7; Mirashi 35. The language is Middle Indic with a number of unique features that indicate a different linguistic milieu. The same pillar features an inscription of the Kadamba king Śivaskandavarman, similar in paleography and language; see [78]. Late third century.
52. *Banavāsi inscription of the time of Hāritīputra Viṇhukaḍḍa Cuṭukulānanda Sātakarṇi, year 12. LL* 1186; Gai 1975–1976; Mirashi 37; Tsu.Bana.1. The donor is a Mahābhojī (*mahābhuviya*). Gai understood *siva-khada-nāga-siriya* to be the name of the donor, but Mirashi thinks it refers to the donor's son, who is said to be the *yuvarāja.* Mirashi's interpretation is implausible. Late third century.

Ikṣvākus

53. *Reṇṭāla inscription of Cāntamūla, year 5.* Sankaranarayanan 1967; *Andhra,* pp. 186–188. Erection of a pillar. Ca. 230 CE.

54. *Kesanapalli inscription of the time of Cāntamūla, year 13.* Sankaranarayanan 1970; *Andhra,* p. 178; Tsu.Kesa.16. Dedication of a pillar in the *mahācaitya.* Ca. 238 CE.
55. *Nāgārjunakoṇḍa pillar inscriptions of the time of Vīrapuruṣadatta, year 6.* Vogel 1929–1930: 15–21; Sircar 98–100; *Andhra,* pp. 137–151; Tsu.Naga.1–17. These pillars belong to the *mahācaitya* at Nāgārjunakoṇḍa. The donors include Cātiśrī, sister of Cāntamūla and mother-in-law of Vīrapuruṣadatta; Aḍavi-Cātaśrī, daughter of Cāntamūla; Cula-Cātiśrī, wife of a military officer; Rudradharabhaṭṭārikā, the daughter of a Mahārāja of Ujjayinī and queen of Vīrapuruṣadatta; Bappaśrī, a niece of Cāntamūla's and also a queen of Vīrapuruṣadatta; and Chaṭhiśrī, another niece of Cāntamūla's and queen of Vīrapuruṣadatta. One inscription (C2) mentions that Ānanda, who established the foundations of the *mahācaitya,* belonged to a community of teachers of the *dīgha* and *majjhima* (*nikāyas*) and the five *mātukas*. Ca. 246 CE.
56. *Nāgārjunakoṇḍa inscription of the time of Vīrapuruṣadatta, year 14.* Vogel 1929–1930: 22–23; Sircar 101; *Andhra,* pp. 152–155; Tsu.Naga.41. Private donation of a stone *maṇḍapa,* for the benefit of the teachers of Tāmrapāṇi, who are said to have converted Kaśmīra, Gandhāra, Cīna, Cilāta, Tosali, Aparānta, Vaṅga, Vanavāsi, Yavana, Damila, Palura, and Tāmrapāṇi. Ca. 254 CE.
57. *Nāgārjunakoṇḍa inscription of the time of Vīrapuruṣadatta, year 15. Andhra,* pp. 163–164 Tsu.Naga.21–22. Ca. 255 CE.
58. *Nāgārjunakoṇḍa inscriptions of the time of Vīrapuruṣadatta, year 18.* Vogel 1929–1930: 21–22; Sircar 102; *Andhra,* pp. 151–152. Addition of a stone *maṇḍapa* to the Mahācaitya by Cātiśrī, sister of Cāntamūla and mother-in-law of Vīrapuruṣadatta, for the benefit of the Aparamahāvinaseliyas. Ca. 258 CE.
59. *Nāgārjunakoṇḍa inscription of the time of Vīrapuruṣadatta, year 18. Andhra,* pp. 159–160; Tsu.Naga.18. Ca. 258 CE.
60. *Uppugundur inscription of the time of Vīrapuruṣadatta, year 19.* Chhabra 1959–1960*b*; *Andhra,* pp. 183–184; Tsu.Uppu.1. Ca. 259 CE.
61. *Nāgārjunakoṇḍa inscription of the time of Vīrapuruṣadatta, year 20.* Vogel 1931–1932: 63–64; Sircar 1963–1964*a:* 1A; *Andhra,* p. 159 and pp. 168–169; Tsu.Naga.49. Memorial pillar of Cāntamūla, erected by royal women (who are listed). Sircar read *vijaya* and dated the inscription to 273 CE; the reading *viṃsaya* may be better. Ca. 260 CE.
62. *Jaggayyapeṭa inscription of the time of Vīrapuruṣadatta, year 20. Jag.,* p. 108; *Andhra,* pp. 180–181, Tsu.Jagg.1. Private donation of pillars. Ca. 260 CE.
63. *Nāgārjunakoṇḍa inscriptions of the time of Ehuvula Cāntamūla, year 2.* Vogel 1929–1930: 23–24, 1931–1932: 62–63; Sircar 103. *Andhra* pp. 156–158, Tsu. Naga.42–43. Donation of a *vihāra* by Bhaṭṭidevā, a wife of Vīrapuruṣadatta and mother of Ehuvula Cāntamūla. One of the inscriptions (G2) uses double consonants relatively consistently. Ca. 267 CE.
64. *Nāgārjunakoṇḍa inscription of the time of Ehuvula Cāntamūla, year 8.* Sircar 1963–1964*a:* 2A–B; *Andhra,* pp. 164–166, Tsu.Naga.53–54. Ca. 273 CE.
65. *Allūru inscription of the time of Ehuvula Cāntamūla, year 8.* Srinivasan 1971*a*; *Andhra,* pp. 185–186; Tsu.Allu.2. Ca. 273 CE.

66. *Nāgārjunakoṇḍa inscription of the time of Ehuvula Cāntamūla, year 11.* Vogel 1929–1930: 24–25; Sircar 104; *Andhra,* p. 158; *Ikṣvākus* 42, Tsu.Naga.45. Donation of a pillar and a *vihāra* by Kodabalaśrī, a queen of Vīrapuruṣadatta, for the benefit of the Mahīśāsakas. Ca. 276 CE.
67. *Nāgārjunakoṇḍa inscription of the time of Ehuvula Cāntamūla, year 11.* Chhabra 1959–1960*a*; *Ikṣvākus* 41. Construction of a temple to Sarvadeva. The inscription is in Sanskrit (one *anuṣṭubh* and one *sragdharā* verse). Ca. 276 CE.
68. *Nāgārjunakoṇḍa inscription of the time of Ehuvula Cāntamūla, year 13.* Sircar 1963–1964*a:* No. 3; *Ikṣvākus* 43. Memorial pillar (*chaya-thabh*[*o*]) of Mahāsenāpati Kumāra Elī Ehavūladāsaṃnaka, a stepbrother of Ehuvula Cāntamūla's. Ca. 278 CE.
69. *Nāgārjunakoṇḍa inscription of the time of Ehuvula Cāntamūla, year 16.* Sircar 1961–1962: No. 1; *Ikṣvākus* 44. In Sanskrit. Records the construction and endowment of a temple of Puṣpabhadrasvāmin by Ehuvula Cāntamūla's son, the *mahārājakumāra* and *mahāsenāpati* Vīrapuruṣadatta. Ca. 281 CE.
70. *Nāgārjunakoṇḍa inscription of the time of Ehuvula Cāntamūla, year 24.* Sircar 1963–1964*a:* No. 4; *Andhra,* p. 155; *Ikṣvākus* 45 Tsu.Naga.55. In Sanskrit. Records the installation of an image of the Buddha. Ca. 289 CE.
71. *Pātagaṇḍigūḍem plates of Ehuvula Cāntamūla.* Ramachandra Murthy 1999; Falk 1999–2000; *Andhra,* pp. 191–193. Endowment of structures at the *mahāvihāra.* Ca. 265–290 CE.
72. *Nāgārjunakoṇḍa inscription of the time of Ehuvula Cāntamūla.* Sircar 1963–1964*a:* 1B; *Andhra,* pp. 156. Ca. 265–290 CE.
73. *Nāgārjunakoṇḍa inscription of the time of Ehuvala Cāntamūla.* Narasimhaswami 1951; *Andhra,* p. 174. Mentions Khaṃḍuvulā, one of Ehuvala Cāntamūla's wives. Ca. 265–290 CE.
74. *Gurzāla inscription of the time of Rudrapuruṣadatta, year 4.* Nilakantha Sastri 1941; *Ikṣvākus* 48; Tsu.Gurz.1. A donation to the god Haṃpurasvāmin. The king's name is read *ruḷapurisadāta.* Ca. 294 CE.
75. *Nāgārjunakoṇḍa inscription of the time of Rudrapuruṣadatta, year 11.* Sircar 1961–1962, no. 2; *Andhra,* p. 169; *Ikṣvākus* 49; Tsu.Naga.63. Memorial pillar of Vammabhaṭṭā, the mother of Rudrapuruṣadatta and daughter of a Mahākṣatrapa. Ca. 301 CE.
76. *Phaṇigiri inscription of the time of Rudrapuruṣadatta, year 16.* Skilling and von Hinüber 2011. A hymn in praise of the Buddha in Sanskrit. Ca. 306 CE.
77. *Nāgārjuṇakoṇḍa inscription of an unknown year.* Sircar 1963–1964*a:* 17–18; *Ikṣvākus* 71; Tsu.Naga.56. Fragmentary inscription, of which only the last of ten verses (in the *vaṃśastha* meter) is preserved. It is in Sanskrit and connected with the main Buddhist monastery. Late third or early fourth century CE.

Kadambas

78. *Maḷavaḷḷi inscription of an unknown king. LL* 1196; Gai 1. This is inscribed on the same pillar as the record of Hāritīputra Viṇhukaḍḍa Cuṭukulānanda Sātakarṇi [51]. Sircar 1939: 248 thinks the inscription might belong to

Mayūraśarman or his immediate successor; Gai thinks it belongs to a predecessor of Mayūraśarman. Ca. 330 CE.

79. *Candravalli inscription of Mayūraśarman.* Sircar 68; Gai 2. Sircar reads a list of vanquished enemies in Prakrit; Gai more plausibly reads a description of the tank (*taṭākaṃ*) in Sanskrit. Ca. 330–360 CE.
80. *Tāḷagunda inscription of* Śāntivarman. Sircar 69; Gai 4; Srinivasan 1971*b*. Gives the genealogy of the Kadamba kings from Mayūraśraman, and mentions one Sātakarṇi in verse 33 (as a worshipper at a temple of Bhava). Ca. 455–470 CE.

Pallavas

81. *Mañcikallu inscription of Siṃhavarman.* Sircar 1957–1958. Early fourth century.
82. *Maidavolu plates of Śivaskandavarman.* Hultzsch 1900–1901. Issued to an official at Dhānyakaṭa (Amarāvati) while Śivaskandavarman was a *yuvarāja*. Grant of a village to two Brāhmaṇas. First inscriptional mention of Āndhra (*aṃdhapatīya*). Early fourth century.
83. *Hirehaḍagali plates of Śivaskandarvarman.* Bühler 1892*b*; *LL* 1200. Confirmation and supplement of an earlier donation of a village in the district of *sātāhani*. The last sentence, a *maṅgala*, is in Sanskrit. Early fourth century.
84. *British Museum plates. Sircar* 66. There is a reference to *siri-vijaya-khandavamma-mahārājassa* in the first line, but the relationship of this plate to the Pallava king of that name is uncertain because of textual difficulties. Early fourth century.
85. *Copper Plate of Viṣṇugopavarman, year 1.* Reddy and Reddy 2000. Mid-fourth century CE?

Śālaṅkāyanas

86. *Ēlūru Grant of Devavarman, year 13.* Hultzsch 1907–1908. Ca. 320–340 CE.
87. *Kānukollu Grant of Nandivarman, Year 14.* Krishna Rao 1955–1956. Third quarter of fourth century CE.
88. *Dhārikāṭūra Grant of Acaṇḍavarman, year 35.* Sircar 1965–1966. Last quarter of fourth century CE.
89. *Penugoṇḍa Grant of Hastivarman, year 2.* Sircar 1963–1964*b*. End of fourth century CE.

Vākāṭakas

90. *Vāśim copper plates of Vindyaśakti II, year 37.* Sircar 59; *Vākāṭakas* 23. Ca. 392 CE.
91. *Pune plates of Prabhāvatīguptā, year 13 (of Pravarasena II).* Sircar 60. Prabhāvatīgupta was the daughter of Candragupta II (Vikramāditya), and the wife of the Vākāṭaka king Rudrasena, who predeceased her. She ruled as regent until her sons Dāmodarasena and later Pravarasena II assumed the throne. Ca. 433 CE.
92. *Ṛddhapur plates of Prabhāvatīguptā, year 19 (of Pravarasena II).* Sircar 61; *Vākāṭakas* 8. Ca. 439 CE.

93. *Miregāṃv plates of Prabhāvatīguptā, year 20 (of Pravarasena II).* Shastri 2000. Ca. 440 CE.
94. *Rāmṭek* praśasti *of the time of Pravarasena II.* Bakker and Isaacson 1993. On the occasion of the construction of a temple to Viṣṇu at Rāmagiri (Rāmṭek). Bakker and Isaacson argue that it was commissioned by the daughter of Prabhāvatīguptā after the latter's death and thus belongs to the later reign of Pravarasena II. Ca. 440–452 CE.
95. *Ajaṇṭā inscription of the time of Hariṣeṇa.* Sircar 63; *Vākāṭakas* 25; Tsu.Ajan.52. Probably inscribed by Hariṣeṇa's minister Varāhadeva. Refers to Vindhyaśakti as the founder of the Vākāṭaka dynasty (*vākāṭakavaṅśaketuḥ*). End of fifth century CE.

Kṣatrapas and Ābhīras

96. *Mathurā inscription of the time of Śoḍāsa.* Lüders 1937–1938. The date is in Middle Indic, but the following verse in the *bhujaṅgavijṛmbhita* meter is in Sanskrit. Mid- first century CE.
97. *Nāsik inscription of Uṣavadāta, years 42 and 45 of Nahapāna. LL* 1133; *ICN* 12; Sircar 58; Mirashi 38; Tsu.Nasi.12. Donation and endowment of a cave at Triraśmi/Tiraṇhu (Pāṇḍulena). Ca. 74 and 77 CE.
98. *Nāsik inscription of Dakṣamitrā, wife of Uṣavadāta. LL* 1132; *ICN* 11; Sircar 60; Mirashi 42; Tsu.Nasi.11. Dakṣamitrā's donation of a cell. Ca. 70–78 CE.
99. *Kārle inscription of Uṣavadāta. LL* 1099; *ICK* 13; Sircar 61; Mirashi 39; Tsu. Karl.26. Ca. 70–78 CE.
100. *Nāsik inscription of Uṣavadāta. LL* 1131; *ICN* 10; Sircar 59; Mirashi 43; Tsu. Nasi.10. Records Uṣavadāta's excavation of a cave. Ca. 70–78 CE.
101. *Nāsik inscription of Dakṣamitrā, wife of Uṣavadāta. LL* 1134; *ICN* 13; Mirashi 41; Tsu.Nasi.13. Dakṣamitrā's donation of a cell. Ca. 70–78 CE.
102. *Nāsik inscription of Uṣavadāta. LL* 1135; *ICN* 14a; Mirashi 40; Tsu.Nasi.14. Details the religious patronage of Uṣavadāta. Ca. 70–78 CE.
103. *Junnar inscription of the time of Nahapāna, year 46. LL* 1174; *Junnar* 25; Sircar 62; Mirashi 44; Tsu.Junn.3. Records Ayyama's donation of a cistern. Ca. 78 CE.
104. *Junāgaṛh inscription of Rudradāman, year 72 (Śaka).* Kielhorn 1905–1906; *LL* 965; Sircar 67; Mirashi 51. Records the restoration of the embankments of Sudarśana lake after a flood, with a long *praśasti* of Mahākṣatrapa Svāmi Rudradāman. 150 CE.
105. *Nāsik inscription of the time of* Ābhīra *Māḍharīputra* Īśvarasena, *year 9. LL* 1137; *ICN* 15; Tsu.Nasi.16. The donor, Viṣṇudattā, is the daughter of a Śaka named Agnivarman. Mid-third century CE.
106. *Kānherī inscription of the time of Māḍharīputra Svāmi Śakasena. ASWI-K* 19; *LL* 1002; Gokhale 42; Tsu.Kanh.42. Names Hālaṇikā as the donor of the cave. Mid-third century CE.
107. *Nāgārjunakoṇḍa inscription of the time of Vāsiṣṭhīputra Ābhīra Vasuṣeṇa, year 26* (reading of the year very uncertain). Sircar 1961–1962; Salomon 2013. Installation of an image of Viṣṇu (*aṣṭabhujasvāminaḥ*) on Seṭagiri by Mahāgrāmika

Mahātalavara Mahādaṇḍanāyaka Śivaseba, a vassal of the above-named king's. Mention is made of the Śaka Rudradāman of Avanti and Viṣṇurudra Śivalānanda Sātakarṇi of Vanavāsi, both of whom were previously unable to move the image from its location in Saṃjayantīpurī. Ca. 340 CE.

APPENDIX C

Fragments of Early Prakrit Grammars

These fragments are all in Prakrit *gāthās*, in whole or in part, that bear on the grammatical characterization of Prakrit. The first group containts fragments attributed to Harivṛddha. The second contains fragments with no attribution. The third group contains testimonia. I can make no claims to completeness: the Jain commentarial literature is vast, and I rely largely on the findings of A. N. Upadhye (1931–1932) and Hiralal Jain (1945).

FRAGMENTS ATTRIBUTED TO HARIVṚDDHA

These fragments are collected from the following materials:

- *Ratnaśrīṭīkā* (RāŚrīṬī) of Ratnaśrījñāna on Daṇḍin's *Kāvyādarśa* (see *Mirror of Literature* in the bibliography). Written in 931. This appendix reflects most of the suggestions of Bhayani 1973. Some of Ratnaśrījñāna's quotations are preserved by Saṅgharakkhita in his *Mahāsāmi-ṭīkā* on the *Subodhālaṃkāra* (ed. Padmanabh Jaini [Oxford, 2000]).
- *Ṭippaṇī* (KāAṬi) of Namisādhu on Rudraṭa's *Kāvyālaṃkāra* (see *Ornament of Literature* in the bibliography). Written in 1069. Other readings are given by Kulkarni 1988 = PVSWP.

1. *Ratnaśrīṭīkā* on 1.33 (p. 23).
   कथं तद्भवं तस्मात् संस्कृतात् †वर्णान्यत्वेन† उत्पत्तिर्यस्य तत्तद्भवं शब्दभवमित्यर्थः । तच्च **महिन्द-सिन्धव-बहिरादिकं** यथोक्तं हरिवृद्धेन ।
   mahiṃda-, *siṃdhava-*, *bahira-*, etc. [are *śabdabhava* words.]

2. *Ratnaśrīṭīkā* on 1.33 (p. 23).

तत्समम् तेन संस्कृतेन समं तत्समम्, प्राकृतशब्दमपीत्यर्थः । तच्च **हरि-हर-कमलादिकं** यथोक्तं तत्रैव ।

hari-, hara-, kamalā-, etc. [are *śabdasama* words.]

3. *Ratnaśrīṭīkā* on 1.33 (p. 23).

देशी प्राकृतं महाराष्ट्रप्रसिद्धम् । तदुक्तम्—

मरहट्ठ-देस-संकेअएहि सद्देहि भण्णए देसी इति ।

मरहट्ठ] Bhayani; **मरहट्ठा** RāŚrīṬī
संकेअएहि] Bhayani; **संकेतएहि** RāŚrīṬī

Deśī is expressed through words that are conventionally recognized in the region of Mahārāṣṭra.

4. *Ratnaśrīṭīkā* on 1.33 (p. 23). The *deśī* words in this passage have been restored by Bhayani on the basis of Hemacandra's *Deśīnāmamālā*.

तच्च **बोक्कण-कंकेल्लिचिरिड्डिहिल्ल-सित्थादिकं** यथोक्तं तत्रैव ।

बोक्कण] Bhayani; **वोक्कण** RāŚrīṬī
चिरिड्डिहिल्ल] Bhayani; **चिरिहिरहिर** RāŚrīṬī
सित्था] Bhayani; **सिच्छा** RāŚrīṬī

bokkaṇa- ("crow"), *kaṃkelli-* ("Aśoka tree"), *ciriḍḍihilla-* ("curds"), *sitthā-* ("bowstring"), etc. [are *deśī* words.]

5. *Ratnaśrīṭīkā* on 1.34 (p. 24). Although not explicitly attributed to Harivṛddha, the context makes the attribution very probable.

महाराष्ट्राः कुन्तल-मुलकाश्मक-विदर्भ-†महियाचरत्रवैश्या†दि-प्रभेदाः7 आश्रयः अधिष्ठानं यस्यां तां महाराष्ट्राश्रयां भाषां वाचं प्रकृष्टं प्राकृतेषु शोभनतमं प्राकृतं विदुः उपदिशन्ति बहुज्ञाः । तदुक्तम्—

†ऊह इअ विविह-भासा परिरि हिअअं य† मोत्तूणं ।
मरह[ट्ठभासिअं चे]अ अत्थि गहिअं कइल्लेहि ॥

कुन्तल . . . प्रभेदाः] conj.; **कुन्तलामुरलासकविदर्भमहियाचरत्रवैश्यादिप्रभेदाः** RāŚrīṬī
मरह[ट्ठभासिअं चे]अ] conj.; **मरहअठिअया अ** RāŚrīṬī

. . . it is the language of Mahārāṣṭra that poets have accepted.

6. *Ratnaśrīṭīkā* on 1.33 (p. 24).

ननु सामान्यभाषापि प्राकृतप्रकारोऽस्ति । यदुक्तं हरिवृद्धेन—

अण्णेहि अ एएहि अ सरिसं चिअ होइ सामण्णे इति ।

चिअ] **चअ** RāŚrīṬī

That which these and the others have in common is in the category of "Common" (*sāmānya*).

7. *Ratnaśrīṭīkā* on 1.34 (p. 24). Bhayani restored *musumūria* on the basis of *Siddhahemacandra* 8.4.106, which teaches this root as a substitute for *bhañj-*.

व्यवह्रियते [शि]क्षणं व्यवहारः [तत्र] प्रवर्तते एभिरिति सा च **मुसुमूरिअ-मूअच्छिअच्छिकेत्यादिका** यथोक्तं <u>हरिवृद्धेन</u> ।

मुसुमूरिअ] Bhayani, **मुसुमुरिअ** RāŚrīṬī

broken . . .

8. *Ratnaśrīṭīkā* on 1.34 (pp. 24–25). Although not explicitly attributed to Harivṛddha, the context makes the attribution very likely.

तदुक्तम्—

सद्दभवा सद्दसमा देसि त्ति अ तिण्णि पाअअण्णेहि ।
सामण्ण-पाअअ-सहिअ †आया अअय इतराणि आउ† ॥

पाअअण्णेहि] Bhayani; आ अ अण्णेहि RāŚrīṬī
पाअअ-सहिअ] Bhayani; ययाअ इसहि RāŚrīṬī

"Derived," "Identical," and "Regional" are the three [recognized] by those who know Prakrit;
With the addition of "Common Prakrit" . . .

9. *Kāvyālaṃkāraṭippaṇī* 2.19 (p. 17) = PVSWP p. 2.

तथा ह्यष्टौ हरिणोक्ताः यथा—

महुरं फरुसं कोमलमोजस्सिं निट्ठुरं च ललियं च ।
गंभीरं सामण्णं च अट्ठ भणिईओ नायव्वा ॥

फरुसं] PVSWP; परुसं KāAṬi
अट्ठ] PVSWP; अद्ध KāAṬi
भणिईओ] conj.; भणितिउ PVSWP, भणिती उ KāAṬi
नायव्वा] PVSWP; नायच्चा KāAṬi

The sweet, the harsh, the soft, the powerful, the severe, the playful, the profound, and the general: these are the eight *bhaṇitis*.

UNATTRIBUTED FRAGMENTS

These fragments are collected from the following sources:

- The *Nāṭyaśāstra* (NāŚā) ascribed to Bharata (see *Treatise on Theater* in the bibliography). Dates very approximately to between the second and fourth centuries CE. It contains a concise grammar of Prakrit, partially composed in Prakrit, at the beginning of the seventeenth chapter. Nitti-Dolci 1972 [1938] and Alsdorf 1975 [1941] made corrections to the reading of the first edition of the Baroda text, which have not been taken into account in subsequent editions. My apparatus only refers to the readings of the second edition; that edition can be consulted for variants in the manuscripts of the *Nāṭyaśāstra* (of which there are an enormous amount).
- The *Gāthālakṣaṇa* (GāLa) of Nanditāḍhya (see *Definition of the Gāthā* in the bibliography). Date unknown; a quotation of a verse from Rājaśekhara, if it is not an interpolation, would put him after the tenth century.
- The Śvetāmbara commentarial literature, especially that of Jinadāsa (seventh century), Haribhadra (ca. eighth century) and Malayagiri (twelfth century) on the *Nandisūtra, Anuyogadvārasūtra, Daśavaikālikasūtra, Āvaśyakasūtra*, and *Sūryaprajñapti*. Fragments of Prakrit grammars in these texts were first noted by Upadhye 1931–1932.
- The Digambara commentarial literature, especially the *Dhavalā* of Vīrasena on the *Ṣaṭkhaṇḍāgama* of Puṣpadanta and Bhūtabali (completed in 816), and the *Jayadhavalā* (JaDha) of Vīrasena and Jinasena on the *Kaṣāyaprābhṛta* of

Guṇabhadra (completed in 823). Most of the citations from these sources were noted by Jain 1945.

- Prakrit grammars, namely, the *Prākṛtalakṣaṇa* (PrāLa) ascribed to Caṇḍa (see *Definition of Prakrit* in the bibliography) and the *Prākṛtasaṃjīvinī* (PrāSaṃ) of Vasantarāja on Vararuci's *Prākṛtaprakāśa* (see *Light on Prakrit* in the bibliography). Vasantarāja probably lived in the eleventh century (see chapter 7). The *Prākṛtalakṣaṇa* is more of a text tradition than a single text, and different manuscripts have different rules, examples, glosses, and so on.

1. Cited by Haribhadra in his *Vṛtti* to the *Nandisūtra* 74 (p. 57 l. 12); also in his commentary on the *Daśavaikālikasūtra* (only the second *pāda*) and Malayagiri's commentary on the *Nandisūtra* (only the second *pāda*), the Āvaśyakasūtra (see Jain 1945 and Upadhye 1931–1932), and the *Sūryaprajñapti* (see Weber 1868: 273). Nitti-Dolci 1972 [1938]: §841 notes a different version of the same verse cited in the commentary to *Prākṛtalakṣaṇa* 2.13 (दुवयणे बहुवयणं चउत्थीविभत्तीए छट्ठी भण्णए । जह हत्था तह पाया वंदामि देवाहिदेवाणं ॥).

   बहुवयणेण दुवयणं छट्ठिविभत्तीइ भण्णइ चउत्थी ।
   जह हत्था तह पाया नमोत्थु देवाहिदेवाणं ॥

   The plural replaces the dual, and the sixth case replaces the fourth case.
   For example, "hands" and "feet," and "reverence to the Jinas."

2. Cited by Haribhadra in his *Vṛtti* to the *Nandisūtra* 51 (p. 28 l. 19).

   ए होइ अयारंते पयम्मि बीयाऐ बहुसु पुल्लिंगे ।
   तइयाइसु छट्ठी-सत्तमीण एक्कम्मि महिलत्थे ॥

   E occurs at the end of a word whose stem ends in *a* in the masculine accusative plural and in the instrumental, genitive, and locative of the feminine singular.

3. *Nāṭyaśāstra* 17.6 = *Gāthālakṣaṇa* 4. Nitti-Dolci (1972 [1938]: §839) notes the close similarity to *Prākṛtalakṣaṇa* 2.10 (एदोद्रलोपा विसर्जनीयस्य).

   एओआरपराइ अ अंकारपरं च पाअए णत्थि ।
   वसआरमज्झिमाइ अ कचवग्ग-तवग्ग-णिहणाइं ॥

   पराइ अ conj.; पराणिअ NāŚā, पराइं GāLa
   अंकारपरं च GāLa (and Alsdorf); अं आरपरं अ NāŚā, अंआरपरं अ Nitti-Dolci

   The sounds after *e* and *o* (i.e., *ai* and *au*),
   as well as the sounds after *anusvāra* (i.e., *visarga*), do not exist in Prakrit.
   Likewise the sounds between *v* and *s* (i.e., *ś* and *ṣ*)
   and the final sounds in the velar, palatal and dental groups (i.e., *ṅ*, *ñ* and *n*).

4. *Nāṭyaśāstra* 17.7. Also cited in the *Dhavalā* (*pādas ab*) and the *Jayadhavalā* (*pādas cd*); see Jain (1945).

   वच्चंति कगतदयवा लोवं अत्थं च से वहंति सरा ।
   खघथधभा उण हत्तं उवेंति अत्थं च मुंचंता ॥

   वच्चंति . . . वहंति सरा] NāŚā; Dha reads वच्चंति कगतदयवा लोवं अत्थसरा; Jain emends to तिट्ठंति अट्ठ सरा
   लोवं] JaDha; लोपं NāŚā
   च] conj; अ NāŚā

The sounds *k, g, t, d, y* and *v* are lost, and the vowel that follows them bears their meaning.
The sounds *kh, gh, th, dh,* and *bh* become *h* and leave their meaning (?).

5. *Nāṭyaśāstra* 17.8.
उप्परहुत्तरआरो हेटा हुत्तो अ पाअए णत्थि ।
मोत्तूण भद्र-वोद्रह-रुद्र-ह्रद-चन्द्र-जाईसु ॥

    हुत्तो] conj.; हुत्तौ NāŚā
    रुद्र] Alsdorf; पद्र NāŚā and Nitti-Dolci

Whether it comes first or last, *r* as part of a consonant cluster does not exist in Prakrit.
Exceptions include words of the type *bhadra-, vodraha-, rudra-, hrada-,* and *candra-*.

6. *Nāṭyaśāstra* 17.9.
खघथधभाण हआरो मुह-मेह-कहा-वहू-पहूएसु ।
कगतदयवाण णिच्चं वीयम्मि ठिओ सरो होइ ॥
h replaces *kh, gh, th, dh,* and *bh* in words like *muha-* (*mukha-*), *meha-* (*megha-*), *kahā-* (*kathā-*), *vahū-* (*vadhū-*) and *pahū-* (*prabhu-*).
The following vowel always stands in for the sounds *k, g, t, d, y,* and *v* after they disappear.

7. Malayagiri's commentary to the *Nandisūtra* (the second half of a *gāthā*). Cited in Upadhye 1931–1932.
मतुवत्थम्मि मुणिज्जह आलं इल्लं मणं तह य ॥
Know that *-ālaṃ, -illaṃ,* and *-maṇaṃ* are possessive suffixes.

8. Vasantarāja, *Prākṛtasaṃjīvinī* on 4.34. I have restored the verse heavily; it is evidently a *gāthā*, but the latter half of the first line is very corrupt. Although this verse does not pertain directly to Prakrit grammar, it bears on the regional characterization of Prakrit.
मरहट्ठदेसभासाऍ [संकहिइ जो पसिद्धसोहग्गं] ।
सो तावेण ण सावइ कविअणचिरसाइअं भणिअं ॥

    भासाऍ] conj.; भासाअ PrāSaṃ
    संकहिइ जो पसिद्धसोहग्ग] conj.; संकइ जो राहिअ स्संदेहिइ जा गो हिअं पसिद्धं PrāSaṃ. I take संदेहिइ to be an explanatory gloss on संकहिइ. The rest of the pāda is jumbled and unmetrical.
    तावेण] conj.; दावेण PrāSaṃ
    सावइ; conj. metri causa; सावेइ PrāSaṃ

He who doubts the well-known beauty of the regional language of Mahārāṣṭra—does he not thereby curse the words that have been savored for so long by so many poets?

9. *Prākṛtalakṣaṇa* (manuscript C), commentary to 2.14; see Nitti-Dolci 1972 [1938]: §842. The verse describes the "root sounds" (*mūlavaṇṇa-*), that is, the phonological inventory of Sanskrit.
तेत्तीस विंजणाइं च सत्तवीसइ सरा तहा भणिया ।
चत्तारि य जोगवहा चउसट्ठी मूलवण्णा ॥

च सत्तवीसइ] conj. metri causa; सत्तवीस PrāLa

Thirty-three consonants, twenty-seven vowels,
and four combining sounds makes sixty-four root sounds.

10. *Dhavalā* 9: 95 (only the last half); *Jayadhavalā* (see Jain 1945).

कीरइ पयाण काण वि आई-मज्झंत-वण्ण-सर-लोव ।

Some words undergo an elision of an initial, medial or final consonant or vowel.

11. The first few words are cited widely: by Jinadāsa (*Anuyogadvārasūtra-cūrṇi,* p. 128), by Haribhadra (*Anuyogadvāra-vivṛti,* p. 187), by Vīrasena (*Dhavalā,* vol. 8, p. 90; vol. 9, p. 95; vol. 10, p. 2; vol. 13, pp. 243 and 337). The complete verse is cited only in the *Jayadhavalā* (see Jain 1945). Since it allows for the substitution of any vowel by any other vowel, it must have been very useful for exegetical purposes.

एए छच्च समाणा दोण्णि अ संझक्खरा सरा अट्ठ ।
अण्णोण्णस्स विरोहा उवेंति सव्वे समाएसं ॥

The eight vowels—these six simple vowels and two compound vowels—
come in place of each other without any restraint (so Jain).

12. *Jayadhavalā* (see Jain 1945).

दीसंति दोण्णि वण्णा संजुत्ता अह व तिण्णि चत्तारि ।
ताणं दुव्वल-लोवं काऊण कमो पजुत्तव्वो ॥

When two, letters are joined, or three, or four,
elide the weakest of them, and continue the process.

13. *Jayadhavalā* (see Jain 1945). This transforms voiceless into voiced sounds, which is relatively rare except in Jain texts and in (in the limited context of *t* to *d*) in Prakrit used on the stage. As the verse currently stands it is an *upagīti/gātha* (both halves have just one light syllable in their sixth *gaṇa*).

वग्गे वग्गे आई अविट्ठया दोण्णि जे वण्णा ।
ते णेयय णिय वग्गे तइअत्तणयं उवणमंति ॥

In every class the two letters that stand at the beginning
are variously changed to the third letter of that class.

TESTIMONIA

1. *Vṛttajātisamuccaya* 2.8–9. Note that the commentator Gopāla notes that "according to some people Vṛddhakavi is Harivṛddha" (*vṛddhakavir harivṛddha iti kecit*).

भुअआहिवसालाहणवुड्ढकइनिरूविअं इमं दइए ।
णिहणणिरूपविअधुवअम्मि वत्थुए गीइआ णत्थि ॥

In the opinion of Bhujagādhipa, Sātavāhana, and Vṛddhakavi,
when a strophic *vastuka* features a *dhruvakā* in its definition, there is no need for a *gītikā*.

भुअआहिवसालाहणवुड्ढकइनिरूविआण दुवईण ।
णामाइं जाइं साहेमि तुज्झ ताइं विअ कमेण ॥

I will tell you in sequence all the names for the *dvipadas*
defined by Bhujagādhipa, Sātavāhana, and Vṛddhakavi.

2. *Sarasvatīkaṇṭhābharaṇa* 1.99 (ex. 133), p. 93 = Śṛṅgāraprakāśa 9.266, p. 507.

   अम्हारिसा वि कइणो हलिवुड्ढहालपमुहा वि ।
   मण्डुक्क-मक्कडा वि हु होंति हरी सप्पसिंहा वि ॥
   People like me are poets
   Just as much as Harivṛddha and Hāla.
   Don't we call frogs and monkeys *hari*,
   besides snakes and lions?

3. *Karpūramañjarī* pp. 9–10 (ed. Ghosh). The *vidūṣaka* complains about the servant girl Vicakṣaṇā.

   विदूषकः । [सक्रोधम्] ता उज्जुअं ज्जेव किं ण भण्णइ अम्हाणं चेडिआ हरिउड्ढ-णन्दिउड्ढ-पोट्टिस-हाल-प्पहदीणं पि पुरदो सुकइ त्ति ।

   हरिउड्ढ . . . प्पहदीणं] Konow lists many variants on these names, but the most significant is हरि-बम्हसिद्धि-ओड्डीस-पालित्तअ-चंपअराअ-मल्लसेहराणं, read by witnesses STU.

   VIDŪṢAKA: [*Angrily.*] Well, why don't you come right out and say it? That this servant girl of ours is a better poet than even Harivṛddha, Nandivṛddha, Poṭṭisa, and Hāla?

NOTES

CHAPTER 1. PRAKRIT IN THE LANGUAGE ORDER OF INDIA

1. Foucault 1994 [1966]: xxiv.

2. Mīrzā Khān, *Gift from India* (1936 [1676]), 53: *bebāyad dānist ki zabān-i ahl-i hind mutaʿaddid ast. ammā ānchi badān kitābhā o dīvānhā taṣnīf tuwān kard, o maṭbūʿ-i ṭabʿ-i salīm o ẕihn-i mustaqīm bāshad, bar sih gūnah ast.* M. Ziauddin's English translation is on p. 34. See also Keshavmurthy 2013.

3. See Pollock 2011: 29 and 2006*a*: 89–105.

4. "More or less" because the third position, the vernacular, was often filled by a language called Apabhramsha, which many people did in fact think of as a vernacular.

5. Mīrzā Khān, *Gift from India*, 53–54: *duyum parākirt . . . o madḥ-i mulūk o wuzarāʿ o akābir beshtar badīn zabān goyand. o ān zabān-i ʿālam ast, yaʿni ʿālam-i ki zīr zamīn ast. o ān-rā pātāl-bānī goyand . . . o nāg-bānī nīz nāmand . . . yaʿnī zabān-i ahl-i asfal us-sāfilīn o mārān ki zamīnīyān o suflīyānand. o ān murakkab ast az sahāskirt, ki sābiq maẕkūr shud, o bhākhā, ki baʿd az īn maẕkūr shawad.* The translation here is based on Ziauddin's.

6. See the end of chapter 7.

7. Foucault 1994 [1966]: xv.

8. Quoted in Crowley 1996: 39.

9. There are a few reliable guides: von Hinüber 2001 and two works by Jagdishchandra Jain (1961, in Hindi; 2004, in English).

10. Saussure 2011 [1959]: 20–23.

11. Linguistic areas are spaces in which genetically unrelated languages share grammatical features; see Emeneau 1956.

12. *Mirror of Literature* 1.32; see the discussion in chapter 5.

13. Kaviraj 1992; Pollock 2003, 2006*a*.

14. Social science has naturalized these categories to the extent that they are used constantly and promiscuously in Indological scholarship, often without recognition of or attention to the domains and problems through which they were theorized in the first place (thus it has become common to speak of Sanskrit language practices "legitimating" political power without reference to Weber, or of Sanskrit language practices serving the purposes of "distinction" without reference to Bourdieu).

15. For language ideology, see Woolard 1994; for philology as a corrective to social theory, see Pollock 2006*a:* 497–524.

16. Foucault 2009 [1961]: xxviii; Sakai 1992: 4–5; Sakai 2009: 77. For the regimentation of discursive practices in classical India, see Pollock 1989.

17. Pollock 1996, 2006*a:* 37–280.

18. Gadamer 2004 [1960]: 287–288. The original reads "eine ausgezeichnete Weise des Geschichtlichseins selbst, den geschichtlichen Vorzug der Bewahrung, die—in immer erneuerter Bewährung—ein Wahres sein läßt" (Gadamer 2010 [1960]: 292).

19. *Necklace of Sarasvatī* 2.17, the second example (p. 144) = *Recognition of Śakuntalā* 3.13.

20. *Seven Centuries,* and the difficult problem of its date and authorship, is discussed in chapter 3.

21. W175 in *Seven Centuries* (unless otherwise noted I cite verses from Weber's edition of the text and using his numeration); *Light on Suggestion,* p. 16 (Kāvyamālā ed.); see Ingalls, Masson, and Patwardhan 1990: 83, whose translation I cannot improve upon. For Ānandavardhana's "revolution" see McCrea 2008.

22. See Abhinavagupta's commentary on Ānandavardhana's *Light on Suggestion,* pp. 84, 90–92 in the Ingalls, Masson and Patwardhan translation; the *Explanation of the Suggestion Verses* by Ratnākara, who reproduces Abhinavagupta's notes (as noted by Masson and Patwardhan 1974); Dundas 1985: 17. Bhoja's discussion of the verse seems to show no awareness of the controversy generated by Ānandavardhana's *Light.*

23. Although the use of Prakrit in these domains still stands in need of explanation, it is notable that they are the same domains in which vernacular texts would later appear; see Pollock 2011: 29; Jain 2004: 425–478; Bhattacharyya 1947; Chintamani 1971.

24. For general introductions to Jainism, see von Glasenapp 1999; Jaini 1979; Dundas 2002 [1992].

25. See, e.g., Cox 2006 and Hopkins 2002. For Jain literature in Prakrit, consult Chaudhari 1973.

26. Bhoja (eleventh century), *Illumination of the Erotic,* p. 398: *sāhityasya sarvapārṣadatvāt* (Pollock 2006*a:* 430 n. 103); Bhoja is adapting Rājaśekhara (tenth century), *Analysis of Literature,* p. 38: *sarvapārṣadatvāt kāvyavidyāyāḥ.*

27. *Message Poem,* vv. 3 (*micchadeso*), 4 (*kulakamalo pāiyakavvesu*). I am aware of the real possibility of anachronism in using the word "Hindu" (e.g., Hawley 1991; Lorenzen 1995), but I use it to refer to a variety of systems of belief and practice (Shaivism, Vaishnavism, "Vedic" and "Puranic" Hinduism) that acknowledge, however nominally, the authority of the Vedas.

28. Bāṇabhaṭṭa (seventh century) calls *Seven Centuries* an "inexhaustible treasury" (*Deeds of Harṣa,* v. 12).

29. A verse in praise of Yaśovarman of Ankor (ca. 900 CE) refers to a Prakrit court epic by Pravarasena (Barth 1885: 254[434]e, LVII B v. 7): *yena pravarasenena dharmasetuṃ vivṛṇvatā* (ed. *vivṛṇvata*) | *paraḥ pravaraseno 'pi jitaḥ prākṛtasetukṛt* ||: "He, called Pravarasena because of his excellent army, produced a Bridge of Dharma, and thereby conquered that other Pravarasena who merely produced a common bridge" (with a pun on both *pravarasena-* and *prākṛtasetu-*, both "a common bridge" and "the Bridge in Prakrit." Prakrit in Java is discussed in chapter 6.

30. See the discussion in chapter 3.

31. See chapter 7.

32. On "homeless texts" see Tavakoli-Targhi 2001: 8–15. Contrast the case of Sanskrit today: to combat what they see as a nefarious neocolonialist ideology in mainstream scholarship, some right-wing Hindus have sought to claim "ownership" (*adhikāra*) of Sanskrit, by which they mean the exclusive right to make claims about its history.

33. The more successful examples are Syādvāda Mahāvidyālaya in Benares, founded in 1905, and the National Institute for Prakrit Studies and Research in Śravaṇabeḷagoḷa, founded in 1991. Thanks to John Cort for discussing these institutions with me.

34. Hoernle 1880*a*: 313, a useful summary of the history of scholarship on Prakrit up to that date. The emphasis is mine.

35. Lassen 1837: 7.

36. Both Goldschmidt's and Weber's editions were accompanied by several ancillary studies (Goldschmidt 1873, 1874, 1875, 1878, 1879, 1881, 1883*a*, 1883*b*, 1885; Weber 1870, 1874, 1883).

37. Pischel 1874, 1879, 1981 [1900].

38. In the text just below, I refer to Jacobi 1886 (to which Jacobi 1908–1909 is related). Jacobi's editions of Jain texts include Jacobi 1879 and 1884; his *Kleine Schriften* were edited by Bernhard Kölver in 1970.

39. For important collections of their papers, see *Upadhye Papers* (Mysore, 1983) and Bhayani's *Indological Studies* (Ahmebad, 1993 and 1998).

40. Jacobi 1886: §1; it is updated by Masica 1991: 50–55.

41. See Salomon 1995: 301: "The basic assumption is that there is and always ways an absolute dichotomy between 'Sanskrit' and 'Prakrit' or, in modern terms, of OIA [Old Indo-Aryan, AO] versus Middle Indo-Aryan (MIA)." This assumption is made, e.g., by Sankunni Nair (1995: 71–89).

42. Pollock 2006*a*: 61, citing Renou 1956: 84.

43. The term "simultaneous order" is T.S. Eliot's (1982: 37). For the languages of the *Kuvalayamālā*, see Upadhye 1963–1964.

44. So Katre 1964: 2–3.

45. For Émile Senart's "Monumental Prakrit" and "Sinhalese Prakrit," see Salomon 1998: 76–77 and 151. "*Leṇa* Prakrit" refers to the language of the rock-cut caves or *leṇa*s (Sanskrit *layana-*) in the usage of Richard Pischel (1981 [1900]: §7). "*Stūpa* Dialect" was proposed by Heinrich Lüders (1911: 62). For the relationship between Prakrit and "Buddhist Hybrid Sanskrit" see Edgerton 1936. On "Niya Prakrit" see Burrow (1935–1937). Sankunni Nair (1995: 72) suggests that the *Cullavagga* of the Pali canon uses the terms "Sanskrit" and "Prakrit," but this is incorrect; his reference is rather to the well-known *sakāya niruttiya* passage, for which see Brough 1980 and Levman 2008–2009.

46. Pischel 1981 [1900]: §§1–2; von Hinüber 2001: §1. One of Pischel's favorite quotations comes from Pṛthvīdhara's commentary on *Little Clay Cart* (p. 1): *mahārāṣṭryādayaḥ kāvya eva prayujyante* "Mahārāṣṭrī and the other Prakrit languages are only used in poetry" (see Pischel 1873: 397). Pṛthvīdhara, however, did not mean what Pischel apparently thought he meant. *Kāvye,* I believe, is in contrast to *nāṭake;* Mahārāṣṭrī is not used in theater (and therefore not used in *Little Clay Cart*), because it is used exclusively in "literature heard" (*śravyakāvya*), that is, literature meant to be read or recited rather than performed onstage. (Pṛthvīdhara seems to be right when it comes to earlier plays, but wrong about the later plays.)

47. With one exception: the *saṭṭaka,* or Prakrit play, although this genre could easily be considered a dramatization of existing Prakrit genres of lyric poetry and song. For more on this genre, see chapter 7.

48. For the idea that theatrical languages are considered Prakrit secondarily, see the discussion of Daṇḍin's *Mirror of Literature* in chapter 5.

49. Daṇḍin, *Mirror of Literature* 1.34: *mahārāṣṭrāśrayāṃ bhāṣāṃ prakṛṣṭaṃ prākṛtaṃ viduḥ | sāgaraḥ sūktaratnānāṃ setubandhādi yanmayam ||*. The spelling Māhārāṣṭrī is a scholarly convention inaugurated by Jacobi (1886); see Abhyankar 1955 for the historically more accurate spelling "Mahārāṣṭrī".

50. This periodization is explicitly ventured by George Grierson (1927: 122): "It may be taken as a convenient date for fixing the memory, that these Prakrits were dead languages by, in round numbers, 1000 A.D."

51. *Seven Centuries,* W2; *Taraṅgalolā,* v. 13 (there is a metrical problem here and I propose to read *pāaavayaṇanibaddhaṃ* or something like it instead of *pāyayaṭṭhaṃ ca nibaïṃ*); *Līlāvaī,* v. 43; *Kuvalayamālā,* p. 4 l. 11; *Vajjālagga, gāhāvajjā* (vv. 9–18).

52. *Brilliance of the Connoisseurs,* v. 5: *siṃgāra-bhāva-suhaā sarasā varasuṃdari vva somālī | koḍḍa-maṇoraha-jaṇaṇī haraï maṇaṃ pāauttī hu ||*.

53. See chapter 5. The only case that I know of in which the word "Prakrit" is used to refer to Buddhist scripture is in the Spitzer manuscript (Franco 2004); for its use in reference to Jain scripture, see the "three myths" discussed in chapter 3.

54. Deleuze and Guattari 1986: 26.

55. See chapter 5.

56. The historical framework is Sheldon Pollock's (1996, 1998, 2006*a*).

57. For reviews of the "origins of *kāvya*" question, see Pollock 2006*a:* 77ff., focusing on an ethnohistorical moment of invention in Vālmīki's *Rāmāyaṇa* and a (later) process of "desacralization" of Sanskrit under the Śaka rulers of Gujarat; Jamison 2004, focusing on the continuities between *kāvya* and the *Ṛg Veda* (she acknowledges the "Middle Indic" origins of *kāvya,* however, on pp. 145–147); Boccali 1999 and Rossella 2011, focusing on the *Songs of the Buddhist Monks and Nuns* in Pali.

58. Garrez 1872.

59. Javanese stands somewhat apart, although it is closer to this first group than the second. Tamil and Malayalam form a group somewhat apart because of their reliance on an independent grammatical tradition in Tamil. For more on these two groups, see chapter 6.

60. I am thinking of the critique of Rousseau and Saussure in Derrida 1997 [1976].

61. Tambling 1988.

62. Although Prakrit is very often conflated with vernacular speech, both in premodernity (see the verse of Haribhadra discussed in chapter 3) and by modern scholars (e.g., Granoff 1989*b:* 330).

63. As people did to protest compulsory Hindi education in Tamil Nadu (Ramaswamy 1997: 1) or demand the formation of a state for Telugu-speaking regions (Mitchell 2009: 1).

64. There are exceptions: Viśvanātha, the seventeenth-century scribe of the *Moonlight of the Essence of the Bridge* (*Setutattvacandrikā*), a synthetic commentary on *Rāvaṇa's Demise,* was clearly well acquainted with Prakrit. In the Jaisalmer collections there are several old manuscripts that were revised and corrected by scholars such as Pradyumna Sūri (mid-thirteenth century) who were similarly well acquainted with Prakrit. But I can attest that these are exceptions.

65. Ghanaśyāma, *River of Amazement:* "Some self-styled scholars have made the mistake of reading the Prakrit phrase *viddhasālabhajjiā* instead of *viddhasālabhaṃjiā* on account of their belief that the circle on top of the letter bha, which usually represents nasalization, is a scribal mistake in some of the manuscripts for a circle to the side of the letter, which represents the doubling of the following consonant, and understanding this phrase as 'the wife and the brother-in-law that has been beat up' [*viddha-syāla-bhāryā,* the middle word now being a mild vulgarity in most Indian languages—AO], they claim that it is out of character with the poet, with the sentiment of the play, and with what actually happens in the play, as well as indecent. But they have wasted their time with this debate, since their theory is contradicted by Vicakṣaṇā's line in the third act, in which she says 'a statue (*śālabhañjikā*) was created in imitation of her,' and hence the title of the play is *Viddhasālabhaṃjiā,* 'The Pierced Statue'" (*kvacit pustaka-prasūtyantareṣu lekhaka-hasta-doṣa-vaśād akṣara-mastaka-pārśvānusvāra-dvitva-vyañjaka-bindu-viśvāsena viddha-sāla-[bhajji]ā iti prākṛta-bhāṣā-pāṭham āśaṃkya viddha-syāla-bharyeti kavi-bhāva-nāṭikārtha-viruddham asaṃgataṃ ca vadanti paṇḍita[ṃ]manyāḥ kecid. bhrānta-pratiyoginas tu tucchāḥ, tṛtīyāṅka-praveśake "tadaṇuvādiṇī sālabhaṃjīā ṇimmāvidā" iti vicakṣaṇā-vākya-virodhād iti dik. tathā ca viddha-sālabhaṃjieti nāma yasyāḥ*). The commentary is ascribed to Ghanaśyāma's wives Sundarī and Kamalā, but I believe that Ghanaśyāma ghost-wrote it, or that his wives somehow learned how to uncannily replicate their husband's pretentious style.

66. Bloch 1893 and the critical review of Konow 1894, which refers to Hoernle 1873: 210; Pischel 1981 [1900]: §22; Hillebrandt 1984 [1912].

67. There is some slight evidence that Bhāsa was also a Prakrit poet; see Krishna Moorthy 1946.

68. Printz 1921. See A. N. Upadhye's n. 35 in the introduction to *Kaṃsa's Demise* and the work of Anna Aurelia Esposito (2004, 2008, 2010*a*, 2010*b*).

69. Von Hinüber 2001: §59: "zwischen den Handschriften und den Grammatikern einen gangbaren Mittelweg zu suchen." See also Steiner 1997: 157–208 and 2001, echoing Hoernle 1873: 210.

70. See Mārkaṇḍeya's *Sum-Total of Prakrit* 3.77 and Konow 2007 [1901]: 202; on the latter, see Ghosh's edition (the avowed purpose of which is to correct Konow's unwarranted interventions in the text) and Salomon 1982; *Mirror of Literature* 6.158*cd*–159: "Men who are not low, whose souls are purified [*saṃskṛta*], speak Sanskrit; women of that status should use Śaurasenī, but they should use Mahārāṣṭrī in verses" (*puruṣāṇām anīcānāṃ*

saṃskṛtaṃ saṃskṛtātmanām | śaurasenī prayoktavyā tādṛśīnāṃ ca yoṣitām | āsām eva tu gāthāsu mahārāṣṭrīṃ prayojayet |). See chapter 5 regarding Rājaśekhara's fourfold model of language.

71. And this was the view of the first generation of European scholars to read Prakrit: "Volkssprache" (Westergaard 1862: 86); "volkstümliche Charakter" (Weber 1870: 14).

72. Grierson 1927: 123.

73. Ibid., 121. Grierson's "Aryan" is what anglophone linguists after World War II called "Indo-Aryan"; I follow the lead of Hermann Jacobi in calling this language-family "Indic."

74. Ghatage 2000 [1936]: 105. Ghatage is echoing the idea of "literarische Ausbildung" that was earlier formulated by, e.g., in Bloch 1893: 12.

75. Lacôte 1908: 42: "Ainsi, les prâkrits, au sens étroit que donnent les grammairiens à ce terme, n'ont pas de réalité linguistique, ou, plus exactement, il n'en ont qu'une indirecte." The chapter in which Lacôte writes this is titled "Caractère artificiel des prâkrits."

76. Besides Bloch 1970 [1914]: 15, see Konow 1894: 473: "Das litteräre Prakrit ist meiner Ueberzeugung nach nie eine lebendige Sprache gewesen" (in my opinion literary Prakrit has never been a living language). And see too Konow 2007 [1901]: 191.

77. *Kuvalayamālā* §246 (pp. 152–153); see also Master 1950; Upadhye 1963–1964; Chojnacki 2008*a*: 447–450.

78. Pischel 1900: §6; my translation differs slightly from Jha's (Pischel 1981 [1900]).

79. On Pali, see von Hinüber 1982; on Ardhamāgadhī, see Jacobi 1884. Pischel developed the idea of artificiality in conversation with other scholars in an early review (1873).

80. Schleicher quoted in Crowley 1996: 11. One can also compare the titular metaphor of *The Life of Language* by William Dwight Whitney, a Sanskrit scholar who was instrumental in the establishment of linguistics as a discipline independent from philology.

81. "It is generally assumed that dramatic Prākrits do not represent the actual speech of the people they are supposed to typify. Nevertheless, they are based upon it and they remain for us pieces of valuable evidence regarding phonology, morphology and syntax of Middle Aryan dialects. This value diminishes with time" (Bubenik 1996: 15). Along the same lines, see Bloch 1970 [1914] and 1965 [1934].

82. Kloss 1967: 39.

83. Deshpande 1993.

CHAPTER 2. INVENTING PRAKRIT: THE LANGUAGES OF POWER

1. "That man should speak at all is nature's act, / but how you speak—in this tongue or in that— / she leaves to you and to your preference" (https://digitaldante.columbia.edu/dante/divine-comedy/paradiso/paradiso-26).

2. See Pollock 2006.

3. Dante, *On Vernacular Eloquence* 17.2 (Botterill 1996).

4. The parallel between the Sātavāhanas and the Kuṣāṇas (but not the literary cultures over which they presided) was explored by Lévi 1936; see Ollett 2017 for further reflections.

5. The chronology of the Sātavāhana dynasty was a lively topic of Indological discussion starting with Pargiter 1913 and lasting into the 1970s. Almost all of this scholarship is based on Ussherian tabulations of the *purāṇas* and, toward the end of this period, on extremely

creative construals of the epigraphic evidence. The abundant numismatic evidence led to no convincing chronology until Shailendra Bhandare's dissertation (1999).

6. The numismatic evidence analyzed by Bhandare (1999, 2006, 2011) and Joe Cribb (1998, 2000) largely corroborates the chronology that Dehejia 1972 derived from inscriptional paleography and formal comparison of architectural elements. Shastri 1999 more or less concurs with these results.

7. In appendix B, the inscriptions have been given serial numbers, cited in these notes in square brackets, e.g., [1] refers to "Kanaganahalli inscription of the time of Vāsiṣṭhīputra Śrī Chimuka Sātavāhana, year 16."

8. [6] and [7].

9. On the *dakṣiṇāpatha,* see Neelis 2011: 205–226. On political and economic integration and urbanization during the Sātavāhana period, see Ray 1986, Morrison 1995, Sinopoli 2001, Parabrahma Sastry 2008, and Skinner 2012.

10. This title is applied to an unknown king (probably Śrī Sātakarṇi) at Nāṇeghāṭ [6], to Gautamīputra Śrī Sātakarṇi at Sannati [11], to Vāsiṣṭhīputra Śrī Puḷumāvi at Nāsik [18], and to Śrī Sātakarṇi (probably Vāsiṣṭhīputra Śrī Sātakarṇi) in the Junāgaṛh inscription [104]. It supplies the title to Gokhale 2008, *Lord of Dakṣiṇāpatha,* a collection of essays on the Sātavāhanas.

11. General treatments of rock-cut architecture include Dehejia 1972 and Nagaraju 1981; see also Rees 2011.

12. See Bakker 2007: 21; the image gallery of the Kuṣāṇa rulers at Māṭ, near Mathurā, is a later example (see Lüders 1961: 131–147), as is the one at Surkh Kotal (Fussman 1989); on these see also Rosenfield 1967. For the representation of the Sātavāhanas at Kanaganahalli, see below in the text.

13. "Poetry of politics": Pollock 1996: 198.

14. The donations to the priests are called *dakhinā* (*dakṣiṇā*), and those to the spectators are called *pasapaka* (*prāsarpaka*).

15. The first legible invocation (line 1) reads *namo dhaṃmasa;* something has been lost prior to this. See Minkowski 2008 for the introductory verses of literary texts, with which the invocations of inscriptions (commonly *sidhaṃ* in this period) bear some relation, as yet undetermined . For the Vedic and post-Vedic connotations of *dharma*, see Olivelle 2004: 82.

16. See, e.g., *Āpastambaśrautasūtra* 21.5.10 and 21.8.7 and *Baudhāyanaśrautasūtra* 8.5.

17. For a good bibliographic introduction to the enormous scholarly literature on Aśoka's inscriptions, see Falk 2006.

18. See the *Compendium of the Essence of Figures in Literature* 1.3 of Udbhaṭa for the definition of *chekānuprāsa.*

19. *Caritabrahmacariyāya* could also refer to her study of the Vedas. Bühler (followed by Sircar and Mirashi) inserted word breaks to read *yañā hutā dhūpanasugaṃdhā,* but the following letter *ya* guarantees that this is another long compound describing Nāganikā (so also Gokhale 2004–2006: 250); see the bibliography for [6]. See the *Ornament of Literature* of Bhāmaha 2.8 and Udbhaṭa's *Compendium* 1.8–10 for *lāṭānuprāsa.* Some of the more interesting controversies surrounding the interpretation of this inscription have involved the eligibility of women to perform *śrauta* sacrifices; see Sankaranarayanan 1999.

20. Daṇḍin calls power (*ojas*) the "essence of literary prose" (*gadyasya jīvitam*) in his *Mirror of Literature* 1.80. *Treatise on Theater* 16.105 reads: *samāsavadbhir bahubhir vicitraiś ca padair yutam | sānurāgair udāraiś ca tad ojaḥ parikīrtyate* ||. I follow Abhinavagupta's insightful commentary in my interpretation of this verse. I follow Amarasiṃha (*ojo dīptau bale*, 3.3.234) in translating *ojas* as "power," where a more conventional translation might be "vigor"; the word is cognate with the word "august."

21. Tieken 2006; see chapter 4.

22. The term *apratihatacakra-* was used by Khāravela, across the Deccan in Odisha, within a generation of the Nāṇeghāṭ inscription. It was also used by Indo-Parthian ruler Gondophares, of the middle of the first century BCE, and the Kṣatrapa Rājūvula of Mathurā, in the early first century CE (Rosenfield 1967: 152). It is probably referenced in the epithet *apatihatasaṃkapa-* "whose resolve to sacrifice was never impeded," of the Ikṣvāku rulers of Nāgārjunakoṇḍa (late third century CE).

23. As noted by Jacobi (1886: §13), who makes what I consider a faulty historical inference about this difference (see below in the text).

24. The term "linguistic volume" is Gramsci's (Lo Piparo 2010: 27).

25. The reading and translation are from Nakanishi and von Hinüber 2014; see [25] for the other label inscriptions. See Fynes 1995 on the religious patronage of the Sātavāhanas. Zin 2013 wonders why rulers who were not themselves Buddhists were so prominently depicted in the Buddhist art of Kanaganahalli. For the phrase *mahācaitya* applied to the *stūpa* at Kanaganahalli, see Skilling 2016.

26. The inscriptions of Hāthībāḍā and Ghosuṇḍī in the early first century BCE speak of the construction of a structure for worship of Saṃkarṣaṇa and Vāsudeva; see Salomon 1998: 87.

27. Tieken 2008: 371 n. 82. Compare the surprise of Ācārya (1982: 27) at Gautamī Balaśrī's eulogy of her son at Nāsik: *yah sacmuc āścarya kī bāt hai ki svayaṃ ko 'ek brahmaṇa' aur 'khatiyadapamānamadana' kahne vāle tathā vaidik evaṃ bhāgavatdharm kā punaruddhār karne vāle sātavāhan nareśoṃ ne prākṛt ko rājbhāṣā kā gaurav pradhān kiyā* ("It is really a matter of surprise that the Sātavāhana kings, who called themselves 'unique Brāhmaṇas' and 'destroyers of the pride and arrogance of the Kṣatriyas' and oversaw a resurgence of Vedic and Bhāgavata religion, made Prakrit into the major language of state").

28. See Pollock 2006*a*: 39–50; see also the Vedic prohibition on writing in *Aitareya Āraṇyaka* 5.3.3, "he should not learn when he has eaten flesh, or seen blood, or a dead body, or done what is unlawful, or anointed (his eyes) or oiled or rubbed his body, or had himself shaved, or bathed, or has put on colour, or put on a wreath, or had intercourse, or written, or obliterated writing" (trans. Keith 1909: 301–302; thanks to Pashaura Singh for drawing my attention to this passage).

29. Scholarship sometimes still refers to this dynasty as the "Cedis" (e.g., Fitzgerald 2009), on the basis of a rather difficult reading in Khāravela's Udayagiri inscription [46]. The records of other kings, however, use the title Mahāmeghavāhana (see appendix A).

30. See [46]. Lüders (1911: 62) had already recognized in this inscription an early *praśasti*. Some scholars have been troubled by the fact that Khāravela's inscription is in a western language rather than an eastern language, and have postulated either that Khāravela employed a western scribe (Barua 1929: 163) or that his aversion to the language of the people of Magadha was greater than his aversion to the language of the Sātavāhanas (Witzel 2006:

466). But there was only one language in which serious claims about political power could be advanced in Khāravela's time, and that was the western Middle Indic used also by the Sātavāhanas. In its year-by-year organization, Khāravela's inscription recalls those of Aśoka and ultimately, if indirectly, that of Darius as Behistun (Pollock 2006*b:* 180–181).

31. Line 4: *dutiye ca vase acitayitā sātakaṇiṃ pacima-disaṃ haya-gaja-nara-radha-bahulaṃ daṃḍaṃ pathāpayati kañhabeṃnāgatāya senāya vitās[e]ti asika-nagaraṃ* ("And in the second year, without a care for Sātakarṇi, he sent his forces, with plentiful horses, elephants, infantry, and chariots, to the west, and when his army had reached the Krishna and Wainganga rivers, he terrified the city of Ṛṣika"). Reading *asika* for Barua's *asaka* and *kañhabeṃnāgatāya* with Jayaswal (1929–1930) instead of Barua's *ka[liṃgā]gatāya ca.* Nath 1990 has convincingly identified Ṛṣikanagara (*asikanagara*) with the town of Adam in northeastern Maharashtra.

32. See Cox 2013: 136 for a short discussion of these compounds. One example is *bh[ī]ta-tasite ca nikhita-chata-bhiṃgāre hita-ratana-sāpateye sava-raṭhika-bhojake pāde vaṃdāpayati*, literally, "he made all of the Raṭṭhikas and Bhojakas, having been first terrified and then trembling, having had their parasols and pitchers cast away, having had their jewels and riches taken away, to bow at his feet."

33. An example is *haya-gaja-nara-radha-bahulaṃ*, cited in n. 30 above. I have tried and failed to find examples in this inscription of metrical prose such as the *veḍha* discussed by Jacobi 1885 and Mette 1973.

34. Of its literary qualities, the repetition of the key word *caka* in different senses (*apatihata-caka-vāhana-balo caka-dhar[o] guta-cako pavata-cako*), a kind of *lāṭānuprāsa*, can be mentioned.

35. *sava-pāsaṃḍa-pūjako sava-devāyatana-saṃkāra-kārako* in line 17; *sava-gharavāsinaṃ ca sava-rāja-bhatakānaṃ ca sava-gahapatikānaṃ ca [sava]-bamhaṇānaṃ ca pāna-bhojanaṃ dadāti arahatānaṃ [samaṇānaṃ ca] [pāna-bhojanaṃ] dadāti [sata-sahase-hi]* in line 9.

36. [18]. My argument presupposes a date of ca. 84 CE for the death of Gautamīputra Śrī Sātakarṇi, which is supported by a variety of evidence (Seeley and Turner 1984; Bhandare 1999; Cribb 1992, 1998, 2000; Shastri 1996*c*). The essential points of this argument, however, are compatible with the older date of ca. 124 CE (Sircar 1966).

37. [11]; see figure 5. Nakanishi and von Hinüber restore [*vaseṭhi*] instead of [*gotami*] in the king's metronymic, which is inexplicable in view of the parallels to the Nāsik inscription. I do not know where the Sannati stela is currently located (it is not at the Gulbarga museum, where many of the other stelae from Sannati are housed).

38. ". . . *khatiya-dapa-māna-mada-nasa-saka-yavana-palhava-nisūdanasa dhama-pajita-kara-viniyoga-karasa kitāparādhe pi satu-jane apāṇa-hisā-rucisa dijāvara-kuṭuba-vivadhanasa khakharāta-vasa-niravasesa-karasa sātavāhana-kula-yasa-patithāpana-karasa sava-maḍalābhivādita-ca[ra]ṇasa vinivatita-cātuvaṇa-sakarasa aneka-samarāvajita-satusaghasa aparājita-vijaya-patāka-satujana-dupadhasanīya-puravarasa kula-purisa-parаparā-gata-vipula-rāja-sadasa. . .*" Later sources identify the sounds of royalty as five drums (*pañcamahāśabda*).

39. There are interesting recollections of this story in the Jain tradition. The commentaries on the *Āvaśyaka* (see Balbir 1993*a:* 60) and the *Prabandha of Pādalipta* relate that the Sātavāhana king sent an agent to Nahapāna in Bharuch who prevailed upon Nahapāna

to spend all of his money on religious donation; when Nahapāna ran out of money, the Sātavāhana king besieged Bharuch and killed Nahapāna. See also Klatt 1882: 252, which notes that Nabhovāhana (Nahapāna) ruled for forty years according to Jain chronology (such a duration is corroborated by his series of portrait coins). For the most detailed narrative of this conflict, based primarily on numismatic evidence, see Bhandare 1999.

40. This range—from highly composite to highly analytic over the course of a single sentence—would become typical of later prose-poetry in Sanskrit, such as Subandhu and Bāṇa.

41. "This is deliberate art, however little we may admire it," Keith 1920: 50 concedes. Winternitz 1985 [1920]: 38 asserts that the inscription has "all the characteristics of the style of ornate prose." Kane 1961: 336 says that the Nāsik inscription "exhibits the same traits" as the literary prose of Rudradāman's Junāgaṛh inscription.

42. A few specific echoes can be singled out. "The one whose mounts have drunk from the waters of the three oceans" (*ti-samuda-toya-pīta-vāhanasa*) is echoed in a similar title, "overlord of the three oceans" (*trisamudrādhipataye*) applied to a king named Sātavāhana who briefly appears in Bāṇa's *Deeds of Harṣa* (seventh century CE). Another title, "the single archer" (*ekadhanudharasa*), recurs as a title of Dilīpa in Kālidāsa's *Dynasty of Raghu* (3.31, fifth century CE).

43. Pollock, who coined the term "poetry of politics," recognizes in the Nāsik inscription a "quasi *praśasti*" (Pollock 2006*a:* 79 n. 11).

44. Lévi 1904: 170.

45. [100]. For the distinction between expressive and documentary purposes, see Pollock 2006*a:* 117–118. For the Nāsik inscription of Uṣavadāta, see Salomon 1998: 89–90. Damsteegt 1978: 212 distinguishes a "eulogy" in "almost pure Sanskrit" from the rest of the inscription. "[T]he language of the concluding part is different from that of the rest of the record," Sircar 1965: 167 n. 2 observes. Uṣavadāta tried to write in correct Sanskrit but "fell back into the traditional Prākṛt" after a few lines, Witzel 2006: 467 claims, overlooking the functional differentiation. Tieken 2006: 108 n. 29 ignores this inscription.

46. [99].

47. Bronkhorst 2014.

48. See the prohibitions in the *Aitareya Āraṇyaka* mentioned above.

49. [96], [12].

50. *Seven Centuries* W272: *kīraṃti ccia ṇāsaï uae reha vva khalaaṇe mettī | sā uṇa suaṇammi kaā aṇahā pāhāṇareha vva ||* ("friendship with wicked people is destroyed as soon as it's made, like a letter drawn on water, but friendship with good people is like a letter carved onto stone"). On this text, see chapter 3.

51. Pollock 2006*a:* 72.

52. [12]; Bhandare 1999: 135.

53. [104].

54. The suggestion of Witzel 2006: 467 that the Kṣaharātas tried and failed "to imitate the classical Sanskrit used by their Kṣatrapa neighbors" (i.e., Rudradāman), is based on an outdated chronology (that of Sircar 1965). Nahapāna lived about a hundred years before Rudradāman.

55. According to Lubin 2005: 94, the Kṣatrapas "demonstrate[d] the legitimacy of [their] rule by embracing the sacral authority of the brahmins." Witzel 2006: 467 invokes a general

rule that "outsiders chose to follow local, native tradition and religion strenuously as they wanted to legitimize themselves in the eyes of their subjects (and neighbors)." Neither defines legitimation or justifies the extension of legitimation theory from twentieth-century Europe to first-century India.

56. Lévi 1904: 174. Pollock similarly argues that these foreigners "sought to turn Sanskrit into an instrument of cultural-political power of a new sort" (2006*a:* 72).

57. Rapson 1908 [1967]: xci and Sircar 1963–1964*c* call the language "Dravidian Prakrit"; it has since been interpreted as Tamil (Panneerselvam 1969; Krishnan 2002) or Telugu (Sarma 1973). Comparison with early Tamil inscriptions confirms their interpretation as Tamil (Mahadevan 2003: 199).

58. Damsteegt 1978, 1989.

59. This is the view of Damsteegt 1978; see p. 223 for the influence of Mathurā and p. 208 for the influence of Brahmanical culture).

60. The Sanskrit form is *kṣatrapasya;* the Gāndhārī forms are *kṣatrapasa* and *kṣatravasa* (see http://gandhari.org/n_dictionary.php). All Middle Indic languages (including Gāndhārī) have the ending *-assa,* written *-asa* in the Brāhmī and Kharoṣṭhī scripts of this period.

61. [28]; [104], line 12: *dakṣiṇāpathapates sātakarṇer dvir api nīrvyām avajītyāvajītya* [sic] *saṃbaṃdhā*[*vi*]*dūra*[*ta*]*yā anutsādanāt prāptayaśasā.*

62. In this connection, it is worth mentioning a relief at Kanaganahalli that depicts the Sātavāhana ruler Puḷumāvi (probably Vāsiṣṭhīputra Śrī Puḷumāvi) making a gift of the city of Ujjayinī, the most important city of the Kārdamaka Kṣatrapas, to an otherwise-unknown "Ajayanta" (see [25]). Evidently there is much we do not know about the history of relations between the Sātavāhanas and their northern neighbors.

63. Pollock 2006*a:* 72.

64. Pischel's remark that "many a famous Sanskrit work, I think, will turn out to be an imitation of a Prâkrit original" (1886: 13 n. 1) should thus be modified to reflect translation on the level of discourse rather than on the level of the individual work. I thank Sheldon Pollock for the reference.

65. Sircar 1939; for a more recent statement of the same view, see Menon 1996: 251.

66. [105].

67. [55], taking as a representative sample the inscription that Vogel labels as C3 (of the Buddha): *sidhaṃ namo bhagavato devarāja-sakatasa supabudha-bodhino savaṃñuno sava-satānukampakasa jita-rāga-dosa-moha-vipamutasa mahāgaṇi-vasabha-*[*gaṃ*]*dha-hathisa samma-sam*[*budh*]*asa dhātuvara-parigahitasa*; (of Śrī Cāntamūla): *mahārajasa virūpakhapati-mahāsena-parigahitasa hiraṇa-koṭa-go-satasahasa-hala-satasaha*[*sa-*]*dāyisa savathesu apatihata-saṃkapasa vāsiṭhiputasa ikhākusa siri-cātamūlasa.* Note the linking of the two passages by the word *parigahitasa,* and the connection between *apatihata-saṃkapasa* and the *apratihata-cakasa* of Nāṇeghāṭ and the *apatihata-bala-vāhano* of Udayagiri. A longer eulogy of the Buddha is found in inscription G. For a new study of the Ikṣvāku inscriptions, we look forward to the results of a research project directed by Stefan Baums, Arlo Griffiths, Ingo Strauch, and Vincent Tournier.

68. No Sanskrit inscription is dated to the reigns of Śrī Cāntamūla (r. ca. 225–240) or Vīrapuruṣadatta (r. ca. 240–265); Sanskrit inscriptions appear in the reign of Ehuvula Cāntamūla (r. ca. 265–290) and Rudrapuruṣadatta (r. ca. 290–315). One of Vīrapuruṣadatta's

wives was Rudradharabhaṭṭārikā, "daughter of the *mahārāja* of Ujjayinī" (*ujanikā-mahārabalikā mahādevi rudradharabhat[ā]rikā,* in [55], inscription B5), and one of Ehuvula Cāntamūla's wives—and the mother of Rudrapuruṣadatta—was Vammabhaṭṭa, "the daughter of a Mahākṣatrapa" in [75].

69. [107]. For this reading and interpretation see Salomon (2013): *saṃjayapur[ī]to yo rāj[ā] bhi āva[nta]kena śakena Rudradām[e]na vānavāsakena [ca] viṣṇurudraśivalānanda[sāta] karṇṇinā [s]th[ā]nāto pi na cālito.*

70. [80], verse 33 (in an obscure *mātrāsamaka* meter):

> *sayiha bhagavato bhavasyādidevasya siddhyālaye siddha-gāndharvva-rakṣo-gaṇais sevite vividha-niyama-homa-dīkṣā-parair brāhmaṇai snātakai stūyamāne sadā-mantra-vādaiś śubhaiḥ* |
> *sukṛtibhir avanīścarair ātma-niśśreyasaṃ prepsubhis sātakarṇyādibhiś śraddhayābhyarccite idam urusalilopayogāśrayaṃ bhūpatix kārayām* āsa *kākusthavarmmā taḍākam mahat* ||

71. Pischel 1981 [1900]: 8 n. 5.

72. For the loss of initial *s* see Burrow 1947; the pronunciation of post-nasal or intervocal stops as voiced is a general feature of many South Dravidian languages (such as Tamil) in which voice is not contrastive.

73. These are found in the inscriptions of the Sālaṅkāyanas [86, 87, 88] (the relatively late inscription of Hastivarman II [89] shows a promiscuous mixture of Sanskrit and Middle Indic words), the Vāśim plates of the early Vākāṭakas [90], and the Pātagaṇḍigūḍem plates of Ehuvula Cāntamūla [71].

74. [51], [52].

75. [90], [83], [71], [84], [86], [87], [88]. The one (very early) exception to the rule is Rāmgaṛh (Falk 1991).

76. Compare the observation of Sankaranarayanan (2009: 49): "Now, if one chooses to compare the elegant poetic language of the Sanskrit inscriptions of the early Guptas . . . on the one hand and the colourless prose of the Prakrit records of the last phase of the Prakrit age . . . on the other, one cannot easily escape the conclusion that it was the ardent desire for poetry on the part of kings of the age and of their favourite court poets that must have been responsible for this change-over in medium."

77. See Pollock 2006*a:* 115–161 on *praśasti.* Sircar 1939 already appreciated the influence of the Sātavāhanas on subsequent political discourse.

78. *ti-samuda-toya-pīta-vāhanasa* [18]; *trisamudranātha-* (in the Kevala Narasiṃha temple inscription [95]), *catur-udadhi-salilāsvādita-yaśā* (in the Pune plates of Prabhāvatīgupta [91]).

79. Salomon 1998: 85–86.

80. See Salomon 2001; Salomon 1995: 302: "the tendency has been . . . to view, and sometimes dismiss, the hybrids as some sort of exceptional and 'artificial' linguistic construction, or to attribute them to some vaguely stated 'influence' of Prakrit on Sanskrit or vice versa." For the problems of hybridity, see Flood 2009: 150–151; for a criticism of Franklin Edgerton's expansive definition of "Buddhist Hybrid Sanskrit," see Brough 1954.

81. Strauch 2012: 150; see also Bronkhorst 2010, 2014.

82. See, with deep reservations, Bronkhorst 2011: 18: according to its reading of early Indian sources, "different languages, each exhibiting its own structure, do not exist. Ultimately there is only Sanskrit, and other languages in principle share its structure." In this

connection it is interesting to note that a Bactrian inscription of Kaniṣka (Sims-Williams 2004) from Rabatak around 130 CE refers to the "Indian" (υνδοοαο, *hindwa*) forms of several names.

83. Sanskritization "did not only involve a linguistic shift within the boundaries of Buddhist literature but... also ... a cultural change which implied a more intensive confrontation with new branches of non-Buddhist literature composed in Sanskrit," Strauch 2012: 151 rightly says of Gandharan Buddhist literature.

84. These processes had been known in some form to earlier scholars (Jacobi 1886 calls the first *Ausbildung* and the second *Verschriftlichung*).

CHAPTER 3. INVENTING PRAKRIT: THE LANGUAGES OF LITERATURE

1. Bakhtin 1981: 295.

2. Alsdorf 2006 [1965]: 15–16. The only comprehensive history of Prakrit literature that I know is Jain 1961, which is organized into Jain and non-Jain sections (Jain 2004 presents much of the same material in English). For the conceit of "two histories" and its critical potential see Kaviraj 2003 and especially Chakrabarty 2000.

3. Winternitz 1985 [1920]: 37; Keith 1920: 223–226; Lienhard 1984: 64. For the golden age see Müller 1883; the idea is reprised in Ingalls 1976.

4. Bühler 1890; Lévi 1908 contains a short aperçu of the discovery and reception of Aśvaghoṣa's works (and was followed in 1909 by Haraprasad Shastri's discovery of Aśvaghoṣa's poem titled *Handsome Nanda*).

5. See Wright 1966, which uses the designation "non-classical," partly as a provocation.

6. Jacobi 1894.

7. Pollock 1996, 2006*a*.

8. Jacobi 1908–1909.

9. Warder 1990 [1974]: §§613–662; Pollock 2006*a*: 77ff.

10. Comm. on *Prakrit Piṅgala* v. 1 (p. 2 in Kāvyamālā edition): *saṃskṛte tv ādyakavir vālmīkiḥ, prākṛte śālivāhanaḥ, bhāṣākāvye piṅgalaḥ.*

11. *Seven Centuries of Āryās* v. 38: *prākṛtamayaṃ nibandhaṃ vitanvatā śālavāhananṛpeṇa | kāvyānām itareṣāṃ tadvikṛtitvaṃ kathitam arthāt ||*.

12. Joglekar 1946.

13. One exception is the Jain monk Rājaśekhara. He is forced to conclude that Sātavāhana is a family name (*sātavāhanakramikaḥ sātavāhana iti*) by a chronological discrepancy: one king of this name, he says, was a contemporary of Vikramāditya in 57 BCE, and another was a contemporary of Kālakācārya in 466 CE (*Twenty-four Prabandhas*, p. 152).

14. Hāla is seventeenth on the unified list provided by Pargiter 1913: 36, preceded by Ariṣṭakarṇa (a name that must either be a corruption or a false Sanskritization) and followed by Mantalaka (who is mentioned in the label inscriptions at Kanaganahalli [25].)

15. Shobhana Gokhale (1988) claimed to have discovered a coin of Hāla, but Chandrashekhar Gupta (1993) showed that her reading is impossible. For the need to supplement the *purāṇas* with material sources in the evaluation of their historical claims, see Bhandare 2006.

16. A minister named Hāla is mentioned in an inscription from Kuḍā [45], probably from the first century CE. A similar form, Hālaka, is attested on a Brāhmī label on

an *ostrakon* from Egypt dating to around the second century CE (Salomon 1991: 733). The feminine form Hālaṇṇikā is attested from Kanheri [106]. For the derivation see the introduction to Upadhye's edition of the *Līlāvaī,* p. 43, Sircar 1968: 207, and Warder 1990 [1974]: §771. Gopalachari 1941: 42 derives the name from *sātakarṇi* rather than from *sātavāhana.* Warder identifies Hāla with Vāsiṣṭhīputra Śrī Puḷumāvi, evidently because he was one of the dynasty's greatest kings and most likely to have patronized a great work of literature.

17. In one of his Sanskrit lexicons, the *Wishing-Stone of Meanings,* Hemacandra lists *Hāla* and *Sātavāhana* as synonyms (3.376). Similarly, Kṣīrasvāmin, in his commentary to *Amara's Treasury* 2.8.2, quotes a verse that gives *Hāla* and *Śālivāhana* as synonyms. In his *Garland of Regional Nouns,* Hemacandra lists *Hāla* as a synonym of *Sālāhaṇa* (8.66), *Kuṃtala* as a synonym of *Hāla* (2.36), and *Caüraciṃdha* as another synonym of *Hāla* (3.7). In the latter two cases, Hemacandra explains *Hāla* as *Sātavāhana* in his Sanskrit commentary. Hemacandra evidently thought, along with Rājaśekhara before him, that Hāla-Sātavāhana was a king of the Kuntala region in what is now northern Karnataka. The name Caturacihna means that he used the signature *catura,* a fact for which Hemacandra is the only authority. Hāla and Sātavāhana are used interchangeably in the *Līlāvaī* of Kautūhala and the *Twenty-four Prabandhas* of Rājaśekhara.

18. Sources for these stories (many of which have been assembled by Upadhye 1970: 6–12 and Ācārya 1982) include, from Jain narrative literature, *Twenty-four Prabandhas*), pp. 136ff., *Wishing-Stone of Prabandhas,* pp. 10ff., *Collection of Old Prabandhas,* pp. 11ff.; *Many Places of Pilgrimage* (pp. 59ff.), as well as the related *prabandha*s of Pālitta and Nāgārjuna in these texts and in *Deeds of the Promoters;* the *Līlāvatī* of Kautūhala and the *Vīracarita* (Jacobi 1876); the relevant sections of the Kashmiri versions of the *Great Story* (Kṣemendra's *Cluster of Blossoms from the Great Story* and Somadeva's *Ocean of the Rivers of Story*); and sections of Bāṇa's *Deeds of Harṣa* and Daṇḍin's *Avantisundarī.*

19. *Twenty-four Prabandhas,* pp. 147–148.

20. Weber 1874: 348: *prākṛtamayaṃ gadyapadyamayaṃ kāvyaṃ kartum upacakramire.*

21. For "collective effervescence" see Durkheim 1995 [1912].

22. *Wishing-Stone of Prabandhas,* pp. 10–11: *sa śrīsātavāhanas taṃ pūrvabhavavṛttāntaṃ jātismṛtyā sākṣātkṛtya tataḥprabhṛti dānadharmam ārādhayan sarveṣāṃ mahākavīnāṃ viduṣāṃ ca saṅgrahaparaḥ catasṛbhiḥ svarṇakoṭībhir gāthācatuṣṭayaṃ krītvā saptaśatīgāthāpramāṇaṃ sātavāhanābhidhānaṃ saṅgrahagāthākośaṃ śāstraṃ nirmāpya nānāvadātanidhiḥ suciraṃ rājyaṃ cakāra.*

23. *Seven Centuries* W3: *satta saāiṃ kaïvacchaleṇa koḍīa majjhaārammi | hāleṇa viraïāiṃ sālaṃkārāṇa gāhāṇaṃ* ||. Numbers prefixed with W refer to Weber's 1881 *editio princeps,* from which I take the text unless otherwise noted. A crore is ten million.

24. This interpretation was proposed by Sohoni 1964.

25. *Seven Centuries* W467: *āvaṇṇāi kulāiṃ do ccia jāṇaṃti uṇṇaïṃ ṇeuṃ | gorīa hiaadaïo ahavā sālāhaṇaṇariṃdo* ||. The first word may mean "connected with Pārvatī" (*āparṇa*) or "fallen on hard times" (*āpanna*); the idea is that it's impossible for anyone (other than Śiva himself) to enhance the status of Pārvatī's family by marriage, since she is the daughter of the already exalted Himālaya mountain. The verse is unanimously ascribed to Poṭṭisa, whom tradition regards as a minister of Sātavāhana (a role he plays in the romance *Līlāvatī*), although the printed text of Pītāmbara's commentary mistakenly associates the author name with the preceding verse.

26. For the language of Aśvaghoṣa's dramas, see Lüders 1911. Lenition is the softening of consonants (such as the intervocalic *t* in *mata*, softened to *mada* and finally *maa*); see the discussion in chapter 4. Weber 1881; Keith 1920: 224; and Jacobi 1886: §14 argue for this.

27. Nitti-Dolci 1972 [1938]: §214.

28. For the conservatism of the inscriptional language, see Warder 1968.

29. Bhandarkar 1917: 189. The word *horā* (from Greek ὥρα) could have been introduced as early as the second century BCE, when Greeks began to play an important role on the Indian political scene. It is discussed at length in Sphujidhvaja's *Yavanajātaka* ("Greek Genethlialogy"), which was composed in 149 CE. For the seven-day week, see Bennedik 2007, who does not mention *Seven Centuries*. I thank Somadeva Vasudeva for the reference.

30. See Sircar 1969, who likewise maintained that Candragupta II was the "first" Vikramāditya. Legends about King Sātavāhana make him a rival and contemporary of Vikramāditya (as in the *Vīracarita*).

31. A first-century date has long been favored by people uninfluenced or unconvinced by Weber's and Bhandarkar's arguments; see, e.g., Smith 1902: 660; Konow 1894. See also Gopalachari 1941, cited in n. 33 below.

32. Mirashi 1947, 1960*a*, 1960*b*. See Sohoni 1999 for a criticism.

33. See Mirashi 1947. I do not know where he cites Pītāmbara's commentary from, but the verses he mentions as 616, 617, and 618 are found as 619, 620, and 621 in the edition of Jagdish Lal Shastri (matching the numeration of Weber's 1881 edition). W619, W620, and W621 appear in Bhuvanapāla and Ājaḍa's recension in a different position and are assigned completely different authors. Pītāmbara attributes W95 to Vākpatirāja, but the corresponding name is spelled as Bappayarāya in Ājaḍa's commentary, and assigned to W96. The form Vākpatirāja found in Pītāmbara and Bhuvanapāla may be a false Sanskritization; I strongly suspect that the original form was Bapparāya, the name of an author who is quoted in *Svayambhū's Meters* (4.2.7). Only W621 and W95 (as well as W96) are common to all recensions in Weber's edition. The idea of a first- or second-century "kernel" is also found in Gopalachari 1941: 42.

34. A manuscript of Bhuvanapāla's commentary at the Lalbhai Dalpatbhai Institute of Indology in Ahmedabad notes in the margin that Poṭṭisa, to whom W4 is ascribed, was Hāla's minister.

35. The quotation is from Zumthor 1992 [1972]: 5–6, in reference to twelfth-century Europe. Tieken 2001: 111 also suspects that "the gāthās were composed only at the moment of their inclusion in the Sattasaī."

36. Novetzke 2008.

37. See *Songs of the Buddhist Nuns (Therīgāthā)*, trans. Hallisey, p. xxiii.

38. Verse 468 of the *Topical Anthology* (*Vajjālagga*), compiled some time after *Seven Centuries*, memorializes Hāla: "They say women are faithful if they come from good families. But that's not true: they are faithful if they have a good husband. Even when Hāla went to heaven, the Godāvarī river did not leave her master's place, the city of Pratiṣṭhāna" (*purisavisesena saïttaṇāi na kulakkameṇa mahilāṇa | saggaṃ gae vi hāle na muyai golā païṭṭhāṇaṃ* ||, reading *païṭṭhāṇaṃ* as both *pratiṣṭhānaṃ* and *pati-sthānaṃ*).

39. Desai 1985: 18–28 records the common interpretation of couples (*mithunas*) as auspicious symbols in sculptural art of the Sātavāhana period, but also notes their decorative function and the prominence of the erotic (*śṛṅgāra*) in the decorative program of rock-cut

caves and *stūpas*; see also Meister 1979: fn. 1. I know of no art-historical study of the stelae from Sannati and environs (for images, see Sarma and Varaprasada Rao 1993). For Kanaganahalli, see Poonacha 2013 and Zin 2013.

40. See Ali 2004: 72 and Chakladar 1990 [1929]: 30–33. The most convincing argument for this date is the fact that the text refers to Kuntala Sātakarṇi (possibly belonging to the so-called Banavāsi branch of the Sātavāhanas, who ruled in the third century) and the Ābhīras (who also ruled over various parts of India immediately after the breakup of the Sātavāhana empire in the third century), but not to the Guptas.

41. For these legends see Lévi 1903; see now Ollett 2017.

42. See Wilden 2014: 8, placing the earliest collections in the first century CE.

43. *Seven Centuries*, W2: *amaaṃ pāuakavvaṃ paḍhiuṃ souṃ ca je ṇa āṇaṃti* | *kāmassa tattatattiṃ kuṇaṃti te kaha ṇa lajjaṃti* || (Tieken reads *taṃta-* for *tatta-*). Note that this is missing from the recension of Bhuvanapāla and Ājaḍa (and of Upādhyāya Lakṣmīdhara, who follows their recension for the first hundred verses).

44. Tieken 2001: 73–79; Khoroche and Tieken 2009: 2–6.

45. *Kāma Sūtra*, p. 53: *veśyābhavane sabhāyām anyatamasyodavasite vā samānavidyābuddhiśīlavittavayasāṃ saha veśyābhir anurūpair ālāpair āsanabandho goṣṭhī, tatra caiṣāṃ kāvyasamasyā kalāsamasyā vā*. *Analysis of Literature*, p. 55: *tatra yathāsukham āsīnaḥ kāvyagoṣṭhīṃ pravarttayet bhāvayet parīkṣeta ca, vāsudeva-sātavāhana-śūdraka-sāhasāṅkādīn sakalān sabhāpatīn dānamānābhyām anukuryāt*.

46. Jacobi 1886: §14, also Bühler 1890 and Konow 1894, all of whom place the origins of *kāvya* in the forgotten past; Zumthor 1992 [1972]: 35.

47. See, e.g., Mirashi 1960*a*: "the poets belonged to all ranks of the society from the king to the peasant." Weber 1881 calls the Prakrit of *Seven Centuries* a *lebendige Volkssprache* (xxiii). For further examples, see Tieken 2001: 54. For a critical response, see Boccali 2009.

48. *Seven Centuries*, W169: *ṇikkammāhi vi chettāhi pāmaro ṇea vaccae vasahiṃ* | *muapiajāāsuṇṇaïagehadukkhaṃ pariharaṃto* ||.

49. That this work represents a collection of popular songs is highly improbable," Beames 1872: 222 observes. "Although they are full of allusions to rural scenery and occupations, they appear to bear no greater marks of being real songs of the peasantry, than the insipid couplets of the bergers and bergères of Louis XIV's court did to the utterances of the gaunt starving peasantry of France at that epoch."

50. Tieken 2001: 79; emphasis added.

51. Like many other readers of this literature (including the traditional commentators), I find little in the verse or even in the conventions of reading Prakrit poetry to recommend Tieken's interpretation. But the word "empty," or more precisely "emptied out" (*suṇṇaïa*), does invite a comparison with the empty temples where *Seven Centuries*' villagers often have their liaisons, and might add to the farmer's disappointment.

52. Cf. Friedhelm Hardy's note in his introduction to Govardhana's *Seven Centuries of Āryās* (p. xxi): "Albrecht Weber, the first scholar who worked seriously on the *Sattasaī*, mistakenly thought that Hala's collection represented 'peasant poetry' merely because farmers are spoken of in some of the verses. In fact, the opposite is true: in Hala, peasants are specifically marked because they are outside the poets' own milieu."

53. Tieken too considers clever speech to be one of *Seven Centuries'* themes, but this is an "exception" to the general pattern (2001: 68–72). For the date of Bhuvanapāla, see Vasudeva and Chiarucci 2011.

54. Smith 1985: 100.

55. For the expansion of trade and guilds under the Sātavāhanas, see Ray 1986.

56. Gutzwiller 2006: 401.

57. Cf. Winternitz 1985 [1920]: 108: "these Prākrit lays are not in fact folk-songs in the real sense of the word, but probably popular models of imitated creations of Indian ornate poets, who strove not only for describing the life and activity, above all the life of love, but would also reflect in the feelings and sentiments of the country girls and country lads, the herdsmen and cowherdesses, the female gardener, miller's wife, the hunter and the labourer." Lienhard 1973: 115 observes: "there can be no doubt that the *Sattasaī* presents a poetry of very elaborate design and an extremely refined taste and thus is far from being unconventional and simple."

58. *Seven Centuries,* W637: *dhaṇṇā vasaṃti ṇīsaṃkamohaṇe vahalasaddalavaīe* | *vāaṃdolaṇahallaṃtaveṇugahaṇe giriggāme* ||. I translate the reading of Bhuvanapāla (679), which seems better than the vulgate reading (which has *pattala* for *saddala* and *oṇavia* for *hallaṃta*).

59. Ibid., W638: *papphullagharakalaṃbā ṇidhoasilāalā muiamorā* | *pasaraṃtojjhara-kalaalamaṇoharā iha giriggāmā* ||. I again follow Bhuvanapāla (680).

60. For a discussion of the logic of the commentaries on *Seven Centuries,* see Dundas 1985. For Abhinavagupta's contention that one can only appreciate these verses by reconstructing the "speaker's meaning" from the context, see the discussion in chapter 4 below. For the debate, which focused on the ninth-century *Light on Suggestion* and its claim that "suggestion" (*dhvani*) is the key to literary meaning, see McCrea 2008.

61. *Seven Centuries,* W705 might also be mentioned, although it occurs only in Pītāmbara's text and a few other versions of the vulgate: *gāmāruha mhi gāme vasāmi ṇaaraṭṭhiiṃ ṇa āṇāmi* | *ṇāariāṇaṃ païṇo haremi jā homi sā homi* || ("I grew up in the village, I live in the village, and I know nothing of city life. But I snatch away the husbands of city women. I am what I am."). For an argument against Tieken's ironic readings that is based on this second level of meaning, see Boccali 1990: 24–25.

62. See, e.g., *Seven Centuries,* W174: *vaṃkacchipecchirīṇaṃ vaṃkullavirīṇa vaṃkabhamirīṇaṃ* | *vaṃkahasirīṇa puttaa puṇṇehi jaṇo pio hoi* || ("Their glances are crooked. Their speech is crooked. Their walk is crooked. Their laugh is crooked. You have to be really lucky, my boy, to end up as their lover.").

63. Jineśvara, *Treasury of Gāthā-Jewels,* 255: *vaṃkabhaṇiyāiṃ katto katto addhacchipicchiyavvāiṃ* | *ūsasiyaṃ pi muṇijjaï chaïllajaṇasaṃkule gāme* ||.

64. *Seven Centuries,* W720 (found only in some versions of the text, including the manuscripts Weber calls ξπχRST as well as Bhuvanapāla 534): *diṭṭhāi jaṃ ṇa diṭṭho saralasahāvāi jaṃ ca ṇālavio* | *uvaāro jaṃ ṇa kao taṃ cia kaliaṃ chaïllehiṃ* ||.

65. Here is Bhuvanapāla: "She does not want just anyone to figure out that she is attracted to him. But the very means by which she conceals her feelings ends up guiding the inference of clever people" (*iyaṃ asminn anurakteti mā kaścid ajño jānātv iti ya eva svābhiprāyagopanopāyas tasyāḥ sa eva chekalokasya tadīyāśayonnayanaṃ jātaṃ*).

Patwardhan, in his translation, has reached the exact opposite conclusion: "clever observers drew their own conclusions (about her vanishing love for him)."

66. *Seven Centuries,* W163: *vaṃkaṃ ko pulaïjjaü kassa kahijjaü suhaṃ va dukkhaṃ va | keṇa samaṃ va hasijjaü pāmarapaüre haaggāme* || ("Who will send me a crooked glance? Who can I tell my joy and sorrow? Who will I laugh with, in this damned village filled with farmers?").

67. Ibid., W428: *parimalaṇasuhā garuā aladdhavivarā salakkhaṇāharaṇā | thaṇaā kavvālāa vva kassa hiae ṇa laggaṃti* ||. The verse is 428 in Bhuvanapāla and 431 in Pītāmbara. For the technical term *lakṣaṇa* in this verse, see Raghavan 1973 [1942]: 2. Compare the *cāṭu* verse cited in Shulman and Narayana Rao 1998: 61: *saṅgītaṃ sāhityaṃ ca sarasvatyāḥ stanadvayaṃ | ekam āpātamadhuraṃ anyad ālocanāmṛtaṃ* ||.

68. A.K. Warder (1990 [1974]) was convinced that "embrace" is a technique characteristic of later literature, and he suspects verses that employ "embrace" of not being original. I do not share his skepticism. For the history of "embrace," see Bronner 2010, who argues that it became a central technique in Sanskrit prose, as opposed to an occasional device, with Subandhu's *Vāsavadattā* in the sixth century CE. See the discussion of W364 in the text just below.

69. W364: *ko 'ttha jaammi samattho thaïuṃ vitthiṇṇa-ṇimmaluttuṅgam | hiaaṃ tujjha ṇarāhiva gaaṇaṃ ca paoharaṃ mottum* ||. The term *paohara* means both "cloud" and "breast," and the adjectives apply to both the sky and the king's heart (*vitthiṇṇa* means "extensive" and "generous"; *ṇimmala* "clear" and "pure"; *uttuṃga* "elevated" and "noble"). Bhuvanapāla (314) notes *svāminaṃ kavir upagāthayitum idam āha,* "the poet says this in order to eulogize his lord."

70. *Seven Centuries,* W726 (only in χ, R, S, and Ājaḍa's comm.): *amiamaaṃ cia hiaaṃ hatthā taṇhāharā saaṃhāṇaṃ | caṃdamuhi kattha ṇivasaï amittadahaṇo tuha paävo* ||. χ is alone in reading *caṃdamuhi;* the others read *caṃdamuha.* Weber considers the construal with a king to be indisputably better (*unstreitig besser*) than the construal with a woman. Ājaḍa notes that the adjective *amittadahaṇo* can also be given another meaning, "neither Sūrya nor Agni."

71. *Deeds of Harṣa* 14: *avināśinam agrāmyam akarot sātavāhanaḥ | viśuddhajātibhiḥ kośaṃ ratnair iva subhāṣitaiḥ* ||. The word *jāti* can refer to the origin of the jewels or the metrical form in which *Seven Centuries'* verses are composed (alternatively, to the trope of "pure description," better known as *svabhāvokti,* sometimes found in its verses).

72. *Kuvalayamālā* p. 3: *bhaṇiivilāsavaïttaṇacollikke jo karei halie vi | kavveṇa kiṃ paütthe hāle hālā-viyāre vva* ||. The verse is difficult to understand; Chojnacki 2008*b* suggests reading *bollikke* ("inclined to talking," or so this word seems to mean in its only other occurrence in the *Kuvalayamālā*).

73. See, e.g., Jacobi 1886: §14, cited in nn. 26 and 46 above.

74. Tieken 2001: 78.

75. Hart 1975, 1976.

76. I thus agree with Siegfried Lienhard, who was one of the first to highlight these parallels, commenting: "I do not think that an obvious solution can be found for this problem at present" (1973: 116). See also Lienhard 1971. Tieken 2001 argues exactly the opposite of Hart, viz. that Tamil poetry is modeled on Prakrit poetry. For a recent exposition of the aesthetics of early Tamil poetry, see Shulman 2016.

77. See Mayilainātar's *urai* on *Naṉṉūl* v. 48 (*ceyvittōṉāṟ peyar peṟṟaṉa cātavākaṉam iṉantiraiya mutalāyiṉa)* and Nakkīraṉār's *urai* on the first section of *Iṟaiyaṉār Akapporuḷ*. See also Zvelebil 1973. I thank Blake Wentworth for his comments on these passages; he suggests that in the understanding of Mayilainātar and Nakkīraṉār, the *Cātavākaṉam* should have been a Tamil poem.

78. See Mirashi 1963: xxix. Mirashi has discussed the literary activities of the Vākāṭakas in several publications (e.g., 1945, 1960*a*). The fragments of *Hari's Victory* can be consulted in Kulkarni 1991.

79. Mirashi 1951; note the reference to *vacchomī* (*vatsagulmī*) at the beginning of Rājaśekhara's *Karpūramañjarī*.

80. *Rāvaṇa's Demise* 1.10: *parivaḍḍhaï viṇṇāṇaṃ saṃbhāvijjaï jaso viḍhappaṃti guṇā* | *suvvaï suurisacariaṃ kiṃ taṃ jeṇa ṇa haraṃti kavvālāvā* ||.

81. Besides the edition, see Jain 1961: 381–393; 1977, 1997. The author of the *Wanderings*, who held the title *vācaka*, was different from Saṅghadāsa Kṣamāśramaṇa, who composed a *bhāṣya* on the *Bṛhatkalpasūtra*. The *Great Story* is connected to Sātavāhana in its Kashmiri versions (the *Ocean of the Rivers of Story* and *Cluster of Blossoms from the Great Story*), but not elsewhere.

82. *Wanderings, Kahuppattī* (pp. 1–26); on p. 1, *guruparaṃparāgayaṃ vasudevacariyaṃ saṃgahaṃ vannaïssam*.

83. Winternitz 1972 [1927]: 475: "for the Jains, more than any other sect, have in their writings, and especially in their exceptionally comprehensive narrative literature, never addressed themselves exclusively to the learned classes, but made an appeal to other strata of the people also." Alsdorf 2006 [1965]: 15: "The Jains, however, have always possessed a particular affinity for Prākrit as well as for the later popular languages."

84. Piotr Balcerowicz (2001) argues that of the two philosophical works ascribed by tradition to "Siddhasena," the *Right-minded Reasoning* (*Sanmatitarka*) in Prakrit is more than a century older than the *Incarnation of Logic* (*Nyāyāvatāra*) in Sanskrit; he calls the author of the former Siddhasena Divākara and the author of the latter Siddhasena Mahāmati.

85. See Granoff 1989*b*: 340ff.; 1990.

86. Haribhadra Sūri, *Daśavaikālika Ṭīkā: bāla-strī-mūḍha-mūrkhāṇāṃ nṝṇāṃ cāritrakāṅkṣiṇām* | *anugrahārthaṃ tattvajñaiḥ siddhāntaḥ prākṛtaḥ* kṛtaḥ || (quoted in Gandhi 1927: 73). For Haribhadra's dates, see Jinavijaya 1988 [1919].

87. *Endless Stream of Likenesses and Births*, vv. 51–53: *saṃskṛtā prākṛtā ceti bhāṣe prādhānyam arhataḥ* | *tatrāpi saṃskṛtā tāvad durvidaghdahṛdi sthitā* || *bālānām api sadbodhakāriṇī karṇapeśalā* | *tathāpi prākṛtā bhāṣā na teṣām api bhāsate* || *upāye sati kartavyaṃ sarveṣāṃ cittarañjanam* | *atas tadanurodhena saṃskṛteyaṃ kariṣyate* ||.

88. See the discussion of the *Sthānāṅgasūtra* in chapter 5.

89. See Ghosal 1969.

90. See his grammar, Pischel 1981 [1900]: §§16–21.

91. See Punyavijaya 1968: 18: "The *Vedas* are a monopoly of the *Brāhmaṇas*, that is, no one else can understand them; in opposition to this, Lord Mahāvīra and Buddha proclaimed that knowledge should be easily accessible to all without any discrimination whatsoever."

92. Alsdorf 2006 [1965]: 15–16.

93. Jacobi 1879: 17; see also Alsdorf 2006 [1965]: 19.

94. Such as the use of -*o* rather than -*e* in the masculine nominative singular, the loss of sibilant clusters (-*mmi* rather than -*ṃsi*), and the advanced lenition of intervocalic consonants (*kaa*- rather than *kaḍa*-).

95. See, e.g., Alsdorf 2006 [1965].

96. Von Hinüber 2001: §53.

97. Warder 1990 [1974] is the exception, since the canonical literature of the Jains does not fall under its scope. Jain Māhārāṣṭrī texts are treated by Winternitz in a separate volume from classical literature, and they are absent in Keith's and Lienhard's histories. Jain's (1961) chapter on narrative literature (*kathāsāhitya*) includes all Jain authors, and its chapter on poetry (*kāvyasāhitya*) involves all non-Jain authors (with the exception of Hemacandra).

98. One exception is Abhinanda.

99. Jacobi 1908.

100. Warner 2002.

101. Although Vimala never names Vālmīki, there is no doubt that Vālmīki's *Rāmāyaṇa* was his primary source and the object of his critique (Chandra 1970: 234ff.; Kulkarni 1990: 218ff.).

102. *Deeds of Padma* 1.8: *nāmāvaliyanibaddhaṃ* āyariyaparaṃparāgayaṃ *savvaṃ* | *vocchāmi paümacariyaṃ ahāṇupuvviṃ samāseṇa* ||; cf. also 118.102.

103. Ibid. 2.105ff., especially 117 (*aliyaṃ pi savvam eyaṃ uvavattiviruddhapaccayaguṇehiṃ* | *na ya saddahanti purisā havanti je paṇḍiyā loe* ||); 3.8ff. (*paümacariyaṃ mahāyasa ahayaṃ icchāmi pariphuḍaṃ souṃ* | *uppāiyā pasiddhī kusatthavādīhi vivarīyā* ||"), especially 3.15 (*na ya rakkhaso tti bhaṇṇaï dasāṇaṇo ṇeya* āmisāhāro | *aliyaṃ ti savvam eyaṃ bhaṇaṃti jaṃ kukaïṇo mūḍhā* ||).

104. E.g., Ghatage 1934–1935*b*: "But in all these species of literature Jainism cannot claim originality in both conception and execution"; Kulkarni 1990: 5, without protest: "Modern scholars like Jacobi, Glasenapp and Winternitz hold that *the mythology of the Jains is to a great extent derivative*" (italics in original).

105. *Taraṅgavatī* probably mentioned that it was composed in Prakrit: *Taraṅgalolā* v. 13 has *pāyayaṭṭhaṃ ca nibaïṃ* [there is a metrical problem here, so perhaps read *pāyaya-vayaṇa-nibaddhaṃ*, or something similar] *dhamma-kahaṃ suṇaha jaï na dubbuddhī* | *jo dhammaṃ suṇaï sivaṃ so jama-visayaṃ na pecchihii* ||: "If your mind is up to it, listen to this religious story composed in Prakrit, for the one who listens to the auspicious *dharma* will not see Yama's realm." Vimala possibly refers to the language of his *Deeds of Padma* in v. 1.31 (*suttāṇusārasarasaṃ raïyaṃ gāhāhi pāyaḍaphuḍatthaṃ* | *vimaleṇa paümacariyaṃ saṃkheveṇaṃ nisāmeha* ||), although *pāyaḍa*- probably means "clear" (*prakaṭa*) rather than "Prakrit" (*prākṛta*).

106. See the extensive discussion of Pampa's Kannada *Bhāratam* (ca. 950) in *Language of the Gods* (Pollock 2006*a*: 354–363), and p. 384 for the reference to the "first vernacularization of the epic in South Asia" (Peruntēvaṉar's *Pārataveṇpā*).

107. For some of the differences, see Balbir 1989.

108. For the *niryukti*s of the *Āvaśyaka Sūtra*, as well as the best introduction to the *niryukti* literature in general, see Balbir 1993*b*. The word *niryukti*- is the conventional Sanskritization of the Prakrit *nijjutti*-, which represents *nirvyukti*-.

109. Balbir 1993*b:* 39; Dhaky 2004: 138; Schubring 1962: 84. See Dhaky's article for a complete survey of the evidence regarding Bhadrabāhu. For the legend of Bhadrabāhu's migration to the South, see Ohira 1982: 126.

110. In some cases, later texts furnish a *terminus ad quem*, e.g., Jinabhadra's mention of the *Wanderings of Vasudeva* in a commentary dated to 610 CE (Cort 2010: 313). *Taraṅgavatī* and another lost text, *Malayavatī*, are mentioned in a late canonical text, *Anuyogadvārasūtra* (*sūtra* 308), which in turn can only be dated by reference to the Council of Valabhī in the mid-fifth century at which the Śvetāmbara canon was finalized. *Magadhasenā* is mentioned with *Taraṅgavatī* and *Malayavatī* in *Niśīthaviśeṣacūrṇi* (Jain 1961: 376), and Pālitta himself is mentioned as a contemporary of King Muruṇḍa in the somewhat earlier *Niśīthasūtrabhāṣya*, v. 4460.

111. Later Jain traditions fixed Mahāvīra's death at 526 BCE, so 4 CE, or perhaps a couple of generations later (we do not know what date Vimala himself accepted for Mahāvīra's death), would not be far off the mark for *Deeds of Padma*. Jacobi 1918: 59* argued that Vimala's acquaintance with Greek astrology places the text in the third century CE (but see n. 29 above for a critique of these kinds of arguments). See also the introduction to the edition of Jacobi and Jinavijaya; Winternitz 1972 [1927]: 477 n. 3, citing Ernst Leumann's view that a first-century date is "incontestable"; Keith 1920: 34; and Warder 1990 [1974]: §853, noting that Vimala "may be regarded as among the earliest pioneers of Māhārāṣṭrī literature."

112. This section presents a much-abridged version of an argument developed elsewhere (Ollett Forthcoming). For *Taraṅgavatī* and its later abridgements, see Warder 1990 [1974]: §§835–850; Chaudhari 1973: 335ff.; and Jain 1961: 373–381, who notes (373): "suprasiddh pādaliptasūri sab se pahle jain vidvān haiṃ jinhoṃne taraṃgavatī nāmkā svataṃtra kathā-graṃth likhkar prākṛta kathā-sāhitya meṃ ek naī paraṃparā ko janm diyā" ("The well-known Pādalipta Sūri was the first of all Jain scholars to gave birth to a new tradition of Prakrit narrative literature by writing an independent romance called *Taraṅgavatī*"). Leumann 1921 translated the abridgment into German (although his translation focuses on the narrative and thus abridges most of the extended descriptions). The only printed edition is Bhayani's, which also provides a Gujarati translation (the basis for Siṅghavī's Hindi translation); Thomas Oberlies is preparing a new edition (personal correspondence). Thanks to Bhayani's translation, the text is well known in Gujarat and has occasioned some scholarly discussion (see Vijayaśīlacandrasūri 2005).

113. *Taraṅgalolā* 1640: *hāiya-purīya-gacche sūrī jo vīrabhadda-nāmo tti* | *tassa sīsassa lihiyā jaseṇa gaṇinemicaṃdassa* ||. Warder 1990 [1974]: §839 attributes the text to Yaśas. It is sometimes attributed to Nemicandra instead of Yaśas (e.g., by Jain 1961; Chaudhari 1973). The relevant section of Bhadreśvara's *Book of Stories* was included by Harivallabh Bhayani in his edition of *Taraṅgalolā*. See also Malvania 1983, noting that Bhadreśvara produced a synopsis of *Taraṅgavatī* before including it in his *Book of Stories* (p. 82).

114. *Taraṅgalolā* 5–9: *pālittaeṇa raïyā vittharao taha ya desi-vayaṇehiṃ* | *nāmeṇa taraṃgavaī kahā vicittā ya vipulā ya* || *katthaï kuvalāiṃ maṇoramāiṃ aṇṇattha guvila-juyalāiṃ* | *aṇṇattha chakkalāiṃ duppariallāi iyarāṇaṃ* || *na ya sā koi suṇeī na puṇo pucchei neva ya kaheī* | *viusāṇa navara joggā iyara-jaṇo tīe kiṃ kuṇaü* || *to ucceūṇa gāhāo pālittaeṇa raïāo* | *desī-payāiṃ mottuṃ saṃkhittayarī kayā esā* || *iyarāṇa hiyaṭṭhāe mā hohī savvahā vi voccheo* | *evaṃ viciṃtiūṇaṃ khāmeūṇa ya tayaṃ sūriṃ* ||. The translation is tentative.

115. Bhayani 1993*c*.

116. The earliest narrative I refer to is the *Prabandha of Pādalipta* in Prakrit, edited by R.M. Shah from an unfortunately lacunose manuscript dated to 1235 CE (Shah's edition includes a selection from Bhadreśvara's *Book of Stories*). Later sources include the *Deeds of the Promoters* of Prabhācandra, dated to 1278 CE, pp. 28–40, and Jinabhadra's *Collection of Prabandhas*, dated to 1210 CE, pp. 92–95 in the *Purātanaprabandhasaṅgraha.*

117. For the two Nāgarjunas, see White 1996: 61; for two Siddhasenas, see Balcerowicz 2001; and for two Haribhadras, see Williams 1965. For Pālitta, see Dhaky 1974, 2002. I have made a few adjustments to Dhaky's argument (e.g., he thinks that the third Pālitta lived in the later tenth century, but I put him in the later eleventh or twelfth). The biographical sources are dealt with in greater detail in Ollett Forthcoming.

118. Dhaky 1974.

119. See *Prabandha of Pādalipta* vv. 272ff. (where Nahapāna is called Naravāhana; I suspect that *naranāha* is also a modernization of *ṇahavāṇa*); the *Book of Stories* by Bhadreśvara (twelfth century) calls the king Nahavāhana (see p. 95). On this conflict, see chapter 2.

120. For example *Tilakamañjarī* 23: *prasannagaṃbhīrapathā rathāṅgamithunāśrayā* | *puṇyā puṇāti gaṅgevā gāṃ taraṅgavatī kathā* || ("The meritorious story of *Taraṅgavatī*, where pairs of ruddy shelducks reside, purifies the earth like the Ganges, with its *clear and deep waters / clear and profound style*").

121. The name Muruṇḍa suggests the period of Śaka and Kuṣāṇa supremacy in Pāṭaliputra before the Guptas (possibly contemporaneous with the Sātavāhanas), and three Rāṣṭrakūṭa kings named Kṛṣṇa ruled from Mānyakheṭa in the eighth, ninth, and tenth centuries. As noted above, the hagiographical accounts conflate details from the lives of three different Pālittas.

122. *Prabandha of Pādalipta,* vv. 317–318. See also the story of Pādaliptasūri in *Deeds of the Promoters*, v. 332 (*kathā taraṅgalolākhyā vyākhyātābhinavā puraḥ*); *Twenty-Four Prabanadhas*, p. 28 (*ekāṃ ca taraṅgalolāṃ nāma campū rājño 'gre navāṃ nirmāpya sadasi vyācakhye prabhuḥ*). The fact that these *prabandhas* call the work *Taraṅgalolā* suggests that this later redaction of the *Taraṅgavatī* was already available in the thirteenth century.

123. *Kuvalayamālā*, p. 3: *pālittaya-sālāhaṇa-chappaṇṇaya-sīha-ṇāya-saddehi* | *saṃkhuddha-muddha-sāraṃgao vva kaha tā payaṃ demi* ||. The Chappaṇṇayas are a mysterious group of poets, presumably of the Sātavāhana age, who are sometimes mentioned in later works (by Daṇḍin, Abhinavagupta, etc.). A collection of Prakrit verses published by Upadhye (as an appendix to his edition of the Saptaśatīsāra of Vemabhūpāla) circulated under the title *Verses of the Chappaṇṇayas* (*Chappaṇṇayagāhāo*), although this work is evidently later and different form the work that Abhinavagupta knew. See Bhayani 1993*e*; Balbir and Besnard 1993–1994; Balbir 1995–1996.

124.Ibid., p. 3: *ṇimmala-maṇeṇa guṇa-garuyaeṇa paramattha-rayaṇa-sāreṇa* | *pālittaeṇa hālo hāreṇa va sahaï goṭṭhīsu* || *cakkāya-juvala-suhayā rammattaṇa-rāya-haṃsa-kaya-harisā* | *jassa kula-pavvayassa va viyaraï gaṃgā taraṃgavaī* ||. The last verse might rather be translated as a *samāsokti*, as Chojnacki does (2008*b*: 28): "Elle donne le bonheur avec ses paires de tadornes—ses stances—, et apporte la joie avec ses oies royales—sa grâce –, cette Ondine qui émane du noble Pādalipta comme la Gaṅgā du Mont noble, j'ai nommé la *Taraṃgavaī*."

125. *Deeds of Rāma,* opening of chap. 33: *hālenottamapūjayā kavivṛṣaḥ śrīpālito lālitaḥ khyātiṃ kām api kālidāsakṛtayo nītāḥ śakārātinā | śrīharṣo vitatāra gadyakavaye bāṇāya vāṇīphalaṃ sadyaḥ satkriyayābhinandam api ca śrīhāravarṣo 'grahīt* ||. Pālita is an alternative Sanskritization of the Prakrit name Pālitta.

126. I include, e.g., the aorist in *-īa,* which is completely absent from both "courtly" Prakrit and Jain Prakrit of a later date, as well as suffixed pronouns such as *tayaṃ,* and a first-person present in *-aṃ* (see the extract cited below in the text for some examples, and see Bhayani 1993*c;* for comparison to the language of the *Wanderings of Vasudeva,* see Alsdorf 1936 and Esposito 2011).

127. The features are the use of the hiatus filler *y* (called *ya-śruti*) and the use of dental rather than retroflex nasals in word-initial position and word-interally when geminated; both are typically found in Jain Prakrit texts, and they are mentioned by the Jain grammarian Hemacandra, but they are also found, e.g., in the two poems about the tortoise that holds up the earth that Bhoja had inscribed in the eleventh century (see chapter 7). Hoernle had these doubts already in 1880; see his note on p. iv of his edition of Caṇḍa's *Definition of Prakrit.*

128. *Taraṅgalolā* 43–50: *na ya suviṇae na leppe na cittakamme kahāsu ya bahūsu | diṭṭhā va suyā va mae ajjā iva suṃdarā mahilā || lāyaṇṇeṇa ghaḍiyā kā ṇu hu sohagga-maṃjarī iṇamo | pattā va caṃda-joṇhā rūva-guṇa-samaṇṇiyā ihaïṃ || kiṃ hojja payāvaïṇā iṇamo vara-juvaï-savva-sāreṇa | rūva-guṇa-samāüttā savvāyara-nimmiyā suyaṇu || jaï tāva erisaṃ se muṇḍiya-bhāvāe hojja lāyaṇṇaṃ |* āsīya *gihittaṇae rūva-sirī kettiyaṃ maṇṇe || bhūsaṇa-rahiesu vi kiha va tāva jalla-maïlesu aṃgesu | jattha ṭhiyā me diṭṭhī tatto na varajjaï caleuṃ || savvaṃgesu animisā pecchaṇalolā mae surūvaṃ ti | laggaṃtī laggaṃtī kahiṃci hiṃvāviyā diṭṭhī || ajjāe kaṃti-jutte aṇaṇṇa-sarise maṇa-pāsāya-kare | accharasāṇaṃ pi bhave maṇoraho erise rūve || mottūṇa ṇa paüma-vaṇa-saṃḍaṃ gahiya-nevacchā | gharamaïgayā bhagavaī dāṇa-guṇa-paḍoccayā lacchī* ||." There are various textual problems and uncertainties.

129. *Seven Centuries* W234: *jassa jahiṃ cia paḍhamaṃ tissā aṃgammi ṇivaḍiā diṭṭhī | tassa tahiṃ cea ṭhiā savvaṃgaṃ keṇa vi ṇa diṭṭhaṃ* || (trans. Khoroche and Tieken 2009: "On whichever part of her body / One's eye falls first / There it stays. / No one has ever seen the whole of her body"); W271: *kaha sā ṇivvaṇṇijjaü jīa jahāloiammi aṃgammi | diṭṭhī duvvalagāi vva paṃkapaḍiā ṇa uttaraï* || (trans. ibid.: "How can I describe her? / Once you see her body / You cannot take your eyes off it: / They are like a helpless cow / Stuck in the mud").

130. See Bhayani 1993*c* and the discussion of the *gajjaṃte khe* verse in chapter 4.

131. *Deeds of the Promoters, Deeds of Pādalipta Sūri,* v. 38: *aṃbaṃ taṃbacchīe apupphiyaṃ pupphadaṃtapaṃtīe | navasālikaṃjiyaṃ navavahūi kuḍaeṇa me dinnaṃ* ||. This story is also related in Jinabhadra's *Prabandhāvalī* (in *A Collection of Old Prabandhas*) and in Rājaśekhara's *Twenty-four Prabandhas* (p. 25); it was probably in the missing portion of the *Prabandha of Pādalipta.* I read the story somewhat differently than most of the Sanskrit sources, which connect it to Pālitta's power of flight (*pādalepa*); the Prakrit sources, especially the version in Bhadreśvara's *Book of Stories,* does not mention the power of flight at all, which I understand to be a later addition.

132. Warder 1990 [1974]: §839.

133. Sohoni 1999. Later Jain texts naturally have Hāla convert to Jainism.

134. Hoernle 1880*b:* lxii.

135. On Nāgārjuna and Sātavāhana, see Lévi 1936: 101ff.. Walser 2005 identifies the king, plausibly in my view, with Gautamīputra Yajñaśrī Sātakarṇi (see Warder 1968 for the suggestion that it is Vāsiṣṭhīputra Śrī Puḷumāvi). The later Jain traditions that make Nāgārjuna a student of Pālitta (see Granoff 1994) are probably based on the figure that M. A. Dhaky calls "Pādalipta II," a Jain adept associated with Śatruñjaya around the seventh or eighth century, who may indeed be connected to the adept (*siddha*) and alchemist Nāgārjuna.

136. See appendix C.

137. Pollock 1995.

CHAPTER 4. THE FORMS OF PRAKRIT LITERATURE

1. As Saussure preferred to think of language in general: "language is a form and not a substance"(2011 [1959]: 122).

2. Busch 2011*b*: 65–101.

3. See, e.g., Mark Twain's "The Awful German Language"; David Sedaris, "Easy, Tiger" (*New Yorker*, July 11 & 18, 2011, www.newyorker.com/magazine/2011/07/11/easy-tiger); and http://languagelog.ldc.upenn.edu/nll/?p = 23816. French and Italian have fared much better in terms of foreign-language clichés.

4. See the introduction.

5. Auerbach 1993 [1958]: 249.

6. Zumthor 1992 [1972]: 50; Swiggers 2009: 135.

7. Grierson 1927: 123, quoted in chapter 1.

8. *Brilliance of the Connoisseurs*, v. 5: *siṃgāra-bhāva-suhaā sarasā varasuṃdari vva somālī | koḍḍa-maṇoraha-jaṇaṇī haraï maṇaṃ pāauttī hu ||*.

9. *Vajjālagga*, v. 28: *desiyasaddapaloṭṭaṃ mahurakkharachaṃdasaṃṭhiyaṃ laliyaṃ | phuḍaviyaḍapāyaḍatthaṃ pāiyakavvaṃ paḍheyavvaṃ ||*. See also chapter 5 for a similar verse from the same collection. Patwardhan understands the Prakrit name Jayavallaha to represent Jayavallabha, but I think Jagadvallabha is more likely.

10. Not that Prakrit alone had "sweet syllables": the phrase (*madhurākṣara-*) is used, e.g., of Siddhārtha's speech (in Sanskrit) to his horse Kanthaka (*Story of the Buddha* 5.74).

11. See Tieken 2006, citing *Treatise on Theater* 16.104: *bahuśo yac chrutaṃ vākyaṃ uktaṃ vā punaḥ punaḥ | nodvejayati yasmād dhi tan mādhuryam iti smṛtam ||*.

12. Beames 1872: 223.

13. See *Light on Prakrit* 1.9 (ten words). I argued (2012) that *jahā* was metrically reshaped to *jaha* in order to fit into the optimal template of the moraic trochee.

14. See *Light on Prakrit* 1.2 (nine words, of which seven involve prefixes: *sām-iddhi, pāḍi-siddhi, pā-siddhi, āhi-āa, pā-sutta, pāḍi-vaā, pā-aḍa; mānaṃsiṇī,* from *manasvinī,* is almost certainly contaminated with *māna-*, and *sārisa,* from *sadṛśa,* has the typical lengthening of pronominal stems like *mādṛśa-*, *tvādṛśa-*, etc.). See Pischel 1896, 1897; Jacobi 1893, 1898 (also translated into English in Jacobi 1960).

15. The difference between the number of phonemes of Prakrit and the number of "root phonemes" (*mūlākṣaras*) of Sanskrit is noted, e.g., in the beginning of the recently discovered *Praśnavyākaraṇa* (see Acharya 2007), of which Jagat Ram Bhattacharya is currently preparing an edition.

16. In some manuscripts, only *ṇ* is written; in others, *n* is written when it stands at the beginning of a word or when doubled, and *ṇ* is written elsewhere.

17. See, in general, Bronner 2010. One example is *sāraṅga* in Kālidāsa's *Cloud Messenger,* v. 21 (see Mallinātha's comment thereon).

18. *Ornament of Literature* 2.19–21; *Necklace of Sarasvatī* 2.82–86. For Harivṛddha, see appendix C. For some comments on these modes, known as *vṛttis* to some authors, see Raghavan 1973.

19. Such as *praüga-* "foreyoke" and *titaü-* "sieve."

20. *Necklace of Sarasvātī* 2, ex. 191 (p. 240) = *Rāvaṇa's Demise* 1.56. I cite the verse from *Rāvaṇa's Demise* because the text of the *Necklace of Sarasvatī* is very imperfect.

21. Commentary on the above-quoted verse in the *Necklace of Sarasvatī* (p. 240): *seyaṃ mūrdhanyānāṃ prathama-caturtha-pañcama-dvitais tadāvṛttyā ca prāyo jāyate.* The sound *ṭ* and *ḍh,* which seem to be specifically required by Bhoja's characterization, are absent altogether from the verse he quotes, and the sound *ṇ* is repeated only in the word *ṇisaṇṇa-*.

22. Bhoja defines the *ākṣiptikā dhruvā* in his *Necklace of Sarasvatī* as a verse that serves to introduce a particular melody, and he cites a Prakrit *gāthā* as an example (Raghavan 1963: 370).

23. For example, *Līlāvaī* 66: *kuvaī vi vallaho paṇaïāṇa taha ṇayavaro vi sāhasio | paraloya-bhīruo vi hu vīrekka-raso taha cceya* ||. King Sātavāhana is described as "beloved to his wives, although he is a bad husband (or: lord of the earth); strenuously active, although his enemies have been humbled (or: devoted to statecraft); delighting in acts of valor, although afraid of the world beyond (or: afraid of rebirth in hell for conduct unbefitting to his life as a king)." For bitextual techniques such as "embrace" (*śleṣa*), and the poetic movements that formed around them, see Bronner 2010.

24. See, e.g., *Collection of Mora- and Syllable-Counting Meters* 4.29 (the other varieties are scattered throughout this chapter) and *Teaching on Meter* 4.25–28. Bhoja refers to an older view among scholars that the *galitaka* verses of the three major Prakrit court epics are interpolations. Hemacandra has reproduced Bhoja's comment, although he takes Sarvasena to task for including pointless descriptions in the *galitaka* verses of *Hari's Victory,* so we may assume that he did not subscribe to the view that the *galitakas* were interpolated. See Raghavan 1963: 802–803 and *Teaching on Literature,* pp. 461–462.

25. *Rāvaṇa's Demise* 9.82 (reading *rāaeṇa* for Goldschmidt's unmetrical *rāeṇa*). For *yamaka,* see Soehnen-Thieme 1995 and Tubb 2015. Kālidāsa's systematic *yamaka* compositions in the *Dynasty of Raghu,* discussed by Tubb, may well be influenced by the systematic *yamaka* compositions found in earlier Prakrit court epics such as *Hari's Victory.*

26. For the *deśī* vocabulary of *Rāvaṇa's Demise,* see Roy 1998.

27. For the *gāthā* in Prakrit literature in general, see Vyas 1962: §§161–162. The *Vajjālagga* has a *gāthāvrajyā* (vv. 9–18 in Patwardhan's edition), and the *Treasury of Gāthā-Jewels* has a section titled *kāvyapraśaṃsā* (vv. 19–29) that includes several verses about *gāthās.*

28. Pollock 2006*a*: 288.

29. Horsch 1966.

30. For Avestan verse, see most recently Kuemmel 2013. For Indo-European verse, see Meillet 1923, Kurylowicz 1970, and Nagy 1974.

31. Some authors counted 81,920,000 "surface forms" of the *gāthā* (*Definition of the Gāthā* 51; *Mirror for Poets* 2.6); others rightly disputed this number, because it did not take

co-occurrence constraints into account (Govinda on Virahāṅka's *Collection of Mora- and Syllable-Counting Meters* 4.107). See Cappeller 1872: 81–85 for examples of the manipulation of these possibilities for poetic effect.

32. See Ollett 2012. The general idea is that the *gaṇa* is parsed into moraic trochees (either a heavy syllable or two light syllables), and those *gaṇas* in which a moraic trochee begins on the first mora are unsyncopated, while those in which a moraic trochee begins on the second mora are syncopated.

33. See Ollett 2013 and also Cappeller 1872: 72–85, noting that Charles Philip Brown had jokingly translated these variants as Καλλιόπη, Καλλιπύγη, and Περικάλη in his *Sanskrit Prosody and Numerical Symbols Explained* (London: Trübner, 1869). For Sanskrit verses that exemplify the *jaghanacapalā* pattern, see Emeneau 1955.

34. *Brilliance of the Connoisseurs,* v. 25 (folio 3). *Rasas* and *bhāvas* belong to the technical vocabulary of Indian aesthetic theory, on which see Pollock 2016.

35. Alsdorf 2006 [1965]: 74–105; 1966, 1968; see also Bruhn 1996. On the old *āryā,* see Jacobi 1970 [1884]. Warder 1967 has a useful discussion of the *gāthās* in the Pali canon as a whole, but he does not elicit the consequences for internal chronology as clearly as Alsdorf. I do not, by the way, agree with all of Alsdorf's conclusions—he sometimes argues that a text is later simply because it does not seem to represent "authentic" Buddhism or Jainism (Alsdorf 2006 [1965]: 90–91)—but the general chronological scaffolding seems secure.

36. Alsdorf 2006 [1965]: 74; Norman 1987.

37. See Jacobi 1970 [1884]; 1970 [1886]; Schubring 2004; Alsdorf 2006 [1965], 1966, 1968; Hart 1975; Norman 1987.

38. On Magadhan culture see Bronkhorst 2007.

39. Geiger 1956 [1916]; von Hinüber 1996.

40. The classic work on Buddhist Hybrid Sanskrit is Franklin Edgerton's dictionary (1993 [1953]).

41. Vyas 1962 notes (§161): *uttarī bhārat meṃ mātrik gāthāoṃ kā pracār īsvīṃ san ke śurū ke āspās kī den hai* ("the proliferation of *gaṇa*-counting meters in North India is a contribution of around the beginning of the common era").

42. Balbir 1993*b:* 53–55.

43. Punyavijaya 1968: 19–20; see the discussion of "myths of continuity" in chapter 3.

44. See Charles Hallisey's introduction (xxiii) to his translation of *Songs of the Buddhist Nuns* (2015); Lienhard 1975; Boccali 2007; Rossella 2011.

45. Rossella 2011: 7; K. R. Norman (300 BCE, cited in Hallisey's translation of *Songs of the Buddhist Nuns*, p. xxxiii).

46. Smith 1949–1950.

47. The *Definition of the Gāthā* is dated to the tenth century or later, since in its present form it contains a quotation from Rājaśekhara's *Karpūramañjarī.* But it also shares some verses with texts that are indisputably older (see appendix C), and "Nanditāḍhya" is cited by a commentator on ʿAbd ur-Raḥmān's *Message Poem* for verse forms that are not discussed in the *Definition* in its present form. Probably there were several versions of Nanditāḍhya's treatise.

48. See Velankar's discussion in his introduction to the text (he considered them to be original).

49. *Ratnāvalī* 1.13–15; see Svayambhū's *Meters* 4.1 (*pūrvabhāga*, p. 114). I have taken the reading from Svayambhū; editions of the *Ratnāvalī* I have consulted—no critical edition yet exists—read the language more in the convention of theatrical Prakrit (Śaurasenī).

50. *Anuyogadvāra Sūtra* 271: *pariyarabaṃdheṇa bhaḍam jāṇejjā, mahiliyaṃ nivasaṇeṇaṃ | sittheṇa doṇapāgaṃ, kaviṃ ca egāi gāhāe ||*.

51. See Bāṇa's verse praising *Seven Centuries* (quoted in chapter 3), as well as *Treasury of Gāthā-Jewels* 2. V. 7 of *Brilliance of the Connoisseurs* is relevant here, and I provide the text because it has not yet been published: *vimalo suvaṇṇa-gaḍhio ṇāṇālaṃkāra-bharia-bahalattho | vaïroaṇeṇa raïo gāhā-raaṇassa rehae koso |*. The reading *-raaṇāṇa* makes better sense.

52. *Mirror of Literature* 1.13.

53. Read *kośo 'py anekabhinnārthagāthāgrathito gāthākośaḥ kṛṣṇasāraḥ tārāgaṇa iti* with Upadhye 1974.

54. Bhoja, *Illumination of the Erotic* 11.353–354 (p. 674). Bhoja is followed by Hemacandra in his *Teaching on Literature* 8.12–13 (with the *Crest-Jewel of Ornaments* thereon), who also brings in Abhinavagupta's remarks on the *paryā/paryāya*.

55. Acarya 1982: 128–154.

56. Ingalls 1965: 44–45. For Ravigupta's little-known anthology of *āryā* verses, composed sometime before it was translated into Tibetan in the ninth century, see Hahn 2007.

57. On the Chappaṇṇayas, see Balbir and Besnard 1993–1994 and Bhayani 1993*e*.

58. Mirashi 1960*b* argued that the text was originally titled *A Treasury of Gāthās* (*Gāthākośa*); and see too Sohoni 1999; Acarya 1982: 56–57.

59. Joglekar 1946.

60. Tieken 1978; Schubring 1955. Balbir 1995 studied these formal structures as they are found in Jain literature and showed that they were known to Indian readers (as "chain-composition" or *śṛṅkhalābandha*).

61. *Ornament of Literature* 1.30.

62. See Bhayani 1993*a* on the *Gāthāmuktāvalī* and 1993*b* on *vajjā/paryāya*. The Sanskrit word *vrajyā* is a back-formation from the Prakrit *vajjā*.

63. Bappabhaṭṭi, *Constellation* v. 46: *susiyattaṇa-bahulakkhaya-sirīsa-jaladugga-vāraṇārīhiṃ | gāhāhiṃ pasaṃsaṃtaṃ vādi kahaṃ taṃ pasaṃsemo ||*. I have not translated the keywords because all of them involve double meanings.

64. So Bhayani (introduction to the *Constellation*, p. 7): "This was a traditional device to record and protect the authorship of stray verses." See also Upadhye 1974.

65. Vv. 26 and 27 (folio 3).

66. Gadamer 2004 [1960]: 110–119; the (specious) distinction between meaning and significance is E. D. Hirsch's (1967).

67. Ex. 36 on *Mirror for Poets* 2.8.7. See Bhayani 1993*c*.

68. *Siddhahemacandra* 8.1.187, about the transformation of aspirates into *h* (*anāder ity eva, gajjaṃti khe mehā*) and 8.3.132, about the use of *ātmanepada* endings. See also Bhayani 1998: no. 73.

69. Bhoja, *Illumination of the Erotic* 10.226 (p. 571; see also Kulkarni 1988: no. 136, p. 69); *Necklace of Sarasvatī* 3.153 (p. 383; see also Kulkarni 1988: no. 98, p. 359).

70. See v. 319 of the *Prabandha of Pādalipta*.

71. Svayambhū's *Meters* 1.4 (*pūrvabhāga*) = W75: *ua pommarāamaragaasaṃvaliā ṇahaalāu oaraï | ṇahasirikaṃṭhabbhaṭṭha vva kaṃṭhiā kīrariṃcholī ||*. See Keith 1920: 223 n.

5; Tripathi 1984: 294; Winternitz 1985 [1920]: 114 n. 3; and, more optimistically, Pischel 1981 [1900]: §13.

72. *Seven Centuries* W394: *maragaasūīviddhaṃ va mottiaṃ piaï āaaggīvo* | *moro pāusaāle taṇaggalaggaṃ uaaviṃduṃ* ||.

73. Abhinavagupta, *New Dramatic Art*, v. 1, p. 281 (commentary on the *rasasūtra*): *tadupajīvanena muktake, tathā ca tatra sahṛdayāḥ pūrvāparam ucitaṃ parikalpya* īdṛg *atra vaktāsminn avasare ityādi bahutaraṃ pīṭhabandharūpaṃ vidadhate, tena ye kāvyābhyāsap rāktanapuṇyādihetubalādibhiḥ sahṛdayās teṣāṃ parimitavibhāvādyunmīlane 'pi parisphuṭa eva sākṣātkārakalpaḥ kāvyārthaḥ sphurati*. I follow the translation in Pollock 2016 in interpreting this passage .

74. In the commentary on verse 1.4c of Ānandavardhana's *Light on Suggestion*.

75. On *kiḷavis*, see Wilden 2006: 158–185.

CHAPTER 5. FIGURING PRAKRIT

1. Sakai 2009: 83.
2. Jakobson 1959: 233.
3. Sakai 1997, 2009.
4. Sakai 2009.
5. *Phaedrus* 265e: τὸ πάλιν κατ᾽ εἴδη δύνασθαι διατέμνειν κατ᾽ ἄρθρα ᾗ πέφυκεν, καὶ μὴ ἐπιχειρεῖν καταγνύναι μέρος μηδέν, κακοῦ μαγείρου τρόπῳ χρώμενον "[the alternative to classing different elements together under classes is] being able to distinguish them again by their classes, where the joints are, and trying not to make a hack-job of any piece like a bad butcher."
6. "Diese Vorstellung nun von einem allgemeinen Verfahren der Einbildungskraft, einem Begriff sein Bild zu verschaffen, nenne ich das Schema zu diesem Begriffe" (Kant 1998 [1787]: 242 = A140, B179). Cf. Brian Stock's formulation (1998: 13): "A schema is a pattern of information already shaped in discursive or narrative form in the mind."
7. As an example of the general kind of "mediating representations" that schemas provide, recall Goethe's experiments with the "morphology" of plants. Goethe attempted to redescribe plants that he encountered in nature as formal or morphological modifications of each other, such that all plants could be related in this manner as modifications of an originary template (an *Urpflanze*). The template is the necessary starting point for any possible plant, which both bounds the category and encompasses all of its internal diversity. It is not a composite picture of actual plants, but a mediating representation: "if [Schiller] takes for an idea what to me is an experience," Goethe wrote, "then there must, after all, prevail some mediation, some relationship between the two." See Heller 1952: 5, cited in Monk 1990.
8. "Dieser Schematismus unseres Verstandes, in Ansehung der Erscheinungen und ihrer bloßen Form, ist eine verborgene Kunst in den Tiefen der menschlichen Seele, deren wahre Handgriffe wir der Natur schwerlich jemals abraten, und sie unverdeckt vor Augen legen werden" (Kant 1998 [1787]: 242 = A141, B189).
9. To take just one example, the texts discussed in Deshpande 1993 largely belong to the period before "Sanskrit" and "Prakrit" were used as names of languages.
10. Pollock 1996, 2003, 2006a.
11. Sakai 2009.

12. Quoted in Kahrs 1992: 245 from Grierson's review of Pischel's *Grammatik der Prakrit-Sprachen.*

13. See Srimannarayana Murti 1993. According to traditional glosses. *Mādhava's Commentary on Verbal Roots* glosses *saṃskaroti* as *alaṃkaroti* "adorn, elaborate" (p. 511). The *Kāśī Commentary* glosses the term *saṃskāra* several times as "attributing excellence to something that already exists" (*sata utkarṣādhānaṃ saṃskāraḥ,* e.g., on *Aṣṭādhyāyī* 4.4.3).

14. The word is derived from the base *prakṛti* with the suffix *aṆ*. The relevant *sūtras* are *prāg dīvyato 'ṇ* (4.1.83), *tatra bhavaḥ* (4.3.53), and *tata āgataḥ* (4.3.74). The difference in meaning between "existing in" or "come from" the source will be discussed below.

15. Pollock 2006*a:* 45.

16. *Rāmāyaṇa* 5.28.18–19ab: *yadi vācaṃ pradāsyāmi dvijātir iva saṃskṛtām | rāvaṇaṃ manyamānā māṃ sītā bhītā bhaviṣyati || avaśyam eva vaktavyaṃ mānuṣaṃ vākyam arthavat* |. See Cardona 1998: 646; von Hinüber 2001: §2.

17. Kloss 1967; Bronkhorst 2011: 15–18.

18. See Bakhtin 1981: 295, quoted at the beginning of chapter 3, and Pollock 2006*a:* 45.

19. *Sthānāṅga Sūtra* 553 (7.74), p. 674 l. 5 (*sakkatā pāgatā ceva duvidhā bhaṇitīo āhitā*); *Anuyogadvāra Sūtra* 260 (*gāthā* 53), p. 305 l. 3 (*sakkayā pāyayā ceva bhaṇiīo hoṃti duṇṇi u*). I would guess that these *gāthās* date to sometime between the second and the fourth century CE.

20. *Birth of Kumāra* 7.90 (in Kale's edition with Mallinātha's commentary) or 7.89 (in Murti's edition with Vallabhadeva's commentary): *dvidhā prayuktena ca vāṅmayena sarasvatī tan mithunaṃ nunāva | saṃskārapūtena varaṃ vareṇyaṃ vadhūṃ sukhagrāhyanibandhanena* ||.

21. Vallabha ad loc.: *varaṃ pāṇigrahītāraṃ saṃskārapūtena saṃskṛtena, vadhūṃ tu sukhenākleśena grāhyaṃ bodhyaṃ nibandhanaṃ racanā yasya tena, prākṛtenety arthaḥ.* Mallinātha quotes Vallabhadeva almost verbatim in his commentary to this verse.

22. Prakrit is "devoid of the quality of *saṃskāra*" in the *Treatise on Theater, saṃskāra-guṇa-varjita.* In *On Sentence and Word* 1.147, Bhartṛhari also defines a deviant form (*apabhraṃśaḥ*) as "devoid of *saṃskāra*" (*śabdaḥ saṃskārahīno yo gaur iti prayuyukṣite | tam apabhraṃśam icchanti viśiṣṭārthaniveśanam* ||), and we will see later that he framed this definition with Prakrit in mind.

23. *Gauḍa's Demise* 65: *ummillaï lāyaṇṇaṃ paaa-cchāyāe sakkaa-vaāṇaṃ | sakkaa-sakkārukkarisaṇeṇa paaassa vi pahāvo* ||. I do not accept Leendert van Daalen's translation of *paaa* as "the subject under discussion" and *sakkaa* "perfect" in Bodewitz and van Daalen 1998: 42–43. The word *paaa* can be derived from *prākṛta* by Vararuci's rule *ad āto yathādiṣu vā* (*Light on Prakrit* 1.10), and his commentator Vasantarāja actually includes the word *prākṛta-* in the *yathādi-gaṇa* (see *Resuscitation of Prakrit* p. 13).

24. See, e.g., *Līlāvatī,* vv. 41–43. See also the passage from the *Kuvalayamālā* discussed below in the text.

25. The original text is quoted in chapter 3.

26. I thus understand all significations of the compound *pāua-kavvaṃ* at once: *prākṛtānāṃ kāvyam, prākṛtaṃ cedaṃ kāvyaṃ ca,* and *prākṛtabhāṣāmayaṃ kāvyam.*

27. *Kāma Sūtra,* p. 53: *veśyābhavane sabhāyām anyatamasyodavasite vā samānavidyābuddhiśīlavittavayasāṃ saha veśyābhir anurūpair ālāpair āsanabandho goṣṭhī, tatra kāvyasamasyā kalāsamasyā vā. tasyām ujjvalā lokakāntāḥ pūjyāḥ, prītisamānāś cāhāritāḥ.* See the discussion in chapter 3.

28. Ibid., p. 60: *nātyantaṃ saṃskṛtenaiva nātyantaṃ deśabhāṣayā | kathāṃ goṣṭhīṣu kathayaṃl loke bahumato bhavet* || (the verse is also quoted by Bhoja at *Necklace of Sarasvatī* 2.12, p. 142).

29. Yaśodhara's comment (*nātyantam iti, kaścid eva saṃskṛtaṃ vetti deśabhāṣāṃ ca*) means that people who know both Sanskrit and the regional language are rare, and that one should switch between them in order to avoid boring or alienating those who only know one language. But the point of the verse as I understand it is that knowledge of both languages is normative.

30. *Vajjālagga*, v. 29: *lalie mahurakkharae juvaījaṇavallahe sasiṃgāre | saṃte pāiyakavve ko sakkaï sakkayaṃ paḍhiuṃ* ||. The same verse is quoted in the *Treasury of Gāthā-Jewels*, v. 20.

31. *Karpūramañjarī* 1.7 (p. 5 in the edition of Konow; Ghosh's edition lacks this verse): *parusā sakkaabandhā pāuabandho vi suumāro | purisamahilāṇaṁ jettiam ihantaraṃ tettiam imāṇaṃ* ||.

32. Jayasiṃhasūri, *Explanation of the Garland of Advice*, p. 4: *salalia-paya-saṃcārā payaḍiya-mayaṇā suvaṇṇa-rayaṇellā | marahaṭṭhayabhāsā kāmiṇī ya aḍavī ya rehaṃti* ||.

33. *Vajjālagga*, v. 7: *sakkayam asakkayaṃ pi hu attho soyārasaṃgamavaseṇa | appuvvarasavisesaṃ jaṇei jaṃ taṃ mahacchariaṃ* ||.

34. Pollock 2006*a*: 50. Note that Pollock considers Sanskrit and "the Prakrits as we know them" to have been "equally high diglossically," that is, jointly positioned far above the "protoregional speech forms."

35. Govardhana, *Seven Centuries of Āryās* 52: *vāṇī prākṛtasamucitarasā balenaiva saṃskṛtaṃ nītā | nimnānurūpanīrā kalindakanyeva gaganatalam* ||. See Knutson 2014: 47–71 for more about Govardhana's poetics. The verse was discussed by Pischel 1874: 31 and Weber 1881: xxvi.

36. Bhartṛhari, *On Sentence and Word* 1.154: *daivī vāg vyatikīrṇeyam aśaktair abhidhātṛbhiḥ | anityadarśināṃ tv asmin vāde buddhiviparyayaḥ* ||.

37. Bhartṛhari, *Light* on the *Great Commentary: kecid evaṃ manyante. ya evaite prākṛtāḥ śabdāḥ ta evaite nityāḥ. prakṛtau bhavāḥ prākṛtāḥ* (see Houben 1994a: 4; Kahrs 1992: 241).

38. Commentary (*vṛtti*) traditionally ascribed to Bhartṛhari on *On Sentence and Word*, p. 238: *anityavādinas tu ye sādhūnāṃ dharmahetutvaṃ na pratipadyante, mallasamayādisadṛśīṃ sādhuvyavasthāṃ manyante, te prakṛtau bhavaṃ prākṛtaṃ sādhūnāṃ śabdānāṃ samūham ācakṣate. vikāras tu paścād vyavasthitaḥ yaḥ sabhinnabuddhibhiḥ puruṣaiḥ svarasaṃskārādibhir nirṇīyata iti*: "But people who say that Sanskrit is non-eternal do not accept that correct words are a source of merit, and instead think that determining a word's correctness, like scoring a wrestling match, depends on conventions. They explain Prakrit as a collection of correct words, since it 'originates in the source.' The modifications that confused people have subsequently imposed upon it are clearly perceptible in the cause of special accents and so on." See Houben 1997: 337; Kahrs 1992: 24. Note, incidentally, that the *anityadarśins* referred to in *On Sentence and Word* 1.154 do not maintain that language as such is non-eternal, but only that the Sanskrit language is non-eternal, as against Houben 1994a: 7, 1997: 338 and Bronkhorst 1993: 407.

39. As maintained by Houben 1994*a*. Cf., e.g., the Jain monk Namisādhu's discussion of Prakrit in his commentary (dated 1068) to Rudraṭa's *Ornament of Literature* 2.12, as well as

Prabhācandra's attack on the position that only Sanskrit words properly denote their meanings in his *Moon to the Night-Lily of Reasoning,* discussed briefly in Dundas 1996.

40. Thus I disagree with Houben's assertion that *prākṛta* in this context "may include all kinds of spoken and written prakritic languages and varieties . . . perhaps including those we would consider non-Indo-aryan" (Houben 1996: 185).

41. *Karpūramañjarī* 1.8 (Konow) or 1.7 (Ghosh): *atthavisesā te ccia saddā te ccea pariṇamantā vi | uttiviseso kavvaṃ bhāsā jā hou sā hou ||.*

42. The verse answers the producer's question about why the author of the *Karpūramañjarī* "abandoned Sanskrit and started a work in Prakrit" (*tā kiṃ ti sakkaaṃ pariharia pāiabandhe paaṭṭo kaī, Karpūramañjarī* p. 3; Ghosh mistakenly reads *pāīa-*).

43. *Treatise on Theater* 14.2ab: *vāci yatnas tu kartavyo nāṭyasyeṣā tanuḥ smṛtā* |. Different are the minor forms (*uparūpakāṇi*), defined in later texts, which are "minor" precisely because they privilege song and dance over verbal representation.

44. The *Treatise on Theater* offers "the first fully enunciated theory of 'Sanskrit'" (Ali 2004: 171) and contains "the first textual usage of the term Sanskrit to refer to a language or discrete style of speech" (ibid., n. 88; see also Srimannarayana Murti 1993). For a walk-through of the *Treatise on Theater*'s account of language, see Lidova 2012.

45. The word *pāṭhyam* consists of the root *paṭh* ("in the sense of an audible voice," *vyaktāyāṃ vāci*) followed by the *kṛt* suffix *ṆyaT. New Dramatic Art,* 2: 365–366: *pāṭhaviśeṣam arhati, yatnena vā paṭhanīyaṃ, viśiṣṭena rūpeṇa vā paṭhanārhaṃ, āntaracittavṛttivaśād eva vā tathā paṭhituṃ śakyaṃ, ācāryayatnena vā paṭhanīyam iti pāṭhyam.*

46. *Treatise on Theater,* 14.5ab: *dvividhaṃ hi smṛtaṃ pāṭhyaṃ saṃskṛtaṃ prākṛtaṃ tathā.*

47. Ibid., 17.2: *etad eva viparyastaṃ saṃskāraguṇavarjitam | vijñeyaṃ prākṛtaṃ pāṭhyaṃ nānāvasthāntarātmakam ||.*

48. *New Dramatic Art,* 2: 366: *tatra prākṛtasya sāmānyalakṣaṇam āha. saṃskṛtam eva saṃskāraguṇena yatnena parirakṣārūpeṇa varjitaṃ prākṛtaṃ, prakṛter asaṃskārarūpāyā āgatam.*

49. Ibid.: *nanv apabhraṃśānāṃ ko niyama ity āha—nānā yāny avasthāntarāṇi deśaviśeṣās teṣv ātmā niyatasvabhāvo yasyāṃ, deśaviśeṣeṣu prasiddhyā niyamitam ity eva saṃskṛtā eva vācakāḥ, anumānāt tv anye, te tv anyatve prasiddhiṃ gatā ity uktam.* The word on which Abhinavagupta's interpretation depends, *avasthāntaram,* is a generic description of internal differentiation in the *Treatise on Theater* and applies to everything from theater itself to moustaches.

50. *Treatise on Theater* 17.7: *trividhaṃ tac ca vijñeyaṃ nāṭyayoge samāsataḥ | samānaśabdaṃ vibhraṣṭaṃ deśīgatam athāpi ca ||.*

51. For the Prakrit verses quoted therein, see appendix C. Vv. 17.6–9 are Prakrit *gāthās,* parts of which are also quoted in the *Definition of the Gāthā* of Nanditāḍhya (date unknown) and the *Dhavalā* and *Jayadhavalā* commentaries by Vīrasena and Jinasena (composed in ninth-century Karnataka). They are likely adopted from an earlier grammar, possibly Harivṛddha's (see chapter 5). Vv. 17.10–23 are composed in Sanskrit *āryās.* For more on the *Treatise on Theater*'s grammar of Prakrit see Nitti-Dolci 1972 [1938]: 61–92.

52. *Explanation of the System* 1.3.6.12 (p. 237): *māgadha-dākṣiṇātya-tad-apabhraṃśa-prāyāsādhu-śabda-nibandhanā hi te*; later on in the same discussion (p. 239): *kimuta yāni prasiddhāpabhraṣṭadeśabhāṣābhyo 'py apabhraṣṭatarāṇi bhikkhave ity evamādīni,*

dvitīyābahuvacanasthāne hy ekārāntaṃ prākṛtaṃ padaṃ dṛṣṭaṃ, na prathamābahuvacane saṃbodhane 'pi [we observe the ending *-e* in a Prakrit word in the accusative plural, but not in the nominative plural or the vocative], *saṃskṛtaśabdasthāne ca kakāradvayasaṃyogo 'nusvāralopaḥ, ṛvarṇākārāpattimātram eva prākṛtāpabhraṃśeṣu dṛṣṭaṃ na ḍakārāpattir api.* See also Yoshimizu 2015: 53–54, who reconstructs the passage that Kumārila cites as follows: [*ya*]*thā ukkhitte loḍammi ukkheve atthi kāraṇam* | *paḍaṇe ṇatthi kāraṇam aṇ*[*ṇaṃ*] *ubbhava-kāraṇ*[*āt*] || [I would read *kāraṇā*] [*ev'*]*ime sakkaḍā dhammā* [I would read *saṃkaḍā*] *saṃbhavanti sakāraṇā* | *akāraṇā viṇas*[*s*]*anti aṇ*[*ṇam*] *uppattikāraṇāt* || [again *kāraṇā* is to be preferred]."

53. Lüders 1911.

54. Ghose 1932, 1933.

55. Nitti-Dolci 1972 [1938]: 82 = §325.

56. *New Dramatic Art,* 2: 371–372: *muninā ca dig darśitā, vistāravijijñāsuḥ prākṛtadīpikādikam avalokayet. utpalaviracitāyāṃ ca sūtravṛttau paddhatau ca sphutaṃ pūrṇaṃ ca sarvam astīti tatrādaraḥ kāryaḥ.* See Raghavan 1980 for a short note on Abhinavagupta's knowledge of Prakrit grammar.

57. "The term *prākṛtam,* as referring to the totality of literary Prakrits, which are opposed as a whole to the *saṃskṛtam,* should therefore have arisen in dramatic theory" (Pisani 1957: 188).

58. As noted first by Alsdorf 1975 [1941].

59. *Treatise on Theater* 17.25: *bhāṣācaturvidhā jñeyā daśarūpe prayogataḥ* | *saṃskṛtaṃ prākṛtaṃ caiva yatra pāṭhyaṃ prayujyate* ||.

60. This is Abhinavagupta's interpretation in *New Dramatic Art,* 2: 372: *saṃskṛtaprākṛtarūpaiva bhāṣā vaktṛbhedāc caturvidhā saṃpanneti darśayati saṃskṛtaṃ prākṛtaṃ ca pāṭhyam iti.*

61. Abhinavagupta mentions one interpretation, which he does not agree with, according to which "superlanguage" differs from "noble language" in the same way that Vedic Sanskrit differs from classical Sanskrit: *vaidikaśabdabāhulyād āryabhāṣāto vilakṣaṇatvam asyā ity kecit* (ibid.)

62. See Nitti-Dolci's translation (1972 [1938]: 61–92).

63. *Treatise on Theater* 17.46: *athavā chandataḥ kāryā deśabhāṣā prayoktṛbhiḥ* | *nānādeśasamutthaṃ hi kāvyaṃ bhavati nāṭake* ||.

64. I take 17.45, which assigns Śaurasenī to *śuddhajāti* characters, to belong to this section.

65. *Ten Forms* 2.64–66: *pāṭhyaṃ tu saṃskṛtaṃ nṝṇāṃ anīcānāṃ kṛtātmanāṃ* | *liṅginīnāṃ mahādevyā mantrijāveśyayoḥ* || *strīṇāṃ tu prākṛtaṃ prāyaḥ śauraseny adhameṣu ca* | *piśācātyantanīcādau paiśācaṃ māgadhaṃ tathā* || *yaddeśaṃ nīcapātraṃ yat taddeśaṃ tasya bhāṣitam* | *kāryataś cottamādīnāṃ kāryo bhāvavyatikramaḥ* ||.

66. *Treatise on Theater* 17.62: *atra noktaṃ mayā yat tu lokād grāhyam budhais tu tat*; Rajendran 2005: 219.

67. This point was obvious to D. D. Kosambi (1963: 180).

68. *New Dramatic Art,* pp. 376–377: *sā* [sc. *vibhāṣā*] *tattaddeśa eva gahvaravāsināṃ prākṛtavāsināṃ ca, etā eva nāṭye tu.*

69. Bhavabhūti, *Mālatī and Mādhava* 6.10: *sarale sāhasarāgaṃ parihara rambhoru muñca saṃrambham* | *virasaṃ virahāyāsaṃ soḍhuṃ tava cittam asahaṃ me* || ("You simple girl,

give up your love of excitement. Forget your rash enthusiasm, love. It is horribly worrying, this separation of yours: my heart cannot bear it.")

70. *Treatise on Theater* 17.56: *na barbarakirātāndhradramilādyāsu jātiṣu* | *nāṭyaprayoge kartavyaṃ kāvyaṃ bhāṣāsamāśritam* || (ed. *-ānghra-*, impossibly). This is the original context of the verse, which appears earlier as 17.44.

71. See chapter 7. For Amitagati's Sanskrit translation of the *Dharmaparīkṣā* in the eleventh century, see p. 91 of Upadhye's introduction to the *Kuvalayamālā*. There are earlier works, such as Raviṣeṇa's *Legend of Padma* (678 CE), which may be considered translations *lato sensu,* but are better considered independent retellings (in this case of the *Deeds of Padma* by Vimala Sūri).

72. *Verses of the Chappaṇṇayas,* v. 45: *jo sakkayaṃ na yāṇai suvisuddha-pāiyaṃ pi vottuṃ-je* | *moṇaṃ tu tassa saraṇaṃ, nīsaraṇaṃ ahava parisāe* ||. The last part is a play on words, remarked upon by Balbir and Besnard (1993–1994), meaning both "or, he can leave the assembly altogether" (*nīsaraṇaṃ* from *niḥsaraṇam*) and "or otherwise it's a disaster for the assembly" (*nīsaraṇaṃ* from *niḥśaraṇam*).

73. See the verse quoted above from the *Vajjālagga* ("Sanskrit or other than Sanskrit") and compare Bhāmaha's *Ornament of Literature* 1.28cd (*saṃskṛtāsaṃskṛtā ceṣṭā kathāpabhraṃśabhāk tathā*).

74. See Bronner 2012 on the dates of Bhāmaha and Daṇḍin, and see Pollock 2006*a:* 90–93 on their discussion of literary language.

75. *Ornament of Literature* 1.16cd: *saṃskṛtaṃ prākṛtaṃ cānyad apabhraṃśa iti tridhā.*

76. *Mirror of Literature* 1.10: *taiḥ śarīraṃ ca kāvyānāmalaṅkāraśca darśitaḥ* | *śarīraṃ tāvad iṣṭārthavyavacchinnā padāvalī* ||.

77. Ibid., 32: *tad idaṃ vāṅmayaṃ bhūyaḥ saṃskṛtaṃ prākṛtaṃ tathā* | *apabhraṃśaś ca miśraṃ cety* āhur āptāś *caturvidham* ||.

78. See Bakhtin 1981: 4.

79. See *Analysis of Literature* pp. 5–10, and cf. Vāgbhaṭa's *Ornament* 2.1 (influenced by Rājaśekhara's formulation): *saṃskṛtaṃ prākṛtaṃ tasyāpabhraṃśo bhūtabhāsitam* | *iti bhāśāś catasro 'pi yānti kāvyasya kāyatām* ||.

80. Pollock 2006*a:* 112.

81. *Ornament of Literature* 1.30ab: *anibaddhaṃ punar gāthāślokamātrādi tat punaḥ* (note that *gāthās* are in *Prakrit, ślokas* are in Sanskrit, and *mātrās* are in Apabhramsha); *Mirror of Literature* 1.37: *saṃskṛtaṃ sargabandhādi prākṛtam skandhakādi yat* | *osarādir apabhraṃśo nāṭakādi tu miśrakam* ||.

82. The verbal root *saṃ-khyā* means "to enumerate," and *pari-saṃ-khyā* means "to exclude." See *Mīmāṃsā Sūtra* 1.2.42 (*parisaṃkhyā*).

83. *Ocean of the Rivers of Story* 1.6.147–148: *śrutvaivaitad asaṃbhāvyaṃ tam avocam ahaṃ ruṣā* | *ṣaḍbhir māsais tvayā devaḥ* śikṣitaś *cet tato mayā* || *saṃskṛtaṃ prākṛtaṃ tadvad deśabhāṣā ca sarvadā* | *bhāṣātrayam idaṃ tyaktaṃ yan manuṣyeṣu saṃbhavet* ||. Sten Konow (1894: 477) was one of the first to appreciate the importance of this passage.

84. The language of the ghouls is called the "fourth" at *Ocean of the Rivers of Story* 1.7.29, when Guṇāḍhya greets Kaṇabhūti (*dṛṣṭvā tvāṃ svāgataṃ kṛtvā caturthyā bhūtabhāṣayā*).

85. Charles Malamoud (1981: 36) showed that the final element is a "residue defined negatively by the absence of a characteristic common to the first three terms." His example

is the list of *varṇas*, where the fourth *varṇa*, the Śūdra, is defined by the absence of the ritual entitlements that make each of the first three *varṇas* "twice-born."

86. Rājaśekhara, preface to *Young Rāmāyaṇa*, v. 11: *giraḥ śravyā divyāḥ prakṛtimadhurāḥ prākṛtadhurāḥ subhavyo 'pabhraṃśaḥ sarasaracanaṃ bhūtavacanam | vibhinnāḥ panthānaḥ kim api kamanīyāś ca ta ime nibaddhā yas tv eṣāṃ sa khalu nikhile 'smin kavivṛṣā* || (cited in the introduction to *Analysis of Literature*, p. xliii, and also quoted by Bhoja at *Necklace of Sarasvatī* 2.17, p. 143).

87. *Karpūramañjarī*, p. 3: *savva-bhāsā-cadureṇa*. I doubt that Rājaśekhara had ever personally seen a single work in the language he called Paishachi.

88. *Mirror of Literature* 1.34: *mahārāṣṭrāśrayāṃ bhāṣāṃ prakṛṣṭaṃ prākṛtaṃ viduḥ | sāgaraḥ sūktaratnānāṃ setubandhādi yanmayam* ||.

89. Ibid., 35: *saurasenī ca gauḍī ca lāṭī cānyā tādṛśī | yāti prākṛtam ity eva vyavahāreṣu sannidhim* ||. See Pollock 2006*a*: 91.

90. Uddyotana, *Kuvalayamālā*, p. 70, §137: *āyaṇṇiūṇa ya ciṃtiyaṃ ṇeṇa, 'are, kayarīe uṇa bhāsāe eyaṃ ullaviyaï keṇāvi kiṃ pi? hūṃ, are sakkayaṃ tāva ṇa hoi. jeṇa taṃ aṇeya-paya-samāsa-ṇivāovasagga-vibhatti-liṃga-pariyappaṇā-kuviyappa-saya-duggamaṃ dujjaṇa-hiyayaṃ piva visamaṃ. imaṃ puṇa ṇa erisaṃ. tā kiṃ pāyayaṃ hojja? huṃ, taṃ pi ṇo, jeṇa taṃ sayala-kalā-kalāva-mālā-jala-kallola-saṃkula-loya-vuttaṃta-mahoyahi-mahāpurisa-mahaṇuggayāmaya-ṇīsaṃda-biṃdu-saṃdohaṃ saṃgghaḍiya-ekkekkama-vaṇṇa-paya-ṇāṇārūva-virayaṇā-sahaṃ sajjaṇa-vayaṇaṃ piva suha-saṃgayaṃ. eyaṃ puṇa ṇa suṭṭhu. tā kiṃ puṇa avahaṃsaṃ hohii? hūṃ, taṃ pi ṇo, jeṇa sakkaya-pāyaobhaya-suddhāsuddha-paya-sama-visama-taraṃga-raṃgata-vaggiraṃ ṇava-pāusa-jalaya-pavāha-pūra-pavvāliya-giri-ṇai-sarisaṃ sama-visamaṃ paṇaya-kuviya-piya-paṇaïṇī-samullāva-sarisaṃ maṇoharaṃ. eyaṃ puṇa ṇa suṭṭhu . . .'*

91. It is not certain that the author of *Rogue Stories* (*Dhūrtākhyāna*) is identical to the Haribhadra that Uddyotana identifies as his teacher.

92. Uddyotana, *Kuvalayamālā*, pp. 152–153 (§246). Other examples are given in Upadhye's useful introductory note (pp. 77ff.).

93. Ibid., p. 16, §40: *keettha pāyaya-pāḍhayā, keittha sakkaya-pāḍhayā, aṇṇe avabbhaṃsa-jāṇiṇo*.

94. *Deeds of Padma* 1.2.3: *sakkaẏa-pāẏaẏa-puliṇālaṅkiẏa* (sc. *rāmakahā-ṇaï eha kamāgaẏa* at the beginning of this *kaḍavaka*).

95. *Deeds of King Vikramāṅka* 18.6: *brūmaḥ sārasvata-kula-bhuvaḥ kiṃ nidheḥ kautukānāṃ tasyānekādbhuta-guṇa-kathā-kīrṇa-karṇāmṛtasya | yatra strīṇām api kim aparaṃ janma-bhāṣāvad eva pratyāvāsaṃ vilasati vacaḥ saṃskṛtaṃ prākṛtaṃ ca* ||.

96. Adapted from Williams 1983: 90. Bilhaṇa's fondness for the term *janmabhāṣā* qualifies the claim that "the concept of a mother tongue is a foreign, post-nineteenth century idea in India" (Narayana Rao 2003: 425).

97. *Mirror of Literature* 1.36*cd*: *śāstre tu saṃskṛtād anyad apabhraṃśatayoditam*. The best short introduction to Apabhramsha is Bhayani 1989; Siṃh 1971 [1952] includes a more comprehensive survey.

98. *Mirror of Literature* 1.36*ab*: *ābhīrādigiraḥ kāvyeṣv apabhraṃśa iti smṛtāḥ*. For the Ābhīras, see Sircar 1939: 242; Prakash 1954; and Suryavanshi 1962, and for their connection to Apabhramsha, see Tagare 1942.

99. See Ratnaśrījñāna on *Mirror of Literature* 1.36 (p. 25): *apabhraṃśo 'pi prākṛtavac caturdhā smaryate. yad uktam—śabdabhavaṃ śabdasamaṃ deśīyaṃ sarvaśabdasāmānyam | prākṛtavad apabhraṃśaṃ jānīhi caturvidham* āhitam || *iti.*

100. *Message Poem*, vv. 4, 6 (see the references in chapter 1).

101. Tieken 2008.

102. *New Dramatic Art*, p. 376. One of the "sublanguages" is Ābhīrī, which is named for one of the same communities with which Daṇḍin would associate literary Apabhramsha.

103. See *Illumination of the Erotic*, chap. 3, pp. 164–166 (translated at Pollock 2006*a:* 581–582).

104. Pollock 2006*a:* 133.

105. Narayana Rao 1995: 34–35.

106. For a longer discussion of Paishachi, see Ollett 2014, the key points of which are summarized here; the major contributions to the question include Grierson 1906; Lacôte 1908; Master 1943; Sani 1985; Hinüber 1981, 1985.

107. Barth 1885: 277 [457], lviii C15).

108. See Govardhana, *Seven Centuries of* Āryās, v. xxxiv: *śrīrāmāyaṇabhāratabṛhatkathānām kavīn namaskurmaḥ | trisrotā iva sarasā sarasvatī sphurati yair bhinnā* ||.

109. In Sanskrit: the *Ocean of the Rivers of Story* by Somadeva, the *Cluster of Blossoms from the Great Story* by Kṣemendra, and *Verse Summary of the Great Story* (*Bṛhatkathāślokasaṅgraha*) by Budhasvāmin, for all of which see Lacôte 1908. In Tamil: the *Great Story* (*Peruṅkatai*), for which see Vijayalakshmy 1978, 1981, 1982. In Prakrit: the *Wanderings of Vasudeva* by Saṅghadāsa, for which see Jain 1977.

110. Uttanūr plates of Durvinīta (Ramesh 1984: 82): *devabhāratīnibaddhavaḍḍhakathena.*

111. *Mirror of Literature* 1.38*cd*: *bhūtabhāṣāmayīṃ tv āhur adbhutārthā bṛhatkathā*, accepting the variant *tv āhur* with Ratnaśrījñāna instead of *prāhur.*

112. See *Way of the Poet-King* v. 1.41: *sakkadamuṃ pāgadamum ad' akkuṃ bagedante samaṟi pēḻal munnaṃ*: "From time immemorial, Sanskrit and Prakrit could be used for refined compositions, as one sees fit."

113. Ponna in his *Śāntipurāṇa* (*pēḻva mūṟuvare bhāṣegaḷam;* see Rice 1882: 301) and Nāgavarman in his *Ocean of Meters*: *saṃskṛtaṃ prākṛtam apabhraṃśaṃ paiśācikam emba mūṟuvare bhāṣegaḷoḷ* (Master 1943: 43–44; Pollock 2006*a:* 370).

114. Kuvayalamālā §7, p. 4 l. 12: *koūhaleṇa katthaï para-vayaṇa-vaseṇa sakkaya-ṇibaddhā | kiṃci avabbhaṃsa-kayā dāviya-pesāya-bhāsillā* ||.

115. *Ornament of Literature* 2.12: *prākṛta-saṃskṛta-māgadha-piśācabhāṣāś ca sūrasenī | ṣaṣṭho 'tra bhūribhedo désaviśeṣād apabhraṃśaḥ* ||. See Jacobi 1918: 81*, who also noted that Rudraṭa was the first to express the idea of the "six languages."

116. See Hahn 2012, and see the verse of Bhavabhūti cited above.

117. One of Bhoja's examples (*Necklace of Sarasvatī* 2 ex. 164) praises Viṣṇu (in Sanskrit) and Śiva (in Paishachi) simultaneously: *rucirañjitārihetiṃ jananamitaṃ sāmakāyamakalaṅkam | santamamitaṃ ca mānaya kamalāsanamabhivirājantam* || (for a translation, see Ollett 2014: 444–445).

118. This common knowledge is contained in the following verse: *saṃskṛtaṃ prākṛtaṃ caivāpabhraṃśo 'tha piśācikī | māgadhī śaurasenī ca ṣaḍbhāṣāś ca prakīrtitāḥ* ||. It appears in

some manuscripts of the *Definition of Prakrit* ascribed to Caṇḍa (see Hoernle's ed., p. 52) as well as Amaracandra's *Commentary* on the *Wish-Granting Vine of Literature* (p. 8).

119. See Tieken 2001 on the invention of a Tamil literary tradition under the Pāṇṭiyas. This marks a radical break with preceding language practices and linguistic imaginaries, despite claims that "political Tamil" existed under the Pallavas as well (Francis 2013).

120. Ravikara (also known as Śrīpati) quotes the following verse at the beginning of his commentary on the *Prakrit Piṅgala* that equates regional languages and Apabhramsha: *deśabhāṣāṃ tathā kecid apabhraṃśaṃ vidur budhāḥ | saṃskṛte prākṛte vāpi rūpasūtrānurodhataḥ | apabhraṃśaḥ sa vijñeyo bhāṣā yā yatra laukikī ||*.

CHAPTER 6. KNOWING PRAKRIT

1. On Hemacandra's career and the probable sequence of his works, see Bühler 1936.

2. A reading list on the disciplinary identity of philology would start with Pollock 2009 and Pollock, Elman, and Chang 2014. I find Auerbach's (1961 [1948]: 9–37) description of the discipline to be the most straightforward (I owe my acquaintance with this text to Yashin 2011). On philology in India, see Ciotti 2013: 29–34; Pollock 2014; Cox 2016.

3. As done, e.g., by Subrahmanyam 2011. For "model of" and "model for," see Geertz 1993 [1973].

4. "Centripetal" is a term of Bakhtin's (1981); see also Crowley 1996: 39ff., and for general surveys, Joseph 2004, 2006.

5. For the idea of grammars of culture, see Pollock 1985, 1989.

6. The distinction between interlingual and intralingual is based on Jakobson 1959.

7. See Joseph 2006: 19: "Grammarians don't 'discover' verb conjugations; neither do they invent them out of whole cloth; we don't actually have a word for what they do."

8. Pischel 1981 [1900]: §34; Nitti-Dolci 1972 [1938].

9. In the following I make a few meager additions to the material gathered by H. C. Bhayani (1975 [reprinted in his *Indological Studies* in 1993] and 1997).

10. Vaidya 1926–1927: 66.

11. Svayambhū quotes a verse of Hāla as an example of the *śārdūlavikrīḍita* verse form at 1.47.2 of his *Meter,* and a verse of Sālāhaṇa as an example of the *udgīti* verse form at 1.4.2 (*pūrvabhāga*). He also refers to the *dhavalas* of Sālāhaṇa at 8.18. Virahāṅka refers to Sālāhaṇa as an authority (along with Bhuaāhiva = Bhujagādhipa and Vuḍḍhakaï = Vṛddhakavi, see below in text) on *dvipadī,* a kind of strophic form, at *Collection of Mora- and Syllable-Counting Meters* 2.8–9.

12. See *River of Amazement,* p. 102 (*madhye syād antarantareti śālivāhanaḥ*; *antarantarā* is used in a Sanskrit verse, but Ghanaśyāma often quotes Sanskrit lexica to explain Prakrit words, and I see no reason why the reverse should not be true), p. 117 (*ettaham ettatthaṇīti śālivāhanaḥ*), and p. 157 (*milāamāṇety etat hasamāṇā hasantī ca hasamāṇeti dig iti prākṛtacandrikāyāṃ śālivāhanokteḥ sādhīyaḥ*). As noted in chapter 1, the *River of Amazement* is ascribed to Ghanaśyāma's wives Sundarī and Kamalā.

13. On points of Prakrit grammar Ghanaśyāma defaults to Vararuci's *Light on Prakrit,* which was presumably more comprehensive.

14. All of the Prakrit-language fragments of Prakrit grammars discovered to date are collected in appendix C (Nitti-Dolci 1972 [1938]: §845 referred to them as "some āryās on

grammatical generalities and some isolated sūtras"). Harivṛddha and Sātavāhana are mentioned together in a verse quoted by Bhoja (in both the *Necklace of Sarasvatī* and the *Illumination of the Erotic*), in a passage from Rājaśekhara's *Karpūramañjarī*, and in the *Collection of Mora- and Syllable-Counting Meters*, which are given as testimonia in the aforementioned appendix. See also Bhayani 1975. The name "Old Hari" also provides some slight evidence for the poet's antiquity. For the date of the *Definition of the Gāthā*, see the discussion in chapter 4.

15. Nitti-Dolci 1972 [1938]: 221–222 = §845.

16. The similarities between the *Mirror* and Bhāmaha's *Ornament* indicate a direct borrowing, and there are arguments to be made that Bhāmaha borrowed from the *Mirror* rather than the other way around.

17. For Svayambhū see Bhayani 1989: 26–28. Svayambhū's ninth-century date is based on a reference to the Seuṇas, who formed their own polity in the region of present-day Pune only in the second quarter of the ninth century. For Virahāṅka, see Velankar's introduction, §20.

18. Later biographies attribute his use of this signature to the suicidal depression that he felt after the death of two of his nephews (Granoff 1989*a:* 109); for Haribhadra's date see Jinavijaya 1988 [1919] and Williams 1965. The twelfth-century commentator on the *Collection,* Gopāla, provides no information about Virahāṅka.

19. See the introduction to the *Prakrit Lakṣmī* by Bühler and Klatt 1879.

20. See Renou 1938: 167: "il est devenu courant, à partir d'une certaine époque, de citer «honoris causa» des grammariens, soit fictifs, soit du moins n'ayant eu aucune part dans la confection des sūtra où leur nom est allégué" [it became standard, starting from a certain time, to cite some grammarians *honoris causa* who were either fictional or at least had no part in producing the *sūtra*s that bear their name].

21. Upadhye 1941*b,* 1956.

22. See Raghavan 1950 and Pischel 1981 [1900]: §31. The fragments quoted by Malayagiri are the very un-Pāṇinian *vyatyayo 'py āsām* (sc. *vibhaktīnām*) and *liṅgaṃ vyabhicāry api.* Konow (1894) believed that Pāṇini really did write a Prakrit grammar.

23. See pp. 124–130 of Acharya's edition of Mārkaṇḍeya's *Sum-Total of Prakrit.*

24. See seminal discussion of the *Light on Prakrit* in Nitti-Dolci 1972 [1938], with the observation that the text was often simply called the *Prākṛtasūtra*s by (some) premodern authors. Westergaard (1862: 82–88) lists nine different Kātyāyanas. Kātyāyana as a minister of Nanda appears in the *Kalpanāmaṇḍatikā* of Kumāralāta (Lévi 1908, who incorrectly attributed the text to Aśvaghoṣa), *Ocean of the Rivers of Story* of Somadeva, *Avantisundarī,* and the Jain *niryukti*s discussed by Balbir 1989: 513. For *Both Go to Meet,* see Venkatacharya (1968); for *Gāthāśataka,* extant only in Tibetan translation, see Hahn 1983. For the traditions that identify Vararuci with the grammarian Kātyāyana, see Nitti-Dolci 1972 [1938]: 2; Scharfe 1977: 162; Bloch 1893: 9; and *A Cluster of Blossoms* vv. 3–4 on 1.1, as well as the *Ocean of the Rivers of Story* 1.2.1: *nāmnā vararuciḥ kiṃ ca kātyāyana iti śrutaḥ.*

25. See Gornall 2014: 530 for a "broader 'grammatisation'" that includes Pali.

26. Pollock 2006*a:* 169–171. Kumāralāta is, incidentally, the earliest source for the legend of Vararuci-Kātyāyana in his *Kalpanāmaṇḍatikā.*

27. On the topical organization of the *Kātantra,* see Liebich 1919: 10. The list of topics, however, is very different: the *Kātantra* deals with *sandhi,* nouns, and verbs; the *Light*

with the transformations affecting vowels, single consonants, conjunct consonants, then a "mixed" set of rules, and then nominal morphology, verbal morphology, verbal roots, and indeclinables. See the opening verse of the *Resuscitation of Prakrit*. For *taddhita* suffixes in the *Kātantra* see Cardona 2008. For the overlap in technical terminology (*āmantraṇa*- for "vocative," *bhūta*- for "past," *bhaviṣyat*- for "future," etc.), see Renou 1938: 164–165. An early lexicon was also ascribed to Vararuci (Liebich 1919: 12).

28. Alsdorf 1975 [1941]: 140, following Nitti-Dolci, summarizes the *Light*'s importance as follows: "Auf Vararucis Beschreibung der Māhārāṣṭrī gehen die Māhārāṣṭrī-Abschnitte sämtlicher andern Grammatiken zurück, auch Hemacandras, auch der östlichen: Vararuci spielt hier eine Rolle, die cum grano salis der Pāṇinis für das Sanskrit vergleichbar ist" [the Māhārāṣṭrī sections of all the other grammarians go back to Vararuci's description, including Hemacandra's and the eastern grammarians: Vararuci plays a role here that is more or less comparable to Pāṇini's for Sanskrit]. Similarly, Renou 1938: 160. Alsdorf's emphasis is directed against Grierson, who believed that Vararuci belonged exclusively to the "eastern" school of Prakrit grammarians.

29. Nitti-Dolci 1972 [1938]: §269, §272, §275. This was already obvious to Bloch (1893: 11–12): "Jedenfalls ist es klar, dass Vararucis regeln sich auf die sprache der Mahārāshṭrī-literatur beziehen, und da Hāla von anfang an als standard werk dieser poesie galt, wird er sicher auch einbegriffen werden müssen" [in any case it is clear that Vararuci's rules are confined to the language of Mahārāṣṭrī literature, and since Hāla was the standard work of this poetry from the beginning, he surely must have been included as well].

30. *Light on Prakrit* 6.23 (*īa bhūte*); Alsdorf 1936: 325; Balbir 1989: 510.

31. *Light on Prakrit* 5.92 (*ṅau ca maï mae*); Esposito 2011: 37.

32. Jacobi 1908–1909.

33. Nitti-Dolci 1972 [1938]: §273. The best reference remains the conspectus edition of Baladeva Upādhyāya (1972), which prints the recensions of Vasantarāja (and the anonymous *Cluster of Blossoms*) and Bhāmaha separately.

34. *New Dramatic Art*, 4: 385 (comm. on 32.382): *apare vararucyādipraṇītaprākṛtalak ṣaṇānvitaṃ śaurasenyādideśabhāṣādyatiriktaṃ prākṛtam evārdhasaṃskṛtaṃ iti manyante.* This confirms that the version of *Light* known to Abhinavagupta did not define Śaurasenī; Bhāmaha's commentary also does not extend to the chapter on Śaurasenī.

35. See the introduction to Ghosh's edition of the *Wish-Granting Tree of Prakrit* (pp. xvii–xviii) for further arguments against the identification of Bhāmaha with the Kashmiri poetician. For Abhinavagupta's remarks, see *New Dramatic Art* on *Treatise on Theater* 17.17 (p. 372).

36. See the chapter on the eastern grammarians in Nitti-Dolci 1972 [1938], who edited Puruṣottama's Prakrit grammar.

37. Alsdorf 1975 [1941]: 141; Upadhye 1941*b*: 169 n. 27; Ghosal 1969. See also Upadhye 1931–1932: 51, who expected the Jain monk Śubhacandra (sixteenth-century Rajasthan) to discuss Jain varieties of Prakrit and was disappointed.

38. Upadhye 1941*b*: 171 calls Grierson a "sentimental propagandist of his terminology."

39. Nitti-Dolci 1972 [1938]: §§415ff.

40. Grierson imagined the history of Prakrit grammar to be an elaboration of two contraposed "base texts," Vararuci in the east and Hemacandra in the west, as noted above. But

even Nitti-Dolci comes close to suggesting that there were "two independent theories" of Prakrit, as Renou 1938: 161 points out.

41. *Treatise on Theater* 17.3; *Mirror of Literature* 1.33ff. with Ratnaśrījñāna's commentary. See appendix C for these passages.

42. Ratnaśrījñāna's commentary on the *Mirror of Literature*, p. 23: *tataścaikaprakāraṃ saṃskṛtaṃ, prākṛtaṃ tv anekaprakāram*. Somewhat later in the tenth century, Dhanika uses almost exactly the same words in his commentary to *Ten Forms* 2.65*ab* (p. 132): *tadbhavaṃ tatsamaṃ deśīty anekaprakāraṃ prākṛtam*.

43. I use Daṇḍin's terminology only because it has become the most commonly cited. Harivṛddha uses *saddasama*, and Bharata *samānaśabda*, for Daṇḍin's *tatsama*; for *tadbhava*, Harivṛddha has *saddabhava* and Bharata has *vibhraṣṭa*; for *deśī*, Harivṛddha has *desī* and Bharata has *deśīgata*. For other synonyms of these words see Acharya's introduction (p. 56) to his edition of the *Sum-Total of Prakrit*. I use the term "derived" as a functional description of the category. E.G. Kahrs (1992) protests too much that "*tadbhava* in the sense of 'derived from Sanskrit' was a feat of Western authors" (245), since "derivation"—not necessarily in the sense of descent through time, but in the sense of systematic transformation through grammatical rules—is precisely what the category refers to, especially in its synonyms *vibhraṣṭa-*, *vikārin-*, *tajja-*, etc. See also Pollock 2004: n. 19.

44. Masica 1991: 65, referring to Vertogradova 1978.

45. The "meta-linguistic" character of the *tatsama–tadbhava–deśī* distinction has been obvious to scholars such as Lisa Mitchell (2009: 103).

46. Masica 1991: 65–66, noting that R.L. Turner criticized the use of this terminology in his Gune lectures.

47. See Drocco 2012.

48. Kahrs 1992; I agree fully with Houben's (1994*b*) response.

49. Commentary on Rudraṭa's *Ornament of Literature*2.12: *sakalajagajjantūnāṃ vyākaraṇādibhir anāhitasaṃskāraḥ sahajo vacanavyāpāraḥ prakṛtiḥ, tatra bhavaṃ saiva vā prākṛtam*.

50. *Garland of Regional Nouns* 1.4: *aṇāipāiyapayaṭṭabhāsā-*.

51. Namisādhu does so only indirectly, since Prakrit is not one of the languages for which he gives explicit rules: he notes that the rules he supplies for the other languages involve "exceptions" (*apavādas*) to the rules that operate on Prakrit, which in turn relate Prakrit to Sanskrit. One example is that "in Paiśācikā, there is no elision of the letters *k*, *g*, *c*, *j*, *t*, *d*, *p*, and *y*" (*tathā kagacajatadapayādīnāṃ paiśācikyāṃ svaraśeṣābhāvo 'bhihitaḥ*), implying that such an elision does obtain in Prakrit.

52. *Siddhahemacandra* on 8.1.1: *prakṛtiḥ saṃskṛtaṃ, tatrabhavaṃ tata āgataṃ vā prākṛtaṃ. saṃskṛtānantaraṃ prākṛtam adhikriyate. saṃskṛtāntaraṃ ca prākṛtasyānuśāsanaṃ siddhasādhyamāna-bheda-saṃskṛta-yoner eva tasya lakṣaṇaṃ, na deśyasyeti jñāpanārthaṃ. saṃskṛtasamaṃ tu saṃskṛtalakṣaṇenaiva gatārthaṃ. prākṛte ca prakṛti-pratyaya-liṅga-kāraka-samāsa-saṃjñādayaḥ samṣkṛtavad veditavyāḥ*. See Pischel 1981 [1900]: §8 for the meaning of *siddha* and *sādhyamāna* in this context.

53. The reference is to Pāṇini's *sūtras* 4.3.53 and 4.3.74; see Kahrs 1992, also discussing this passage in detail. I agree with Kahrs that his alternative translation ("like [the body of rules] for the origin") is "less convincing."

54. *Resuscitation of Prakrit* on *Light on Prakrit* 4.35. Mārkaṇḍeya divides Prakrit into Sanskrit-identical and Sanskrit-derived only, and ascribes the third category of Regional to "some people" (*Sum-Total of Prakrit*, p. 4).

55. See Drocco 2012: 125, with references to Pischel 1981 [1900]: §9: "The Indians include under the deśya or deśī class very heterogenous elements."

56. *Garland of Regional Nouns*, introduction.

57. E.g., *pāsaṃ* "eye" from **pāśa-*, from the same root as *paśyati* "see" (cited by Pischel 1981 [1900]: §9).

58. Hemacandra includes a large number of "Regional" words in his grammar as verbal substitutes (*dhātvādeśas*) simply in order to teach them with *anubandhas*—diacritical markers that convey information about how the form is used—that the format of his lexicon does not accommodate.

59. *Sum-Total of Prakrit*, commentary, p. 4: *deśe deśe narendrāṇāṃ janānāṃ ca svake svake | bhaṅgyā pravartate yasmāt tasmād deśyaṃ nigadyate* ||. I have not been able to trace this very in any extant work of Bhoja's, although he is known to have written a Prakrit grammar that is no longer extant (according to Kumārasvāmin in his commentary to the *Pratāparudrīya*).

60. Music is one other discourse that was constitutively concerned with the regional (cf. Mataṅga's *Bṛhaddeśī*), although here, too, regionality seems to be defined negatively, in contrast to an earlier transregional tradition, rather than through the particular practices of a particular place.

61. *Garland of Regional Nouns* 1.1 (Sanskrit commentary); *Prakrit Lakṃsī* 278 (*kaïṇo aṃdha-jaṇa-kivā-kusala tti payāṇamaṃtimā vannā | nāmaṃmi jassa kamaso teṇesā viraiyā desī* ||: "This *deśī* was composed by the poet whose name consists of the last letters of the words *aṃdha, jaṇa, kivā,* and *kusula*"); Pṛthvīdhara's commentary on *Little Clay Cart*, p. 27.

62. Harivṛddha: *marahaṭṭhadesasaṃkeaehi saddehi bhaṇṇae desī* (see appendix C).

63. This is also clear in Ratnaśrījñāna's introduction to the quotation (on *Mirror of Literature* 1.33, p. 23): *deśī prākṛtaṃ mahārāṣṭraprasiddham*.

64. See Garrez 1872 and Bloch 1970 [1914]; the word *marāṭhī* is derived from *mahārāṣṭrī*.

65. A rethinking of the concept of the "vernacular" on global-comparative lines has been necessitated by the work that the concept does in the writing of Sheldon Pollock, among others; see Cohen 2011. One useful starting point would be Somerset 2003. Here, however, I confine myself to the commonsense ("vernacular") concept of the vernacular and its links to the social and the political.

66. In his Aihoḷe inscription of 634 CE, Pulakeśin II is said to have acquired sovereignty over "the three Mahārāṣṭrakas and their ninety thousand villages"(*agamad adhipatitvaṃ yo mahārāṣṭrakāṇāṃ navanavatisahasragrāmabhājāṃ trayāṇām*), and he was called "king of the Mahārāṣṭras" by Xuánzàng in 640–641 CE. The plural is important here, although not guaranteed by the Chinese. Later on, in 931 CE, Ratnaśrījñāna (p. 24) enumerated several regions as constituents of Mahārāṣṭra, including Kuntala, Aśmaka, and Vidarbha (although the text is corrupt here; see appendix C). For the formation of a vernacular polity under the later Yādava kings, see Schmiedchen 2014 and Novetzke 2016.

67. H. C. Bhayani (1973) was the first to notice this distinction, although he did not quite understand the significance of *sāmaṇṇa*.

68. See Bhuvanapāla on verse 112 (W104) of *Seven Centuries: cīe iti sāmānyabhāṣāśrayeṇa śabdaprayogaḥ. lokaḥ kila cīyaśabdena citām* āha. *tadbhava-tatsama-deśī-sāmānyabhāṣāśrayena caturvidhaṃ prākṛtaṃ pūrvācāryāḥ smaranti.* The *pūrvācāryas* must include Harivṛddha.

69. *Mirror of Literature* 1.35: *śaurasenī ca gauḍī ca lāṭī cānyā ca tādṛśī | yāti prākṛtam ity eva vyavahāreṣu sannidhim* ||. See also Ratnaśrījñāna's commentary thereon, where these remarks of Harivṛddha are cited.

70. *Prakrit Grammar* of Trivikramadeva 1.1.1: *siddhir lokāc ca;* Appayya Dīkṣita III's commentary thereon is *prākṛtaśabdānāṃ madhye ete prayojyā ete na prayojyā iti vyavasthāyāḥ siddhiḥ niścayo na kevalaṃ vakṣyamāṇasūtrebhya eva, kiṃtu kāvyajñalokavyavahārād api syāt, tenātra śāstre sūtrānanuśiṣṭo 'pi kāvyābhiyuktavyavahārastho hrasva eṄ sādhur iti siddham* ("The determination of whether linguistic forms should or should not be used in Prakrit does not only come from the following rules, but also from the actual practice of those who know literature, and therefore in this grammar whatever has not been explicitly taught by a rule—for example the use of a short *e* or *o* vowel—is correct if it occurs in the usage of literary authorities").

71. Pollock 2004: 401.

72. Vararuci, *Light on Prakrit:* 8.23: *śeṣaṃ saṃskṛtāt.*

73. See *Sum-Total of Prakrit* 3.77; Ghanaśyāma's criticisms are scattered throughout his commentaries on the plays of Kālidāsa and Bhavabhūti (the *Saṃjīvanī* on the *Recognition of Śakuntalā* is listed in the bibliography).

74. Rāma Pāṇivāda's commentary on 1.42: *kathaṃ tarhi 'aha soūṇa taṃ porā ṇārāaṇam uvaṭṭhiaṃ' iti prayoga iti cet bāhulakād iti brūmaḥ. nanu bāhulakaṃ bāhulakam iti tatra tatrodghoṣyate. na ca jñāyate kiṃ pramāṇam iti. satyam. 'ḍāḍhādayo bahulam' iti vakṣyate. tatra yogavibhāgaḥ kariṣyate. tathā ca bahulam iti sūtraṃ sarvavidhiśeṣatvena vyākhyāsyate. tena prayogānusāreṇa bahulaśabdopādānāt siddham iṣṭam.* Also 4.34: *evaṃ kṛte kiṃ kṛtaṃ bhavatīti pauravādiprayogāḥ sādhavo bhavantīty akhilam avadātam.*

75. For "lack of rigor," see Renou 1938: 165; the sentiment is common.

76. Nara 1979; Busch 2011; Cort 2015.

77. On these regimes, see Cohn 1996; Trautmann 2006.

78. See Dvivedi 2008 [1952], who is somewhat critical of these forward-tilting histories.

79. Hunter 2015: 740; *Virāṭaparvan*, pp. 7–8: *umilva maṅgalā niṅ mañjavākna byāsamata, maṅgala niṅ mikəta prakṛta nikeṅ virāṭaparva saṅ kathā* (reading *niṅ mikəta* with Fokker instead of *nimitta* with Juynboll).

80. The text is the so-called *Chandakaraṇa* or *Candrakiraṇa*. See Lokesh Chandra 1997: 182: *ujar parakṛta mvaṅ saṅaskṛta.*

81. Cf. Pollock 2004: 406: "The striving for the specification of the vernacular particular from within the dominating Sanskrit epistemological universal; the quest for discipline in the putatively lawless dialectal; the search for a new authority upon which this discipline could be founded; the royal court as the social site par excellence for the production of systematic vernacular knowledge—this entire culture-power complex of vernacularity finds its most condensed expression in the production of Kannada grammar." See also p. 412 of the same article.

82. *Jewel-Mirror of Language* 174: *padavidhi kannaḍakaṃ sakkadakkam illādyarinde sanduvan aṟid' i- | rpudu birudāvaḷiyoḷ pēḻvudu peṟavaṟoḷ āgad' idu viruddha-samāsam* ||:

"Kannada words should not be joined with Samskrita words to form a compound. But some compounds, made by ancient poets are to be retained in usage; such compounds can be used in titles also. Nowhere else the use of such compounds is permitted" (trans. Kedilaya).

83. See *Way of the Poet-King* 1.51ff. and *Analysis of Literature* (of Nāgavarman), v. 55; the latter verse is quoted in the *Jewel-Mirror* at an earlier point (102).

84. *Jewel-Mirror of Language* 299: *sakkadamaṃ maṛegoḷḷade cokkaḷikeyin accagannaḍaṃ bēḻpara ka- | yvokka nidhiy' enip' apabhraṃśakkam dēśīyapadakam uṇṭu samāsam* ||: "For those who, without resorting to Samskrita, want to use pure Kannada, these *tadbhava* words, their compounds, and the *tatsama* compounds form a handy treasure. With these words and compounds, *dēśīya* (pure Kannada) words can be joined to form compounds" (trans. Kedilaya). The term *samasaṃskṛtaṃ*, which is defined in v. 80, had already been used in *Way of the Poet-King* (1.51 and 1.55).

85. Badiger 1978 thinks that the words in the *apabhraṃśaprakaraṇa* are actually Prakrit words that had been borrowed into Kannada (see also Nagarajaiah 1994 and Khadabadi 1981); this chapter clearly, however, has a generative rather than descriptive purpose.

86. "Likely": see the discussion of Nannaya and Appakavi below in the text.

87. *Ornament of the* Āndhra *Language,* v. 7ab: *saṃskṛta-prākṛtādi-lakṣaṇamu jeppi tenugunaku lakṣaṇamu jeppakuniki.*

88. Ibid., v. 19: *tatsamambun āga dadbhavambanan acca-tenugun āga mariyu dēśyam anaga | grāmyabhāṣan āga galavaidu teragulu vēṟe vēṟe vāni vistarintu* ||; v. 27ab: *tatsamambu dakka takkina nālagun acca-tenugul' andur' akhila-janulu* |. See also Mitchell 2009: 103.

89. In her edition of *Ornament of the Āndhra Language* (pp. 24–25), Ainavolu suggests that *accatenugu* refers to common vocabulary items (*tala* "head," *nela* "moon," *vēsavi* "summer," etc.), while *dēśitenugu* refers to words of the poetic vocabulary (*eṟukuva* "knowledge," etc.).

90. *Wishing-Stone* 1.46–47; Mitchell 2009: 103. The phrase *anyadeśaja-*, which I translate as "of foreign origin" (literally, "originating in another place"), slightly complicates her argument that "the foreign" as a category is absent from premodern Telugu grammars.

91. *Ocean of Meters,* v. 70: *int' aṟupid' ubhayabhāṣeyoḷaṃ toḍarade sarva-viṣaya-bhāṣādigaḷiṃ | mun tiḷupidapaṃ ninag'* ān *antarisade kīḻ idaṃ payo-ruha-vadanī*; also v. 296. In other texts, *ubhayabhāṣā* refers to Sanskrit and the regional vernacular; see *Ornament of the Āndhra Language,* v. 5, and the discussion of the "new duality" in chapter 7.

92. Pollock 1998, 2004.

93. Virahāṅka discusses the *jāti*s in Prakrit and the *vṛtta*s in Sanskrit (the latter in the fifth chapter).

94. The descent of Prakrit meters from Tamil originals was entirely self-evident to George Hart (1975), but a detailed study—which would take into account the other metrical systems of South India besides Tamil—remains to be done.

95. Mitchell 2009: 108; Pollock 2004: 402.

96. For Urdu as a mixed language, see Bangha 2005. For Malayalam I follow Freeman 1998, which mentions the Prakrit genealogy of *maṇipravāḷam* only in a footnote (no. 28).

97. In the *praśasti* to the text: *prāyaḥ prākṛtabhāratyāṃ kvacit saṃskṛtamiśrayā | maṇipravālanyāyena prokto 'yaṃ granthavistaraḥ* ||. I thank Sarah Pierce Taylor for the reference.

98. *New Dramatic Art,* 4: 385 (comm. on 32.382): *trivargaprasiddhaṃ padamadhye saṃskṛtaṃ madhye deśabhāṣādiyuktaṃ tad eva kāryam, dakṣiṇāpathe maṇipravālam iti prasiddham, kāśmīre śāṭakulam iti.* See also Ezhuthachan 1971.

CHAPTER 7. FORGETTING PRAKRIT

1. "The learned delight in the Sanskrit language; / nobody can relish the flavor of Prakrit. / Regional speech is sweet to everyone, / so that's the kind of Avahaṭṭha I'll speak." Cited from McGregor 1984: 30; the translation is my own.

2. Jineśvara Sūri quotes this verse in the following form in his *Treasury of Gāthā-Jewels* (1194 CE), v. 21: *pāiyakavvaṃ paḍhiuṃ gumpheuṃ taha ya kujjayapasūṇaṃ | kuviyaṃ ca pasāheuṃ ajja vi bahave na yāṇaṃti ||*. Jayaratha (later twelfth century) quotes it in the following form on p. 7 of his *Analysis* of Ruyyaka's *Totality of Ornaments: pāuabaṃdhaṃ paḍhiuṃ baṃdheuṃ taha a kujjakusumāiṃ | poḍhamahilaṃ ca ramiuṃ virala ccia ke vi jāṇaṃti ||*.

3. E.g., Siddharṣi (see chapter 3).

4. The opposition dates to around 1540 (Alessandro Citolini's *Lettera in difesa della lingua volgare*), and it is conspicuously absent from earlier discussions of Latin and the vernaculars in Renaissance Italy. See Faithfull 1953; Mioni 2004. On the "death of Sanskrit," see Pollock 2001.

5. Alsdorf 2006 [1965]: 15–16.

6. Pollock 1998; 2006*a:* pt. 2.

7. Phukan 2001: 37.

8. Pollock 2006*a:* 390–391; 2011: 24–25.

9. Pischel 1905–1906, reprinted with translation in Kulkarni 2003; Upadhye 1975–1976.

10. Bhoja is also credited with a Prakrit grammar that is now lost.

11. See Bhayani 1996 for a fragmentary poem on the theme of *māna* (another fragmentary poem is titled *kodaṇḍa,* "the bow") and Katare 1952 for an inscribed verse of *Seven Centuries,* and see Disalkar 1960: 292 for inscriptional Prakrit more generally.

12. The Prakrit poet Dhanapāla, who was earlier patronized by Bhoja's uncle Vākpati Muñja, was patronized by Bhoja later in life.

13. Pollock 2006*a:* 346; Tieken 2008.

14. The inscription, dated to the reign of the Cāḷukya king Vijayāditya Satyāśraya, is edited in Panchamukhi 1941: 2–3.

15. Yashaschandra 2003: 581 .

16. Rice 1882: 301, 304; *Ornament of the* Āndhra *Language,* v. 5. For Ketana and Tikkana, see Narayana Rao 2003: 393.

17. Narayana Rao 1995: 28; 2003: 398.

18. *Deeds of Manu,* vv. 7–8.

19. Raghavan 1963: 824.

20. See Dvivedi 2008 [1952] and Siṃh 1971 [1952].

21. McGregor (1984: 30), followed by Tieken (2008: 358).

22. Nara 1979: 6, taking *ko* in the sense of *kovi.*

23. The final line of the verse, "that's why one should compose in *such* an Avahaṭṭha," refers to the *desila vayanā* mentioned previously, as Thibaut d'Hubert rightly suggests (personal communication).

24. Rice (1882: 301).

25. The text was edited by A. N. Upadhye; unbeknownst to him, it seems, Weber also consulted this text for his edition of *Seven Centuries* (it is his "second Telugu recension").

26. Somasekhara Sarma 1948: 469; Narayana Rao and Shulman 2012: 22.

27. Vema, *Essence of the Seven Centuries*: *hālaḥ prāk saptaśatīṃ gāthākoṭer vyadhatta saṃprati tu | so 'yaṃ vemabhūpālas tasyā api śatakam āharat sāram ||*.

28. See Ghatage 1934–1935; Jain 1981: 38, and the comprehensive Jain 1961.

29. Yashaschandra 2003: 584–585; Bangha 2012.

30. Cort 2009.

31. *Epitome of Queen Līlāvatī*, pp. 26–28.

32. A.N. Upadhye's introduction to vol. 2 of the *Kuvayalamālā*, p. 96; Christine Chojnacki is preparing a paper on these abridgments (see also Chojnacki 2012, 2016).

33. Ghatage 1934–1935: 42.

34. Cort 2015; on the *Essence for Gommaṭa* (*Gommaṭasāra*), see also Upadhye 1983; 1990: 263 .

35. I owe this observation to Sheldon Pollock. Abhinavagupta cites Prakrit and Apabhramsha verses (and composes his own) in many of his works, but when commenting upon the Prakrit and Apabhramsha verses in Ānandavardhana's *Light on Suggestion*, he typically provides a Sanskrit gloss.

36. Richard Pischel tentatively identifies this Vasantarāja with another, the Reḍḍi king Kumāragiri (r. 1386–1402), who was deposed by the very same Pedakomaṭi Vema that we encountered earlier as the author of *Essence of the Seven Centuries* (see Pischel 1874: 17–18). Thanks to an old manuscript of Vasantarāja's commentary held at Cambridge, and brought to my attention by Vincenzo Vergiani (see MS Or. 84 at https://cudl.lib.cam.ac.uk/view/MS-OR-00084/1), we know that the author is the same as the author of the *Vasantarājaśakuna*, who was patronized by Candradeva (probably the Gāhaḍavāla king who ruled from 1089 to 1103, and at any rate earlier than Ballālasena in the twelfth century, who quotes the *Vasantarājaśakuna*).

37. Lakṣmīdhara wrote a commentary on Jayadeva's twelfth-century classic *Gītagovinda* that is ascribed in one manuscript to the Vijayanagara king Tirumala (r. 1565–1572 CE).

38. For a recent overview of Śeṣa Kṛṣṇa's career, see Benke 2010.

39. See *Moonlight of Prakrit* 9.36 (referring to the *Moonlight of Words* [*Padacandrikā*]).

40. Raghavan 1941.

41. See Upadhye's introductions to the *Candralekhā*, as well as Naikar 1998 and the forthcoming PhD dissertation of Melinda Fodor (Paris).

42. For the story of this rivalry, especially as reported in the *Pṛthvirāj Rāso*, see Talbot 2016.

43. *Candralekhā* of Rudradāsa, Upadhye's Introduction, p. 58: "the result has fallen far short of what a drama really should be".

44. For Ghanaśyāma in general, see Chaudhuri 1943; Mainkar 1970; Shukla 1985; Yutaka 2007.

45. Upadhye 1955.

46. Ghanaśyāma, Ānandasundarī 1.8: *pākhaṃḍo ṇa mahaṃ tidikkhaï viḍo sīlāi vijjaṃ jaḍo jaṃ jaṃ jassa sudullahaṃ khidisu so taṃ taṃ muhā ṇiṃdaï | (huṃ, avahido suṇāhi) te savve uṇa ekka-desa-kaïṇo je ekka-bhāsā-caṇā so saṃpuṇṇa-kaī vihāi bhuvaṇe jo savva-bhāsā-kaī ||*.

47. See pp. xxxiv–xxxix of Upadhye's introduction to *Kaṃsa's Demise.*

48. These commentaries on *Rāvaṇa's Demise* by Pravarasena are discussed by Krishnakanta Handique in his introduction to his 1976 translation, and most recently by Acharya 2006, noting a manuscript of Harṣapāla's commentary.

49. Rāmadāsa, *Light on Rāma's Bridge,* p. 2: *dhīrāṇāṃ kāvyacarcācaturimavidhaye vikramādityavācā yaṃ cakre kālidāsaḥ kavikusumavidhuḥ setunāmaprabandham* | *tadvyākhyā sauṣṭhavārthaṃ pariṣadi kurute rāmadāsaḥ sa eva granthaṃ jallālīndrakṣitipativacasā rāmasetupradīpam* ||.

50. Harṣapāla's commentary, second verse: *tena prākṛtakovidaiḥ saha samālocya prasannākṣaram saṃkṣepād akarod idaṃ vivaraṇaṃ śrīharṣapālo nṛpaḥ* ||.

51. Pollock 2014: 119.

52. See *Prakrit Piṅgala* 1.71, 1.190, 1.204. Similar "accidental anthologies" are discussed in chapter 4.

53. Siṃh 1997 [1956]; Vyas 1962; Nara 1979; Bubeník 1998.

54. *Prakrit Piṅgala* 1.1: *paḍhamabbhāsataraṃḍo*; Lakṣmīnātha offers three alternatives for *-bbhāsa-*, but favors *bhāṣā.* For the boat image, see *Mirror of Literature* 1.12.

55. E.g., *Prakrit Piṅgala* 1.177 (*jaṃpaï piṃgala vīra*), 1.191 (*piṃgaleṇa paāsio*), 1.194 (*bhaṇaï phaṇiṃdo vimalamaī*), etc.

56. See Busch 2011*a* on "Hindi literary beginnings." For Piṅgala as the first poet of *bhāṣā* (or *narabhāṣā*), see Lakṣmīnātha's commentary on *Prakrit Piṅgala* 1.1 and Keśavadāsa, *Garland of Meters* (*Chandamālā*) 2.4; I thank Allison Busch for the reference. Both the *Adornment of Language* (*Vāṇībhūṣaṇa*) and the *Pearl of Meters* (*Vṛttamauktika*) are Sanskrit reworkings of the *Prakrit Piṅgala* (the latter based heavily on the former); Keśavadāsa too works the introductory verses of the *Prakrit Piṅgala,* perhaps from a Sanskrit source, into the beginning of the second section of his *Garland of Meters.*

57. Lakṣmīnātha's commentary to *Prakrit Piṅgala* 1.1. The earliest citation I have found for the conceit of Piṅgala as a Nāga is Halāyudha's commentary (middle of the tenth century) on the *Chandaḥ Sūtra.* Earlier authors refer to him, among them Śabara, Virahāṅka, and the author (Mitradhara?) of the *Chandoviciti* discovered in Turfan (Schlingloff 1958), but not as a *nāga* (unless he is the authority to whom Virahāṅka refers as *bhuaāhiva*).

58. Siṃh 1997 [1956]: §30, who cites Bhikhārīdāsa's *Examination of Literature,* v. 15: *braja māgadhī milai amara nāga yavana bhākhāni* | *sahaja pārasī hūṃ milai ṣaṭa vidhi kahata bakhāni* ||. If this argument is correct, we should not expect to find Prakrit designated as the language of the snakes in the early Mārū-Gūrjar literature (of the twelfth and thirteenth centuries), which I have not consulted. Some Prakrit texts do seem to have a lot to do with snakes (e.g., *Hara's Belt,* a compendium of medical and magical knowledge of the tenth century, whose title refers to the serpent Vāsuki), but do not represent Prakrit as the language of the snakes, as far as I am aware.

BIBLIOGRAPHY

PRIMARY SOURCES

Amara's Treasury (*Amarakośa* [*Nāmaliṅgānuśāsana*]) of Amarasiṃha: (1) *The Nâmalingânuśâsana (Amarakosha) of Amarasimha, with the Commentary (Amarakoshodghâtana) of Kshîrasvâmin.* Edited by Krishnaji Govind Oka. Poona [Pune]: Law Printing Press, 1913. (2) *Amara's Nāmaliṅgānuśāsanam with the Commentary Amarakośodghāṭana of Bhaṭṭa Kṣīrasvāmin.* Edited by Har Dutt Sharma and N.G. Sardesai. Poona Oriental Series 43. Poona [Pune]: Oriental Book Agency, 1941.

Analysis of Literature (*Kāvyamīmāṃsā*) of Rājaśekhara: *Kāvyamīmāṁsā of Rājaśekhara.* Edited by C.D. Dalal and Pandit R.A. Sastry. Revised and enlarged by K.S. Ramaswami Sastri Siromani. Gaekwad's Oriental Series 1. Baroda [Vadodara]: Oriental Institute, 1934.

Analysis of Literature (*Kāvyāvalōkanaṃ*) of Nāgavarman: *Nāgavarma viracitaṃ Kāvyāvalōkanaṃ.* Edited by H. Dēvīrappa. Bengaluru: Kannaḍa Sāhitya Pariṣattu, 2004.

Āpastambaśrautasūtra: The Śrauta Sútra of Ápastamba belonging to the Taittiríya Samhitá. Edited by Richard Garbe. Calcutta [Kolkata]: Asiatic Society, 1902.

Aṣṭādhyāyī of Pāṇini: *Pâṇini's Grammatik.* Edited by Otto Böhtlingk. Leipzig: Haessel, 1887.

Ānandasundarī of Ghanaśyāma: *Ghanaśyāma's Ānandasundarī.* Edited by A.N. Upadhye. Benares [Varanasi]: Motilal Banarsidass, 1955.

Anuyogadvāra Sūtra: Anuyogadvārasūtram, with Three Commentaries: Jinadāsa Gaṇi Mahattara's Cūrṇi, Haribhadra Sūri's Vivṛti, and Maladhāri Hemacandra Sūri's Vṛtti. Edited by Jambūvijaya. 2 vol. Jaina Āgama Series 18. Bombay [Mumbai]: Śrī Mahāvīra Jaina Vidyālaya, 1999–2000.

Baudhāyanaśrautasūtra: The Baudhāyanaśrautasūtra. Edited by C.G. Kashikar. New Delhi: Indira Gandhi National Centre for the Arts, 2003.

Birth of Kumāra (*Kumārasaṃbhava*) of Kālidāsa: (1) *Kálidása's Kumârasambhava.* Edited by M.R. Kale. With Mallinātha's commentary. Bombay [Mumbai]: Standard Publishing

Co., 1917. (2) *Vallabhadeva's Kommentar (Śāradā-Version) zum Kumārasambhava des Kālidāsa*. Edited by Mulakaluri Srimannarayana Murti. Supplementband zum Verzeichnis der Orientalischen Handschriften in Deutschland. Wiesbaden: Steiner, 1980.

Brilliance of the Connoisseurs (*Rasikaprakāśana*) of Vairocana: Asiatic Society of Calcutta MS G-4825.

Candralekhā of Rudradāsa: *Rudradāsa's Candralekhā*. Edited by A. N. Upadhye. Bombay [Mumbai]: Bharatiya Vidya Bhavan, 1967.

Collection of Mora- and Syllable-Counting Meters (*Vṛttajātisamuccaya*) of Virahāṅka: *Kavi Virahāṅka Kṛta Saṭīka Vṛttajātisamuccaya*. Edited by H. D. Velankar. Rājasthāna Purātana Granthamālā 61. Jodhpur: Rājasthāna Prācyavidyā Pratiṣṭhāna, 1962.

Collection of Old Prabandhas (*Purātanaprabandhasaṅgraha*): *Purātanaprabandhasaṅgraha*. Edited by Jina Vijaya Muni. Singhi Jain Series 2. Calcutta [Kolkata]: Siṅghī Jaina Jñānapīṭha, 1936.

Commentary on the Wish-Granting Vine of Literature (*Kāvyakalpalatāvṛtti*) of Amaracandra: *Kāvyakalpalatāvṛtti with Sūtras (Text) of Arisinha by Amara-Chandra Yati*. Edited by Jagannath Sastri Hoshing. Benares [Varanasi]: Vidya Vilas Press, 1931.

Compendium of the Essence of Figures in Literature (*Kāvyālaṃkārasārasaṅgraha*) of Udbhaṭa: *Kāvyālaṅkāra-sāra-saṅgraha of Udbhaṭa*. Edited by Narayana Daso Banhatti. Bombay Sanskrit and Prakrit Series 79. Poona [Pune]: Bhandarkar Oriental Research Institute, 1982.

Constellation (*Tārāgaṇa*) of Bappabhaṭṭi: *Tārāyaṇa (Tārāgaṇa): An Anthology of Bappabhaṭṭi's Prakrit Gāthās Compiled by Śāṅkuka*. Edited by H. C. Bhayani. Prakrit Text Series 24. Ahmedabad: Prakrit Text Society, 1987.

Cloud Messenger (*Meghadūta*) of Kālidāsa: *The Meghadûta of Kâlidâsa, With the Commentary (Saṃjîvanî) of Mallinâtha*. Edited by M. R. Kale. Bombay [Mumbai]: Bombay Vaibhav Press, 1934.

Cluster of Blossoms from the Great Story (*Bṛhatkathāmañjarī*) of Kṣemendra: *The Bṛihatkathâmañjarî of Kshemendra*. Edited by Paṇḍit Śivadatta and Kâshînâth Pâṇdurang Parab. Kāvyamālā 69. Bombay [Mumbai]: Nirṇaya-Sâgara Press, 1901.

Cluster of Blossoms of Prakrit (*Prākṛtamañjarī*): See *Light on Prakrit*.

Descent of Forms for Prakrit (*Prākṛtarūpāvatāra*) of Siṃharāja: *Prakritarupavatara: A Prakrit Grammar Based on the Valmiki sutra, by Simharaja, son of Samudrabandhayajvan*. Edited by E. Hultzsch. London: Royal Asiatic Society, 1909.

Deeds of Harṣa (*Harṣacarita*) of Bāṇabhaṭṭa: *Bâṇabhaṭṭa's Biography of King Harshavardhana of Sthâṇîśvara*. Edited by A. A. Führer. Bombay [Mumbai]: Government Central Press, 1909.

Deeds of King Vikramāṅka (*Vikramāṅkadevacarita*) of Bilhaṇa: *The Vikramânkadevacarita: A Life of King Vikramâditya–Tribhuvana Malla of Kalyāṇa*. Edited by Georg Bühler. Bombay [Mumbai]: Government Central Book Depot, 1875.

Deeds of Padma (*Paümacariya*) of Vimala Sūri: *Ācārya Vimalasūri's Paumacariyam*. Edited by Hermann Jacobi and revised by Muni Punyavijayaji. 2 vols. Ahmedabad: Prakrit Text Society, 2005. Originally published by H. Jacobi in 1914.

Deeds of Padma (*Paümacariu*) of Svayambhū: *Paumacariu of Svayambhūdeva*. Edited by H. C. Bhayani. Singhi Jain Series 34. Bombay [Mumbai]: Bhāratīya Vidyā Bhavan, 1953.

Deeds of Rāma (*Rāmacarita*) of Abhinanda: *Ramacarita of Abhinanda*. Edited by K.S. Rāmaswāmi Śāstrī Śiromaṇi. Gaekwad's Oriental Series 46. Baroda [Vadodara]: Oriental Institute, 1930.

Deeds of the Promoters (*Prabhāvakacarita*) of Prabhācandra: *Prabhāvaka Charita of Prabhāchāndrācharya*. Edited by Jinavijaya. Ahmedabad: Siṅghī Jaina Granthamālā, 1940.

Definition of the Gāthā (*Gāthālakṣaṇa*) of Nanditāḍhya: Printed as an appendix in *Kavidarpaṇa*, ed. H. D. Velankar. Jodhpur: Rajasthan Oriental Research Institute, 1962.

Definition of Prakrit (*Prākṛtalakṣaṇa*) of Caṇḍa: *The Prákṛita-Lakshaṇam or Chaṇḍa's Grammar of the Ancient (Ársha) Prakrit*. Edited by A. F. Rudolf Hoernle. Calcutta [Kolkata]: Asiatic Society, 1880.

Dhavalā of Vīrasena: See *Ṣaṭkhaṇḍāgama*.

Dispeller of Disputes (*Vigrahavyāvartanī*) of Nāgārjuna: *Nāgārjunakṛtā Vigrahavyāvarttanī svopajñavṛttyā sametā*. Edited by Kāśīprasāda Jāyasavāla and Rāhula Sāṃkṛtyāyana. Patna: Bihar and Orissa Research Society, 1937.

Distilled Essence (*Saṃkṣiptasāra*) of Kramadīśvara: *Prākṛtādhyāya (The Prākṛta Book of the Saṃkṣiptasāra)* by Kramadīśvara. Edited by Satya Ranjan Banerjee. Prakrit Text Series No. 22. Ahmedabad: Prakrit Text Society, 1980.

Dynasty of Raghu (*Raghuvaṃśa*) of Kālidāsa: (1) *The Raghuvamśa of Kálidása, with the Commentary (the Sanjîvanî) of Mallinâtha*. Edited M.R. Kale. Bombay [Mumbai]: Gopal Narayen, 1922. (2) *The Raghupañcikā of Vallabhadeva: Being the Earliest Commentary on the Raghuvaṃśa of Kālidāsa*. Edited by Dominic Goodall and Harunaga Isaacson. Groningen: E. Forsten, 2003.

Endless Stream of Likenesses and Births (*Upamitibhavaprapañca*): *Śrīmatsiddharṣisādhuviracitā Upamitibhavaprapañcakathā*. Edited by Śāha Nagīna Bhāī Ghelā Bhāī Javherī. Śreṣṭi Devacandra Lālabhāī Jainapustakoddhāra 46. Mumbai: Nirṇaya-Sāgara Press, 1918.

Epitome of Queen Līlāvatī (*Līlāvatīsāra*) of Jinaratna Sūri: *The Epitome of Queen Lilavati by Jinaratna*. Edited and translated by R.C.C. Fynes. New York: New York University Press, 2005.

Essence of the Saṃhitās (*Saṃhitāsāra*) of Śaṅkuka: see Slouber 2011.

Examination of Literature (*Kāvyanirṇaya*) of Bhikhārīdāsa: *Bhikhārīdāsa Granthāvalī, dvitīya khaṇḍa (Kāvyanirṇaya)*. Edited by Viśvanāthaprasāda Miśra. Kāśī [Varanasi]: Nāgarīpracāraṇī Sabhā, 1957.

Explanation of the Garland of Advice (*Dharmopadeśamālāvivaraṇa*) of Jayasiṃha Sūri: *Upadēśamālāvivaraṇa of Jayasiṃasūri*. Edited by Lālcand Bhagavāndās Gāndhī. Singhi Jain Series 28. Bombay [Mumbai]: Bharatīya Vidyā Bhavan, 1949.

Exposition of the Six Languages (*Ṣaḍbhāṣāvivaraṇa*) of Bālasarasvatī: Adyar Library and Research Centre, Adyar, Chennai, MS TR 451.

Explanation of the Suggestion Verses (*Dhvanigāthāpañjikā*) of Ratnākara: *Śrīrājānakaratnākaraviracitā Dhvanigāthāpañcikā*. Edited by Bṛjeśakumāraśukla. Lakhanaū: Akhila-Bhāratīya-Saṃskṛta-Pariṣad, 1999. See also Masson and Patwardhan 1974.

Explanation of the System (*Tantravārttika*) of Kumārila Bhaṭṭa: See *Mīmāṃsā Sūtras*.

Exposition of the Sūtras on the Ornaments of Literature (*Kāvyālaṃkārasūtravṛtti*) of Vāmana: *The Kâvyâlankâra-Sûtras of Vâmana with His Own Vṛitti*. Edited by Paṇḍit Durgâprasâda and Kâśînâth Pâṇḍurang Parab, revised by Wâsudev Laxmaṇ Shâstrî Paṇśîkar. 3rd rev. ed. Kâvyamâlâ 15. Bombay [Mumbai]: Nirṇaya-Sâgar Press, 1926.

Extensive Play of the Bodhisattva (*Lalitavistara*): *Lalita Vistara*. Edited by S. Lefmann. Halle: Buchhandlung des Waisenhauses, 1908.

Gauḍa's Demise (*Gaüḍavaho*) of Vākpatirāja: *Gaüḍavaho* by Vākpatirāja. Edited by N. G. Suru. Prakrit Text Series 18. Ahmedabad: Prakrit Text Society, 1975.

Garland of Meters (*Chandamālā*) of Keśavadāsa: *Chandamālā*, pp. 431–456 in *Keśava-graṃthāvalī, khaṇḍa* 2. Edited by Viśvanāthaprasāda Miśra. Allahabad: Hindustani Academy, 1955.

Garland of Regional Nouns (*Deśīnāmamālā*) of Hemacandra: *Hemachandra's Deśīnāmamālā*. Edited by R. Pischel. 2nd ed. rev. P. V. Ramanujaswami. Bombay Sanskrit Series 17. Poona [Pune]: Bhandarkar Oriental Research Institute, 1938.

Gift from India (*Tuḥfat al-Hind*) of Mīrzā Khān: *A Grammar of the Braj Bhākhā by Mīrzā Khān (1676 A.D.)*. Edited and translated by M. Ziauddin. Calcutta [Kolkata]: Visva-Bharati Book-shop, 1936.

Great Commenary (*Mahābhāṣya*) of Patañjali: *Patanjali's Vyâkaraṇa-Mahâbhâshya*. Edited by F. Kielhorn. 3 vols. Bombay [Mumbai]: Government Central Book Depôt, 1880–1884.

Hara's Belt (*Haramekhalā*) of Mādhuka: (1) *The Haramekhala of Māhuka*. Edited by K. Sāmbaśiva Śāstrī. (Chapters 2–4 only.) Trivandrum Sanskrit Series 124. Trivandrum: Government Press, 1936. (2) *Śrīḥ Mādhukadhīrasahāyapaṇḍitaviracitā Haramekhalā Saṭīkā (Pūrvakhaṇḍaḥ)*. Edited by Kṛṣṇaprasādaśarman. Kathmandu: Nepal Government Press, 1972.

Hari's Victory (Harivijaya) of Sarvasena: See Kulkarni 1991.

Illumination of the Erotic (*Śṛṅgāraprakāśa*) of Bhojadeva: *Śṛṅgāraprakāśa* [*Sāhityaprakāśa*] *by Bhojarāja*. Edited by Rewāprasāda Dwivedī. 2 vols. New Delhi: Indira Gandhi National Centre for the Arts, 2007.

Iṟaiyaṉār Akapporuḷ: *Iṟaiyaṉār Akapporuḷ mūlam Nākkīraṉār uraiyuṭaṉ*. Edited by Pavāṉantam Piḷḷai. Madras [Chennai], 1916.

Jewel-Lamp of Prakrit (*Prākṛtamaṇidīpikā*) of Appayya Dīkṣita III: *Prākṛtamaṇidīpa of Appayyadīkṣita*. Edited with a commentary by T. T. Srinivasagopalacharya. Mysore: Government Press, 1953.

Jewel-Mirror of Language (*Śabdamaṇidarpaṇa*) of Keśava: See Kedilaya 1964–1977.

Kāma Sūtra of Vātsyāyana: *Śrīvātsyāyanapraṇītaṃ Kāmasūtram, Yaśodharaviracitayā Jayamaṅgalākhyayā ṭīkayā sametam*. Edited by Durgāprasāda. 2nd ed. Mumbai: Nirṇaya Sāgara Yantrālaya, 1900.

Kaṃsa's Demise (*Kaṃsavaho*) of Rāma Pāṇivāda: *Rāma Pāṇivāda's Kaṁsavaho (A Prākrit Poem in Classical Style)*. Edited by A. N. Upadhye. 2nd ed. Delhi: Motilal Banarsidass, 1968 [1940].

Karpūramañjarī of Rājaśekhara: (1) *Karpūramañjarī (The Prakrit Play of Rājaśekhara)*. Edited by Manomohan Ghosh. Calcutta [Kolkata]: University of Calcutta, 1939. (2) *Rāja-çekhara's Karpūra-mañjarī*. Edited by Sten Konow. Translated by Charles Rockwell Lanman. Harvard Oriental Series 4. Cambridge, Mass.: Harvard University, 1901.

The Kāśī Commentary (*Kāśikāvṛtti*) of Vāmana and Jayāditya: see http://gretil.sub.uni-goettingen.de/gretil/1_sanskr/6_sastra/1_gram/jvkasixu.htm. Based on Aryendra Sharma's edition (Hyderabad, 1969–1985).

Kuvalayamālā of Uddyotanasūri: *Uddyotana-sūri's Kuvalayamālā, Part I.* Edited by A. N. Upadhye. Singhi Jain Series 45. Bombay [Mumbai]: Bhāratīya Vidyā Bhavana, 1959.

Kuvalayamālā's Story (*Kuvalayamālākathā*) of Ratnaprabhasūri: *Uddyotana-sūri's Kuvalayamālā, Part II: Ratnaprbha-sūri's* [sic] *Kuvalayamālā Kathā.* Edited by A. N. Upadhye. Singhi Jain Series 46. Bombay [Mumbai]: Bharatiya Vidya Bhavan, 1970.

Light on Prakrit (*Prākṛtaprakāśa*) of Vararuci: (1) *Vararuciracitaḥ Prākṛtaprakāśaḥ Sañjīvanī Subodhinī Manoramā Prākṛtamañjarī ceti ṭīkācatuṣṭayena Hindībhāṣānuvādena ca sametaḥ.* Edited by Baladeva Upādhyāya. Sarasvatībhavana-Granthamālā 102. Varanasi: Vārāṇaseya-Saṃskṛta-Viśvāvidyālaya, 1972. (2) *The Prákṛita-Prakáśa: or, the Prákṛit Grammar of Vararuchi, with the Commentary (Manoramá) of Bhámaha.* Edited by Edward Byles Cowell. Hertfort: Stephan Austin, 1854. (3) *Prakṛta-Prakasa* [sic] *of Vararuci with Bhāmaha's Commentary Manoramā.* Edited by P. L. Vaidya. Poona [Pune]: Oriental Book Agency, 1931. (4) *The Prākṛtaprakāśa of Vararuci with the Commentary of Rāmapāṇivāda.* Edited by C. Kunhan Raja and K. Ramachandra Sarma. Madras [Chennai]: Adyar Library, 1946. (5) *The Prākṛta-Prakāśa of Vararuci, Text Edited for the First Time with a New Commentary Entitled Prākṛta-pāda-ṭīkā by Nārāyaṇa Viydāvinoda.* Edited by Satya Ranjan Banerjee. Calcutta [Kolkata]: Sanskrit Pustak Bhandar, 1975.

Light on Rāma's Bridge (*Rāmasetupradīpa*) of Rāmadāsa: See *Rāvaṇa's Demise* (6).

Light on Suggestion (*Dhvanyāloka*) of *Ānandavardhana:* See Ingalls et al. 1990.

Light on the Great Commentary (*Mahābhāṣyadīpikā*) of Bhartṛhari: *Mahābhāṣyadīpikā of Bhartṛhari.* Edited by K. V. Abhyankar and V. P. Limaye. Poona [Pune]: Bhandarkar Oriental Research Institute, 1967.

Līlāvaī of Kautūhala: *Līlāvaī: A Romantic Kāvya in Māhārāṣṭrī Prākrit of Koūhala with the Sanskrit Vṛtti of a Jaina Author.* Edited by A. N. Upadhye. Singhi Jain Series 31. 2nd ed. (1st ed. 1949). Bombay [Mumbai]: Bharatiya Vidya Bhavan, 1966.

Little Clay Cart (*Mṛcchakaṭika*) of Śūdraka: *The Mṛichchhakaṭika of Śûdraka with the Commentary of Pṛithivîdhara.* Edited by Kâshinâth Pâṇḍurang Parab. Bombay [Mumbai]: Nirṇaya Sâgar Press, 1900.

Mādhava's Commentary on Verbal Roots (*Mādhavīyadhātuvṛtti*) of Sāyaṇa: *The Mādhavīya Dhātuvṛtti [A Treatise on Sanskrit Roots based on the Dhātupāṭha of Pāṇini] by Sāyaṇācārya.* Edited by Dwarikadas Shastri. Prāchya Bhāratī Series 1. Varanasi: Prāchya Bhāratī Prakāshan, 1964. http://sanskritlibrary.org/Sanskrit/Vyakarana/Dhatupatha/index2.

Mālatī and Mādhava (*Mālatīmādhava*) of Bhavabhūti: *Mahākavi-śrībhavabhūtiviracitam Mālatīmādhavam 'Candrakalā'-saṃskṛta-hindī-ṭīkopetam.* Edited by Śrīśeṣarājaśarman Śāstri. Varanasi: Chaukhamba Sanskrit Series Office, 1998.

The Many Places of Pilgrimage (*Vividhatīrthakalpa*) of Jinaprabhasūra: *Vividha Tīrtha Kalpa of Jinaprabha Sūri.* Edited by Jinavijaya. Singhi Jain Series 10. Shantiniketan: Siṅghī Jaina Jñānapīṭha, 1934.

Message Poem (*Sandeśarāsaka*) of ʿAbd ur-Raḥmān: (1) *Abdala-Rahamāna-kṛta Saṃdeśarāsaka.* Edited by H. C. Bhayani. Ahmedabad: Prakrit Text Society, 1999. Revision of the text published by Bhayani, together with Jinavijaya Muni, in the Singhi Jain Series in 1945. (2) *Abdularahamāna-kṛta Saṃdeśa Rāsaka.* Edited by Hazārīprasāda Dvivedī and Viśvanātha Tripāṭhī. Bombay [Mumbai]: Hindī-Grantha-Ratnākara, 1965.

Mīmāṃsā Sūtras of Jaimini: *Śrīmajjaiminipraṇītam Mīmāṃsādarśanam*. Edited by Subbāśāstrī. Ānandāśramagranthāvalī 97. 6 vols. Pune: Ānandāśramamudraṇālaya, 1929–1934.

Miragāvatī of Quṭban: "The Miragāvatī of Kutabana: Avadhī Text with Critical Notes." Edited by D. F. Plukker. PhD thesis, University of Amsterdam, 1981.

Mirror for Poets (*Kavidarpaṇa*): *Kavidarpaṇa*. Edited by H. D. Velankar. Jodhpur: Rajasthan Oriental Research Institute, 1962.

Mirror of Figures (*Alaṃkāradappaṇa*): *Alaṁkāradappaṇa*. Edited by H. C. Bhayani. L. D. Series 120. Ahmedabad: Lalbhai Dalpatbhai Institute of Indology, 1999.

Mirror of Literature (*Kāvyādarśa*) of Daṇḍin: (1) *Kāvyalakṣaṇa of Daṇḍin (also known as Kāvyādarśa) with Commentary Called Ratnaśrī of Ratnaśrījñāna*. Edited by Anantalal Thakur and Upendra Jha. Darbhanga: Mithila Institute of Post-Graduate Studies and Research in Sanskrit Learning, 1957. (2) *Ācāryadaṇḍiviracitaḥ Kāvyādarśaḥ* (with the commentaries of Vādijaṅghāladeva and Taruṇavācaspati). Edited by D. T. Tatacharya. Tirupati: Tiruvādi Śrinivās Mudrālaya, 1936.

Mirror of Literature (*Sāhityadarpaṇa*) of Viśvanātha: *Sāhityadarpaṇa of Viśvanātha*. Edited by P. V. Kane. 2nd ed. Bombay [Mumbai]: Nirṇaya Sāgara Press, 1923.

Moon to the Night-Lily of Reasoning (*Nyāyakumudacandra*) of Prabhācandra: *Nyâya Kumud Chandra of Śrîmat Prabhâchandrâchârya*. 2 vols. Edited by M. Kumar Nyaya Shastri. Mâṇik Chandra Digambara Jain Series 38. Bombay [Mumbai]: Mâṇik Chandra Digambara Jain Series, 1938–1941.

Moonlight of Prakrit (*Prākṛtacandrikā*) of Śeṣa Kṛṣṇa: *Śrīśeṣakṛṣṇakṛtā Prākṛtacandrikā Svopajñavṛttisahitā*. Edited by Subhadropādhyāya. Varanasi: Bhāratīya Vidyā Prakāśan, 1969.

Moonlight of the Essence of the Bridge (*Setutattvacandrikā*): See *Rāvaṇa's Demise* (4).

Moonlight of the Six Languages (*Ṣaḍbhāṣācandrikā*) of Lakṣmīdhara: *The Shaḍbhâshâchandrikâ of Lakshmîdhara*. Edited by Rāo Bahādur Kamalāśaṅkar Prâṇaśaṅkar Trivedî. Bombay [Mumbai]: Government Central Press, 1916.

Nandi Sūtra of Devavācaka: *Nandisūtraṃ by Shrī Devavācaka with the Vṛtti by Shrī Haribhadrācarya and Durgapadavyākhyā on Vṛtti by Shrī Śrīcandrācārya and Viṣamapadaparyāya on Vṛtti*. Edited by Muni Shrī Punyavijayajī. Ahmedabad: Prakrit Text Society, 1966.

Naṉṉūl: *Naṉṉūl mūlamum Mayilai Nātar uraiyum*. Edited by U. Ve. Cāminātaiyār. 2nd ed. Madras [Chennai]: Kapīr Accukkūṭam, 1946.

Necklace of Sarasvatī (*Sarasvatīkaṇṭhābharaṇa*) of Bhoja: *The Saraswatī Kaṇṭhābharaṇa by Dhāreshvara Bhojadeva with Commentaries of Rāmsimha (I-III) and Jagaddhara (IV)*. Edited by Paṇḍit Kedārnāth Śarmā and Wāsudev Laxmaṇ Śāstrī Paṇśīkar. Kāvyamālā 94. Bombay: [Mumbai] Nirṇaya Sāgar Press, 1934.

New Dramatic Art (*Abhinavabhāratī*) of Abhinavagupta: See *Treatise on Theater*.

Niśītha Sūtra and *Bhāṣya*: *Sthavira-puṃgava-śrī-visāhagaṇi-mahattara-praṇītaṃ sabhāṣyaṃ niśītha-sūtram*. Edited by Upādhyāya Kavi Śrī Amaramuni Jī Mahārāj and Muni Śrī Kanhaiyālāla Jī. Āgama Sāhitya Ratnamālā Nos. 3–6. 4 vols. 2nd ed. Delhi: Bhāratīya Vidyā Prakāśana, 1982.

Ocean of Meters (*Chandombudhi*) of Nāgavarman: *Nāgavarma's Canarese Prosody*. Edited by F. Kittel. Mangalore: Basel Mission Book & Tract Depository, 1875.

Ocean of the Rivers of Story (*Kathāsaritsāgara*) of Somadeva: *The Kathâsaritsâgara of Somadevabhatta*. Edited by Paṇdit Durgâprasâd and Kâśînâth Pâṇdurang Parab. 2nd ed. Bombay [Mumbai]: Nirṇaya-Sâgara Press, 1903.

On Sentence and Word (*Vākyapadīya*) of Bhartṛhari: *Vākyapadīyaṃ*. Edited by Raghunātha Śarmā. Sarasvatībhavana-granthamālā 91. Varanasi: Saṃpūrṇānanda Saṃskṛta Viśvavidyālaya, 1988.

Ornament of the Āndhra Language (*Āndhrabhāṣābhūṣaṇamu*) of Ketana: *Andhra Bhaashaa Bhuushanamu*. Edited and translated by Usha Devi Ainavolu. Vijayawada: Emesco, 2009.

Ornament of Literature (*Kāvyālaṅkāra*) of Bhāmaha: *Kāvyālaṅkāra of Bhāmaha*. Edited by C. Sankara Rama Sastri. Sri Balamanorama Series 54. Mylapore, Madras [Chennai]: Sri Balamanorama Press, 1956.

Ornament of Literature (*Kāvyālaṅkāra*) of Rudraṭa: *Śrīrudraṭapraṇītaḥ Kāvyālaṃkāraḥ Namisādhukṛtayā ṭippaṇyā sametaḥ*. Edited Durgāprasāda and Vāsudeva Śarman Paṇaśīkara. Kāvyamālā 2. Mumbai: Nirṇaya-Sāgara Press, 1909.

Phaedrus of Plato. In *Platonis Opera*, ed. John Burnet. Oxford: Oxford University Press, 1903. www.perseus.tufts.edu/hopper/text?doc=Perseus%3Atext%3A1999.01.0173%3Atext%3DPhaedrus.

The Pierced Statue (*Viddhaśālabhañjikā*) of Rājaśekhara. See *River of Amazement*.

Poem of Cihna (*Śrīcihnakāvya*) of Kṛṣṇalīlāśuka: *Śrīcihnakāvyam Govindābhiṣekanāmnā prasiddhaṃ Śrīkṛṣṇalīlāśukamuniviracitaṃ Durgaprasādayatikṛtavivaraṇopetam*. Edited by K. Raghavan Piḷḷa. Trivandrum: Paurastyabhāṣāgaveṣaṇahastalikhitagranthaprasādhanakāryālayādhyakṣa, 1971.

Prabandha of Pādalipta: In *Ajñātakartṛka Prabandha-catuṣṭaya* (*Prākṛtabhāṣānibaddha*). Edited by Ramaṇīka M. Śāha. Ahmedabad: Kalikāla-sarvajña Śrīhemacandrācārya Navama Janma-śatābdi Smṛti Saṃskāra-śikṣaṇa-nidhi, 1994.

Prakrit Grammar (*Prākṛtānuśāsana*) of Puruṣottamadeva: (1) *Le Prākṛtānuśāsana de Puruṣottama*. Edited by Luigia Nitti-Dolci. Paris: Société Asiatique, 1938. (2) See *Wish-Granting Tree of Prakrit* of Rāmaśarman.

Prakrit Grammar (*Prākṛtaśabdānuśāsana*) of Trivikramadeva: *Prakrit Grammar of Trivikrama*. Edited by P. L. Vaidya. Sholapur: Jaina Saṁskṛti Saṁrakṣaka Saṁgha, 1954.

Prakrit Lakṣmī (*Pāialacchī*) of Dhanapāla: *The Pâiyalachchhî Nâmamâlâ: A Prakrit Kosha by Dhanapâla*. Edited by Georg Bühler. Göttingen: Peppmüller, 1879.

Prakrit Piṅgala (*Prākṛtapiṅgala* or *Prākṛtapaiṅgala*): (1) *Prākṛtapaiṅgalam*. Edited by Bholāśaṅkara Vyāsa. Prakrit Text Series 2 & 4. 2 vols. Ahmedabad: Prakrit Text Society, 2007 [1959 and 1962]. Reprint. With the commentaries *Piṅgalasāravikāśinī* of Ravikara, *Piṅgalapradīpa* of Lakṣmīnātha Bhaṭṭa, and *Piṅgalaprakāśa* of Vaṃśīdhara. (2) *Prākṛtapiṅgalasūtrāṇi Lakṣmīnāthabhaṭṭaviracitayā vyākhyayānugatāni*. Edited by Śivadatta Śarmā and Kāśīnātha Śarmā. Kāvyāmālā 41. Mumbai: Nirṇaya-sāgara Press, 1894.

Rambhāmañjarī of Nayacandra Sūri: *Nayacandrasūri's Rambhāmañjarī*. Edited by Ram Prakash Poddar. Vaishali: Research Institute of Prakrit, Jainology, and Ahimsa, 1976.

Ratnāvalī of Harṣa: *Śrīharṣadevaviracitā Ratnāvalī-nāṭikā*. Edited by Śrīparameśvaradīna Pāṇḍeya. 2nd ed. Varanasi: Caukhambā Surabhāratī Prakāśana, 1981.

Rāvaṇa's Demise (*Rāvaṇavaha*) of Pravarasena: (1) *Pravarasena's Setubandha*. Translated by Krishna Kanta Handiqui. Delhi: DK Printworld, 2014. This is a convenient combination of (2) and (3) below, but unfortunately adds nothing except typos. (2) *Râvaṇavaha oder Setubandha.* Edited by Siegfried Goldschmidt. Strassburg: Trübner, 1880. (3) *Pravarasena's Setubandha.* Translated by Krishna Kanta Handiqui. Ahmedabad: Prakrit Text Society, 1979. (4) *Rāvaṇavaha-mahākāvyam.* Edited by Radhagovinda Basak. Calcutta [Kolkata]: Sanskrit College, 1959. (5) Harṣapāla's commentary. Nepalese-German Manuscript Preservation Project, microfilm reel E 1407–6 (191 folios). (6) Rāmadāsa's *Light on Rāma's Bridge (Rāmasetupradīpa). The Setubandha of Pravarasena.* Edited by Pandit *Śivadatta,* Kāśīnāth Pāṇḍurang Parab and Vāsudev Laxmaṇ Śāstrī Paṇśīkar. Kāvyamālā 49. Bombay [Mumbai]: Nirṇaya Sāgar Press, 1935.

Recogntion of Śakuntalā (*Abhijñānaśākuntala*) of Kālidāsa: *Abhijñānaśākuntalam Mahākaviśrīkālidāsapraṇītaṃ Nāṭakaratnam, Kāṭayavemabhūpaviracitayā Kumāragirirājīyayā vyākhyayā samanvitam.* Edited by C. Sankara Rama Sastri. Mylapore, Madras [Chennai]: Balamanorama Press, 1947.

Resuscitation of Prakrit (*Prākṛtasaṃjīvanī*) of Vasantarāja: see *Light on Prakrit.*

River of Amazement (*Camatkārataraṅgiṇī*) of Sundarī and Kamalā (and Ghanaśyāma): *The Contribution of Women to Sanskrit Literature,* vol. 1: *(Drama): The Camatkāra-taraṅgiṇī of Sundarī and Kamalā and the Prāṇapratiṣṭhā of Their Husband Ghanaśyāma, Commentaries on the Viddha-śālabhañjikā of Rājaśekhara.* Edited by Jatindra Bimal Chanduri. Calcutta [Kolkata]: Calcutta Oriental Press, 1943.

Way of the Poet-King (*Kavirājamārgaṃ*) of Śrīvijaya: *Śrī Nṛpatuṅgadevānumatam appa Śrīvijayakṛta Kavirājamārgam.* Edited by M. V. Sītārāmayya. Bengaluru: B. M. Śrī Smāraka Pratiṣṭhāna, 1994.

Ṣaṭkhaṇḍāgama of Puṣpadanta and Bhūtabali: *The Ṣaṭkhaṇḍāgama of Puṣpandata and Bhūtabali, with the Commentary Dhavalā by Vīrasena.* 16 vols. Edited by Hiralal Jain. Vols. 1–12 published in Amraoti (Amravati): Jaina Sāhitya Uddhāraka Fund Kāryālaya, 1939–1955. Vols. 13–16 published in Solapur: Jaina Samskrit Samrakshaka Sangha, 1993–1995.

Seven Centuries (*Sattasaī*) by Hāla: (1) *Das Saptaçatakam des Hâla.* Edited by Albrecht Weber. Leipzig: Brockhaus, 1881. Supplements, and is supplemented by, several other publications: Weber 1870 (reviewed by Garrez 1872), Weber 1874, and Weber 1883. (2) *Śrīsātavāhanaviracitā Gāthāsaptaśatī Gaṅgādharabhaṭṭaviracitayā Ṭīkayā Sametā.* Edited by Vasudeva Śarman. 2nd ed. Mumbai: Nirṇaya Sāgara Press, 1911. (3) *Hāritāmrapītāmbara's Gāthāsaptaśatīprakāśikā: A Hitherto Unpublished Commentary on Hāla's Gāthāsaptaśatī.* Edited by Jagdish Lal Shastri. Lahore: the editor, 1942. (4) *Sātavāhanācī Gāthāsaptaśatī.* Edited Sadāśiv Ātmārāma Jogaḷekara. 2nd ed. Pune: Prasāda Prakāśana, 1978. (5) *Saptaśatīsāra with Bhāvadīpikā of Vema Bhūpāla along with the Chappaṇṇaya-Gāhāo.* Edited by A. N. Upadhye. Kolhapur: Shivaji University, 1970. (6) *Hāla's Gāhākosa (Gāthāsaptaśatī) with the Sanskrit Commentary of Bhuvanapāla.* Edited by M. V. Patwardhan. Vol. 1, Ahmedabad: Prakrit Text Society, 1980. Vol. 2, Delhi: B. L. Institute of Indology, 1988. (7) Premarāja's commentary (*Sāhityajanmāvani*): MS 181 of 1879–1881 at the Bhandarkar Oriental Research Institute, Pune. (8) Ājaḍa's commentary: MS 385 of 1887–1891 at the Bhandarkar Oriental Research Institute, Pune. (9) Bhuvanapāla's commentary (*Chekoktivicāralīlā*): MS 76 at the Kaiser Library, Kathmandu (Nepalese–German Manuscript Preservation Project Microfilm Reel C 0006–12). (10) Upādhyāya Lakṣmīdhara's commentary: MS tr. 715/kāvya 18 at the National

Archives, Kathmandu (Nepalese-German Manuscript Preservation Project Microfilm Reel B 0018–13).

Seven Centuries of Āryās (*Āryāsaptaśatī*) of Govardhana: (1) *Seven Hundred Elegant Verses.* Translated by Friedhelm Hardy. New York: New York University Press and the JJC Foundation, 2009. (2) *The Āryāsaptaśatī of Govardhanāchārya.* Edited by Paṇḍit Durgāprasād and Kāśīnāth Pāṇḍurang Parab and Vāsudev Laxmaṇ Śāstrī Paṇśīkar. 3rd rev. ed. Kāvyamālā 1. Bombay: [Mumbai] Nirṇaya Sāgar Press, 1934.

Seven Centuries of Āryās (*Āryāsaptaśatī*) of Viśveśvara: *Āryāsaptaśatī Parvatīyaśrīviśveśvar apaṇḍitaviracitā.* Edited by Viṣṇu Prasāda Bhaṇḍāri. Chowkhambā Sanskrit Series 315. Benares [Varanasi]: Vidya Vilas Press, 1924.

Siddhahemacandra of Hemacandra: (1) *Hemacandra's Grammatik der Prâkritsprachen.* Edited by Richard Pischel. Halle: Waisenhaus, 1877. (2) *Prakrit Grammar of Hemacandra, Being the Eighth Chapter of his Siddhahemacandra.* Edited by P. L. Vaidya. Poona [Pune]: Hanuman Press, 1928.

Songs of the Buddhist Nuns (*Therīgāthā*): *Therigatha: Poems of the First Buddhist Women.* Edited and translated by Charles Hallisey. Murty Classical Library of India 3. Cambridge, Mass.: Harvard University Press, 2015.

Śṛṅgāramañjarī of Viśveśvara: see Upadhye 1961.

The Statue (*Pratimānāṭaka*) of Bhāsa: *Pratimānāṭaka,* on the Multimediale Datenbank zum Sanskrit-Schauspiel maintained by Matthias Ahlborn, www.bhasa.indologie.uni-wuerzburg.de/index.html.

Story of Manu (*Manucaritramu*) of Allasāni Peddana: *The Story of Manu.* Translated by Velcheru Narayana Rao and David Shulman. Cambridge, Mass.: Harvard University Press, 2015.

Story of Udayasundarī (*Udayasundarīkathā*) of Soḍḍhala: *Udayasundarîkathâ of Soḍḍhala.* Edited by C. D. Dalal and Embar Krishnamacharya. Baroda [Vadodara]: Central Library, 1920.

Sum-Total of Prakrit (*Prākṛtasarvasva*) of Mārkaṇḍeya: *Mārkaṇḍeya's Prākṛta-sarvasva.* Edited by Krishna Chandra Acharya. Prakrit Text Series 11. Ahmedabad: Prakrit Text Society, 1968.

Svayambhū's Meters (*Svayambhūchandas*): *Mahākavi Svayambhū Kṛta Svayambhūchanda.* Edited by H. D. Velankar. Rājasthāna Purātana Granthamālā 37. Jodhpur: Rājasthāna Prācyavidyā Pratiṣṭhāna, 1962.

Taraṅgalolā: Saṃkhitta-Taraṃgavaī-Kahā: An Early Abridgement of Pādalipta's Taraṃgavaī with Gujarati Translation. Edited by H. C. Bhayani. L. D. Series 75. Ahmedabad: Lalbhai Dalpatbhai Institute of Indology, 1979.

Taraṅgavatī of Pālitta: see preceding entry (*Taraṅgalolā*).

Teaching on Meter (*Chandonuśāsana*) of Hemacandra: *Chando'nuśāsana of Hemachandrasūri.* Edited by H. D. Velankar. Singhi Jain Series 49. Bombay [Mumbai]: Bharatiya Vidya Bhavan, 1961.

Teaching on Literature (*Kāvyānuśāsana*) of Hemacandra: *Kāvyānuśāsana [with Alaṁkāracūḍāmaṇi and Viveka] by Ācārya Hemacandra with Two Anonymous Ṭippaṇas.* Edited by Rasiklal C. Parikh and V. M. Kulkarni. 2nd ed. Bombay [Mumbai]: Sri Mahavira Jaina Vidyalaya, 1964.

Ten Forms (*Daśarūpaka*) of Dhanañjaya and the *Avaloka* of Dhanika: *The Daśarūpaka of Dhanaṃjaya, with the Commentary Avaloka by Dhanika and the Sub-Commentary Laghuṭīkā by Bhaṭṭanṛsiṃha.* Edited by T. Venkatacharya. Madras [Chennai]: Adyar Library and Research Centre, 1969.

Tilakamañjarī of Dhanapāla: *The Tilaka-Mañjarī of Dhanapāla.* Edited by Bhavadatta Śāstrī and Śivadatta. Kāvyamālā 85. Bombay: [Mumbai] Nirṇaya Sāgara Press, 1938.

Totality of Figures (*Alaṃkārasarvasva*) of Ruyyaka: *The Alañkārasarvasva* [sic] *of Rājānaka Ruyyaka with the Commentary of Jayaratha.* Edited by Girijāprasād Dvivedi. Kāvyamālā 35. Bombay [Mumbai]: Nirṇaya Sāgar Press, 1939.

Treasury of Āryās (*Āryākośa*) by Ravigupta: *Ācāryaravigupta-viracitā Lokasaṃvyavahārapravṛttiḥ.* Edited by Vijayapālaśāstrī. Garli, Himachal Pradesh: Rāṣṭriya-Saṃskṛta-Saṃsthānam (Veda-Vyāsa Campus), 2012.

Treasury of Gāthā-Jewels (*Gāthāratnakośa*) of Jineśvara: *Jineśvarasūri's Gāhārayaṇakosa.* Edited by Amritlal M. Bhojak and Nagin J. Shah. L. D. Series 52. Ahmedabad: Lalbhai Dalpatbhai Institute of Indology, 1975.

Treasury of Subhāṣita-Jewels (*Subhāṣitaratnakośa*) of Vidyākara: *The Subhāṣitaratnakoṣa compiled by Vidyākara.* Edited by D. D. Kosambi and V. V. Gokhale. Cambridge, Mass.: Harvard University Press, 1957.

Treatise on Power (*Arthaśāstra*): *The Kauṭilīya Arthaśāstra.* Edited by R. P. Kangle. University of Bombay Studies in Sanskrit, Prakrit and Pali 1. Bombay [Mumbai]: University of Bombay, 1960.

Treatise on Theater (*Nāṭyaśāstra*) of Bharata: *The Nāṭyaśāstra of Bharatamuni. With the Commentary Abhinavabhāratī by Abhinavaguptācārya.* 4 vols. Vadodara [Baroda]: Oriental Institute, 1992–2006. Vol. 1 (chaps. 1–7), 4th ed. by K. Krishnamoorthy, 1992. Vol. 2 (chaps. 8–18), 2nd ed,.by V. M. Kulkarni and T. Nandi, 2001. Vol. 3 (chaps. 19–27), 2nd ed. by V. M. Kulkarni and T. Nandi, 2003. Vol. 4 (chaps. 28–36), 2d ed. by V. M. Kulkarni and T. Nandi, 2006.

Twenty-four Prabandhas (*Caturviṃśatiprabandha*) of Rājaśekhara: *Caturviṁśati-Prabandha or Prabandhakośa by Rājaśekharasūri.* Edited by Hiralal Rasikdas Kapadia. Forbes Gujarati Sabhā Series 12. Bombay [Mumbai]: Forbes Gujarati Sabhā, 1932.

Unlocking Amara's Treasury (*Amarakośodghāṭana*) by Kṣīrasvāmin: see *Amara's Treasury.*

Urvaśī Won by Valor (*Vikramorvaśīya*) by Kālidāsa: *The Vikramorvaśīya of Kālidāsa.* Edited by H. D. Velankar. New Delhi: Sahitya Akademi, 1961.

Vāgbhaṭa's Ornament (*Vāgbhaṭālaṅkāra*): *The Vāgbhatālankāra of Vāgbhata with the Commentary of Simhadevagaṇi.* Edited by Kedāranātha Śāstrī and Wāsudev Laxmaṇ Śāstrī Paṇśīkar. 5th ed. Bombay: [Mumbai] Nirṇaya-Sāgara Press, 1933.

Vajjālagga of Jagadvallabha: (1) *Jayavallabha's Vajjālaggaṃ.* Edited by M. V. Patwardhan. Prakrit Text Series 14. Ahmedabad: Prakrit Text Society, 1969. (2) *Jayavallabhakṛta dharma, artha, aura kāma ke jīvana-mūlyoṃ kā anupama prākṛta sūkti-kośa Vajjālaggaṃ.* Edited by Viśvanātha Pāṭhaka. Varanasi: Pārśvanātha Vidyāśrama Śodha Saṃsthāna, 1984.

Uṣā and Aniruddha (*Usāṇiruddha*) of Rāma Pāṇivāda: *Rāmapāṇivāda's Usāṇiruddhaṁ.* 1st ed. by A. N. Upadhye. 2nd ed. by V. M. Kulkarni. Ahmedabad: Sharadaben Chimanbhai Educational Research Centre, 1996.

Verses of the Chappaṇṇayas (*Chappaṇṇaya-Gāhāo*): (1) *Saptaśatīsāra with Bhāvadīpikā of Vema Bhūpāla, along with the Chappaṇṇaya-Gāhāo (Text and Chāyā).* Edited by A. N. Upadhye. Shivaji University Sanskrit and Prakrit Series 3. Kolhapur: Shivaji University, 1970. (2) See Balbir and Besnard 1993–1994.

Virāṭaparvan: *Wirâṭaparwwa: Oudjavaansch prozageschrift.* Edited by H. H. Juynboll. 's-Gravenhage: Martinus Nijhoff, 1912.

Wanderings of Vasudeva (*Vasudevahiṇḍi*) of Saṅghadāsa: *Pūjyaśrīsaṅghadāsagaṇivācaka-vinirmitaṃ Vasudevahiṇḍiprathamakhaṇḍam.* Edited by Caturavijaya and Puṇyavijaya. Bhavnagar: Bhāvanagarasthā Śrījainaātmānandasabhā, 1930.

Wish-Granting Cow of Prakrit (*Prākṛtakāmadhenu*) of Laṅkeśvara: See *Wish-Granting Tree of Prakrit* of Rāmaśarman.

Wish-Granting Tree of Prakrit (*Prākṛtakalpataru*) of Rāmaśarman: *Rāmaśarman's Prākṛta-Kalpataru.* Edited by Manomohan Ghosh. Calcutta [Kolkata]: Asiatic Society, 1954.

Wishing-Stone of Meanings (*Abhidhānacintāmaṇi*) of Hemacandra: *Kalikālasarvajña-śrihemacandrācāryaviracitaḥ Abhidhānacintāmaṇiḥ Svopajñaṭīkāsahitaḥ.* Edited by Haragovindadāsa and Becaradāsa. Bhavnagar: Vidyā Vilāsa Press, 1894.

Wishing-Stone of Prabandhas (*Prabandhacintāmaṇi*) of Merutuṅga: *Prabandhacintāmaṇi.* Edited by Jinavijaya. Singhi Jain Series 1. Shantiniketan: Siṅghī Jaina Jñānapīṭha, 1931.

Wishing-Stone of the Āndhra Language (*Āndhraśabdacintāmaṇi*). *Āndhraśabdacintāmaṇiḥ: A Grammar of the Telugu Language in Sanskrit.* Translated by R. V. S. Sundaram and Deven Patel. Mysore: Central Institute of Indian Languages, 2016.

Yugapurāṇa: See Mitchiner 1986.

SECONDARY LITERATURE

Abhyankar, K. V. 1955. "Mahārāṣṭrī Prakrit." *Annals of the Bhandarkar Oriental Research Institute* 36: 373–376.

Ācārya, Hari Rām. 1982. *Mahākavi Hāl aur Gāhāsatsaī.* Jaipur: Śaraṇ Book Depot.

Acharya, Diwakar. 2006. "A Brief Note on Harṣapāla's Commentary on the Prakrit Kāvya *Setubandha.*" *Newsletter of the Nepalese-German Manuscript Cataloguing Project* 2: 2–4.

———. 2007. "The Original *Paṇhavāyaraṇa / Praśnavyākaraṇa* Discovered." *International Journal of Jaina Studies (Online)* 3 (6): 1–10.

Ali, Daud. 2004. *Courtly Culture and Political Life in Early Medieval India.* Cambridge: Cambridge University Press.

Alsdorf, Ludwig. 1936. "The *Vasudevahiṇḍi*, a Specimen of Archaic Jaina-Māhārāṣṭrī." *Bulletin of the School of Oriental Studies* 8 (2/3): 319–333. Also in id., *Kleine Schriften*, ed. Albrecht Wezler, 56–70 (Wiesbaden: Steiner, 1975).

———. 1966. *The Āryā Stanzas of the Uttarajjhāyā: Contributions to the Text History and Interpretation of a Canonical Jaina Text.* Abhandlung der Geistes- und Sozialwissenschaftlichen Klasse; Jahrgang 1966 No. 2, Akademie der Wissenschaften und der Literatur, Mainz. Wiesbaden: Steiner.

———. 1968. *Die Āryā-Strophen des Pali-Kanons, metrisch hergestellt und textgeschichtlich untersucht.* Abhandlung der Geistes- und Sozialwissenschaftlichen Klasse, Jahrgang 1967 No. 4, Akademie der Wissenschaften und der Literatur, Mainz. Wiesbaden: Steiner.

———. 1975 [1941]. "Zur Kenntnis der Prakrit-Grammatiker." In id., *Kleine Schriften*, ed. Albrecht Wezler, 563–567. Wiesbaden: Steiner.

———. 2006 [1965]. *Jaina Studies: Their Present State and Future Tasks*. Mumbai: Hindi Granth Karyalay.

Auerbach, Erich. 1961 [1948]. *Introduction aux études de philologie romane*. Frankfurt a. M.: Vittorio Klostermann.

———. 1993 [1958]. *Literary Language and Its Public in Late Latin Antiquity and in the Middle Ages*. Princeton, N.J.: Princeton University Press.

Badiger, P. B. 1978. "The Study of Prakrit Grammar for Understanding the Tadbhava Words in Kannaḍa." In *Proceedings of the Seminar on Prakrit Studies (1973)*, edited by K. R. Chandra, 53–57. Ahmedabad: Lalbhai Dalpatbhai Institute of Indology.

Bakhtin, M. M. 1981. *The Dialogic Imagination: Four Essays*. Translated by Michael Holquist. Austin: University of Texas Press.

Bakker, Hans. 2007. "Monuments to the Dead in Ancient North India." *Indo-Iranian Journal* 50: 11–47.

Bakker, Hans, and Harunaga Isaacson. 1993. "The Ramtek Inscriptions II: The Vākāṭaka Inscription in the Kevala-Narasiṃha Temple." *Bulletin of the School of Oriental and African Studies* 56 (1): 46–74.

Balbir, Nalini. 1989. "Morphological Evidence for Dialectal Variety in Jaina Māhārāṣṭrī." In *Dialectes dans les littératures indo-aryennes: Actes du colloque international, Paris, 16–18 septembre 1986*, ed. Colette Caillat, 503–525. Paris: Collège de France.

———. 1993*a*. "Stories from the Āvaśyaka Commentaries." In *The Clever Adulteress and Other Stories: A Treasury of Jain Literature*, ed. Phyllis Granoff, 17–74. New Delhi: Motilal Banarsidass.

———. 1993*b*. Āvaśyaka-Studien *1: Introduction générale et traductions*. Stuttgart: Franz Steiner.

———. 1995. "Formes et usages de la concaténation en prakrit." In *Sauhṛdya-maṅgalaṃ: Studies in Honour of Siegfried Lienhard on His 70th Birthday*, ed. M. Juntunen, W. L. Smith, and C. Suneson, 5–25. Stockholm: Association of Oriental Studies.

———. 1995–1996. "La tradition manuscrite des Chappaṇṇayagāhāo." *Bulletin d'études indiennes* 13–14: 35–50.

Balbir, Nalini, and M. Besnard. 1993–1994. "Les strophes des connaisseurs (*Chappaṇṇayagāhao*), Anthologie gnomique en prakrit." *Bulletin d'études indiennes* 11–12: 235–354.

Balcerowicz, Piotr. 2001. "The Two Siddhasenas and the Authorship of the *Nyāyāvatāra* and the *Saṃmatitarkaprakaraṇa*." *Journal of Indian Philosophy* 29 (3): 351–378.

Bangha, Imre. 2005. "Rekhta, Poetry in Mixed Language: The Emergence of Khari Boli Literature in North India." In *Before the Divide: Hindi and Urdu Literary Culture*, ed. Francesca Orsini, 21–84. New Delhi: Orient BlackSwan.

———. 2012. "Maru Gurjar and Madhyadeśī: The Hindī Ādikāl." Paper presented at the 11th International Conference on Early Modern Languages in North India, Shimla. Forthcoming in *Texts and Traditions in Early Modern North India*, ed. John Stratton Hawley, Anshu Malhotra and Tyler Williams.

Barth, M. A. 1885. *Inscriptions sanscrites du Cambodge*. Paris: Imprimerie nationale.

Barua, Benimadhab. 1929. *Old Brāhmī Inscriptions in the Udayagiri and Khaṇḍagiri Caves.* Calcutta [Kolkata]: University of Calcutta.

Beames, John. 1872. *A Comparative Grammar of the Modern Aryan Languages of India,* vol. 1: *On Sounds.* London: Trübner.

Benke, Theodore. 2010. "The Śūdrācāraśiromaṇi of Kṛṣṇa Śeṣa: A 16th Century Manual of Dharma for Śūdras." Ph.D. thesis, University of Pennsylvania.

Bennedik, Susanne. 2007. "Die Siebenplanetenwoche in Indien." Ph.D. thesis, Rheinischen Friedrich-Wilhelms-Universität zu Bonn.

Bhandare, Shailendra. 1999. "Historical Analysis of the Sātavāhana Era: A Study of Coins." Ph.D. thesis, University of Bombay.

———. 2006. "Numismatics and History: The Maurya-Gupta Interlude in the Gangetic Plain." In *Between the Empires: Society in India, 300 to 400,* ed. Patrick Olivelle, 67–112. Oxford: Oxford University Press.

———. 2011. "Linking the Past: Overstruck Coins and the Chronology of the Sātavāhanas." In *Felicitas: Essays in Numismatics, Epigraphy and History in Honour of Joe Cribb,* ed. Shailendra Bhandare and Sanjay Garg, 53–63. Mumbai: Reesha Books.

———. 2016. "Money and the Monuments: Coins of the Sada Dynasty of the Coastal Andhra Region." In *Amaravati: The Art of an Early Buddhist Monument in Context,* ed. Akira Shimada and Michael Willis, 37–45. London: British Museum.

Bhandarkar, D. R. 1917. "Vikrama Era." In *Commemorative Essays Presented to Sir Ramkrishna Gopal Bhandarkar,* 187–194. Poona [Pune]: Bhandarkar Oriental Research Institute.

Bhattacharyya, Dinesh Chandra. 1947. "New Light on Vaidyaka Literature." *Indian Historical Quarterly* 23: 123–155.

Bhayani, Harivallabh C. 1973. "Some Further Light on Harivṛddha, and His Novel Classification of Literary Prakrit and Apabhraṁśa." *Vidyā (Humanities Section)* 16 (1): 1–6.

———. 1975. "The Prakrit Poets Harivṛddha, Sātavāhana, and Āḍhyarāja." *In Sanskrit and Indological Studies: Dr. V. Raghavan Felicitation Volume,* ed. R. N. Dandekar, R. K. Sharma, Mandan Mishra, Satyavrat, and S. S. Janaki, 61–76. Delhi: Motilal Banarsidass.

———. 1989. *Apabhraṃśa Language and Literature: A Short Introduction.* Delhi: Bhogilal Leherchand Institute of Indology.

———. 1993*a*. "*Gāthā-muktāvalī:* A Newly-Discovered Recension of Hāla's *Sapta-śataka.*" In *Indological Studies: Literary and Performing Arts, Prakrit and Apabhraṃśa Studies,* 139–161. Ahmedabad: Parshva Prakashan.

———. 1993*b*. "*Paryāyabandha* and *Saṁghāta.*" In *Indological Studies: Literary and Performing Arts, Prakrit and Apabhraṁśa Studies,* 3–9. Ahmedabad: Parshva Prakashan.

———. 1993*c*. "Some Prakrit Verses of Pādalipta and the Authenticity of the *Taraṁgalolā.*" In *Indological Studies: Literary and Performing Arts, Prakrit and Apabhraṃśa Studies,* 129–138. Ahmedabad: Parshva Prakashan.

———. 1993*d*. "The Prakrit poets Harivṛddha, Sātavāhana and Āḍhyarāja." In *Indological Studies: Literary and Performing Arts: Prakrit and Apabhraṃśa Studies,* 162–177. Ahmedabad: Parshva Prakashan.

———. 1993*e*. "The *Ṣaṭprajñaka-gāthā* and *Hṛdayavatī.*" In *Indological Studies: Literary and Performing Arts, Prakrit and Apabhraṁśa Studies,* 10–19. Ahmedabad: Parshva Prakashan.

———. 1996. *Rāula-Vela of Roḍa*. Ahmedabad: Parshva Prakashan.

———. 1997. "Deśya Lexicography Prior to Hemacandra." *Journal of the Asiatic Society of Bombay* 72: 36–41.

———. 1998. "The Sources of the Prakrit Illustrations of the *Siddhahemaśabdānuśāsana*." In *Indological Studies: Literary and Performing Arts, Prakrit and Apabhraṁśa Studies*, 60–84. Ahmedabad: Parshva Publication.

Bloch, Jules. 1965 [1934]. *Indo-Aryan from the Vedas to Modern Times*. Translation by Alfred Master of *L'indo-aryen du Véda aux temps modernes*. Paris: Adrien-Maisonneuve.

———. 1970 [1914]. *The Formation of the Marāṭhī Language*. Translated by D. R. Chanana. Delhi: Motilal Banarsidass.

Bloch, Theodor. 1893. *Vararuci und Hemacandra*. Güttersloh: Bertelsmann.

Boccali, Giuliano. 1990. "Poesie delle campagne e poesia d'arte nella *Sattasaī*." In *Le settecento strofe*, ed. Guiliano Boccali, Daniela Sagramoso, and Cinzia Pieruccini, 7–29. Brescia: Paideia.

———. 1999. "Rain Poems and the Genesis of *kāvya*." In *Pandanus '98: Flowers, Nature, Semiotics*, ed. Jaroslav Vacek and Blanka Knotková-Čapková, 13–41. Prague: Signeta.

———. 2007. "La relazione a epica tradizionale e poesia d'arte: Resulti acquisiti, problemi aperti." In *Vestigia antiquitatis: Atti dei seminari del dipartimento di scienze dell'antichità dell'Università degli studi di Milano*, ed. Isabella Gualandri, 147–160. Milan: Cisalpino.

———. 2009. "*Sattasaī*, between Nature and Court Poetry." *Pandanus* 3 (2): 63–74.

Bodewitz, Henk W., and Leendert A. van Daalen. 1998. "Vākpatirāja's *Gauḍavaha*." *Wiener Zeitschrift für die Kunde Südasiens* 42: 40–66.

Botterill, Steven, ed. 1996. *De vulgari eloquentia of Dante Alighieri*. Cambridge Medieval Classics, No. 5. Cambridge: Cambridge University Press.

Bronkhorst, Johannes. 1993. "Buddhist Hybrid Sanskrit: The Original Language." In *Aspects of Buddhist Sanskrit: Proceedings of the International Symposium on the Language of Sanskrit Buddhist Texts*, ed. Kameshwar Nath Mishra, 396–414. Sarnath: Central Institute of Higher Tibetan Studies.

———. 2007. *Greater Magadha*. Leiden: Brill.

———. 2010. "The Spread of Sanskrit." In *From Turfan to Ajanta: Festschrift for Dieter Schlingloff on the Occasion of His Eightieth Birthday*, ed. Eli Franco and Monika Zin, 117–140. Kathmandu: Lumbini International Research Institute.

———. 2011. *Language and Reality: On an Episode in Indian Thought*. Revised translation by Michael S. Allen and Rajam Raghunathan. Brill's Indological Library, No. 36. Leiden: Brill.

———. 2014. "Misunderstood Origins: How Buddhism Fooled Modern Scholarship—and Itself." In *The Complex Heritage of Early India*, ed. D. N. Jha, 307–315. Delhi: Manohar.

Bronner, Yigal. 2010. *Extreme Poetry: The South Asian Movement of Simultaneous Narration*. New York: Columbia University Press.

———. 2012. "A Question of Priority: Revisiting the Bhāmaha-Daṇḍin Debate." *Journal of Indian Philosophy* 40: 67–118.

Brough, John. 1954. "The Language of the Buddhist Sanskrit Texts." *Bulletin of the School of Oriental and African Studies* 16 (2): 351–375.

———. 1980. "Sakāya Niruttiyā: Cauld kale het. " In *Die Sprache der ältesten buddhistischen Überlieferung/The Language of the Earliest Buddhist Tradition*, ed. Heinz Bechert, 35–42. Göttingen: Vandenhoeck & Ruprecht.

Bruhn, Klaus. 1996. "Ludwig Alsdorf's Studies in the *Āryā*." *Berlin Indologische Studien* 9/10: 7–53.

Bubeník, Vít. 1996. *The Structure and Development of Middle Indo-Aryan Dialects*. Delhi: Motilal Banarsidass.

———. 1998. *A Historical Syntax of Late Middle Indo-Aryan (Apabhraṃśa)*. Amsterdam: John Benjamins.

Burrow, Thomas. 1935–1937. "The Dialectal Position of the Niyā Prakrit." *Bulletin of the School of Oriental Studies* 8: 419–436.

———. 1947. "Dravidian Studies VI: The Loss of Initial c/s in South Dravidian." *Bulletin of the School of Oriental and African Studies* 12 (1): 132–147.

Busch, Allison. 2011*a*. "Hindi Literary Beginnings." In *South Asian Texts in History: Critical Engagements with Sheldon Pollock*, ed. Yigal Bronner, Whitney Cox, and Lawrence McCrea, 203–225. Ann Arbor, Mich.: Association for Asian Studies.

———. 2011*b*. *Poetry of Kings: The Classical Hindi Literature of Mughal India*. Oxford: Oxford University Press.

Bühler, Georg. 1890. *Die indische Inschriften und das Alter der Indischen Kunstpoesie*. Sitzungsberichte der Philosophisch-Historischen Classe der Kaiserlichen Akademie der Wissenschaften, vol. 122. Vienna: Kaiserliche Akademie der Wissenschaften.

———. 1892*a*. "A New Inscription of the Andhra King Yajñaśrî Gautamiputra." *Epigraphia Indica* 1: 95–96.

———. 1892*b*. "A Prâkrit Grant of the Pallava King Śivaskandavarman." *Epigraphia Indica* 1: 2–10.

———. 1936. *The Life of Hemacandrācārya*. Shantiniketan: Siṅghī Jaina Jñānapīṭha.

Cappeller, Carl. 1872. *Die Ganachandas: Ein Beitrag zur Indischen Metrik*. Leipzig: Hüthel & Legler.

Cardona, George. 1998. *Pāṇini: His Work and Its Traditions*. Delhi: Motilal Banarsidass.

———. 2008. "Theoretical Precedents of the Kātantra." In *Linguistic Traditions of Kashmir: Essays in Memory of Paṇḍit Dinanath Yaksha*, ed. Mrinal Kaul and Ashok Aklujkar, 300–367. Delhi: D. K. Printworld.

Chakladar, Haran Chandra. 1990 [1929]. *Social Life in Ancient India: Studies in Vātsyāyana's Kāma Sūtra*. New Delhi: Asian Educational Services.

Chakrabarty, Dipesh. 2000. "The Two Histories of Capital." In *Provincializing Europe*, 47–71. Princeton, N.J.: Princeton University Press.

Chandra, K. R. 1970. *A Critical Study of Paumacariyaṁ*. Muzaffarpur: Research Institute of Prakrit, Jainology and Ahimsa.

Chaudharī, Gulāb Candra. 1973. *Jaina Sāhitya kā Bṛhad Itihāsa: Bhāga 6, Kāvya-sāhitya*. Varanasi: Pārśvanātha Vidyāśrama Śodha Saṃsthāna.

Chaudhuri, J. B. 1943. "Sanskrit Poet Ghanaśyāma." *Indian Historical Quarterly* 19: 237–251.

Chhabra, B. C. 1959–1960*a*. "Nagarjunakonda Inscription of Ehavalasri's Time." *Epigraphia Indica* 33: 147–149.

———. 1959–1960*b*. "Uppugundur Inscription of Virapurisadata's Time, Year 19." *Epigraphia Indica* 33: 189–191.

Chintamani, B. M. 1971. "Notices of Thirteen MSS in Prākṛt with Special Reference to Their Scientific and Technological Contents." *Indian Journal of History of Science* 6 (2): 168–172.

Chojnacki, Christine. 2008*a*. *Kuvalayamālā: Roman jaina de 779 composé par Uddyotanasūri*, vol. 1: *Étude*. Marburg: Indica et Tibetica Verlag.

———. 2008*b*. *Kuvalayamālā: Roman jaina de 779 composé par Uddyotanasūri*, vol. 2: *Traduction et annotations*. Marburg: Indica et Tibetica Verlag.

———. 2012. "Remodeling Jain Novels in Medieval Times: Means and Motivations." Talk at the 12th World Sanskrit Conference in New Delhi.

———. 2016. "Charming Bouquet or Wedding Garland? The Structures of the Jain Heroine 'novel' in Prakrit from *Kuvalayamālā* (779) to *Maṇoramā* (1082)." *Asiatische Studien/Études asiatiques* 70 (2): 365–398.

Ciotti, Giovanni. 2013. "The Representation of Sanskrit Speech-Sounds: Philological and Linguistic Historiographies." Ph.D. thesis, University of Cambridge.

Cohen, Walter. 2011. "The Rise of the Written Vernacular: Europe and Eurasia." *PMLA* 126: 719–729.

Cohn, Bernard. 1996. "The Command of Language and the Language of Command." In *Colonialism and Its Forms of Knowledge: The British in India*, 16–56. Princton, N.J.: Princeton University Press.

Cort, John. 2009. "An Epitome of Medieval Śvetāmbara Jain Literary Culture: A Review and Study of Jinaratnasūri's Līlāvatīsāra." *International Journal of Jaina Studies (Online)* 15 (1): 1–33.

———. 2010. *Framing the Jina: Narratives of Icons and Idols in Jain History*. Oxford: Oxford University Press.

———. 2015. "Making It Vernacular in Agra: The Practice of Translation by Seventeenth-Century Digambar Jains." In *Tellings Not Texts: Singing, Story-telling and Performance in North India*, ed. Francesca Orsini and Katherine Butler Schofield, 61–105. Cambridge: Open Book Publishers.

Cox, Whitney M. 2006. "Making a Tantra in Medieval South India: The *Mahārthamañjarī* and the Textual Culture of Cōḻa Cidambaram." Ph.D. thesis, University of Chicago.

———. 2013. "Literary Register and Historical Consciousness in Kalhaṇa: A Hypothesis." *Indian Social and Economic History Review* 50 (2): 131–160.

———. 2016. *Modes of Philology in Medieval South India*. Leiden: Brill.

Cribb, Joe. 1992. "Numismatic Evidence for the Date of the Periplus." In *Indian Nusmismatics, History, Art and Culture: Essays in the Honor of Dr. P. L. Gupta*, ed. D. W. MacDowall, Savita Sharma, and Sanjay Garg, 131–145. Delhi: Agam Kala Prakashan.

———. 1998. "Western Satraps and Satavahanas: Old and New Ideas of Chronology." In *Ex Moneta: Essays on Numismatics, History and Archaeology in Honour of Dr. David W. MacDowall*, ed. Amal Kumar Jha and Sanjay Garg, 167–182. New Delhi: Harman Publishing House.

———. 2000. "Early Indian History." In *Buddhist Reliquaries from Ancient India*, ed. Michael Willis, 39–54. London: British Museum Press.

Crowley, Tony. 1996. *Language in History: Theories and Texts*. New York: Routledge.

Damsteegt, Th. 1978. *Epigraphical Hybrid Sanskrit: Its Rise, Characteristics and Relationship to Buddhist Hybrid Sanskrit*. Orientalia Rheno-Traiectina, No. 23. Leiden: Brill.

———. 1989. "The Pre-Kuṣāṇa and Kuṣāṇa Inscriptions and the Supercession of Prakrit by Sanskrit in North India in General and at Mathurā in Particular." In *Mathurā: The*

Cultural Heritage, ed. Doris Meth Srinivasan, 298–307. New Delhi: American Institute of Indian Studies.

Dehejia, Vidya. 1972. *Early Buddhist Rock Temples: A Chronology.* Ithaca, N.Y.: Cornell University Press.

Deleuze, Gilles, and Félix Guattari. 1986. *Kafka: Towards a Minor Literature.* Minneapolis: University of Minnesota Press.

Derrida, Jacques. 1997 [1976]. *Of Grammatology.* Baltimore: Johns Hopkins University Press.

Desai, Devangana. 1985. *Erotic Sculpture of India: A Socio-Cultural Study.* New Delhi: Munshiram Manoharlal.

Deshpande, Madhav M. 1993. *Sanskrit and Prakrit: Sociolinguistic Issues.* Delhi: Motilal Banarsidass.

Dhaky, M.A. 1974. "The Architectural Data in the *Nirvāṇakālikā* of Pādalipta-Śūri *[sic]*." *Sambodhi* 3 (1): 11.

———. 2002. "Pādaliptasūri viracita 'Nirvāṇakalikā'no samaya aṇe ānuṣaṅgika samasyāo." In *Nirgranthaitihāsikalekhasamuccaya*, 85–102. Ahmedabad: Śreṣṭhī Kastūrbhāī Lālbhāi Smārak Nidhi.

———. 2004. "Ārya Bhadrabāhu." In *Jambūjyoti (Munivara Jambūvijaya Festschrift)*, ed. M.A. Dhaky and J.B. Shah, 108–155. Ahmedabad: Shresthi Kasturbhai Lalbhai Smarak Nidhi, Sharadaben Chimanbhai Educational Research Centre.

Disalkar, D.B. 1960. "The Influence of Classical Poets on the Inscriptional Poets." *Journal of Indian History* 38: 285–302.

Drocco, Andrea. 2012. "Eternal Sanskrit and the Meaning of the Tripartite Prakrit Terminology *tatsama, tadbhava* and *deśī.*" *Linguistica e filologia* 32: 119–136.

Dundas, Paul. 1985. *The Sattasaī and Its Commentators.* Turin: Indologica Taurinensia.

———. 1996. "Jain Attitudes Towards the Sanskrit Language." In *Ideology and Status of Sanskrit: Contributions to the History of the Sanskrit Language*, ed. Jan E.M. Houben, 137–156. Leiden: Brill.

———. 2002 [1992]. *The Jains.* New York: Routledge.

Durkheim, Emile. 1995 [1912]. *The Elementary Forms of Religious Life.* New York: Free Press.

Dvivedī, Hazārīprasād. 2008 [1952]. *Hindī Sāhitya kā Ādikāl.* New Delhi: Vāṇī Prakāśan.

Edgerton, Franklin. 1936. "The Prakrit Underlying Buddhistic Hybrid Sanskrit." *Bulletin of the School of Oriental and African Studies* 8: 501–516.

———. 1993 [1953]. *Buddhist Hybrid Sanskrit Grammar and Dictionary.* Delhi: Motilal Banarsidass.

Eliot, T.S. 1982. "Tradition and the Individual Talent." *Perspecta* 19: 36–42.

Emeneau, Murray. 1955. "Signed Verses by Sanskrit Poets." In *Suniti Kumar Chatterji Jubilee Volume*, 41–52. Pune: Linguistic Society of India.

———. 1956. "India as a Linguistic Area." *Language* 32 (1): 3–16.

Esposito, Anna Aurelia. 2004. *Cārudatta: Ein indisches Schauspiel: Kritische Edition und Übersetzung mit einer Studie des Prakrits der "Trivandrum-Dramen."* Wiesbaden: Harrassowitz.

———. 2008. "Some Remarks on the Prakrit of the So-called 'Trivandrum plays' as Found in the Manuscripts." In *Proceedings of the XIIth World Sanskrit Conference, Helsinki, July 2003*, ed. Petteri Koskikallio and Asko Parpola. Delhi: Motilal Banarsidass.

———. 2010*a*. "Bermerkungen zu den Schreibkonventionen der in Malayāḷam-Schrift verfassten Dramenmanuskripte sowie zu ihrer relativen Chronologie." In *Indisches Theater: Text, Theorie, Praxis,* ed. Karin Steiner and Heidrun Brückner, 141–154. Wiesbaden: Harrassowitz.

———. 2010*b*. "Textual Criticism Concerning the Keralite Drama Manuscripts." In *Text Genealogy, Textual Criticism, and Editorial Technique,* ed. Jürgen Hanneder and Phillip A. Maas, 269–283. Vienna: Verlag der Österreichischen Akademie der Wissenschaften.

———. 2011. "The Prākrit of the Vasudevahiṇḍī—An Addendum to Pischel's Grammar." *Zeitschrift der Indologie und Südasienstudien* 28: 29–50.

Ezhuthachan, K. N. 1971. "Abhinavagupta on Manipravala." In *Proceedings of the First All India Conference of Dravidian Linguists,* ed. V. I. Subramoniam, 113–114. Trivandrum: St. Joseph's Press.

Faithfull, R. Glynn. 1953. "The Concept of 'Living Language' in Cinquecento Vernacular Philology." *Modern Language Review* 48 (3): 278–292.

Falk, Harry. 1991. "Kunstdichtung in den Höhlen von Rāmgarh." *Asiatische Studien / Études asiatiques* 95 (2): 257–276.

———. 1999–2000. "The Pāṭagaṇḍigūḍem Copper-Plate Grant of king Ehavala Cāntamūla." *Silk Road Art and Archaeology* 6: 275–283.

———. 2006. *Aśokan Sites and Artefacts: A Source-Book with Bibliography.* Mainz: Von Zabern.

———. 2009. "Two Dated Sātavāhana Epigraphs." *Indo-Iranian Journal* 52: 197–206.

Fitzgerald, James. 2009. "No Contest between Memory and Invention: The Invention of the Pāṇḍava Heroes of the Mahābhārata." In *Epic and History,* ed. David Konstan and Kurt A. Raaflaub, 103–121. Malden, Mass.: Wiley-Blackwell.

Flood, Finbar Barry. 2009. *Objects of Translation: Material Culture and Medieval "Hindu-Muslim" Encounter.* Princeton, N.J.: Princeton University Press.

Foucault, Michel. 1994 [1966]. *The Order of Things: An Archaeology of the Human Sciences.* New York: Vintage Books.

———. 2009 [1961]. *History of Madness.* London: Routledge.

Francis, Emmanuel. 2013. "Praising the King in Tamil during the Pallava Period." In *Bilingual Discourse and Cross-Cultural Fertilisation: Sanskrit and Tamil in Medieval India,* ed. Whitney Cox and Vincenzo Vergiani, 359–409. Pondicherry: École française d'Extrême-Orient and Institut français de Pondichéry.

Franco, Eli. 2004. *The Spitzer Manuscript: The Oldest Philosophical Manuscript in Sanskrit.* Vienna: Verlag der Österreichischen Akademie der Wissenschaften.

Freeman, Richard. 1998. "Rubies and Coral: The Lapidary Crafting of Language in Kerala." *Journal of Asian Studies* 57 (1): 38–65.

Fussman, Gérard. 1989. "The Māṭ Devakula: A New Approach to Its Understanding." In *Mathurā: The Cultural Heritage, ed. Doris Meth Srinivasan,* 193–199. New Delhi: American Institute of Indian Studies.

Fynes, R. C. C. 1995. "The Religious Patronage of the Sātavāhana Dynasty." *South Asian Studies* 11: 43–50.

Gadamer, Hans-Georg. 2004 [1960]. *Truth and Method.* New York: Continuum.

———. 2010 [1960]. *Wahrheit und Methode: Grundzüge einer philosophischen Hermeneutik.* Tübingen: Mohr Siebeck.

Gai, G. S. 1975–1976. "Banavasi Inscription of Vinhukada Satakanni, Year 12." *Epigraphia Indica* 34: 239–242.

Gandhi, Lalchandra Bhagawandas. 1927. *Three Apabhraṁśa Works of Jinadattasūri*. Baroda [Vadodara]: Oriental Institute.

Garrez, G. 1872. Review of *Ueber das Saptaçatakam des Hâla* by A. Weber. *Journal Asiatique* 20: 197–220.

Geertz, Clifford. 1993 [1973]. "Religion as a Cultural System." In *The Interpretation of Cultures: Selected Essays*, 87–125. London: Fontana Press.

Geiger, Wilhelm. 1956 [1916]. *Pāli Literature and Language*. Translated by B. Ghosh. Calcutta [Kolkata]: University of Calcutta.

Ghatage, A. M. 1934–1935*a*. "Hymns in Prakrit." *Journal of the University of Bombay* 3: 45–50.

———. 1934–1935*b*. "Narrative Literature in Jaina Māhārāṣṭrī." *Annals of the Bhandarkar Oriental Research Institute* 16 (1–2): 26–43.

———. 2000 [1936]. "Māhārāṣṭrī Language and Literature." In *Amrita*, 95–148. Ahmedabad: Shreshti Kasturbhai Lalbhai Smarak Nidhi.

Ghosal, S. N. 1969. "The Ārṣa Prakrit as Hemacandra Viewed It." *Journal of the Oriental Institute, Baroda* 18 (4): 304–314.

Ghose, Manomohan. 1932. "Prākṛt verses in the Bharata-Nāṭyaśāstra." *Indian Historical Quarterly* 8: 1–52.

———. 1933. "Mahārāṣṭrī—A Later Phase of Śaurasenī." *Journal of the Department of Letters (Calcutta)* 23: 1–24.

Gokhale, Shobhana. 1988. "A Unique Copper-Coin of the Satavahana King Hala." *Journal of the Academy of Indian Numismatics and Sigillography* 6: 65–66.

———. 2004–2006. "The Nāṇeghāṭ Record—A Masterpiece in Ancient Indian Records." *Adyar Library Bulletin* 68–70: 239–260.

———. 2008. *Lord of Dakṣiṇāpatha: Coins, Trade and Trade-Centers under the Sātavāhanas*. Mumbai: Reesha Books.

Goldschmidt, Paul. 1873. *Specimen des Setubandha*. Göttingen: Königliche Gesellschaft der Wissenschaften zu Göttingen.

Goldschmidt, Siegfried. 1874. "Der Infinitiv des Passivs im Prākṛt." *Zeitschrift der Deutschen Morgenländischen Gesellschaft* 28: 491–493.

———. 1875. "Bildungen aus Passiv-Stämmen im Prākṛt." *Zeitschrift der Deutschen Morgenländischen Gesellschaft* 29: 491–495.

———. 1878. "Prākṛtica." *Zeitschrift der Deutschen Morgenländischen Gesellschaft* 32: 99–112.

———. 1879. *Prākṛtica*. Strassburg: Trübner.

———. 1881. "Prākṛtische Miscellen." *Zeitschrift der vergleichende Sprachforschung* 25: 436–438, 610–617.

———. 1883*a*. "Prākṛtica." *Zeitschrift der Deutschen Morgenländischen Gesellschaft* 37: 457–458.

———. 1883*b*. "Prākṛtische Miscellen." *Zeitschrift der vergleichende Sprachforschung* 26: 103–112, 327–328.

———. 1885. "Prākṛtische Miscellen." *Zeitschrift der vergleichende Sprachforschung* 27: 336.

Gopalachari, K. 1941. *Early History of the Andhra Country*. Madras: University of Madras.

Gornall, Alastair. 2014. "How Many Sounds Are in Pāli? Schism, Identity and Ritual in the Theravāda *saṅgha*." *Journal of Indian Philosophy* 42 (5): 511–550.

Granoff, Phyllis. 1989*a*. "Jain Lives of Haribhadra: An Enquiry into the Sources and Logic of the Legends." *Journal of Indian Philosophy* 17 (2): 105–128.

———. 1989*b*. "The Biographies of Siddhasena: A Study in the Texture of Allusion and the Weaving of a Group-Image, Part I." *Journal of Indian Philosophy* 17 (4): 329–384.

———. 1990. "The Biographies of Siddhasena: A Study in the Texture of Allusion and the Weaving of a Group-Image, Part II." *Journal of Indian Philosophy* 18 (4): 261–304.

———. 1994. "Jain Biographies of Nāgārjuna: Notes on the Composition of a Biography in Medieval India." In *Monks and Magicians: Religious Biographies in Asia*, ed. Phyllis Granoff and Koichi Shinohara, 45–66. Delhi: Motilal Banarsidass.

Grierson, George Abraham. 1906. *The Piśāca Languages of North-Western India*. Asiatic Society Monographs, No. 8. London: Royal Asiatic Society.

———. 1927. *Linguistic Survey of India*, vol. 1, pt. 1: *Introductory*. Calcutta [Kolkata]: Government of India.

Gupta, Chandrashekhar. 1992. "Sopara Coin of Gautamīputra Yajña Sātakarṇi and Its Bearing on the Naneghat Inscription of the Reign of Vāsiṣṭhīputra Sātakarṇi: Year 13." In *Numismatic Studies Volume 2*, ed. Devendra Handra, 81–85. New Delhi: Harman Publishing House.

———. 1993. "A Potin Coin of King Satavahana from the Deccan." *Studies in South Indian Coins* 3: 73–80.

Gupta, P. L. 1975. "Nāneghāṭ Inscription of an Unknown Queen—A Historical Study." *Journal of the Epigraphical Society of India* 2: 59–71.

Gutzwiller, Kathryn. 2006. "The Bucolic Problem." *Classical Philology* 101 (4): 380–404.

Hahn, Michael. 1983. "Vararucis Gāthāśataka—eine Analyse." In *Documenta Barbarorum: Festschrift für Walther Hessig zum 70. Geburtstag*, ed. Klaus Sagaster and Michael Weiers, 143–151. Wiesbaden: Harrassowitz.

———. 2007. "Ravigupta and His Nīti Stanzas (I)." In *Minami Ajia Kotengaku—South Asian Classical Studies*, 2: 305–355. Kyushu University Department of Indology.

———. 2012. "Der Bhāṣāśleṣa—eine Besonderheit kaschmirischer Dichter und Poetiker?" In *Highland Philology: Results of a Text-Related Kashmir Panel at the 31st DOT, Marburg 2010*, 77–105. *Studia Indologica Universitatis Halensis*, No. 4. Halle an der Saale: Universitätsverlag Halle-Wittenberg.

Hart, George L. 1975. *The Poems of Ancient Tamil: Their Milieu and Their Sanskrit Counterparts*. Berkeley: University of California Press.

———. 1976. *The Relation between Tamil and Classical Sanskrit Literature*. Wiesbaden: Harrassowitz.

Hawley, Jack. 1991. "Naming Hinduism." *Wilson Quarterly* 15 (3): 20–24.

Heller, Erich. 1952. "Goethe and the Idea of Scientific Truth." In id., *The Disinherited Mind: Essays in Modern German Literature and Thought*, 2–26. Cambridge: Bowes & Bowes.

Hillebrandt, Alfred, ed. 1984 [1912]. *Mudrārākṣasa by Viśākhadatta*. Hildesheim: Georg Olms.

Hirsch, Eric Donald. 1967. *Validity in Interpretation*. New Haven, Conn.: Yale University Press.

Hoernle, A. F. R. 1873. "Genitive Post-positions." *Indian Antiquary* 2: 210–213.

———. 1880*a*. "A Sketch of the History of Prakrit Philology." *Calcutta Review* 71–72: 311–332.

———. 1880*b*. *A Grammar of the Eastern Hindi Compared with the Other Gaudian Languages*. London: Trübner.

Hopkins, Steven Paul Arthur. 2002. *Singing the Body of God: The Hymns of Vedāntadeśika in Their South Indian Tradition*. Oxford: Oxford University Press.

Horsch, Paul. 1966. *Die Vedische Gāthā- und Śloka-Literatur*. Bern: Francke Verlag.

Houben, Jan E. M. 1994*a*. "Bhartṛhari's Familiarity with Jainism." *Annals of the Bhandarkar Oriental Research Institute* 75: 1–24.

———. 1994*b*. "Early Indian Authors and Linguistic Change (Postscript to: Bhartṛhari's Familiarity with Jainism)." Annals of the Bhandarkar Oriental Research Institute 75: 255–256.

———. 1996. "Sociolinguistic Attitudes Reflected in the Work of Bhartṛhari and Some Later Grammarians." In *Ideology and Status of Sanskrit: Contributions to the History of the Sanskrit Language*, ed. Jan E. M. Houben, 157–193. Leiden: Brill.

———. 1997. "Bhartṛhari's Perspectivism (1): The *vṛtti* and Bhartṛhari's Perspectivism in the First *kāṇḍa* of the *Vākyapadīya*." In *Beyond Orientalism: The Work of Wilhelm Halbfass and Its Impact on Indian and Cross-Cultural Studies*, ed. Eli Franco and Karin Preisendanz, 317–358. Amsterdam: Rodopi.

Hultzsch, Eugen. 1900–1901. "Mayidavolu Plates of Sivaskandavarman." *Epigraphia Indica* 6: 84–89.

———. 1907–1908. "Plates of Vijaya-Devavarman." *Epigraphia Indica* 9: 56–59.

Hunter, Thomas. 2015. "A Distant Mirror: Innovation and Change in the East Javanese Kakawin." In *Innovations and Turning Points: Toward a History of Kāvya Literature*, ed. Yigal Bronner, Gary Tubb, and David Shulman, 739–786. New Delhi: Oxford University Press.

Ingalls, Daniel H. H. 1965. *An Anthology of Sanskrit Court Poetry: Vidyākara's "Subhāṣitaratnakośa."* Cambridge, Mass.: Harvard University Press.

———. 1976. "Kālidāsa and the Attitudes of the Golden Age." *Journal of the American Oriental Society* 96 (1): 15–26.

Ingalls, Daniel H. H., Jeffrey Mousaieff Masson, and M. V. Patwardhan. 1990. *The Dhvanyāloka of Ānandavardhana: With the Locana of Abhinavagupta*. Cambridge, Mass.: Harvard University Press.

Jacobi, Hermann. 1876. "Ueber das *Vîracaritram*." *Indische Studien* 14: 97–160. Leipzig: Brockhaus.

———. 1879. *The Kalpasûtra of Bhadrabâhu*. Leipzig: Brockhaus.

———. 1884. *Gaina sûtras*. Oxford: Clarendon Press.

———. 1885. "Indisches Hypermetra und hypermetrische Texte." *Indische Studien* 17: 381–441. Leipzig: Brockhaus.

———. 1886. *Ausgewählte Erzählungen in Mâhârâshṭrî*. Leipzig: Birzel.

———. 1893. "Ueber die Betonung im klassischen Sanskrit und in den Prâkṛit-Sprachen." *Zeitschrift der Deutschen Morgenländischen Gesellschaft* 47: 574–582.

———. 1894. "War das Epos und die profane Litteratur Indiens ursprünglich in Prākṛit abgefaßt?" *Zeitschrift der Deutschen Morgenländischen Gesellschaft* 48: 407–417.

———. 1898. "Der Aksent im Mittelindischen." *Zeitschrift für Vergleichende Sprachforschung* 35: 563–582. Also in id., *Kleine Schriften*, ed. Bernhard Kölver, 73–88 (Wiesbaden: Steiner, 1970).

———. 1908–1909. "Ueber das Prakrit in der Erzählungs-Litteratur der Jainas." *Rivista degli studi orientali* 2: 231–236.

———, ed. 1918. *Bhavisatta Kaha von Dhaṇavāla: Eine Jaina Legende in Apabhraṃśa.* Munich: Verlag der Königlich Bayerischen Akademie der Wissenschaften.

———. 1960 [1893]. "On Accent in the Classical Sanskrit and the Prākrit Dialects." Translated with notes by S. N. Ghosal. *Journal of the Oriental Institute, Baroda* 10: 34–52.

———. 1970 [1884]. "Ueber die Entwicklung der indischen Metrik in nachvedischer Zeit." In id., *Kleine Schriften,* ed. Bernhard Kölver, 142–174. Wiesbaden: Steiner.

———. 1970 [1886]. "Zur Kentniss der Āryā." In id., *Kleine Schriften,* ed. Bernhard Kölver, 198–204. Wiesbaden: Steiner.

Jain, Hiralal. 1945. "Traces of an Old Metrical Prakrit Grammar." In *Bhārata-Kaumudī: Studies in Indology in Honour of Dr. Radha Kumud Mookerji,* 1: 315–322. Allahabad: Indian Press.

Jain, Jagdishchandra. 1961. *Prākṛta Sāhitya kā Itihāsa.* Varanasi: Chaukhambā Vidyābhavana.

———. 1977. *The Vasudevahiṇḍi: An Authentic Jain Version of the Bṛhatkathā.* Ahmedabad: Lalbhai Dalpatbhai Institute of Indology.

———. 1981. *Prakrit Narrative Literature: Origin and Growth.* New Delhi: Munshiram Manoharlal.

———. 2004. *History and Development of Prakrit Literature.* New Delhi: Manohar.

Jain, Kamal. 1997. *Vasudevahiṇḍī: Eka Adhyayana.* Varanasi: Pārśvanātha Vidyāpīṭha.

Jaini, Padmanabh. 1979. *The Jaina Path of Purification.* Berkeley: University of California Press.

Jakobson, Roman. 1959. "On Linguistic Aspects of Translation." In *On Translation,* ed. R. A. Brower, 30–39. Cambridge, Mass.: Harvard University Press.

Jamison, Stephanie. 2004. *The Rig Veda between Two Worlds.* Paris: Collège de France.

Jayaswal, K. P. and R. D. Banerji. 1929–1930. "The Hathigumpha Inscription of Kharavela." *Epigraphia Indica* 20: 71–89.

Jinavijaya. 1988 [1919]. *Haribhadrasūri kā Samaya-Nirṇaya.* 2nd ed. Varanasi: Pārśvanātha Vidyāśrama Śodha Saṃsthāna.

Joglekar, S. A. 1946. "Sātavāhana and Sātakarṇi." *Annals of the Bhandarkar Oriental Research Institute* 27 (3–4): 237–287.

Joseph, John E. 2004. *Language and Identity.* New York: Palgrave Macmillan.

———. 2006. *Language and Politics.* Edinburgh: Edinburgh University Press.

Kahrs, Eivind G. 1992. "What Is a Tadbhava Word?" *Indo-Iranian Journal* 35: 225–249.

Kane, Pandurang Vaman. 1961. *History of Sanskrit Poetics.* Delhi: Motilal Banarsidass.

Kant, Immanuel. 1998 [1787]. *Kritik der reinen Vernunft.* Hamburg: Meiner.

Katare, Sant Lal. 1952. "An Inscribed Sculpture Inspired by Hāla's *Gāthāsaptaśatī.*" *Indian Historical Quarterly* 28: 379–385.

Katre, Sumitra Mangesh. 1964 [1945]. *Prakrit Languages and Their Contribution to Indian Culture.* Pune: Deccan College Postgraduate and Research Institute.

Kaviraj, Sudipta. 1992. "Writing, Speaking, Being: Language and the Historical Formation of Identities in India." In *Nationalstaat und Sprachkonflikte in Süd- und Südostasien,* ed. Dagmar Hellmann-Rajanayagam and Dietmar Rothermund, 25–65. Stuttgart: Steiner.

———. 2003. "The Two Histories of Literary Culture in Bengal." In *Literary Cultures in History: Reconstructions from South Asia,* ed. Sheldon Pollock, 503–566. Berkeley: University of California Press.

Kedilaya, A. Shanker. 1964–1977. "Śabdamaṇidarpaṇa." *Annals of Oriental Research, University of Madras* 19–27: 1–460.

Keith, Arthur Berriedale. 1909. *The Aitareya Āraṇyaka.* Oxford: Clarendon Press.

———. 1920. *A History of Sanskrit Literature.* Oxford: Oxford University Press.

Keshavmurthy, Prashant. 2013. "Tuḥfat ul-Hind." *Perso-Indica: An Analytical Survey of Persian Works on Indian Learned Traditions,* ed. F. Speziale and C. W. Ernst. http://perso-indica.net/work/tuhfat_al-hind-1.

Khadabadi, B. K. 1981. "On the Apabhraṃśa Chapter of the *Śabdamaṇidarpaṇa.*" *Annals of the Bhandarkar Oriental Research Institute* 62: 227–234.

Khoroche, Peter, and Herman Tieken. 2009. *Poems on Life and Love in Ancient India: Hāla's Sattasaī.* Albany: excelsior editions.

Kielhorn, Franz. 1905–1906. "Junagadh Rock Inscription of Rudradaman." *Epigraphia Indica* 8: 36–49.

Klatt, Johannes. 1879. "Dhanapâla's Ṛishabhapañcâçikâ." *Zeitschrift der Deutschen Morgenländischen Gesellschaft* 33: 445–483.

———. 1882. "Extracts from the Historical Records of the Jainas." *Indian Antiquary* 11: 245–256.

Kloss, Heinz. 1967. "'Abstand languages' and 'Ausbau languages.'" *Anthropological Linguistics* 9 (7): 29–41.

Knutson, Jesse Ross. 2014. *Into the Twilight of Sanskrit Court Poetry.* Berkeley: University of California Press.

Konow, Sten. 1894. "Review of Bloch, Vararuci und Hemacandra." *Göttingische gelehrte Anzeigen* 1: 472–482.

Konow, Sten, ed. 2007 [1901]. *Rājaçekhara's Karpūramañjarī.* Translated by Charles Rockwell Lanman. Delhi: Harvard University Press.

Kosambi, D. D. 1963. "Combined Methods in Indology." *Indo-Iranian Journal* 6: 177–202.

Krishna Moorthy, K. 1946. "Bhāsa as a Prakrit Poet." *Indian Historical Quarterly* 22 (1): 73–74.

Krishna Rao, B. V. 1955–1956. "Two Salankayana Charters from Kanukollu." *Epigraphia Indica* 31: 1–10.

Krishna Shastri, H. 1925–1926. "The Kodavali Rock-Inscription of Chandasati; The Second Year of Reign." *Epigraphia Indica* 18: 316–319.

Krishnan, K. G. 2002. "Note on Sātavāhana Bilingual Coins." In *Śrī Subrahmaṇya Smṛtī,* ed. I. K. Sarma, 503–504. New Delhi: Sandeep Prakashan.

Kulkarni, V. M. 1988. *Prakrit Verses in Sanskrit Works on Poetics,* vol. 1: *Text (With Appendixes and index).* Delhi: Bhogilal Leherchand Institute of Indology.

———. 1990. *The Story of Rāma in Jain Literature.* Ahmedabad: Saraswati Pustak Bhandar.

———. 1991. *Bhoja and the Harivijaya of Sarvasena.* Ahmedabad: Saraswati Pustak Bhandar.

Kulkarni, V. M., ed. 2003. *Kūrmaśatakadvayam: Two Prakrit Poems on Tortoise Who Supports the Earth.* L. D. Series, No. 136. Ahmedabad: Lalbhai Dalpatbhai Institute of Indology. Translation of the text as edited by Richard Pischel in *Epigraphia Indica* 8 (1905–1906).

Kuryłowicz, Jerzy. 1970. "The Quantitative Meter of Indo-European." In *Indo-European and Indo-Europeans,* ed. George Cardona, Henry M. Hoenigswald, and Alfred Senn, 421–430. Philadelphia: University of Pennsylvania Press.

Kümmel, Martin Joachim. 2013. "Silbenstruktur und Metrik: Neues zum Altavestischen." Presented at Sprache und Metrik in Diachronie und Synchronie, Munich. www.academia.edu/9573102/Silbenstruktur_und_Metrik_Neues_zum_Altavestischen.

Lacôte, Félix. 1908. *Essai sur Guṇāḍhya et la Bṛhatkathā, suivi du texte inédit des chapitres XXVII à XXX du Nepāla-māhātmya.* Paris: Ernest Leroux.

Lassen, Christian. 1837. *Institutiones linguae Pracriticae.* Bonn: Koenig & Van Borcharen.

Leumann, Ernst. 1921. "Die Nonne: Ein neuer Roman aus dem alten Indien." *Zeitschrift für Buddhismus* 3: 193–234, 272–333.

Levman, Bryan. 2008–2009. "*Sakāya niruttiyā* revisited." *Bulletin d'études indiennes* 26–27: 33–51.

Lidova, Natalia. 2012. "The *Nāṭyaśāstra:* the Origin of the Ancient Indian Poetics." *Cracow Indological Studies* 14: 61–85.

Liebich, Bruno. 1919. *Zur Einführung in die indische einheimische Sprachwissenschaft. I. Das Kātantra.* Sitzungberichte der Heidelberger Akademie der Wissenschaften, Heidelberg: Carl Winter.

Lienhard, Siegfried. 1971. "Palai Poems in Sanskrit and Prakrit." In *Professor K. A. Nilakanta Sastri Felicitation Volume,* ed. Saw. Ganesan, S. Rajam, N. S. Ramaswami, and M.D. Pampath, 416–422. Madras: Professor K.A. Nilakanta Sastri Felicitation Committee.

———. 1973. "*Akapporuḷ* and Sanskrit *Muktaka* Poetry." In *Association internationale des études tamoules/International Association of Tamil Research: Compte-rend de la troisième conférence internationale/Proceedings of the Third International Conference Seminar, Paris 1970,* ed. X.S. Thani Nagayam and François Gros, 111–118. Pondichéry: Institut ançais d'indologie.

———. 1975. "Sur la structure poétique des Theratherîgâthâ." *Journal Asiatique* 263 (3–4): 375–396.

———. 1984. *A History of Classical Poetry: Sanskrit—Pali—Prakrit. A History of Indian Literature,* Wiesbaden: Harrassowitz.

Lo Piparo, Franco. 2010. "The Linguistic Roots of Gramsci's Non-Marxism." In *Gramsci, Language and Translation,* ed. Peter Ives and Rocco Lacorte, 19–28. Lanham, Md.: Lexington Books.

Lokesh Chandra. 1997. "Chanda-karaṇa: the Art of Writing Poetry." In *Cultural Horizons of India,* 140–185. New Delhi: International Academy of Indian Culture and Aditya Prakashan.

Lorenzen, David. 1995. "Who Invented Hinduism?" *Comparative Studies in Society and History* 41 (4): 630–659.

Lubin, Timothy. 2005. "The Transmission, Patronage, and Prestige of Brahmanical Piety from the Mauryas to the Guptas." In *Boundaries, Dynamics and Construction of Traditions in South Asia,* ed. Federico Squarcini, 77–103. Florence: Firenze University Press.

Lévi, Sylvain. 1903. "Notes on the Indo-Scythians." *Indian Antiquary* 32: 381–389, 417–426.

———. 1904. "On Some Terms Employed in the Inscriptions of the Kshatrapas." *Indian Antiquary* 33: 163–174.

———. 1908. "Açvaghoṣa, le sûtrâlaṃkâra et ses sources." *Journal asiatique* 12: 57–184.

———. 1936. "Kaniṣka et Sātavāhana: Deux figures symboliques de l'Inde au premier siècle." *Journal asiatique* 228: 61–121.

Lüders, Heinrich, ed. 1911. *Bruchstücke buddhistischer Dramen.* Berlin: Reimer.

Lüders, Heinrich. 1937–1938. "Seven Brahmi Inscriptions from Mathura and its Vicinity." *Epigraphia Indica* 24: 194–210.

———. 1961. *Mathurā Inscriptions.* Göttingen: Vandenhoeck & Ruprecht.

Mahadevan, Iravatham. 2003. *Early Tamil Epigraphy: from the Earliest Times to the Sixth Century A.D.* Chennai: Cre-A.

Mainkar, T. G. 1970. "Ghanaśyāma, a Prakrit Poet." In *Proceedings of the Seminar in Prakrit Studies, June 23–27, 1969,* ed. R. N. Dandekar and A. M. Ghatage, 171–174. Poona [Pune]: University of Poona.

Malamoud, Charles. 1981. "On the Rhetoric and Semantics of *puruṣārtha.*" *Contributions to Indian Sociology* 15: 33–48.

Malvania, Dalsukh. 1983. "On Bhadreśvarasūri's *Kahāvalī.*" *Indologica Taurinensia* 11: 77–95.

Masica, Colin. 1991. *The Indo-Aryan Languages.* Cambridge: Cambridge University Press.

Masson, Jeffrey Mousaieff, and M. V. Patwardhan. 1974. "*Dhvanigāthāpañjikā.*" *Annals of the Bhandarkar Oriental Institute* 55: 219–225.

Master, Alfred. 1943. "The Mysterious Paiśācī." *Journal of the Royal Asiatic Society* 34–45, 217–233.

———. 1950. "Gleanings from the *Kuvalayamālā Kahā* I: Three Fragments and Specimens of the Eighteen Desabhāsās." *Bulletin of the School of Oriental and African Studies* 13: 410–415.

McCrea, Lawrence J. 2008. *The Teleology of Poetics in Medieval Kashmir.* Cambridge, Mass.: Department of Sanskrit and Indian Studies, Harvard University.

McGregor, Ronald Stuart. 1984. *Hindi Literature from its Beginnings to the Nineteenth Century.* Wiesbaden: Harrassowitz.

Meillet, Antoine. 1923. *Les origines indo-européennes des métres grecs.* Paris: Presses universitaires de France.

Meister, Michael. 1979. "Juncture and Conjunction: Punning and Temple Architecture." *Artibus Asiae* 41 (2–3): 226–234.

Menon, A. G. 1996. "The Use of Sanskrit in South Indian Bilingual Royal Inscriptions: Social, Political, and Religious Implications." In *Ideology and Status of Sanskrit,* ed. Jan E. M. Houben, 249–263. Leiden: Brill.

Mette, Adelheid. 1973. "Veḍhas in *Lalitavistara* und *Divyāvadāna.*" *Wiener Zeitschrift für die Kunde des Morgenländes* 17: 21–42.

Minkowski, Christopher. 2008. "Why Should We Read the Maṅgala Verses?" In *Śāstrārambha: Inquiries into the Preamble in Sanskrit,* ed. Walter Slaje, 1–24. Wiesbaden: Harrassowitz.

Mioni, Alberto M. 2004. "Classical Language—Dead Language / Klassische Sprache—Tote Sprache." In *Sociolinguistics: An International Handbook of the Science of Language and Society / Soziolinguistik: Ein internationales Handbuch zur Wissenschaft von Sprache und Gesellschaft,* ed. Ulrich Ammon, Norbert Dittmar, Klaus J. Mattheier, and Peter Trudgill, 1: 314–322. 2nd ed. Berlin: De Gruyter.

Mirashi, Vasudev Vishnu. 1945. "Some Royal Poets of the Vākāṭaka Age." *Indian Historical Quarterly* 21: 193–201.

———. 1947. "The Date of the *Gāthāsaptaśatī*." *Indian Historical Quarterly* 23: 300–310. Reprinted in id., *Studies in Indology,* 1: 76–88 (Nagpur: Vidarbha Samshodhana Mandala, 1960).

———. 1951. "The Home of the Vākāṭakas." *Annals of the Bhandarkar Oriental Research Institute* 32 (1–4): 1–18.

———. 1960*a*. "Some Ancient Prakrit poets." In id., *Studies in Indology,* 1: 89–95. Nagpur: Vidarbha Samshodhana Mandal.

———. 1960*b*. "The Original Name of the *Gāthāsaptaśatī*." In id., *Studies in Indology,* 1: 70–75. Nagpur: Vidarbha Samshodhana Mandal.

———, ed. 1963. *Inscriptions of the Vākāṭakas.* Corpus Inscriptionum Indicarum, vol. 5. Ootacamund: Government Epigraphist for India.

Mirashi, Vasudev Vishnu. 1975. "The Identity of the Sātavāhana King Śiva-śrī Puḷumāvi." In *Literary and Historical Studies in Indology,* 163–166. Delhi: Motilal Banarsidass.

———. 1977. "Nāṇēghāṭ Inscription Re-examined." *Studies in Indian Epigraphy* 3: 86–89.

Mitchell, Lisa. 2009. *Language, Emotion, and Politics in South India: The Making of a Mother Tongue.* Bloomington: Indiana University Press.

Mitchiner, John E., ed. 1986. *The Yuga Purāṇa.* Calcutta [Kolkata]: Asiatic Society.

Monk, Ray. 1990. *Ludwig Wittgenstein: The Duty of Genius.* New York: Free Press.

Morrison, Kathleen D. 1995. "Trade, Urbanism, and Agricultural Expansion: Buddhist Monastic Institutions and the State in the Early Historic Western Deccan." *World Archaeology* 27 (2): 203–221.

Müller, Max. 1883. *India: What Can It Teach Us?* London: Lovell's Library.

Nagaraja Rao, M. S. 1985. "Brāhmī Inscriptions and Their Bearing on the Great Stūpa at Sannati." In *Indian Epigraphy: Its Bearing on the History of Art,* ed. Frederick M. Asher and G. S. Gai, 41–45. New Delhi: Oxford and IBH Publishing Company.

Nagarajaiah, Hampa. 1994. "Influence of Prakrit on Kannaḍa Language and Literature." In *Jainism and Prakrit in Ancient and Medieval India: Essays for Professor Jagdish Chandra Jain,* ed. N. N. Bhattacharyya, 113–120. Delhi: Manohar.

Nagaraju, S. 1981. *Buddhist Architecture of Western India, c. 250 B.C.–c. A.D. 300.* Delhi: Agam Kala Prakashan.

Nagy, Gregory. 1974. *Comparative Studies in Greek and Indic Meter.* Cambridge, Mass.: Harvard University Press.

Naikar, Chandramouli S. 1998. *The Prakrit Plays of India.* Dharwad: Medha Publishers.

Nakanishi, Maiko, and Oskar von Hinüber. 2014. *Kanaganahalli Inscriptions.* Tokyo: International Research Institute for Advanced Buddhology, Soka University. Supplement to ARIRIAB 17 (2013).

Nara, Tsuyoshi. 1979. *Avahaṭṭha and Comparative Vocabulary of New Indo-Āryan Languages.* Tokyo: Institute for the Study of Languages and Cultures of Asia and Africa.

Narasimha Murthy, A. V. and H. R. Raghunatha Bhat. 1975. "Banavāsi Inscription of Siva Siri Puḷumāvi." *Studies in Indian Epigraphy* 1: 34–39.

Narasimhaswami, H. K. 1951. "Nagarjunikonda Image Inscription." *Epigraphia Indica* 29: 137–139.

Narayana Rao, Velcheru. 1995. "Coconut and Honey: Sanskrit and Telugu in Medieval Andhra." *Social Scientist* 23: 24–40.

———. 2003. "Multiple Literary Cultures in Telugu." In *Literary Cultures in History: Reconstructions from South Asia*, ed. Sheldon Pollock, 383–436. Berkeley: University of California Press.

Narayana Rao, Velcheru, and David Shulman. 2012. *Śrīnātha: The Poet Who Made Gods and Kings*. Oxford: Oxford University Press.

Nath, Amarendra. 1990. "Toponymy of Asaka and Asika." *Indica* 27: 87–96.

Neelis, Jason. 2011. *Early Buddhist Transmission and Trade Networks: Mobility and Exchange within and beyond the Northwestern Borderlands of South Asia*. Leiden: Brill.

Nilakantha Sastri, K. A. 1941. "Gurzala Brahmi Inscription." *Epigraphia Indica* 26: 123–125.

Nitti-Dolci, Luigia, ed. 1938. *Le Prākṛtānuśāsana de Puruṣottama*. Cahiers de la société asiatique, No. 6. Paris: Société asiatique.

———. 1972 [1938]. *The Prākrita Grammarians*. Translated by Prabhākara Jhā. Delhi: Motilal Banarsidass.

Norman, K. R. 1987. "The Origin of the Āryā Metre." In *Buddhist Philosophy and Culture: Essays in honor of N. A. Jayawickrema*, 203–214. Kelaniya, Sri Lanka: Vidyalankara Press.

Novetzke, Christian. 2008. *Religion and Public Memory: A Cultural History of Saint Namdev in India*. New York: Columbia University Press.

———. 2016. *The Quotidian Revolution: Vernacularization, Religion, and the Premodern Public Sphere in India*. New York: Columbia University Press.

Ohira, Suzuko. 1982. *A Study of Tattvārthasūtra with Bhāṣya*. Ahmedabad: Lalbhai Dalpatbhai Institute of Indology.

Olivelle, Patrick. 2004. "The Semantic History of Dharma in the Middle and Late Vedic Periods." In *Dharma: Studies in Its Semantic, Cultural and Religious History*, ed. Patrick Olivelle, 69–89. New Delhi: Motilal Banarsidass.

Ollett, Andrew. 2012. "Moraic Feet in Prakrit Metrics: A Constraint-Based Approach." *Transactions of the Philological Society* 110 (2): 241–282.

———. 2013. "The *gaṇacchandas* in the Indian Metrical Tradition." In *Puṣpikā: Proceedings of the First International Indology Graduate Research Symposium*, ed. Nina Mirnig, Peter Szanto, and Michael Williams, 331–364. Oxford: Oxbow Books.

———. 2014. "Ghosts from the Past: India's Undead Languages." *Indian Economic and Social History Review* 51 (4): 405–456.

———. 2017. "Making It Nice: *Kāvya* in the Second Century." *Journal of Indian Philosophy*, special issue, "Aśvaghoṣa across Boundaries," ed. Roy Tzohar.

———. Forthcoming. "Pālitta and the History of Prakrit Literature." In *Jaina Studies (Proceedings of a Panel at the 16th World Sanskrit Conference in Bangkok, 2015)*, ed. Peter Flügel and Nalini Balbir.

Panchamukhi, R. S., ed. 1941. *Karnatak Inscriptions*, vol. 1. Dharwar: Karnatak Research Institute.

Panneerselvam, R. 1969. "Further Light on the Bilingual Coin of the Sātavāhanas." *Indo-Iranian Journal* 11: 281–288.

Parabrahma Sastry, P. V. 2008. "Society and Economy of the Sātavāhana Age." In *Early Historic Andhra Pradesh, 500 BC—AD 624*, ed. I. K. Sarma, 18–32. New Delhi: Tulika Books.

Pargiter, F. E. 1913. *The Purāṇa Text of the Dynasties of the Kali Age*. London: Oxford University Press.

Phukan, Shantanu. 2001. "'Through throats where many rivers meet': The Ecology of Hindi in the World of Persian." *Indian Economic and Social History Review* 38 (1): 33–58.

Pisani, Vittore. 1957. "On the Origin of *Prākṛtam* and *Pāli* as Language Designations." In *Felicitation Volume Presented to Professor Sripad Krishna Belvalkar,* 185–191. Benares [Varanasi]: M. B. Dass.

Pischel, Richard. 1873. "Review of Beames, *Comparative Grammar of the Modern Aryan Languages of India.*" *The Academy* 4: 397–398.

———. 1874. *De Grammaticis Pracriticis.* Breslau: Adolph Kiepert.

———. 1879. "Die Deçîçabdâs bei Trivikrama." *Beiträge zur Kunde der indogermanischen Sprachen* 3: 235–265.

———, ed. 1886. *Rudraṭa's Çṛṅgâratilaka and Ruyyaka's Sahṛdayalîlâ.* Kiel: Haeseler.

———. 1896. "Der Accent des Prākrit." *Zeitschrift für Vergleichende Sprachforschung* 34: 568–576.

———. 1897. "Der Accent des Prākrit." *Zeitschrift für Vergleichende Sprachforschung* 35: 140–150.

———. 1900. *Grammatik der Prakrit-Sprachen.* Strassburg: Karl Trübner.

———. 1905–1906. "Two Prâkṛit Poems at Dhâr." *Epigraphia Indica* 8: 241–260.

———. 1981 [1900]. *A Grammar of the Prākrit Languages.* Translated by S. Jhā. 2nd ed. Delhi: Motilal Banarsidass.

Pollock, Sheldon. 1985. "The Theory of Practice and the Practice of Theory in Indian Intellectual History." *Journal of the American Oriental Society* 105 (3): 499–519.

———. 1989. "Playing by the Rules: *Śāstra* and Sanskrit Literature." In *Shastric Traditions in Indian Arts,* ed. Anna Libera Dallapiccola, 301–312. Stuttgart: Steiner.

———. 1995. "In Praise of Poets: On the History and Function of the Kaviprasamsa." In *Ānanda Bhārati: Dr. K. Krishnamoorthy Felicitation Volume,* ed. B. Channakeshava and H. V. Nagaraja Rao, 443–457. Mysore: D. V. K. Murthy.

———. 1996. "The Sanskrit Cosmopolis, 300–1300: Transculturation, Vernacularization, and the Question of Ideology." In *Ideology and Status of Sanskrit: Contributions to the History of the Sanskrit Language,* ed. Jan E. M. Houben, 197–248. Leiden: Brill.

———. 1998. "India in the Vernacular Millennium: Literary Culture and Polity, 1000–1500." *Dædalus* 127: 41–74.

———. 2001. "The Death of Sanskrit." *Comparative Studies in Society and History* 42 (2): 392–426.

———. 2003. "Sanskrit Literary Culture from the Inside Out." In *Literary Cultures in History: Reconstructions from South Asia,* ed. Sheldon Pollock, 39–130. Berkeley: University of California Press.

———. 2004. "A New Philology: from Norm-Bound Practice to Practice-Bound Norm in Kannada Intellectual History." In *South Indian Horizons: Felicitation Volume for François Gros,* ed. Jean-Luc Chevillard, 389–406. Pondicherry: Institut français de Pondichéry / École française d'extrême-orient.

———. 2006*a*. *The Language of the Gods in the World of Men: Sanskrit, Culture, and Power in Premodern India.* Berkeley: University of California Press.

———. 2006*b*. "Empire and Imitation." In *Lessons of Empire: Imperial Histories and American Power,* ed. Craig Calhoun, Frederick Cooper, and Kevin Moore, 175–188. New York: New Press.

——. 2009. "Future Philology? The Fate of a Soft Science in a Hard World." *Critical Inquiry* 35 (4): 931–961. Special issue, *The Fate of Disciplines*, ed. James Chandler and Arnold I. Davidson (Chicago: University of Chicago Press).

——. 2011. "The Languages of Science in Early Modern India." In *Forms of Knowledge in Early Modern Asia: Explorations in the Intellectual History of India and Tibet, 1500–1800*, ed. Sheldon Pollock, 19–48. Durham, N.C.: Duke University Press.

——. 2014. "What Was Philology in Sanskrit?" In *World Philology*, ed. Sheldon Pollock, Benjamin A. Elman, and Ku-ming Kevin Chang, 114–136. Cambridge, Mass.: Harvard University Press.

——. 2016. *A Rasa Reader*. New York: Columbia University Press.

Pollock, Sheldon, Benjamin Elman, and Ku-ming Kevin Chang, eds. 2014. *World Philology*. Cambridge, Mass.: Harvard University Press.

Poonacha, K. P. 2013. *Excavations at Kanaganahalli*. New Delhi: Archaeological Survey of India.

Prakash, Buddha. 1954. "The Ābhīras: Their Antiquity, History, and Culture." *Journal of the Bihar Research Society* 40 (3): 249–265.

Printz, Wilhelm. 1921. *Bhāsa's Prakrit*. Frankfurt a. M.: Im Selbstverlag.

Puṇyavijaya, Dalsukh Mālvaṇiā, and Amritlāl Mohanlāl Bhojak. 1968. *Nandisuttam and Aṇuogaddārāiṁ*. Bombay [Mumbai]: Shri Mahāvīra Jaina Vidyālaya.

Raghavan, V. 1941. "Appayya Dīkṣitas II and III." *Proceedings of the All-India Oriental Conference* 10: 176–180.

——. 1950. "Prākṛta Works Known from Bhoja's Śṛṅgāra-prakāśa." In *Siddha-Bhāratī, or, The Rosary of Indology: Presenting 108 Original Papers on Indological Subjects in Honour of the 60th Birthday of Dr. Siddheshwar Varma*, ed. Vishva Bandhu, 199–206. Hoshiarpur: V. V. R. Institute.

——. 1963. *Bhoja's Śṛṅgāra Prakāśa*. Madras: Punarvasu.

——. 1973. "The Vṛttis in Kāvya." In *Studies on Some Concepts of the Alaṃkāra Śāstra*, 201–213. Madras: Adyar Library and Research Centre.

——. 1973 [1942]. *Studies on Some Concepts of the Alaṃkāra Śāstra*. Madras: Adyar Library and Research Centre.

——. 1980. "Abhinavagupta's Polymathy." In *Abhinavagupta and His Works*, 94–98. Varanasi: Chaukhamba Orientalia.

Rajendran, C. 2005. "Sociolinguistic Problems in Nāṭyaśāstra." In *Avaniśrīḥ: Avanindra Kumar Felicitation Volume*, ed. Mithilesh Chaturvedi, Nath Bimali, and Siddharth Shankar Singh, 215–219. Delhi: Vidyānilayam Prakāśan.

Ramachandra Murthy, N. S. 1999. "Pātagaṇḍigūḍem Plates of Ehavala Chāntamūla." *Journal of the Epigraphical Society of India* 25: 114–123.

Ramaswamy, Sumathi. 1997. *Passions of the Tongue: Language Devotion in Tamil India, 1891–1970*. Berkeley: University of California Press.

Ramesh, K. V. 1984. *Inscriptions of the Western Gangas*. New Delhi: Indian Council of Historical Research.

Rapson, Edward James. 1908 [1967]. *Catalogue of the Coins of the Andhra Dynasty, the Western Kṣatrapas, the Traikūṭaka Dynasty and the "Bodhi" Dynasty*. London: Trustees of the British Museum.

Ray, Himanshu Prabha. 1986. *Monastery and Guild: Commerce under the Sātavāhanas.* Delhi: Oxford University Press.

Reddy, A. K. V. S., and N. Krishna Reddy. 2000. "A Newly Discovered Prākrit Copper Plate Grant of Pallava Viṣṇugōpavarman, Year 1." In *Śāṅkaram: Recent Researches on Indian Culture (Professor Srinivasa Sankaranarayanan Festschrift),* ed. S. S. Ramachandra Murthy, B. Rajendra Prasad, and D. Kiran Kranth Choudary, 68–70. New Delhi: Harman Publishing House.

Rees, Gethin. 2011. "A Hiatus in the Cutting of Buddhist Caves in the Western Deccan." *Ancient Asia* 2: 119–134.

Renou, Louis. 1938. "Review of Nitti-Dolci, *Les grammariens prakrits.*" *Journal Asiatique* 230: 159–168.

———. 1956. *Histoire de la langue sanskrite.* Lyon: Éditions IAC..

Rice, Lewis. 1882. "Early Kannada Authors." *Journal of the Asiatic Society of Great Britain and Northern Ireland* 15: 295–314.

Rosen Stone, Elizabeth. 1994. *The Buddhist Art of Nāgārjunakoṇḍa.* Delhi: Motilal Banarsidass.

Rosenfield, John M. 1967. *The Dynastic Arts of the Kushans.* Berkeley: University of California Press.

Rossella, Daniela. 2011. "On the Origins of *Kāvya:* A Never-Ending Story?" *Pandanus* 5 (2).

Roy, Suchitra. 1998. *Reconstructed Grammar of the Setubandha: Exhaustive Study of Vowels Only.* Calcutta [Kolkata]: Punti Pustak.

Sakai, Naoki. 1992. *Voices of the Past: The Status of Language in Eighteenth-Century Japanese Discourse.* Ithaca, N.Y.: Cornell University Press.

———. 1997. *Translation and Subjectivity.* Minneapolis: University of Minnesota Press.

———. 2009. "How Do We Count a Language? Translation and Discontinuity." *Translation Studies* 2 (1): 71–88.

Salomon, Richard. 1982. "The Original Language of the Karpūra-mañjarī." *Wiener Zeitschrift für die Kunde Südasiens* 132: 119–141.

———. 1991. "Epigraphic Remains of Indian Traders in Egypt." *Journal of the American Oriental Society* 111 (4): 731–736.

———. 1995. "On Drawing Socio-linguistic Distinctions in Old Indo-Aryan: The Question of Kṣatriya Sanskrit and Related Problems." In *The Indo-Aryans of Ancient South Asia: Language, Material Culture and Ethnicity,* ed. George Erdosy, 293–306. Berlin: Walter de Gruyter.

———. 1998. *Indian Epigraphy: A Guide to the Study of Inscriptions in Sanskrit, Prakrit and the Other Indo-Aryan Languages.* New York: Oxford University Press.

———. 2001. "'Gāndhārī Hybrid Sanskrit': New Sources for the Study of the Sanskritization of Buddhist Literature." *Indo-Iranian Journal* 44 (3): 241–252.

———. 2013. "Aṣṭabhujasvāmin: A Reinterpretation of the Ābhīra Inscription from Nagarjunakonda." *Indo-Iranian Journal* 56: 397–417.

Sani, Saverio. 1985. "La Paiśācī, lingua di demoni." In *Scritti in onore di Riccardo Ambrosini,* ed. Enrico Campanile, Romano Lazzeroni, and Roberto Peroni, 193–204. Pisa: Giardini.

Sankalia, H. D., S. B. Deo, Z. D. Ansari, and S. Ehrhardt. 1960. *From History to Pre-history at Nevasa (1954–1956).* Poona [Pune]: Deccan College Postgraduate and Research Institute.

Sankaranarayanan, S. 1967. "Rentala Pillar Inscription of Siri-Chantamula, Year 5." *Epigraphia Indica* 37: 29–32.

———. 1970. "Kesanapalli Inscription of Chantamula, year 13." *Epigraphia Indica* 38: 313–318.

———. 1999. "Nānāghāṭ Cave Inscription of Nāgaṃṇikā: A Fresh Study." *Adyar Library Bulletin* 63: 193–211.

———. 2009. "An Earliest [sic] Sanskrit Inscription in South India." In id., *Rare Facets of Ancient Indian History and Culture,* 1: 46–74 . New Delhi: Harman Publishing House, 2009.

Sankunni Nair, M. P. 1995. *Points of Contact between Prakrit and Malayalam.* Trivandrum: International School of Dravidian Linguistics.

Sarkar, H. 1965–1966. "Nagarjunakonda Prakrit Inscription of Gautamiputra Vijaya Satakarni, Year 6." *Epigraphia Indica* 36: 273–275.

———. 1971. "Some Early Inscriptions in the Amaravati Museum." *Journal of Ancient Indian History* 4 (1–2): 1–13.

Sarma, I. K. 1973. "A Coin Mould-Piece from Nāgārjunakoṇḍa Excavations." *Journal of the Economic and Social History of the Orient* 16 (1): 89–106.

———. 1978. "Epigraphical Discoveries at Guntupalli." *Journal of the Epigraphical Society of India* 5: 48–61.

Sarma, I. K., and J. Varaprasada Rao. 1993. *Early Brāhmī Inscriptions from Sannati.* Delhi: Harman.

Saussure, Ferdinand de. 2011 [1959]. *Course in General Linguistics.* New York: Columbia University Press.

Scharfe, Harmut. 1977. *Grammatical Literature,* vol. 5.2 of *A History of Indian Literature.* Wiesbaden: Harrassowitz.

Schlingloff, Dieter. 1958. *Chandoviciti: Texte zur Sanskritmetrik.* Berlin: Akademie Verlag.

Schmiedchen, Annette. 2014. *Herrschergenealogie und religiöses Patronat: Die Inschriftenkultur der Rāṣṭrakūṭas, Śilāhāras und Yādavas (8. bis 13. Jahrhundert).* Leiden: Brill.

Schubring, Walther. 2004. *Mahāvīra's Words.* Ahmedabad: L. D. Institute of Indology. "Translated from the German with much added material" by W. Bollée and J. Soni.

———. 1955. "Jinasena, Mallinātha, Kālidāsa." *Zeitschrift der Deutschen Morgenländischen Gesellschaft* 105: 331–337.

———. 1962. *The Doctrine of the Jainas.* Delhi: Motilal Banarsidass.

Seeley, Nigel J., and Paula J. Turner. 1984. "Metallurgical Investigations of Three Early Indian Coinages: Implications for Metal Trading and Dynastic Chronology." In *South Asian Archaeology 1981: Proceedings of the Sixth International Association of South Asian Archaeologists in Western Europe,* ed. B. Allchin, 331–333. Cambridge: Cambridge University Press.

Seshadri Sastri, P. 1937–1938. "Dharanikota Dharmchakra Pillar Inscription." *Epigraphia Indica* 1972 24: 256–260.

Sharma, M. J. 1975–1976. "Vāsana Inscription of Vāsaṭhīputa Siri Puḷumāvi." *Epigraphia Indica* 41: 154–158.

Shastri, Ajay Mitra. 1993. "On the Velpuru Pillar Inscription of Maha Sada." *Journal of the Epigraphical Society of India* 19: 13–18.

———. 1996*a*. "King Mahasada of Velpuru Inscriptions and Coins." In *Spectrum of Indian Culture: Professor S. B. Deo Felicitation Volume*, ed. C. Margabandhu and K. S. Ramachandran, 353–356. Delhi: Agam Kala Prakashan.

———. 1996*b*. "Mahakhatapa Vasithiputa Isamahisa." In *Numismatic Panorama: Essays in the Memory of Late Shri S. M. Shukla*, ed. K. K. Maheshwari and Biswajeet Rath, 59–65. New Delhi: Harman Publishing House.

———. 1996*c*. "Śaka Era." *Indian Journal of History of Science* 31: 67–88.

———. 1999. "The Purāṇas on the Sātavāhanas: An Archaeological-Historical Perspective." In *The Age of the Sātavāhanas*, ed. Ajay Mitra Shastri, 3–72. New Delhi: Aryan Books International.

Shastri, Ajay Mitra, and K. D. Kawadkar. 2000. "Miregāon Plates of Prabhāvatīguptā, Year 20." *Annals of the Bhandarkar Oriental Research Institute* 81: 135–151.

Shukla, Chitra. 1985. "Three One-Act Plays of Ghanaśyāma." *Journal of the Oriental Institute, Baroda* 35 (1–2): 37–41.

Shulman, David. 2016. *Tamil: A Biography*. Cambridge, Mass.: Harvard University Press.

Shulman, David, and Velcheru Narayana Rao. 1998. *A Poem at the Right Moment: Remembered Verses from Premodern South India*. Berkeley: University of California Press.

Sims-Williams, Nicholas. 2004. "The Bactrian Inscription of Rabatak: A New Reading." *Bulletin of the Asia Institute* 18: 53–68.

Sinopoli, Carla M. 2001. "On the Edge of Empire: Form and Substance in the Satavahana Dynasty." In *Empires: Perspectives from Archaeology and History*, ed. Susan E. Alcock, Terence N. D'Altroy, Kathleen D. Morrison, and Carla M. Sinopoli, 155–178. Cambridge: Cambridge University Press.

Sircar, D. C. 1939. *The Successors of the Sātavāhanas in Lower Deccan*. Calcutta [Kolkata]: University of Calcutta.

———. 1957–1958. "Two Inscriptions from Guntur District." *Epigraphia Indica* 32: 82–91.

———. 1961–1962. "Nagarjunikonda Inscription of the Time of Abhira Vasushena, Year 30." *Epigraphia Indica* 34: 197–204.

———. 1963–1964*a*. "More Inscriptions from Nagarjunikonda." *Epigraphia Indica* 35: 1–36.

———. 1963–1964*b*. "Penugonda Plates of Hastivarman." *Epigraphia Indica* 35: 145–150.

———. 1963–1964*c*. "Silver Coin of Vasisthi-putra Satakarni." *Epigraphia Indica* 35: 247–252.

———. 1965. *Select Inscriptions Bearing on Indian History and Civilization, from the Sixth Century B.C. to the Sixth Century A.D.* 2nd ed. Calcutta [Kolkata]: University of Calcutta.

———. 1965–1966. "Three Copper-Plate Charters." *Epigraphia Indica* 36: 1–18.

———. 1966. "Early Western Satraps and the Date of the Periplus." *Numismatic Chronicle* 6: 241–249.

———. 1968. "The Sātavāhanas and the Chedis." In *History and Culture of the Indian People II: The Age of Imperial Unity*, ed. R. C. Majumdar, chap. 13, 191–215. 4th ed. Bombay [Mumbai]: Bharatiya Vidya Bhavan.

———. 1969. *Ancient Malwa and the Vikramāditya Tradition*. Delhi: Munshiram Manoharlal.

———. 1969–1970. "Some Epigraphic and Manuscript Records." *Journal of Ancient Indian History* 3 (1–2): 30–49.

Sircar, D. C., and Krishnan, K. G. 1961–1962. "Two Inscriptions from Nagarjunikonda." *Epigraphia Indica* 34: 17–22.

Siṃh, Nāmvar. 1971 [1952]. *Hindī ke Vikās meṃ Apabhraṃś kā Yog.* Allahabad: Lokabhāratī.

———. 1997 [1956]. *Pṛthvīrāja Rāso: Bhāṣā aur Sāhitya.* New Delhi: Rādhākṛṣṇa.

Skilling, Peter. 2016. "Caitya, Mahācaitya, Tatāgatacaitya: Questions of Terminology in the Age of Amaravati." In *Amaravati: The Art of an Early Buddhist Monument in Context,* ed. Akira Shimada and Michael Willis, 23–36. London: British Museum.

Skilling, Peter, and Oskar von Hinüber. 2011. "An Epigraphical Buddhist Poem from Phanigiri (Andhrapradesh) om the Time of Rudrapuruṣadatta." *Annual Report of the International Research Institute for Advanced Buddhist Studies* 14: 7–12.

Skinner, Michael. 2012. "Urbanization and Interactions in the Early Historic Deccan: The Sātavāhana, Western Kṣatrapa, and Ikṣvāku Dynasties." Master's thesis, University of Washington.

Slouber, Michael. 2011. "*Śaṅkuka's* Saṃhitāsāra: Edition and Translation of Verses 1–5, 75–85, and 127–154 with an Anonymous Commentary." Master's thesis, University of Hamburg.

Smith, David. 1985. *Ratnākara's Harivijaya: An Introduction to the Sanskrit Court Epic.* Delhi: Oxford University Press.

Smith, Helmer. 1949–1950. "Les deux prosodies du vers bouddhique." *Årsberättelse (Bulletin de la Société Royale des Lettres de Lund),* 1–43.

Smith, Vincent A. 1902. "Andhra History and Coinage I: The Andhra People or Nation, and the Early Andhrabhṛtya Kings." *Zeitschrift der Deutschen Morgenländischen Gesellschaft* 56: 649–675.

Sohoni, S. V. 1964. "First Five Verses of *Gāhā Sattasaī.*" *Journal of the Bihar Research Society* 50: 1–7.

———. 1999. "Hāla and Nāgārjuna." In *The Age of the Sātavāhanas,* ed. Ajay Mitra Shastri, 205–208. New Delhi: Aryan Books International.

Somasekhara Sarma, M. 1948. *History of the Reddi Kingdoms: Circa 1325 A.D. to circa 1448 A.D.* Waltair: Andhra University.

Somerset, Fiona, and Nicholas Watson. 2003. "Preface: On 'Vernacular.'" In *The Vulgar Tongue: Medieval and Postmedieval Vernacularity,* ed. Fiona Somerset and Nicholas Watson, ix–xiii. University Park: Pennsylvania State University Press.

Srimannarayana Murti, M. 1993. "On the Nomenclature 'Saṃskṛta.'" *Adyar Library Bulletin* 57: 58–71.

Srinivasan, P. R. 1971*a*. "An Inscription of Ehavala-Chamtamula from Alluru, Year 8." *Epigraphia Indica* 39 (4): 139–140.

———. 1971*b*. "Note on Talagunda Inscription of Santivarman." *Epigraphia Indica* 39 (2): 71–74.

Steiner, Roland. 1997. *Untersuchungen zu Harṣadevas Nāgānanda und zum indischen Schauspiel.* Swisttal-Odendorf: Indica et Tibetica Verlag.

———. 2001. "Play Editing and Prakrit Grammarians." In*Sources and time = Les sources et le temps: A Colloquium, Pondicherry, 11–13 January 1997,* ed. François Grimal, 63–76. Pondicherry: Institut français de Pondichéry.

Stock, Brian. 1998. *Augustine the Reader: Meditation, Self-Knowledge and the Ethics of Interpretation.* Cambridge, Mass.: Harvard University Press.

Strauch, Ingo. 2012. "The Character of the Indian Kharoṣṭhī Script and the "Sanskrit Revolution": A Writing System between Identity and Assimilation." In *The Idea of Writing:*

Writing across Borders, ed. Alex de Voogt and Joachim Friedrich Quack, 131–168. Leiden: Brill.

Subrahmanyam, P. S. 2011. "The Prakrit Grammatians: Historical Linguists of Ancient India." *Indian Linguistics* 72: 230–242.

Sukthankar, V. S. 1917–1918. "A New Andhra Inscription of Siri-Pulumavi." *Epigraphia Indica* 14: 153–155.

Suryavanshi, Bhagwansingh. 1962. *The Abhiras: Their History and Culture.* Baroda [Vadodara]: Maharaja Sayajirao University of Baroda.

Swiggers, Pierre. 2009. "Les premières grammaires occitanes: Les *Razos de trobar* de Raimon Vidal et le *Donatz proensals* d'Uc (Faidit)." *Zeitschrift für romanische Philologie* 105 (1–2): 134–147.

Söhnen-Thieme, Renate. 1995. "On the Concept and Presentation of "Yamaka" in Early Indian Poetic Theory." *Bulletin of the School of Oriental and African Studies* 58 (3): 495–520.

Tagare, G. V. 1942. "Apabhraṁśa and the Ābhīras." *Annals of the Bhandarkar Oriental Research Institute* 23: 563–567.

Talbot, Cynthia. 2016. *The Last Hindu Emperor: Prithviraj Chauhan and the Indian Past, 1200–2000.* Cambridge: Cambridge University Press.

Tambling, Jeffrey. 1988. *What Is Literary Language?* Philadelphia: Open University Press.

Tavakoli-Targhi, Mohamad. 2001. "Modernity, Heterotopia, and Homeless Texts." In *Refashioning Iran: Orientalism, Occidentalism and Historiography*, 1–17. New York: Palgrave.

Tieken, Herman. 1978. "A Formal Type of Arrangement in the Vulgata of the *Gâthâsaptaśatî* of Hâla." *Studien zur Indologie und Iranistik* 4: 111–130.

———. 2001. *Kāvya in South India: Old Tamil Caṅkam Poetry.* Groningen: Egbert Forsten.

———. 2006. "Aśoka's Fourteenth Rock Edict and the Guṇa *mādhurya* of the Kāvya Poetical Tradition." *Zeitschrift der Deutschen Morgenländischen Gesellschaft* 156: 95–115.

———. 2008. "The Process of Vernacularization in South Asia." *Journal of the Economic and Social History of the Orient* 51: 338–383. Review of Pollock 2006.

Trautmann, Thomas. 2006. *Languages and Nations: The Dravidian Proof in Colonial Madras.* Berkeley: University of California Press.

Tripathi, G. C. 1984. "King Śālivāhana of Mewar and the Problem of the Authorship of the *Gāthāsaptaśatī*." *Journal of the Ganganath Jha Kendriya Sanskrit Vidyapeetha* 40: 285–302.

Tubb, Gary. 2015. "*Kāvya* with Bells On: *Yamaka* in the *Śiśupālavadha*." In *Innovations and Turning Points: Toward a History of Kāvya Literature*, ed. Yigal Bronner, David Shulman, and Gary Tubb, 142–194. New Delhi: Oxford University Press.

Upadhye, A. N. 1931–1932. "Śubhacandra and his Prakrit Grammar." *Annals of the Bhandarkar Oriental Research Institute* 13: 37–58.

———. 1941*a*. "Prākrit Grammar Attributed to Samantabhadra." *Indian Historical Quarterly* 17: 511–516.

———. 1941*b*. "Vālmīki-Sūtras, A Myth." *Bhāratīya Vidyā* 2 (2): 160–176.

———. 1955. "Marāṭhī Elements in a Prakrit Drama." In *Suniti Kumar Chatterji Jubilee Volume*, 147–152. Poona [Pune]: Linguistic Society of India.

———. 1956. "Once Again: Vālmīki-Sūtras, A Myth." *Bhāratīya Vidyā* 15: 28–31.

———. 1961. "*Siṃgāramaṃjarī*: A Saṭṭaka (Authentically edited for the first time)." *Journal of the University of Poona, Humanities Section* 13: 33–76.

———. 1963–1964. "Languages and Dialects Used in the Kuvalayamālā." *Journal of the Oriental Institute, Baroda* 13: 317–325.

Upadhye, A. N., ed. 1970. *Saptaśatīsāra with Bhāvadīpikā of Vema Bhūpāla along with the Chappaṇṇaya-Gāhāo.* Kolhapur: Shivaji University.

Upadhye, A. N. 1974. "Bappa Bhaṭṭi and His *Tārāgaṇa.*" *Sambodhi* 3 (4): 67–72.

———. 1975–1976. "Bhoja and Prakrit Literature: His *Kūrmaśataka.*" *Journal of the Oriental Institute, Baroda* 25: 63–66.

———. 1983. "Gommaṭa." In *Upadhye Papers,* 217–226. Mysore: University of Mysore Prasaranga.

———. 1990. "Prakrit Language and Literature in the South." In *South Indian Studies: Dr. T. V. Mahalingam Commemoration Volume,* ed. H. M. Nayak and B. R. Gopal, 757–766. Mysore: Geetha Book House.

Vaidya, Paraśurāma Lakṣmaṇa. 1926–1927. "Observations on Hemacandra's *Dēsināmamālā.*" *Annals of the Bhandarkar Oriental Research Institute* 8: 63–71.

Varaprasada Rao, J. 1995. "An Early Sanskrit Inscription from Sannati." *Journal of Archaeology* 3 (2): 165–167.

Vasudeva, Somadeva, and Bergljot Chiarucci. 2011. "The Earliest Commentators on the *Gāhākoso:* Tribhuvanapāla's *Chekoktivicāralīlā* and Upādhyāya Lakṣmīdhara's *Saptaśatakaṭīkā.*" *Newsletter of the Nepalese-German Manuscript Cataloguing Project* 7: 46–54.

Venkatacharya, T. 1968. "The Significance of the Title *Ubhayābhisārikā* and the Date of the Play." *Journal of the American Oriental Society* 88 (2): 350–352.

Vertogradova, V. V. 1978. *Prakrity.* Moskow: Nauka.

Vijayalakshmy, R. 1978. "A Study of the Missing Portion at the Beginning of the Perunkatai with Special Reference to Its Relationship to the Brhatkatha." In *South Indian Studies,* ed. R. Nagaswami, 59–76. Madras [Chennai]: Society for Archaeological, Historical & Epigraphical Research.

———. 1981. *A Study of the Peruṅkatai, an Authentic Version of the Story of Udayana.* Madras [Chennai]: International Institute of Tamil Studies.

———. 1982. "The Tamil *Peruṅkatai* and Its Relation to the *Bṛhatkathā.*" *Indo-Iranian Journal* 24: 27–36.

Vijayaśīlacandrasūri. 2005. "Taraṅgavatī Kathā tathā Pādaliptasūri: Jain ke Ajain." *Anusaṃdhāna* 34: 43–48.

Vogel, J.-Ph. 1929–1930. "Prakrit Inscriptions from a Buddhist Site at Nagarjunikonda." *Epigraphia Indica* 20: 1–37.

———. 1931–1932. "Additional Prākṛit Inscriptions from Nāgārjunikoṇḍa." *Epigraphia Indica* 21: 61–71.

von Glasenapp, Helmut. 1999. *Jainism: An Indian Religion of Salvation.* Delhi: Motilal Banarsidass.

von Hinüber, Oskar. 1981. "Die Paiśācī und die Entstehung der Sakischen Orthographie." In *Studien zum Jainismus und Buddhismus: Gedenkschrift für Ludwig Alsdorf,* ed. Klaus Bruhn and Albrecht Wezler, 121–127. Wiesbaden: Franz Steiner.

———. 1982. "Pāli as an Artificial Language." *Indologica Taurinensia* 10: 133–140.

———. 1985. "Pāli and Paiśācī as Variants of Buddhist Middle Indic." *Bulletin d'études indiennes* 3: 61–77.

———. 1996. *A Handbook of Pāli Literature*. Berlin: Walter de Gruyter.

———. 2001. *Das ältere Mittelindisch im Überblick*. Vienna: Österreichische Akademie der Wissenschaften.

Vyas, Bhola Shanker. 1962. *Prākṛita-Paiṅgalaṃ (Bhāṣāśāstrīya aur Chandaḥśāstrīya Anuśīlana)*. Varanasi: Prakrit Text Society.

Walser, Joseph. 2005. *Nāgārjuna in Context: Mahāyāna Buddhism and Early Indian Culture*. New York: Columbia University Press.

Warder, Anthony Kennedy. 1967. *Pali Metre*. London: Pali Text Society.

———. 1968. "The Possible Dates of Pārśva, Vasumitra (II), Caraka and Mātṛceṭa." In *Papers on the Date of Kaniṣka*, ed. A. L. Basham, 327–336. Leiden: Brill.

———. 1990 [1974]. *Indian Kāvya Literature*, vol. 2: *Origins and Formation of the Classical Kāvya*. Delhi: Motilal Banarsidass.

Warner, Michael. 2002. "Publics and Counterpublics." *Public Culture* 14 (1): 49–90.

Weber, Albrecht. 1868. "Ueber den auf der Kön. Bibl. zu Berlin befindlichen Codex der *Sûryaprajnapti* (ms. or. oct. 155)." In *Indische Studien*, vol. 10, ed. Albrecht Weber, 254–316. Leipzig: Brockhaus.

———. 1870. *Ueber das Saptaçatakam des Hāla: Ein Beitrag zur Kenntniss des Prākṛit*. Leipzig: Abhandlung für die Kunde des Morgenlandes

———. 1874. "Zum Saptaçatakam des Hâla." *Zeitschrift der Deutschen Morgenländischen Gesellschaft* 28: 345–436.

———, ed. 1881. *Das Saptaçatakam des Hâla*. Leipzig: Brockhaus.

———. 1883. "Ueber Bhuvanapâla's Commentar zu Hâla's Saptaçatakam." In *Indische Studien* vol. 16, ed. Weber, 1–204. Leipzig: Brockhaus.

Westergaard, Niels Ludvig. 1862. *Ueber den ältesten Zeitraum der indischen Geschichte mit Rücksicht auf die Litteratur: Ueber Buddha's Todesjahr und einige andere Zeitpunkte in der älteren Geschichte Indiens*. Breslau: A. Gosohorsky.

White, David Gordon. 1996. *The Alchemical Body: Siddha Traditions in Medieval India*. Chicago: University of Chicago Press.

Wilden, Eva. 2006. *Literary Techniques in Old Tamil Caṅkam Poetry*. Wiesbaden: Harrassowitz.

———. 2014. *Manuscript, Print, Memory: Relics of the Caṅkam in Tamilnadu*. Berlin: Walter de Gruyter.

Williams, R. 1965. "Haribhadra." *Bulletin of the School of Oriental and African Studies* 28 (1): 101–111.

Williams, Raymond. 1983. *Keywords: A Vocabulary of Culture and Society*. 2nd ed. New York: Oxford University Press.

Winternitz, Maurice. 1972 [1927]. *History of Indian Literature, Part II: Buddhist Literature and Jaina Literature*. New Delhi: Oriental Books Reprint Corporation.

———. 1985 [1920]. *History of Indian Literature, Part III: Part One: Classical Sanskrit Literature, Part Two: Scientific Literature*. Delhi: Motilal Banarsidass.

Witzel, Michael. 2006. "Brahmanical Reactions to Foreign Influences and to Social and Religious Change." In *Between the Empires. Society in India between 300 BCE and 400 CE*, ed. Patrick Olivelle, 457–499. Oxford: Oxford University Press.

Woolard, Kathryn A., and Bambi B. Schieffelin. 1994. "Language Ideology." *Annual Review of Anthropology* 24: 55–82.

Wright, J. Clifford. 1966. *Non-Classical Sanskrit Literature.* London: School of Oriental and African Studies.

Yashaschandra, Sitamshu. 2003. "From Hemacandra to Hind Svarāj: Region and Power in Gujarati Literary Culture." In *Literary Cultures in History: Reconstructions from South Asia,* ed. Sheldon Pollock, 567–611. Berkeley: University of California Press.

Yashin, Veli. 2011. "Euro(tro)pology: Philology, World Literature, and the Legacy of Erich Auerbach." *Yearbook of Comparative Literature* 57: 269–290.

Yoshimizu, Kiyotaka. 2015. "Kumārila's Criticism of Buddhism as a Religious Movement in His Views on the Sources of Dharma." *Acta Asiatica* 108: 43–62.

Yutaka, Ojihara. 2007. "Ghanaśyāma, un acrobate littéraire: Quelques cas typiques tirés de son *Madanasaṃjîvana.*" In *Mémorial Ojihara Yutaka,* 262–269. Toto Bunko Research Library, No. 9. Tokyo: Toyo Bunko.

Zin, Monika. 2013. "Māndhātar, the Universal Monarch, and the Meaning of Representations of the *cakravartin* in the Amaravati School, and of the Kings on the Kanganhalli Stūpa." In *Proceedings of the International Congress "Buddhist Narrative in Asia and Beyond," Chulalongkorn University, Bangkok, 8 to 11 August 2010,* ed. Peter Skilling and Justin McDaniel. Bangkok: Chulalongkorn University.

Zumthor, Paul. 1992 [1972]. *Toward a Medieval Poetics.* Translated by Philip Bennett. Minneapolis: University of Minnesota Press.

Zvelebil, Kamil. 1973. "The Earliest Account of the Tamil Academies." *Indo-Iranian Journal* 15 (2): 109–135.

INDEX

'Abd ur-Raḥmān, 9, 134, 177, 238n47
Abhimānacihna, 109, 146
Abhinanda, 79
Abhinavagupta, 8, 11, 104, 220n20, 229n60; on classification of language, 244n61; on "half-Sanskrit," 168; on *bhāṣā*, *vibhāṣā*, and *apabhraṃśa*, 134; on identity of Sanskrit and Prakrit, 124; on narrative contexts, 108–9; on *paryāya*, 105; on *pāṭhya* (actors' lines), 123–24; Prakrit grammar and, 149–50; on regularity and 'degraded' (*apabhraṃśa*) practices, 163; providing Sanskrit glosses (*chāyās*), 181, 256n35
Ābhīra kings, 45, 133, 203–4, 228n40
Ābhīrī, 126, 247n102
Acharya, Hari Ram, 103, 220n27
Achaemenid empire, 37
Afghanistan, 90
aggregation (*saṅghāta*), 103
Aitareya Āraṇyaka, 220n28
Ājaḍa, 58, 66, 108, 227n33, 230n70
Akbar (Mughal emperor), 1, 185
Ākho, 176
'Alā'uddīn Khilji, 183, 186
alchemy, 8
alliteration (*anuprāsa*), 90–91, 145
Alsdorf, Ludwig, 72, 97, 99, 149, 250n28
Amara's Treasury, 226n17
Amaru, 104
Aṇahilavāda, 151
Analysis of Literature, 164
Ānandasundarī (Ghanaśyāma), 183
Ānandavardhana, 7–8, 10–11, 74, 108, 214n22, 256n35; on *paryāyas*, 105
Āndhrī, 126
anthropology, linguistic, 5, 17
anuṣṭubh meter, 97, 99, 144
Anuyogadvāra Sūtra, 72, 102, 207
apabhraṃśas ("deviations"), 122, 124, 134, 152
Apabhramsha (Avahaṭṭha), 4, 16, 19, 101, 122, 125, 133–34, 136, 140, 175, 213n4; decline in literary productions in, 179; tradition of metrical analysis in, 186; "six languages" schema and, 138, 139; "three languages" schema and, 114, 129, 131–32, 177; vernacular languages and, 161, 162, 166, 177–78, 186
Appakavi, 167
Appayya Dīkṣita III, 159, 182, 253n70
archetype (*prakṛtiḥ*), 54, 134
Ardhamāgadhī, 31, 53, 72, 73, 96, 97, 126; *gāthā* meter in, 100; as "Middle Indic" language, 96
Ariṣṭakarṇa, 225n14
Ariṣṭanemi (Tīrthaṅkara), 145
Arjuna and the Hunter (Bhāravi), 185
Āryanāgahastin, 78, 81
"Aryan" language family, 20, 218n73
Aśoka, 13, 31, 32, 33, 59, 88
Aṣṭādhyāyī (Pāṇini), 147, 148, 151, 160
Aśvaghoṣa, 51, 52, 56, 59, 170, 225n4
Auerbach, Erich, 86

Aurangzeb (Mughal emperor), 1
Ausgewählte Erzählungen in Mâhârâshṭrî (Jacobi), 12
Āvantī, 126
Avantisundarī (Daṇḍin), 78, 104
Āvaśyaka Sūtra, 99, 207, 221n39, 232n108

Bakhtin, Mikhail, 3, 50
Balarāma (deity), 30
Bālasarasvatī, 181
Bāṇa(bhaṭṭa), 5, 66, 74
Bappabhaṭṭi, 103, 104, 105
Bapparāya, 227n33
Beames, John, 88–89, 90, 93
Bengali ("Old Bengali"), 162
Bhadrabāhu, 76, 99, 170
Bhadreśvara, 77, 234n116
Bhagavadgītā, 104
Bhāmaha, 69, 114, 129, 131, 149
Bhandarkar, D. R., 57
bhaṇitis ("modes of speech"), 91
Bharata (mythical sage), 123, 125, 134, 147, 207
Bhāratī (deity), 55
Bhāravi, 74, 185
Bhartṛhari, 104, 121–22, 242n38
Bhāsa, 19
bhāṣā (vernacular literature), 12, 54, 123, 126, 134, 152. *See also* New Indic
bhāṣāśleṣa (verse spoken in two or more languages), 139
bhāṣātraya ("three languages"), 1, 2, 12, 15; archetypal schema and, 114; as enumerative totality, 129, 130
bhāṣyas ("discussions"), 105
Bhaṭṭa Nāyaka, 8
Bhaṭṭa Udbhaṭa, 138
Bhaṭṭi (author of *Bhaṭṭikāvya*), 139, 182
Bhaṭṭoji Dīkṣita, 181
Bhavabhūti, 128, 182
Bhayani, H. C., 12, 78–79, 105, 252n67
Bhikhārīdāsa, 187, 257n58
Bhīma, 79
Bhīma Kāvya, 177
Bhoja, 6–7, 9, 68, 135, 181, 214n22; on alliteration, 91; cosmopolitan culture and, 10; inscribed poems of, 174–75; "regional" category and, 156; on "type" of language, 139
bhujaṅgavijṛmbhita meter, 41
Bhūtabali, 207
Bhuvanapāla, 58, 62, 108, 149, 158, 227n33, 229n65
Bilhaṇa, 133, 246n96
"birth language" (*jātibhāṣā*), 126
"birth languages" (*janmabhāṣā*), 133, 246n96
Birth of Kumāra (Kālidāsa), 116–17, 119
bitextuality, 92
Bloch, Jules, 20, 144, 250n29
Bloch, Theodor, 18
Book of Stories (Bhadreśvara), 77, 234n116, 235n131
Both Go to Meet (Vararuci), 147
"both-poet" (*ubhayakavi*) topos, 176–77, 181
Bourdieu, Pierre, 214n14
Brahmans, 21, 30, 35, 37, 39, 42, 43, 70, 116, 132; Sanskritization and, 47–48
Brāhmī script, 43, 46
Braj Bhāṣā, 25, 85–86, 162, 187
Brilliance of the Connoisseurs (Vairocana), 10, 14, 88, 96, 104, 106; arrangement of verses in, 105
Buddha, 9, 30, 97, 231n91; eulogy of, 45, 223n67; scenes from life of, 59
Buddhaghosa, 97
Buddhism, 6, 9, 30, 43, 58, 70, 170; "culture of writing" and, 48; Kanaganahalli reliefs and, 33, 36; language of scriptures, 124–25; Pali and, 13, 15, 21; Sanskritization and, 47–48, 225n83
"Buddhist Hybrid Sanskrit," 98
Bühler, Georg, 11, 51
Building the Bridge (Pravarasena II), 68, 131. *See also Rāvaṇa's Demise*
Busch, Allison, 85

Cambodia, 9, 137
Cāmuṇḍa Rāya, 180
Caṇḍa, 143, 145, 153, 208, 209–10
Cāṇḍālī, 126
Candragupta II Vikramāditya, 47, 57, 68, 69, 70, 147, 227n30
Candragupta Maurya, 76
Candralekhā (Rudradāsa), 183
Candraprabha, 179
caṅkam poems, 52, 59, 67, 109
capalā verse, 95
Caṣṭana, 44
Cātavākaṉam, 68
Century (Amaru), 104
Chandaḥ Sūtra (Piṅgala), 186, 187
Chappaṇṇayas, 79, 234n123
chekokti ("clever speech"), 62
China, 13, 163
Chojnacki, Christine, 180
Cloud Messenger (Kālidāsa), 104–5
Cluster of Blossoms of Prakrit, A (anonymous), 147, 250n33
coins, 15, 32, 43

languages: *Ausbildung* of, 86, 225n84; "common" (*sāmaṇṇa*), 158–59, 163, 165, 252n67; "eight languages" schema, 136; "fourth" language, 129, 130, 132; "language ideology," 5; nation and, 2–3; natural and cultural histories of, 18–22; natural history of, 22; ontologies of, 16–18; "regional" languages (*deśabhāṣās*), 140, 159, 163, 164; textual languages, 4; theories of literary language, 86–87; as unified objects, 111–12
languages of power, 23, 26–27, 34, 38, 136
Laṅkeśvara, 147
Lassen, Christian, 11
Lāṭī, 131
Legend of Ajitanātha (Ranna), 176
Legend of Padma (Raviṣeṇa), 132, 245n71
Legend of Śāntināthа (Ponna), 176
"*Leṇa* Prakrit," 13, 215n45
Leumann, Ernst, 54
Lévi, Sylvain, 42
lexicography, 141, 152, 156, 168
lexicons, 146, 155
Lienhard, Siegfried, 230n76, 232n97
Life of Language, The (Whitney), 218n80
Light on Prakrit (Vararuci), 11, 24, 139, 147–50, 161, 208, 248n13; as earliest surviving Prakrit grammar, 147; *Manoramā* commentary on, 149, 150; "regional" category and, 155; Vasantarāja's commentary, 181
Light on Suggestion (Ānandavardhana), 7, 11, 74, 107, 108–9, 214n22, 256n35
Light on the Great Commentary (Bhartṛhari), 122
Light on the Regional (*Deśīprakāśa*), 157
Līlāśuka, 184
Līlāvatī (Kautūhala), 8, 14, 58, 82, 226n16
Lineage of Hari (Vimala), 68, 75, 77
linguistics, 16, 22; "internal linguistics," 3; "linguistic area," 4, 213n11; philology distinguished from, 142; sociolinguistics, 17, 112; three-stage model and, 12
Linguistic Survey of India, 2
literarization, 48, 83, 140, 169, 170
Little Clay Cart (Śūdraka), 126, 216n46
Lokanātha, 185
Lüders, Heinrich, 215n45

Māḍharīputra Īśvarasena, 45
Mādhuka, 8
Magadhasenā, 233n110
Māgadhī, 72, 126, 127, 153; described in *Light on Prakrit*, 150; as ectype of Prakrit, 134, 175; iteration and, 134; as "regional" variety of Prakrit, 135; "six languages" schema and, 138, 139
Māgha, 74
Mahābhārata, 58, 75, 137, 176–77, 185
Mahābhāṣya (Patañjali), 23
Mahāmeghavāhana dynasty, 35, 191
Maharashtra, 3, 13, 14, 50, 131, 157–58, 252n66
Mahārāṣṭrī, 11, 14, 19, 131, 145, 150, 216n46, 216n49, 217n70; as linguistic precursor to Marathi, 157; Śaurasenī and, 125. *See also* Prakrit
Mahāvīra, 8–9, 70, 72, 75, 97, 231n91; death of, 77, 233n111
Malamoud, Charles, 245n85
Mālatī and Mādhava (Bhavabhūti), 128
Malayagiri, 207, 208, 209
Malayalam, 10, 162, 168, 184, 216n59
Malayavatī, 233n110
Malvania, Dalsukh, 99
Mammaṭa, 8, 69
Mānaveda II, 183
Maṇḍana, 78
Mantalaka, 225n14
Marathi, 157, 183, 184
Mārkaṇḍeya, 18, 19, 134, 151; corrections to *Karpūramañjarī*, 161; as "eastern grammarian," 147; "regional" category and, 156
Mathurā, 41, 43
Mātṛceṭa, 59
Mauryan dynasty, 29
Mayilaināṭar, 68
McGregor, R. S., 177
medicine, 8
Merutuṅga, 55, 56
Message Poem ('Abd ur-Raḥmān), 134, 177, 238n47
Meter (Svayambhū), 107, 109, 145
Middle Indic, 12, 13, 14, 23, 41, 113, 148, 175; "Age of Middle Indic," 45; as distinct from Sanskrit, 46–47; Dravidian languages and, 166; *gaṇa*-counting verses in, 96; musicality and indeterminacy in, 90; political, 45; regionalization of, 46; Sātavāhana kings and, 39, 169; Aśoka's inscriptions and, 33
Mīmāṃsā Sūtras, 125
Mirashi, V. V., 57–58
Mirror for Poets, 106–7
Mirror of Figures (*Alaṃkāradappaṇa*), 145, 249n16

South Asia Across the Disciplines is a series devoted to publishing first books across a wide range of South Asian studies, including art, history, philology or textual studies, philosophy, religion, and the interpretive social sciences. Series authors all share the goal of opening up new archives and suggesting new methods and approaches, while demonstrating that South Asian scholarship can be at once deep in expertise and broad in appeal.

Extreme Poetry: The South Asian Movement of Simultaneous Narration, by Yigal Bronner (Columbia)

The Social Space of Language: Vernacular Culture in British Colonial Punjab, by Farina Mir (UC Press)

Unifying Hinduism: Philosophy and Identity in Indian Intellectual History, by Andrew J. Nicholson (Columbia)

The Powerful Ephemeral: Everyday Healing in an Ambiguously Islamic Place, by Carla Bellamy (UC Press)

Secularizing Islamists? Jama'at-e-Islami and Jama'at-ud-Da'wa in Urban Pakistan, by Humeira Iqtidar (Chicago)

Islam Translated: Literature, Conversion, and the Arabic Cosmopolis of South and Southeast Asia, by Ronit Ricci (Chicago)

Conjugations: Marriage and Form in New Bollywood Cinema, by Sangita Gopal (Chicago)

Unfinished Gestures: Devadāsīs, Memory, and Modernity in South India, by Davesh Soneji (Chicago)

Document Raj: Writing and Scribes in Early Colonial South India, by Bhavani Raman (Chicago)

The Millennial Sovereign: Sacred Kingship and Sainthood in Islam, by A. Azfar Moin (Columbia)

Making Sense of Tantric Buddhism: History, Semiology, and Transgression in the Indian Traditions, by Christian K. Wedemeyer (Columbia)

The Yogin and the Madman: Reading the Biographical Corpus of Tibet's Great Saint Milarepa, by Andrew Quintman (Columbia)

Body of Victim, Body of Warrior: Refugee Families and the Making of Kashmiri Jihadists, by Cabeiri deBergh Robinson (UC Press)

Receptacle of the Sacred: Illustrated Manuscripts and the Buddhist Book Cult in South Asia, by Jinah Kim (UC Press)

Cut-Pieces: Celluloid Obscenity and Popular Cinema in Bangladesh, by Lotte Hoek (Columbia)

From Text to Tradition: The Naisadhīyacarita and Literary Community in South Asia, by Deven M. Patel (Columbia)

Democracy against Development: Lower Caste Politics and Political Modernity in Postcolonial India, by Jeffrey Witsoe (Chicago)

Into the Twilight of Sanskrit Poetry: The Sena Salon of Bengal and Beyond, by Jesse Ross Knutson (UC Press)

Voicing Subjects: Public Intimacy and Mediation in Kathmandu, by Laura Kunreuther (UC Press)

Writing Resistance: The Rhetorical Imagination of Hindi Dalit Literature, by Laura R. Brueck (Columbia)

Wombs in Labor: Transnational Commercial Surrogacy in India by Amrita Pande (Columbia)

I Too Have Some Dreams: N.M. Rashed and Modernism in Urdu Poetry by A. Sean Pue (UC Press)

The Place of Devotion: Siting and Experiencing Divinity in Bengal-Vaishnavism by Sukanya Sarbadhikary (UC Press)

We Were Adivasis: Aspiration in an Indian Scheduled Tribe by Megan Moodie (Chicago)

Writing Self, Writing Empire: Chandar Bhan Brahman and the Cultural World of the Indo-Persian State Secretary by Rajeev Kinra (UC Press)

Landscapes of Accumulation: Real Estate and the Neoliberal Imagination in Contemporary India by Llerena Searle (Chicago)

Polemics and Patronage in the City of Victory: Vyasatirtha, Hindu Sectarianism, and the Sixteenth-Century Vijayanagara Court, by Valerie Stoker (UC Press)

Hindu Pluralism: Religion and the Public Sphere in Early Modern South India, by Elaine M. Fisher (UC Press)

Building Histories: The Archival and Affective Lives of Five Monuments in Modern Delhi by Mrinalini Rajagopalan (Chicago)

Reading the Mahavamsa: The Literary Aims of a Theravada Buddhist History by Kristin Scheible (Columbia)

Modernizing Composition: Sinhala Song, Poetry, and Politics in Twentieth-Century Sri Lanka by Garrett Field (UC Press)

Language of the Snakes: Prakrit, Sanskrit, and the Language Order of Premodern India by Andrew Ollett (UC Press)

CPSIA information can be obtained
at www.ICGtesting.com
Printed in the USA
LVHW01s0907281017
554126LV00001B/1/P

9 780520 296220